A. C. Swinburne

Frontispiece Swinburne as a young man

A. C. Swinburne

A Poet's Life

RIKKY ROOKSBY

SCOLAR PRESS

Published by
SCOLAR PRESS
Gower House
Croft Road
Aldershot
Hants GU11 3HR
England

Ashgate Publishing Company
Old Post Road
Brookfield
Vermont 05036 – 9704
USA

British Library Cataloguing in Publication Data

Rooksby, Rikky
  A. C. Swinburne: A Poet's Life.
  (Nineteenth Century Series)
  1. Swinburne, Algernon Charles, 1837–1909—Biography.
  2. Poets, English—19th Century—Biography.
  I. Title.
  821.8

  ISBN 1–85928–069–2

Library of Congress Cataloging-in-Publication Data

Rooksby, Rikky.
    A. C. Swinburne: A Poet's Life / Rikky Rooksby.
      p.   cm. (Nineteenth Century)
    Includes bibliographical references and index.
    ISBN 1–85928–069–2 (acid-free paper)
    1. Swinburne, Algernon Charles, 1837–1909—Biography.   2. Poets,
English—19th century—Biography.   3. Critics—Great Britain—
Biography.   I. Title.   II. Series: Nineteenth Century (Aldershot,
England)
PR5513, R66   1997
821'.8—dc21
[B]   96–29712
                                                             CIP
ISBN 1 85928 069 2

This book is printed on acid free paper

Typeset in Sabon by Manton Typesetters, 5–7 Eastfield Road, Louth, Lincolnshire,

Printed in Great Britain at the University Press, Cambridge

Contents

The Nineteenth Century
General Editors' Preface

The aim of this series is to reflect, develop and extend the great bur-
geoning of interest in the nineteenth century that has been an inevitable
feature of recent decades, as that former epoch has come more sharply into
focus as a locus for our understanding not only of the past but of the
contours of our modernity. Though it is dedicated principally to the
publication of original monographs and symposia in literature, history,
cultural analysis, and associated fields, there will be a salient role for
reprints of significant texts from, or about, the period. Our overarching
policy is to address the spectrum of nineteenth-century studies without
exception, achieving the widest scope in chronology, approach and
range of concern. This, we believe, distinguishes our project from comparable ones, and means, for example, that in the relevant areas of
scholarship we both recognize and cut innovatively across such param-
eters as those suggested by the designations 'Romantic' and 'Victorian'.
We welcome new ideas, while valuing tradition. It is hoped that the
world which pre-dates yet so forcibly predicts and engages our own will
emerge in parts, as a whole, and in the lively currents of debate and
change that are so manifest an aspect of its intellectual, artistic and
social landscape.

Vincent Newey
Joanne Shattock

University of Leicester

Illustrations

Acknowledgements

I wish to thank the British Academy for a small personal research grant which facilitated a number of visits within the UK to places associated with Swinburne and libraries with sources of information about him.

I am deeply grateful to Terry L. Meyers for generously allowing me to consult the hundreds of unpublished letters by and to Swinburne which he has patiently transcribed and annotated over the past 25 years, and for providing notes from the Swinburne family Bible. His encouragement and assistance at every stage in the writing of this book have been greatly appreciated. I am equally grateful to Nicholas Shrimpton of Lady Margaret Hall, Oxford, with whom I have had the pleasure of collaborating on several Swinburne projects since 1987, for his invaluable criticism of early drafts of the text, for illuminating the Oxford background of Swinburne's undergraduate years, and for urging me to write this biography in the first place.

My work has been assisted and inspired in a variety of ways by a host of Swinburneians, some of whom I have enjoyed meeting and corresponding with over the past decade. Pre-eminent among them is Cecil Y. Lang, without whose edition of *The Swinburne Letters* a Swinburne biography would be an impossible undertaking. It is a pleasure to acknowledge Margot K. Louis, Timothy A.J. Burnett, Anthony H. Harrison, Len Findlay, John D. Rosenberg, Thais E. Morgan, David G. Riede, Nicholas B. Scheetz, Morito Uemura, Mark Samuel Lasner, Catherine Maxwell, Michael Wilson, and the work of the late John S. Mayfield and Clyde K. Hyder.

I also wish to thank J. Locker Lampson of Sussex, Jennifer Gosse, Raymond Turley, Tony Glynn, John Goodby, photographer Michael R. Dudley, Rachel Chapman, Edward H. Cohen, Irvine Loudon, Ken Dowden, Mary Graham, Michael Allen, Ron Miller, Edward Fenston, Lynne Elson, Neil MacAlpine and Kitty and David Marks. For the opportunity to experience at first hand the places of Swinburne's youth I am grateful to Captain John Browne-Swinburne of Capheaton, Ian Fareham of East Dene Centre, and Reverend Alfred Tedman of Bonchurch and the Harrisons of Northcourt.

For their manifold labours in bringing this book into being, I thank my publisher Alec McAulay and editor Caroline Cornish.

Among the many librarians and libraries consulted, I would like to express my thanks to Alan Tadiello of Balliol College Library; the staff of Pembroke College Library, Worcester College Library, the Bodleian Library, and Radley College; to Michael Meredith at Eton College

Library; the British Library; the Brotherton Collection at Leeds University Library; Hartley Library, Southampton; the Local Studies Library, Newport (Isle of Wight); the Fitzwilliam Museum and Trinity College Library, Cambridge; to the Public Record Office at Kew; the Wellcome Institute for the History of Medicine; East Sussex County Archives; Northumberland Record Office; Hertfordshire County Record Office; Aberdeen City Library, and Mrs Beverley Emery, Royal Anthropological Institute representative at the Museum of Mankind Library.

For support at various stages of my Swinburne endeavours I extend a personal thanks to Ruth Cochrane, Lawrence James, Denys Stephens, Yvonne James, Martin Coyle, Gwyn and Joan Ingli James, Paul Bridges and Sally Ashton, Gillian and John Green, Angela Foster, Lynette Morris, Caroline Ashley and Adrian Chant, Chris and Ann Miles, and, last but by no means least, Rhonda Riachi who ensured that a book started in sadness ended in gladness.

For permission to quote from unpublished material I wish to thank the Henry W. and Albert A. Berg Collection, New York Public Library, Astor, Lenox and Tilden Foundations; Columbia University Library, New York; Princeton University Library; Duke University Library; Beinecke Rare Book and Manuscript Library, Yale University; the Edith S. and John S. Mayfield Collection, Georgetown University Library; Stanford University Library; University of British Columbia Library; the Brotherton Collection, Leeds University Library; the Master and Fellows of Balliol College, Oxford; the Trustees of Benjamin Jowett; the Master and Fellows of Pembroke College, Oxford; the Provost and Fellows of Worcester College, Oxford; the Master and Fellows of Trinity College, Cambridge; the Provost and Fellows of Eton College; the editors of *Notes and Queries*, *Review of English Studies*, and *Victorians Institute Journal*. For permission to quote from the diary of Helen Rossetti Angeli I would like to thank Signora Helen Guglielmini.

The Max Beerbohm caricature is by permission of Mrs Eva Reichmann and the Master and Fellows of Balliol College.

For permission to quote from Swinburne's unpublished writings I am grateful to Reed Consumer Books (William Heinemann Ltd). For quotations from published sources I wish to thank Yale University Press and Oxford University Press, the Clarendon Press, Oxford, Chatto and Windus, Routledge and Kegan Paul, Sphere books, Faber and Faber, Pennsylvania University Press, and for the lines from Thomas Hardy's 'A Singer Asleep', Macmillan.

I welcome correspondence from anyone with further information on Swinburne which might be incorporated into future editions of this book.

In power of imagination and understanding he simply sweeps me away before him as a torrent does a pebble. I'm righter than he is – so are the lambs and the swallows, but they're not his match.

Ruskin

... taking him for all in all, he is the figure of a man interesting, wonderful and admirable because he is quite unlike all other men.

Vanity Fair

I wish I could command storm at will, like a witch. But perhaps it might be rough on other people.

Swinburne

Introduction

'He was dead then. The waving posters said it.' On a summer morning in 1869, people stood murmuring together or blocked pavements as they read the papers. Algernon Charles Swinburne was dead at 32. The poet who had flouted public decency with *Poems and Ballads* three years earlier had died just as the controversy over his latest book threatened to exceed that of 1866, with a question tabled in the House of Commons. The previous afternoon Swinburne had emerged from a restaurant in Leicester Square with several friends, talking in a loud, excited manner and unsteady on his feet. The party had made their way to his publisher John Camden Hotten at 74–75 Piccadilly, with whom Swinburne was to discuss the threats of prosecution made against his novel. As they approached the shop, a man standing near the roadside suddenly stepped toward Swinburne and discharged a pistol at close quarters. The poet fell bleeding and expired a few minutes later. Apprehended by a constable shortly afterward, the assailant, a Mr Newbiggin of the First Church of Christ Carpenter, Shoreditch, was heard to protest that he had done his duty by God and country in ridding the world of a man whose writings were a danger to the moral health of the nation.

This, of course, is invented history in the spirit of one of Swinburne's own hoaxes. He did not die dramatically, felled in the street by an assassin's bullet, and there was no controversy over his novel in 1869 because that novel was never finished. The posters did not wave the news of Swinburne's death until April 1909. He was to outlive Queen Victoria, dying of pneumonia among his books at the age of 72. But the consequences of an earlier end to Swinburne's life are worth imagining. If he had died in 1869, in a blaze of resurgent public censure ignited by the publication of the story we know as *Lesbia Brandon*, or for that matter if he had drowned off Normandy in 1868 or off the Isle of Wight in 1874 (which he nearly did), or succumbed to alcoholic poisoning (which he could have done at almost any time between 1866 and 1879), his current standing would be very different. The dazzling impression of his first books would shine undiminished by the darker mass of his often flawed later output. The legend of the odd but outstandingly gifted young aristocrat who amazed the 1860s would have passed into literary history with all the customary metaphors of shooting stars and flames that tragically consume themselves. One of the finest Victorian poets would never be mistaken as a minor versifier. Swinburne's reputation would have risen steadily, unhindered by the mundane fact of three unglamorous decades in Putney, spent in semi-retirement with Theodore Watts-Dunton — a counter-legend always serviceable for those who wish to substitute ridicule for intelligent appraisal.

The role of Watts-Dunton in Swinburne's life was a mixed blessing, certainly as far as his later fame is concerned. For much of their time at The Pines, Swinburne was happy, healthy and productive. Watts-Dunton banished some of the loneliness from Swinburne's existence as he banished the spectre of an early death through alcoholism. For that much at least, Watts-Dunton deserves commendation. It is also true that he banished some of Swinburne's friends and sources of inspiration. There are elusive hints that in their last years together Watts-Dunton bullied Swinburne, exercising the tyranny some wish to attribute to the whole of their association. I think it possible that further research may yet uncover some ugly tales of life at The Pines. But if in his case the road of excess led, not to wisdom, but to Watts-Dunton, that was in large measure Swinburne's responsibility. He could not achieve self-control and order, and therefore had to live with someone else's by default, or die. The regime at The Pines was the price Swinburne paid for being unable to curb his self-destructive behaviour, an ironic fate for the poet of Liberty who once wrote, 'Save his own soul he hath no star'.

A Swinburne who died before 1879, before Watts-Dunton and The Pines, before the daily walks over Wimbledon Common, before pram-stopping, Bardolatry and patriotic verse, would have been a phenomenon more conducive to lasting fame. The usual speculation, the sense of a great talent prematurely lost, such as clings to the memory of Keats and Shelley, would have helped Swinburne's reputation weather the literary upheavals of modernism. There would probably be two dozen Swinburne biographies (instead of a mere eight, including this), and we would have a properly edited complete works, a published census of his manuscripts, a reliable bibliography, possibly a journal *Swinburne and his Circle*, and all the other scholarly paraphernalia. As it is, we have none of these things, and in consequence the biographer's task is made more difficult. For all his exuberance, Swinburne was in many ways a private and reticent man, surrounded by a family and relatives who, after his death, were determined to guard that privacy and hide those aspects of his life which were in any way unseemly. No-one as much as Swinburne's biographer regrets the bonfires his sister Isabel and his cousin Mary Disney-Leith apparently made of his family letters, letters which would have been of inestimable value in telling us more about his relationships with his mother, father, sisters and brother.

In the past thirty years, awareness of Swinburne's importance to Victorian literature has significantly increased. A number of critical studies have added to our knowledge of his life and have amply demonstrated the vitality and beauty of Swinburne's best writing, and this biography is indebted to the work of many scholars, especially those who have published on Swinburne since 1960. His literary achievement is as various as it is unique. *Poems and Ballads* (1866), *Poems and Ballads, Second Series* (1878), the best of *Songs Before Sunrise* (1871) and the verse tragedy *Atalanta in Calydon* (1865) show him as one of the most original and exciting of nineteenth-century English poets. Contrary to the widely-held prejudice, he did not die as a poet in 1879 when he moved to Putney and quit alcohol and flagellation brothels. Although much of his later poetry is tiresome, inspiration still fitfully struck, often when Swinburne tried to hammer into unity his thoughts on death or contemplated the forces of change in the natural world. There are at least a dozen lengthy poems (topographical and elegiac) as fine as his more well-known lyrics, which do not repeat old themes but move into fresh areas. First among them is *Tristram of Lyonesse*, started as early as 1869 but mostly written after his life had found stability at Putney. Unlike novelists, poets often fail to maintain the inspiration of their twenties and thirties. In so far as a good deal of his later verse lacks interest, Swinburne merely resembles many other poets who lived to a similar age. Despite this, he wrote poems like 'In Memory of John William Inchbold' or 'A Nympholept' or 'The Lake of Gaube' when he was in his fifties and sixties.

But Swinburne should be remembered not just for his poetry but as a leading Victorian critic, pioneering the appreciation of Blake, Baudelaire, the Brontës, a galaxy of Elizabethan and Jacobean dramatists, and of Whitman, Poe, Hugo, Stendhal, Balzac, Flaubert, Gautier, Latouche, and Cladel. His art criticism was influential, notably on the prose of Walter Pater. He defended Meredith's *Modern Love* in 1862, defended Browning from charges of obscurity, and celebrated the work of William Morris and Dante Gabriel Rossetti. A talented satirist, he poked fun at the prevailing taste for didactic moralizing, and extolled freedom of expression in *Notes on Poems and Reviews* (1866) and *Under the Microscope* (1872). His novel *A Year's Letters* and the unfinished *Lesbia Brandon* portrayed the Victorian upper-class he knew as an insider with cool analysis and wit.

In a broader way, Swinburne's influence went far beyond literature. *Poems and Ballads* and much of his work up to the mid-1870s shocked and annoyed many. Gerard Manley Hopkins's description of Swinburne as 'a plague of mankind' indicates that if Swinburne had not existed in Victorian England it would definitely have been necessary to invent him. By expressing anti-Christian, anti-monarchist and erotic sentiments, he not only challenged the limits of art but became an example of courageous dissent. Whatever impulses drove him to write what he did, his perceived 'paganism' and humanism gave countless readers a whetstone on which to sharpen their own rejection of puritanism and dogma. His very name became a watchword against oppression and humbug, heard not only in the United Kingdom and America but in Italy, Germany, France, Hungary and Scandinavia where his works were translated. Swinburne was the most European of Victorian poets. From works like *Atalanta, Poems and Ballads, Songs Before Sunrise*, and later poems such as 'A Nympholept', a line of influence can be drawn to the decadent writers of the 1890s, to Hardy's last novels, to D. H. Lawrence and other modern writers whose work mounted a similar protest. It leads even to avowedly lesbian writers like H. D. who read *Lesbia Brandon* in 1952 and said it sent her into an 'electric coma'. As Swinburne's friend the artist Seymour Kirkup put it, 'he is our champion against tyranny, temporal and spiritual'.

At the centre of the whirlwind was Swinburne himself, Ruskin's 'demoniac youth', described by Burne-Jones:

> ... his sensitive face, his eager eyes, his peculiar nervous excita-
> bility, the flame-like beauty of his wavy mass of hair, his swift
> speech and extraordinary swiftness of thought and apprehension,
> and a certain delightful inconsequence all his own, made him quite
> the most remarkable, certainly the most poetic personality I have
> ever known.

In 1870 the poet Mathilde Blind wrote, 'whenever I happen to meet Swinburne I am struck afresh by the wonderful vitality and verve of the man's mind. His conversation has the same bracing effect upon me as sea-winds have in another, and I am conscious of a vibration after it for days and weeks together.' Max Beerbohm met Swinburne many years later and remarked that as an old man Swinburne had 'the eyes of a god and smile of an elf'.

Swinburne's child-like quality is mentioned by many who knew him at all stages of his life. His love of children was not a malady contracted at The Pines with Watts-Dunton. The Swinburne who played with Kirkup's little girl in the Boboli Gardens in Florence in 1864, or hid under the table to amuse the daughter of Bayard Taylor in 1867, and allowed Morris's children to throw rose-petals over him, had always loved children, as he revered the old. Like Lewis Carroll, Swinburne was comfortable in the presence of children, relating to them without the self-consciousness that gave some of his adult relationships a certain distance and rigidity.

Part of him never grew up, remaining like Reginald Clavering in his play *The Sisters* (1892), described by Mabel as 'The very schoolboy that I knew you first, / On fire with admiration and with love / Of someone or of something always'. He was fixated on the early experience of being birched, which released and reinforced the masochism latent in his nature. He loved or hated with equal passion; the middle ground had no attraction for him, for his was not a temperate spirit. Running through his life is an impulse to mastery or selfless abandon. It seems that Swinburne's central emotional drive was the need to worship and to achieve an ecstatic loss of self. As a boy he expressed this drive through his encounters with the sea and by participating in the ritual of Holy Communion. After he rejected Christianity, he sought that feeling through other means. He made gods of his heroes – Hugo, Landor, Mazzini, Shakespeare – and found abandon and self-transcendence through writing and reading his poetry, through art and beauty, alcohol and flagellation.

Ever a restless spirit, Swinburne always enjoyed the tumult of the elements. As a young man he sped on horseback across the Isle of Wight, Northumberland and North Cornwall. His idea of Paradise was deep water swimming, where he could feel at one with the immeasurable ocean. He was almost as happy spending hours in the dusty light of his relations' country-house libraries. To see Swinburne whole, we have to keep these two sides in view. As John D. Rosenberg has put it, 'the decadent, verbally sophisticated Swinburne was in another part of his being pre-civilized, a wind-worshipper and a sea-worshipper whose poetry springs from sources more antique than words'. He was a strange blend of power, compulsion and innocence for whom Blake's aphorism 'Energy is eternal delight' might have been written.

Swinburne has received more than his share of caricature. All too often this has taken the place of serious assessment. Some accounts, merely imitating others, have pushed caricature so far that as to make it almost impossible to imagine him as a human being at all. Once this level of distortion is reached, it is easy to maintain that Swinburne's writing did not arise from a complex web of experience but simply from reading other people's books. Ignorance of Swinburne's biography has frequently gone hand-in-glove with the trivializing of his best poetry and prose. A fairly typical example in an authoritative literary history of the Victorian period finds that Swinburne's lament in 'Dolores' is merely Byronic wit:

> Time turns the old days to derision,
>   Our loves into corpses or wives;
> And marriage and death and division
>   Make barren our lives.

This poem was composed in the summer of 1865. In the preceding five years Swinburne had suffered the deaths of his idolized grandfather

CHAPTER ONE

A Small Satisfied Pagan

Even on a calm summer's day, the sound of the sea is audible through a half-open casement at the front of East Dene, Bonchurch, Isle of Wight, the house where Algernon Charles Swinburne spent much of his childhood and youth. On a clear night, the moon silvers a vast expanse of water, south-east across the Channel. In winter, the noise of the ocean reverberates across the lawn in front of the house, and salt smears the glass.

The story of Swinburne's life should begin with the sea. It inspired many of his poems, and he knew of no more sublime a word with which to finish a lyric. The son of a naval captain (later Admiral), he enjoyed his father's stories of life on the high seas, even if Swinburne much preferred to be *in* the ocean rather than *on* it. In the waters of Monk's Bay close by East Dene, Captain Swinburne fostered his son's intense love of the sea, as Swinburne later recalled:

> . . . its salt must have been in my blood before I was born. I can remember no earlier enjoyment than being held up naked in my father's arms and brandished between his hands, then shot like a stone from a sling through the air, shouting and laughing with delight, head foremost into the coming wave – which could only have been the pleasure of a very little fellow. I remember being afraid of other things but never of the sea.

The young Algernon spent so much time either swimming or clambering over rocks and playing along the shore that one of his family nicknames was 'Seagull'. In 1851, when Swinburne was fourteen, a family friend observed that 'his delight in the water was incredible'.

This formative love is captured in his unfinished novel *Lesbia Brandon*. Responding to 'the only sight of divine and durable beauty on which any eyes can rest in the world', Herbert Seyton's heart

> opened and ached with pleasure. His face trembled and changed, his eyelids tingled, his limbs yearned all over: the colours and savours of the sea seemed to pass in at his eyes and mouth; all his nerves desired the divine touch of it, all his soul saluted it through the senses. 'What on earth is the matter with him?' said Lord Wariston. 'Nothing on earth,' said his sister; 'it's the sea.'

Herbert's intense love of the sea-shore is closely based on Swinburne's memories of his own unfettered boyhood:

> In a few months' time he could have gone blindfold over miles of beach. All the hollows of the cliffs and all the curves of the sand-hills were friendly to his feet. The long reefs that rang with return-ing waves and flashed with ebbing ripples; the smooth slopes of coloured rock full of small brilliant lakes that fed and saved from sunburning their anchored fleets of flowers, yellower lilies and redder roses of the sea; the sharp and fine sea-mosses, fruitful of grey blossom, fervent with blue and golden bloom, with soft spear-heads and blades brighter than fire; the lovely heavy motion of the stronger rock-rooted weeds, with all their weight afloat in languid water . . . the broader bands of metallic light girdling the greyer flats and swaying levels of sea without a wave; . . . the sharp delicate air about it, . . . the hard sand inlaid with dry and lumi-nous brine; . . . drew his heart back day after day and satisfied it. Here among the reefs he ran riot . . . At other times he would set his face seaward and feed his eyes for hours on the fruitless floating fields of wan green water, fairer than all spring meadows or sum-mer gardens, till the soul of the sea entered him and filled him with fleshly pleasure and the pride of life . . . .

Swinburne's language is both mystical and sensual, testifying to the power of this first passion. His love of the sea is a key to his intellectual and psychological nature. For Swinburne the sea is being itself; the immersion of the swimmer a brief transcending of separateness and recovery of unity with the All. At the same time, contact with the sea is for him deeply erotic. His fictional surrogate Herbert Seyton 'sprang at the throat of waves that threw him flat, pressed up against their soft fierce bosoms and fought for their sharp embraces'. This eroticism is tinged by an association of pain with pleasure: 'the scourging of the surf made him red from the shoulders to the knees, and sent him on shore whipped by the sea into a single blush of the whole skin'. Whatever the effect of later experiences, Swinburne's masochism seems rooted in his temperament. As a child, Swinburne was thrilled by any display of elemental energy:

> . . . my father came once into my bedroom . . . took me out of bed, wrapped . . . in a blanket and carried me through the garden, across the road, through the copse and down the bank to see the place where I had bathed that morning before breakfast, in a clear pool at the bottom of a waterfall – and where there was now neither waterfall nor pool, but one unbroken yellow torrent roar-ing like continuous thunder.

Whatever gifts the gods bestowed on Swinburne, the medical circum-stances of his entry into the world may have contributed to his physical and psychological eccentricities. Swinburne claimed he was 'born all but dead and hardly expected to live an hour'. The fact Swinburne in the same breath says that in this he was like two of his idols, Victor

Hugo and Goethe, raises a question mark against this claim, and his cousin, Mary Disney Leith (née Gordon) also doubted its verity. But the American physician William B. Ober has argued persuasively that Swinburne may have been born prematurely, suffered anoxic brain damage at birth and that his disproportionately large head (at Eton, his hat was the largest in the school) may indicate arrested hydrocephaly.

Ober's view that Swinburne was premature rests in part on the fact that Swinburne was born in London (at 5 a.m., 5 April 1837), at 7 Chester Street, rather than on the Isle of Wight. Surely his mother, Lady Jane Henrietta Swinburne, would have chosen East Dene for her confinement. This is open to the objection that the best medical attention of the time was available in the capital. But more importantly the Swinburnes did not rent East Dene until 1839 and did not purchase it until 1841. This explains why Alice, the second child, was also born in London. Nevertheless, Ober's diagnosis vividly illuminates the odd traits Swinburne exhibited:

> From earliest childhood he had the trick, whenever he grew the least excited, of stiffly drawing down his arms from his shoulders and giving quick vibrating jerks with his hands ... If he happened to be seated at a moment of excitement, he would jerk his legs and twist his feet also, though with less violence ... to the very end of his life, whenever Swinburne was happy, or interested, or amused, he jerked his arms and fluttered his little delicate hands.

Those who met Swinburne often commented on these tremors. Francis Wedmore encountered Swinburne for the first time at Lord Houghton's and recalled: 'being Swinburne, he was of course immediately communicative, enthusiastic and agreeable – his interest in things emphasized a little, or at least the appearance of it, by a slight quivering movement, as if every thought suggested to him some fresh memory, some fresh excitement'. His alarmed mother consulted a specialist, who explained that Algernon had an 'excess of electric vitality' and preventing its expression might be harmful. The drawing down of his arms began with his excitement at watching a spinning top. Ober comments, 'such uncoordinated, involuntary, stereotyped movements of the extremities are best classified as tics, a type of choreiform movement; their perseveration into adult life indicates the continuing nature of the neural discharge that evoked them'. Swinburne's strange floating walk, his difficulty with writing (indicating 'poor motor coordination'), his habit of covering one eye to read more easily, occasional epileptiform fits, and the restless foot and finger tapping, are given a new cohesion by Ober's hypothesis.

When the Swinburnes settled at Bonchurch the Isle of Wight was at the start of its popularity as a resort. A guide book of 1839 praised Ryde as 'one of the most beautiful watering places in the south of England' and recommended the fashionable promenade at Cowes. The railway from London reached Southampton in 1840 and in 1841 directors of the Southampton line organized the first day return from London, which included a cruise around the isle. At Bonchurch a Lloyds signal station for shipping opened in 1847, an esplanade was laid across Ventnor Cove in 1848–50 and docks were constructed at Ryde in 1849. Queen Victoria began to build a residence, Osborne House, on the island in 1845, and Tennyson lived at Farringford from 1853. The island attracted artists and writers drawn by tales of its Mediterranean beauty. Keats had stayed at Carisbrooke in 1817 and Shanklin in 1819, Tennyson visited Bonchurch in 1846 and Dickens was there in 1849, and Macaulay wrote part of his *History of England* in Ventnor in 1850. For a captain in the Royal Navy, it offered the advantage of being near to Portsmouth.

The village of Bonchurch is part of a stretch of land known as the Undercliff, a narrow platform bounded on one side by the ocean and on the other by steep wooded slopes rising hundreds of feet to the downs. Sheltered and warm, it became famous for its health-promoting properties, especially for consumptives. Dr George Martin of Ventnor wrote of its climate and conditions in *The Undercliff of the Isle of Wight* (1849). He praised Bonchurch, 'embosomed in its ivy-clad rocks and trees, giving it the appearance of perpetual summer':

> Take barren rocks, prolific soils, broken masses, elevated cliffs and precipitous descents, an expanded sea, a winding rivulet and tranquil lake, the wild flower-dell and the rich pasture, the peasant's hut, the farmer's yard, and the admired villa; employ the colours of the bow of heaven; let the motions of animated nature be within reach of observation; cover the whole with an expanded arch; light it with a summer's sun, and call it Bonchurch!

East Dene lies at the northern edge of the village. Built by Beazley in the 1820s, the house was said to contain the bedsteads of King John and Sir Walter Raleigh, an organ played by Queen Elizabeth I and wood-panelling from the Spanish Armada. A neighbour of the Swinburnes, William Sewell, wrote:

> It was a lovely place. On a hot day to look out across the smooth lawn under the great trees, with that bright sea always in motion coming up seemingly to the grass. At one side the old Church, buried in trees. Above the Undercliff and the smooth steep of Bonchurch Down. To the East paths wandering off into the Landslip. One often hears the phrase 'fairy land'. But I think I cannot recall anything in its kind and for its size so lovely as East Dene. But it was oppressively beautiful. It was so perfect, that there was no scope for activity of mind. The beauty lay upon you as a load, and I never came out of it without a sense of relief . . .

1.1 East Dene

Here, in the enchanted environs of the large house and its grounds, with some dozen or so housekeepers, servants, governesses and maids, Swinburne's early years were largely spent.

Swinburne's sensibility was also shaped by family connections with the north of England and the aristocratic ancestry of which he was fiercely proud. In a letter of 1875, invited to share something of his birth and career, Swinburne wrote several pages about his Northumbrian and French predecessors. He was proud to be descended from a line of Catholic and Jacobite exiles, 'a family which in every Catholic rebellion from the days of my own Queen Mary to those of Charles Edward had given their blood like water and their lands like dust for the Stuarts'. This was something of an over-statement, even allowing for the two sons of Sir Edward Swinburne (1660–1706), the first baronet, imprisoned for their part in the 1715 rebellion. Geoffrey Scott records that one Swinburne son:

> ... was taken by his monk tutor, Cuthbert Farnworth, from Capheaton in Northumberland, to the Continent, following the family's implication in the '15. Swinburne was educated for some of the time in a college in Belgium, perhaps St. Gregor's, Douai, as an *enfant trouvé*, his real identity hidden until, half a dozen years later, he was discovered through his looks and breeding to be a Swinburne. He was returned to Capheaton where he recognized his old toys. Farnworth, his tutor, later became his chaplain.

The fourth baronet, Algernon's great-grandfather, apparently 'remained staunchly Jacobite, and contributed to the upkeep of Jacobite prisoners in Carlisle Castle'. In *Bothwell* (1874) Swinburne mythologized his ancestry when Mary Stuart invokes the names of those who will 'lay their loyal hands in minds and pledge/Their noble heads for surety ... names,

> That bear the whole might of this northern land
> Upon their blazon, and the grace and strength
> Of their old honour with them to that side
> That they shall serve in; first the two great earls,
> The Dacre, Norton, Swinburne, Markinfield,
> With all their houses ...

The Swinburnes could trace their Northumbrian roots back to the twelfth century, when they were lords of Swinburne Castle. The subsequent country seat of Capheaton Hall near Cambo, about twenty miles inland from the North Sea, was initially restored by Sir Edward in 1668, eight years after he was made a baronet. Robert Trollop produced 'a foursquare design with an air of solid wealth and good sense' and the gardens were laid out by Capability Brown. In 1824 the house was described as 'well-sheltered by thriving woods and plantations; the

1.2 Capheaton (early nineteenth-century engraving)

1.3   Sir John Edward Swinburne

walks, pleasure-grounds, and gardens are extensive, and derive considerable ornament from a large piece of water, of above eighty acres,
planned and executed by the late Sir Edward Swinburne'. This artificial
lake had a boathouse, miniature sailing ships and an island where
parties would picnic.

There had been one earlier writer in the family, Henry Swinburne
(1743–1803), the author of *Travels through Spain* (1779) and *Travels in*

the Two Sicilies (1783–85). But it was Alger.1on's grandfather, Sir John
Edward Swinburne (1762–1860), who fired the boy's imagination. Born
in France, Sir John converted from Catholicism to Protestantism in 1786,
a move that was the culmination of a steady change of religious affilia-
tion at Capheaton. By 1782 the resident Benedictine chaplain had been
given a salary and a house in the village, and was only to say prayers at
the Hall when invited. According to Scott, 'the chaplain believed that he
had been cleared out of Capheaton Hall in the first place because the
family had already become lukewarm in the practice of their religion'. Sir
John Swinburne became MP for Launceston from 1788 to 1790 and
High Sheriff of Northumberland from 1797. His brief experience of the
House of Commons was said to have settled his convictions; he became a
Whig and a Reformer, with no further political ambition. He was President of the Literary and Philosophical Society of Newcastle (1798–1837),
President of the Society of Antiquaries of Newcastle from 1813 until his
death, and a member of the Royal Society of Literature. He assisted the
Revd John Hodgson in his work as historian for the county by contribut-
ing money and material from the family archives. Sir John was 'the model
of a country gentleman, a kind and liberal landlord, an open-handed
contributor to local charities, and the dispenser of warm and generous
hospitality'. Swinburne was proud that his grandfather had known the
painters Turner and Mulready (his brother Edward, Swinburne's great
uncle, had been a painter). 'It was said', wrote Swinburne, 'that the two
maddest things in the North country were his horse and himself', adding,
'he was most kind and affectionate to me always as child, boy, and
youth.' He went on to declare, 'I think you will allow that when this race
chose at last to produce a poet, it would have been at least remarkable if
he had been content to write nothing but hymns and idyls for clergymen
and young ladies to read out in chapels and drawing rooms.' Sir John
married Emilia Bennet, daughter of Richard A. H. Bennet of Beckenham,
Kent, second niece of the late Duchess of Northumberland, in 1787. They
had seven children, at least one of whom, Emily, was tutored in art by
Mulready. She married the diplomat Henry George Ward and accompanied him to Mexico where she produced many sketches of the country
and its people.

   Swinburne's father, Charles Henry (second son of Sir John and Emilia),
was born on 2 April 1797 and entered the Royal Naval College on 18
September 1810; on 12 December 1812 he went to sea on the *Revenge*.
His commissions took him on voyages to Newfoundland, the Cape of
Good Hope, the East Indies and the Mediterranean. Though his service
began in the closing years of the Napoleonic Wars, it seems the most
exciting event of his voyages occurred in July 1831, when, as Commander of the *Rapid*, he sighted an active volcano off the south-west

1.4   Admiral Charles Henry Swinburne

coast of Sicily; a year later it had sunk beneath the waves, creating a dangerous shoal. On 8 July 1835 he advanced to the rank of Captain and retired on half-pay. There is no evidence that he was away at sea during Swinburne's childhood, contrary to suggestions that Algernon was deprived of an effective masculine presence. Charles Henry duly advanced to Rear-Admiral (February 1857), Vice-Admiral (September 1863) and Admiral (October 1867).

Mary Disney Leith described Charles Henry as a disciplinarian,

> as his profession and training required . . . stern he could be when necessary; but a more wise, tender and affectionate father could hardly exist. I do not think he was a great reader of poetry, but he could appreciate what was good . . . Music he loved, and painting also, without practising either art himself, though he could draw and design, and was something of a mechanical genius, devoted to turning and carpentry of all kinds.

William Rossetti found him 'a kindly, conversible man'. To Sewell he was 'too sensible for any extravagances . . . a plain practical man but without Poetry'. The first time Sewell went to see the Swinburnes he spoke to the parents about Algernon's 'fondness for poetry, which the Admiral ridiculed and discouraged'. Then Algernon appeared:

> . . . the moment he came into the room I saw that he was not a common boy. Very small, delicately formed, very small feet and hands, golden hair – it was not red exactly, pale eyes, freckled complexion, feminine features, a shy manner, but not awkward. And the moment you talked to him as if you respected him, he brightened up, and talked freely, especially of his passion for Shakespeare and Italian poetry. And he was then quite a boy.

Sewell urged Swinburne's father not to repress the boy's passion for poetry, but Sewell feared his advice was not heeded and that 'poor Algernon was snubbed, and found no sympathy', instead being left to wander about East Dene, 'sitting by the sea shore, musing among the rocks, and drinking in daily that enervating indolence which scenery and a home of that kind naturally inspired'.

Evidence for an antagonistic relationship between father and son largely rests on a letter Swinburne wrote on 15 January 1870, in which, making a comparison with Shelley, Swinburne admitted there was no doubt that the Admiral had found him an

> afflictive phenomenon . . . before, during, and since my Oxford time; but I do not think you make allowance for the provocation given (as well as received) by a father, who may be kindly and generous, to a boy or man between seventeen and twenty-one or so, with whom he has no deep or wideground of sympathy beyond the animal relation or family tradition. . . . I am sure you can never have felt at that age the irreparable, total and inevitable isolation from all that had once been closest to the mind and thought, and was still closest to the flesh and the memory, the solitude in which one passes from separation to antagonism of spirit (without violent quarrels or open offense, but by pure logical necessity of consequence) the sense that where attraction ends repulsion gradually begins . . . .

In 1869 Swinburne wrote of his father's 'anti-democratic traditions of class and profession'. Elsewhere he described himself as 'a small and not usually good boy of 9 or 10', and was presumably disciplined when, as a family friend remembered, at three years old, 'a pretty-featured, carroty-haired spoilt boy, [he] paid his respects most unpoetically by pricking me with a large pin in a tender place'. In 1909 William Rossetti told his daughter,

> Swinburne was a man of warm family affections: in his early days, however, he used to abuse his Papa in much the same manner as Shelley did – 'I think partly to imitate Shelley'. But he gave up doing so later, 'In his early days he was constantly making some improper joke at his Papa's expense.' He once said to Papa, 'You have never known what it is to live in a family that has no sympathy of understanding of your intellectual pursuits!'. Swinburne's family had no sympathy with his poetry in the beginning – regarding it as mere 'frivolous stuff that it was ridiculous ever to attempt – mere nonsense beneath contempt'.

Alongside this might be set letter 22 of Swinburne's epistolary novel *A Year's Letters* (written *c.* 1861–62) by Captain Harewood to his wayward son Reginald:

> You must be very well aware that for years back you have disgracefully disappointed me in every hope and every plan I have formed with regard to you . . . From childhood upwards, I must once for all remind you, you have thwarted my wishes and betrayed my trust. Prayer, discipline, confidence, restraint, hourly vigilance, untiring attention, one after another failed to work upon you. Affectionate enough by nature, and with no visibly vicious tendencies, but unstable, luxurious, passionate and indolent, you set at nought all guidance . . . At school you were almost hourly under punishment; at home you were almost daily in disgrace . . . So your boyhood passed.

When the novel attained hardcover publication in 1905 Swinburne described Reginald as a 'coloured photograph' of himself – except that 'nothing can possibly be more different than his *parents* and mine'. Swinburne was 68 when he wrote this disclaimer, and his mother and father were dead. Was this parental piety in old age, where absence had made the heart grow forgetful and therefore fonder? Or does the letter of 15 January 1870 express the conflicts of one phase of their relationship? Certainly he had little of which to complain during his thirties, when his father made repeated excursions to London to rescue his son from alcoholic temptation and the onslaught of self-neglect. The critic F. A. C. Wilson suggested Captain Harewood was modelled not on Charles Henry Swinburne but on the father of Swinburne's friend Richard Monckton Milnes.

The relationship with his mother seems to have been warm and close. Lady Jane was born on 19 July 1809 at Barking Hall, Needham, in Suffolk, the daughter of George, the third Earl of Ashburnham (1760–

1830) and his second wife Charlotte Percy (died 1862). Educated at Trinity College Cambridge, George Ashburnham was a Fellow of the Society of Antiquaries and a Knight Grand Cross of the Hanoverian Order. Jane Henrietta had six sisters and five brothers. Brought up partly in Italy, she spent much of her youth among the English expatriates in Florence. Jane Henrietta was maternal, protective, and possessive, but could also be sparkling and witty. She guarded Algernon's early reading, allowing wholesome texts such as the Bible, a bowdlerized Shakespeare and Dickens. She taught him French and Italian, and from her he had the Ashburnham voice, 'exquisitely soft . . . with a rather sing-song intonation'. Swinburne believed he inherited her devotion to babies (to the detriment of his later poetry). Sewell noted 'there was a softness and tenderness and shyness of manner coupled with considerable excitability in Lady Jane which . . . was not exactly the kind of influence required for Algernon'. The Ashburnhams had Northumbrian connections before Charles Henry and Lady Jane Henrietta married on 19 May 1836, for the third Earl's second wife Charlotte Percy was a sister of the Duke of Northumberland. The Ashburnhams had an even longer pedigree than the Swinburnes, pre-dating the Norman conquest. Furthermore, Ashburnham Place in Sussex boasted an exceptional library of rare books and manuscripts, formed by Swinburne's uncle Bertram, the fourth Earl (1797–1878), which outshone even Sir John's at Capheaton. Here was rich soil for the nourishing of a young poet's mind. In *Lesbia Brandon*, Swinburne describes how Herbert 'fell upon the Ensdon library shelves with miscellaneous voracity, reading various books desirable and otherwise, swallowing a nameless quantity of English and French verse and fiction'.

Charles Henry Swinburne and his wife were 39 and 24 respectively when their first child Algernon was born. The Swinburne family Bible tells us that his godparents were Lord Prudhoe, Sir John Edward Swinburne and the Countess of Ashburnham. He was followed by Alice (6 January 1838), Edith (1 December 1840), Charlotte Jane (25 November 1842), Isabel (13 September 1846) and Edward (14 July 1848). Each had a family nickname, used throughout life. Charles was Pino, Jane was Mimmie, Algernon was Hadji, Alice was Ally, Edith was Edie, Charlotte was Wibbie and Isabel Abba. Edith, red-haired like her elder brother, is said to have been Algernon's favourite and one of the tragedies of his life was her death of consumption at the age of 22. Her affection for him is very apparent in the single letter of hers that has so far come to light. She appears, a child of three, in the painting 'Swinburne and His Sisters' by George Richmond.

In adulthood Swinburne's relations with his sisters were affected by his distaste for their High Anglicanism. In 1904 he said, 'in them that creed certainly was compatible with an adorably "beautiful type of character" – which yet, I cannot but think, might have been even better in some ways and happier on the whole with a saner and wider outlook on life and death'. At his mother's funeral, when Swinburne refused to kneel at the grave, Alice forcibly pushed him down by the shoulders, exclaiming, 'Kneel, Algernon, kneel!' A friend of the sisters who knew them in later life commented:

> Alice was the most artistic of the three, Charlotte deeply interested in books, and especially in early printing, Isabel full of genealogical and pedigree lore, great at heraldry, and having at her fingers' ends all the history of some of our more curious peerage successions . . . All of them were very devout members of the extreme High Church section of the Church of England, and deeply concerned at some of their brother's earlier productions, while fully recognizing his incomparable genius . . .

Alice was intelligent, a gifted artist who enjoyed hearing her brother read from his writings. Swinburne dedicated his play *Locrine* (1887) to her. Something of the puritanical force of Isabel's character can be felt in a letter written in middle age to a young woman she befriended: 'I don't like and never will read French stories and my child must let me beg her to be careful how she does, it is so easy to dirty one's mind.' She was 'a person of very definite opinions, and spoke out her mind in no measured terms, especially when she considered that the reputation of her poet brother was concerned'.

Swinburne seems to have had a more distant relationship with Charlotte and Edward. Charlotte was the invalid of the family. When illness stopped her attending Edward's funeral, Swinburne observed, 'it seems hard, for she was always fond of him'. Edward was an 'ardent musician', who spent some time in Germany and in 1879 married his first cousin once removed, Olga Helen Thumann, daughter of Jane Swinburne and Professor Paul Thumann. Like Algernon, Edward was fond of the sea and enjoyed cruises. When he died in 1891, Swinburne said, 'how strong and healthy and happy the poor fellow whom I remember in my school holidays as the brightest of baby boys might and would have been at this hour if instead of the best of friends he had not found the worst of wives'.

In Charlotte's case, no biography of Swinburne has recorded that she was a twin, and that on 25 November 1842 Lady Jane was also delivered of a son, baptized Charles John. But Algernon's first brother died six months later, on 28 May 1843, at 13 Eaton Square, London (a house occupied by the Countess of Ashburnham), of what the registrar elusively noted as 'teething'. The grief of the parents is evident from their memorial to their infant son. The new parish church in Bonchurch has an altar window with two inscriptions: the famous verse of Matthew 18:3, exhorting us to become as children to enter the kingdom of heaven; and another 'in memory of Charles Swinburne, whom, while yet an infant, God called back to himself, and whose parents arranged the setting up of these windows on both sides'.

Algernon was six when his first brother died, old enough to register the sorrow of his mother and father, whatever direct sense of loss he may have felt. He never alluded to Charles John in any letter or poem that has come down to us. It is possible that this has some connection with the many poems about babies he wrote in middle and old age, and with the part of him that, in discussing *The Winter's Tale*, was more moved by the death of Mamilius than anything else in the play. Did the death of Charles John impress a temperament already sensitive to infants? Or did it help to awaken such feelings? In *Lesbia Brandon* Swinburne describes Herbert's feelings about his sister's new-born son:

> ... its helpless and hopeless defects of size and weight, its curious piteous mask of features, its look of vegetable rather than animal life, its quaint motions and soft red overflow of irregular outlines touched and melted him in a singular way: he grew visibly fond of the red and ridiculous lump, and it put out impossible arms and fatuous fingers when he came in sight. Towards all beasts and babies he had always a physical tenderness; a quality purely of the nerves not incompatible with cruelty nor grounded on any moral emotion or conviction.

This may express feelings about Edward, who was born when Swinburne was eleven. When the novel's Lady Wariston has twins, 'a boy and a girl, strong and fat and well-liking, the first-born was eclipsed in all their eyes alike'. The death of her twin brother might also be a factor in Swinburne's antipathy to Charlotte.

Young Algernon had an extended family of cousins. The fourth Earl of and Countess of Ashburnham had eleven children, of whom Bertram (1840), Katherine (1841), John (1845) and William (1847) were closest in age to Swinburne. But by far the most important childhood companion was Mary Julia Charlotte Gordon (later Mrs Disney Leith) who has been called the most significant woman in his life. Born 9 July 1840, she was the only daughter of Sir Henry and Lady Mary Gordon of Northcourt, in the village of Shorwell, eight miles west of East Dene. Her parents had married in August 1839, their marriage settlement naming Charles Henry Swinburne as a trustee, and were godparents to Charlotte Jane. The family links between Mary and Algernon were complex:

> our mothers (daughters of the third Earl of Ashburnham) were sisters; our fathers, first cousins – more alike in characters and

1.5 Northcourt

tastes, more linked in closest friendship, than many brothers. Added to this, our paternal grandmothers – two sisters and co-heiresses – were first cousins to our common maternal grandmother; thus our fathers were also second cousins to their wives before marriage.

Mary's father, Henry Percy Gordon (born 21 October 1806) was Laird of Knockespock, Aberdeenshire. He studied at Peterhouse College, Cambridge, was elected a Fellow of the Royal Society in 1830 and succeeded to his father's baronetcy in 1851. He was deeply involved in local affairs, serving as Deputy Lieutenant of the Isle of Wight. He was also Chairman of the Commission of Highways, and worked on the restoration of Shorwell Church. He tutored the local choir in his house and his plans for flower gardens at Northcourt in the early 1840s still survive. His sister Julia Emily Gordon (1810–96) was a talented watercolourist, who published *Songs and Etchings in Shade and Sunshine* by J. E. G. in 1880.

Henry Percy Gordon taught his daughter mathematics, Greek, Latin, piano, organ and musical composition. She gave music lessons and regularly played the local church organ, in Shorwell and at St Mary's, Inverurie and St Drostan's, Inich, in Scotland. Her grandfather, Sir James Willoughby Gordon, lived four miles down the coast from East Dene, at Niton, in a charming house known as 'The Orchard'. Surrounded by woodland yet close to the sea, the grounds and gardens of this residence inspired several of Swinburne's poems, most notably the 'Dedication' to his play *The Sisters* (1892):

> The shadowed lawns, the shadowing pines, the ways
>   That wind and wander through a world of flowers,
> The radiant orchard where the glad sun's gaze
>   Dwells, and makes most of all his happiest hours,
>   The field that laughs beneath the cliff that towers,
> The splendour of the slumber than enthralls
> With sunbright peace the world within their walls,
> Are symbols yet of years that love recalls.

Here was a world made for children: cool, dark leafy lanes leading down to coves wild or calm, gardens of trellised flowers for hiding, the colours and scents of an orchard, the breezy downs above Bonchurch and Shanklin with their panoramic views. Swinburne later had a rich fund of memories associated with the area between Northcourt and East Dene.

Mary Gordon's recollections of Swinburne went back to 'sitting on the nursery floor together playing with bricks'. She remembered 'seeing Algernon and his eldest sister walking ahead of the rest over the rough grass of the Bonchurch Down – he with that springy, dancing step which he never entirely lost', or riding a small Shetland pony. On

Sundays he gave beautiful readings from the Bible, though there was one passage from the Apostles' Creed he always rendered as 'suffered under Bonchurch Pilate'. He was privileged to have a book at meal-times, and on one occasion 'he made us all into a kind of tableau out of *Dombey and Son*, with himself as Mrs Skewton in her bath chair'. One day the governess hesitated to read a story that involved the drowning of puppies. '"Oh," said Algernon, vehemently, "If it's anything about cruelty to animals, don't read it."' When he and Mary were older they rode together, Swinburne reciting famous poems of the day or Macaulay's *Lays of Ancient Rome*. It was a relationship crucial to the whole course of Swinburne's life.

They were also together at Capheaton and at Mounces, Sir John's shooting-grounds which ran right up to the Scottish border. The Swinburnes would often go north in the late summer to escape the heat of East Dene. There 'a large cousinhood gathered . . . where everything seemed to combine for the delight of youth – a lake to row or sail on, lovely gardens and woods to roam or play in, and . . . abundance of ponies to ride'. Algernon had the occasional tumble but escaped serious injury. Capheaton's delights are evoked in the undergraduate poem 'Hide and Seek':

> Slow sighed the water past the flower-set foreland,
>   Thro' the green glimmer of the windy flags.
> Warm blew the wind from the sunny sleepy moorland,
>   Warm from the heather of the fretted crags.
> Golden hints of broom were dawning on the highland,
>   Golden thoughts of summer stirred in leaf and nest:
> Low sang the river round our windy island,
>   Low the birds murmured of their foliaged rest.

Capheaton served as the model for Lord Cheyne's Lidcombe in *A Year's Letters*, with 'admirable slopes of high bright hill-country behind it, and green sweet miles of park and embayed lake, beyond praise for riding or boating'. Capheaton had the romance of the past. In later years Swinburne would often refer to himself as a 'Borderer', a Northcountryman. His love of Northumberland inspired many poems, his own imitation dialect border ballads, *The Tale of Balen*, parts of *Tristram of Lyonesse*, *The Sisters* and his prose fiction. The contrast between the rugged beauty of the north and the luxuriant leafy environs of the Isle of Wight deeply influenced his outlook. Georges Lafourcade observed that they 'gradually became the poles round which the child's sensibility learned to revolve'.

Out of doors, he was 'a small satisfied pagan', an elemental child, living on his nerves or sinking into languid inactivity; he wanted excitement or nothing, and always to have what he desired immediately. But he enjoyed the devout High Anglicanism of his family, 'having been as child and boy brought up a quasi-Catholic, of course I went in for that as passionately as for other things (e.g. well-nigh to unaffected and unashamed ecstasies of adoration when receiving the Sacrament)'. He was brought up 'with very decided religious principles'. Margot Louis tells us that Lady Jane introduced Swinburne to Newman's Anglican Sermons:

> In 1828, Swinburne's aunt, Elizabeth Swinburne, had married John William Bowden, Newman's close friend; and through her Lady Jane Swinburne sent Newman a token of gratitude for his sermons, which had been 'so great a help to her and hers' ... Moreover ... there is evidence that Swinburne became well read in the works of other literary figures of the High Church, such as J. M. Neale and Richard Chenevix Trench.

In 1866 his father said that in early life his son 'was very reverent and intensely admired all things great and beautiful'. The encounter with the natural world and the Church both fed his impulse to worship.

Bonchurch had its own share of religious controversy during the 1840s, when the Oxford Movement was at its height. One of the prime movers of Church reform in the parish was the sister of William Sewell, Elizabeth, whose moral stories were very popular. The Sewells moved into Sea View (now called Ashcliff), not far from East Dene, and at first Elizabeth 'had an impression that we were going to live there with the nightingales in absolute retirement'. The old Norman church was damp and far too small for the increasing congregation. In 1838 Ventnor had 350 inhabitants; in 1841 this had risen to 900, reaching 2069 by 1847. Bonchurch had 302 inhabitants in 1841. Elizabeth was appalled that Sunday services alternated with those at Shanklin, and that Holy Communion was celebrated only four times a year. Weekday services were unheard of, and many dates in the Christian calendar passed over. Neither were the spartan decor of the church and austerity of the services to her liking, and so she set about changing these. Miss Sewell noted that the village 'was for some time in a chronic state of disturbance in regard to church matters'. She and others, of High Church persuasion, pressed for a monthly Communion. The Revd James White, who owned the land on which the new church was built, did not approve of these developments and satirized the introduction of 'foreign mummeries and superstitions into this quiet parish' under the pseudonym of 'T. Buddle', in *The Edinburgh Magazine* (June 1849). Of feast-days he wrote, 'we must have a new almanac if you come among us much more; for the very days of the week are no longer to be recognised ... The wife of our physician invited us to dinner on the Feast of St. Ollapod, which, after great inquiry, we found meant Monday the 22nd. ' Eventually, in the words of Miss Sewell,

there came an open split between the school committee and the
rector . . . we had a scene in the drawing room at East Dene which
might have been useful to Charles Dickens . . . The position of the
rector . . . was most unfortunate. He stood alone – accused by the
committee of introducing Dissenting books into the school library
without their knowledge. The committee were equally accused by
the rector of introducing books to which he objected. To whom the
right of selection belonged was not clear. The dispute ended by the
books disapproved of by both parties being withdrawn from the
library and put aside; and the succeeding rector . . . burnt them.

The Swinburnes played an important role in financing the building of
the new church (consecrated on 11 December 1848) and provisions
for schooling in the village. Captain Swinburne was Treasurer and
Secretary of the Subscribers to the Bonchurch National School from
1848.

Dickens stayed in Bonchurch from June to late September 1849 at
Winterbourne House. Initially he was delighted: 'from the top of the
highest downs, there are views which are only to be equalled on the
Genoese shore of the Mediterranean; the variety of walks is extraordinary'. Early in August, after two charity sermons were preached for the
school, everyone was 'refreshed with a public tea in Lady Jane
Swinburne's garden'. By late August Dickens's opinion of Bonchurch
had sunk: 'Of all the places I have ever been in, I have never been in one
so difficult to exist in, pleasantly . . . It's not close, I don't know what it
is, but the prostration of it is awful . . . The whole influence of the place
. . . is to reduce and overpower vitality'. Swinburne was noted as 'a
golden-haired lad' Dickens's boys played with. When in 1873 Swinburne
saw this in print, he was excited, for 'it would have been a lark to read
verbatim the reference to the kid just then going to school and taking
his first turn under the birch'.

One of the local people Swinburne remembered from East Dene was
a local fisherman 'whose cottage was on (or just beyond) my father's
property':

> His wife was a favourite of my mother's, and she used to go with
> me on a visit to their cottage half-way down the 'chine' (need I add
> that I always wished to stay and live there?) when I was too small a
> boy to understand what was the matter, or how anybody could
> look unhappy whose house was built in a cleft of the cliff over-
> hanging the sea. But when I was of Etonian age, of course I had to
> be told that my old friend 'Charley' used to drink rather exces-
> sively by fits and starts: for I had seen him, when sent for, enter my
> father's study with exactly the look and bearing of a schoolboy
> entering the flogging room, and found that he took my eagerly
> offered hand in a shame-faced sort of way. My father asked him to
> take the pledge for a time . . .

Swinburne's carefree childhood came to an end in 1848 when he was sent to live at Brooke Rectory, on the western side of the island, to be prepared for Eton by the Revd Foster Fenwick (1790–1858). There he had his own room, as it was considered too far for him to be frequently travelling back to East Dene, and Mary came to see him. Fenwick was surprised by how well read his pupil already was in certain areas. Swinburne's earliest extant letter is to Fenwick's daughter Ulrica (1831–1908), sending a book mark as he travelled to Capheaton in December 1848. Brooke Rectory meant a curtailment of his freedom. He wrote of Herbert Seyton's tutelage at the same age: 'Few children had ever enjoyed eleven years of such idleness and freedom and no seagull likes to have his wings clipped. The scissors must cut close that were to fit this bird for a perch in a school pen.'

CHAPTER TWO

The River and the Block

Swinburne had just turned twelve when he arrived at Eton on 24 April 1849. One of his cousins, Algernon Mitford, later Lord Redesdale, had entered the school in 1846 and was assigned to keep an eye on the new arrival. Redesdale thought his cousin 'a very stay-at-home boy, shy and reserved':

> What a fragile little creature he seemed as he stood there between his father and mother, with his wondering eyes fixed upon me! Under his arm he hugged his Bowdler's Shakespeare ... He was strangely tiny. His limbs were small and delicate; and his sloping shoulders looked far too weak to carry his great head, the size of which was exaggerated by the tousled mass of red hair standing almost at right angles to it ... His features were small and beautiful, chiselled as daintily as those of some Greek sculptor's masterpieces. His skin was very white – not unhealthy, but a transparent tinted white, such as one sees in the petals of some roses ... Another characteristic which Algernon inherited from his mother was the ... exquisitely soft voice with a rather sing-song intonation ... His language, even at that age, was beautiful, fanciful, and richly varied.

Passing through the gate into School Yard, new boys had their first sight of the statue of the King–Founder, Henry VI, and the entrance to the cloisters under Lupton's tower. Soon they became familiar with other Eton landmarks such as Fellows' Pond, Poet's Walk, Sixth Form Bench, the playing-fields with the elms planted in the rule of Charles I, and in the distance Windsor Castle. From 1834 to 1852 the Headmaster was Dr Hawtrey, whom Redesdale described as 'venerable and imposing ... tall and upright ... a traveller, a man of the world, and a linguist, proficient in French, German and Italian'. Hawtrey's time was a time of reform. He founded the School Library, made Mathematics compulsory, and, as numbers jumped from 444 to 777 by 1846, reconstructed the iniquitous Long Chamber.

But to Redesdale Eton in 1846 seemed in many respects little different from the school his father had attended thirty years before:

> With the exception of the new College buildings, only just finished, in Weston's Yard, the outer aspect of the place had undergone no change. There were the same old tumbledown, crazy tenements with weather-stained walls and patched roofs, occupied by tutors and dames. All the sanitary arrangements – save the word! – were

primitively disgusting. Baths were unknown. During the summer months, by the grace of Father Thames, there was bathing in Cuckoo Weir, at Upper Hope, and at Athens, but from September till about May foot-tubs of hot water carried to the various rooms on a Saturday night represented all the cleanliness that was deemed necessary.

Swinburne entered the school in the 'remove' of the Fifth form (the upper division of the Fourth form) and began his progress up the school. Pupils were either Collegers, living in the main building, or Oppidans, who lived in the house of their tutors and enjoyed a somewhat freer life. As an Oppidan, Swinburne was assigned to James Leigh Joynes (1824–1908) and his wife in Keate House, Joynes having returned to Eton the year Swinburne entered. Swinburne later remembered Mrs Joynes as 'so infinitely kind to me, at an age when I most needed kindness'. A. C. Benson, who knew Joynes in the early 1870s, described him as 'modest, kind, and universally popular; and he was gratefully remembered by his schoolfellows for the fact that he set his face firmly and courageously against all bullying and oppression, all improper talk and undesirable habits'. His large head and short stature gave him 'a somewhat gnome-like aspect'. Another old Etonian thought Joynes 'a good scholar and a good disciplinarian, but his intellectual and literary range was limited, and, though he was kind and sympathetic with the boys, he did not make much attempt to adapt himself to their various natures and dispositions'.

Joynes is alleged to have said of Swinburne, 'I did my best for that ungodly boy. He was hopeless. ' Swinburne told Henry Salt of Joynes's 'very sympathetic attitude to a hopeless little prig, as he called himself'. Swinburne sent Joynes a copy of *Atalanta in Calydon*, and was hurt when it went unacknowledged by mischance. On 23 April 1866 Joynes wrote to apologize, 'for I certainly was very much pleased with your thinking of me again now that your literary pursuits have withdrawn you so much from Eton . . . I was attached to you in former times and I believe that you were attached to me'. In later years Joynes regarded his famous pupil's poetry with strong disapproval.

Edmund Warre recalled how Swinburne was invariably late for early school, 'a shock of red unbrushed hair, trailing shoelaces, and an avalanche of books slipping from his arm'. Once, when Swinburne entered a class up a ladder and through the floor, the tutor W. G. Cookesley exclaimed, 'Ha! here's the rising sun at last!'. By contrast, Lord St Aldwyn's vision of 'a horrid little boy, with a big red head and a pasty complexion, who looked as though a course of physical exercise would have done him good', is probably typical of another shade of opinion in the school from those who saw Swinburne as a freak. Nor would it

have helped that he hardly took part in games, and never owned a
cricket bat – though his enthusiasm for walking, swimming and riding
was boundless. Redesdale said Swinburne could swim like a frog, and
was a fearless if inexperienced rider.

Swinburne formed a few close relationships, took comfort from the
maternal care of Mrs Joynes, and pursued his avid love of reading in the
boys' library in Weston's Yard. Redesdale would see him 'sitting perched
up Turk- or tailor-wise in one of the windows . . . with some huge old-
world tome, almost as big as himself, upon his lap, the afternoon sun
setting on fire the great mop of red hair'. In a remarkable letter written
toward the end of his life, Swinburne told Mrs Disney Leith's son-in-
law that he had had a friend with a room in DeRosen's, where he sat on
cushions in the window and read Edgar Allen Poe's 'Descent in the
Maelstrom' when he should have been preparing Thucydides and was
birched as a consequence. For Swinburne it was a time of exciting
discoveries. The intensity of these literary encounters remained with
him. As Gosse wrote, 'almost all Swinburne's literary convictions were
formed while he was at school'. His reading was no longer censored.
According to Redesdale, at home 'not a novel had he been allowed to
open, not even Walter Scott's. Shakespeare he only knew through the
medium of his precious brown Bowdler.'

Classical Greek and Roman literature formed the core of the curricu-
lum, the former taught through the anthology *Poetae Graeci*. Sappho
'took possession of his soul'. Though less fond of Latin verse generally,
and 'pestered' with Horace from twelve to sixteen, he read Catullus
with 'delight and wonder . . . here at last was a poet – a Latin writer –
who was a man and not a schoolbook – a very lovable man too'. His
reading was directed by William Johnson; and another tutor, Henry
Tarver, introduced him to various French authors, most notably Victor
Hugo, whom Swinburne called 'the greatest writer whom the world has
seen since Shakespeare'. Reading Hugo's *Lucrèce Borgia* increased
Swinburne's fascination with the Italian *femme fatale*, while the copy of
Notre Dame de Paris Swinburne received as a school prize he hardly let
out of his sight. Walter Savage Landor's poems gave Swinburne 'inexpli-
cable pleasure and a sort of blind relief'. The holy trinity of Swinburne's
literary worship was completed by Shakespeare, whom he now read in
an unexpurgated text.

Other discoveries included Dr Johnson's *Lives of the English Poets*,
Dodsley's *Great Old Plays*, and Lamb's *Specimens of the English Dramatic Poets*, of which he said, 'that book taught me more than any
other in the world, – that and the Bible'. He read Marlowe in Dyce's
three-volume edition of 1850, and Webster, and was soon steeped in
Elizabethan and Jacobean drama.

> As a lover and student of Cyril Tourneur and all his kind from the
> ripe age of twelve, at which I first read *The Revenger's Tragedy* in
> my tutor's Dodsley at Eton . . . with infinite edification, and such
> profit that to the utter neglect of my school work, to say nothing of
> my duties as a fag, I forthwith wrote a tragedy of which I have
> utterly forgotten the very name (having had the sense at sixteen to
> burn it together with every other scrap of MS. I had in the world),
> but into which I do remember that . . . I had contrived to pack
> twice as many rapes and about three times as many murders as are
> contained in the model . . . It must have been a sweet work, and
> full of the tender and visionary innocence of childhood's fancy.

Swinburne wrote at least three imitation Elizabethan dramas at Eton,
one of which, 'The Unhappy Revenge', survived combustion. The fre-
quency with which he deployed the stage direction 'stabs the king'
became a family joke. When Victoria and Albert visited Eton on 4 June
1851, he wrote the mock-Augustan 'The Triumph of Gloriana'. In 1896
Swinburne recalled how 'my English tutor gave a prize for English
verses on some visit of the Queen's, and that mine was the doggrel
which got it, but which I hope and trust and doubt not went the way of
all waste paper'. In fact, it was preserved by his father.

The serial publication of Dickens's *Bleak House* 'was apt to interfere
with my work rather severely on the first of each month. Don't I
remember how I used to scuttle up to town to Ingalton's after morning
school, to get it'. Swinburne's acute attention to his reading, coupled
with a prodigious memory, enabled him to amaze friends with his
recitations, as Redesdale knew first-hand:

> We used to take long walks together in Windsor Forest and in the
> Home Park, where the famous oak of Herne the Hunter was still
> standing . . . a very favourite goal of our expeditions. As he walked
> along with that peculiar dancing step of his, his eyes gleaming with
> enthusiasm, and his hair – tossed about by the wind, he would
> pour out in his unforgettable voice the treasures which he had
> gathered at his last sitting.

His copies of Arnold's *The Strayed Reveller* and *Empedocles on Etna*
were rarely out of his pockets, and on 26 July 1849 he acquired an
edition of Coleridge.

Yet despite these adventures in literature, Eton must have been a
strange environment to Swinburne, cut off from the company of his
parents and sisters, and far from the sea. In *Lesbia Brandon* Herbert
Seyton leaves Ensdon for school 'in a blind passion of pain, and like one
born alive out of life, or all that was sweet in it':

> It was rather a physical than a sentimental pain, he felt the sharp
> division and expulsion, the bitter blank of change, like a bad taste
> or smell. Away from home and the sea and all common comfort-

able things, stripped of the life-long clothing of his life, he felt as
one beaten and bare . . . It was very bitter and dull to him, to be
taken up and dropped down into the heart of a strange populous
place, beautiful and kindly as he like others should have found it
. . . He had a dear and close friend or two, with whom he rambled
and read verse and broke bounds beyond Datchet or Windsor;
dreaming and talking out the miles of green and measured land
they tramped or shirked over. The seagull grew sick in an aviary,
though (it may be) of better birds. Instead of tender hanging tendrils of woodland he desired the bright straight back-blown copses
of the north; and instead of noble gradual rivers, the turbid inlets
and wintry wildernesses of the sea.

Notice the phrase 'measured land'. Swinburne always desired the wild
and the unbounded. At Eton he had to make do with walks in the
forest and swimming. He thought he knew how the young Shelley
'must have yearned and thirsted after the "waste and solitary places"
near the shore' and was amazed Shelley had neglected swimming
when at Eton, since 'my one really and wholly delightful recollection
of the place and time being that of the swimming lessons and play in
the Thames' (Swinburne's swimming coach was a man named Talbot).
This explains the detail of the 'reaches of the river' in his 'Eton: An
Ode' (1891).

His joy at going north during the summer holidays must have been all
the fiercer. In *The Sisters* (1892) Swinburne has Redgie enthuse for the
times when he raced across the moors 'Till horse and boy were wellnigh
mad with glee/So often, summer and winter, home from school' and ask
rhetorically, 'give the south our streams, would it/Be fit to match our
borders?'. Swinburne admitted, 'I never wrote anything so autobiographical as Redgie's speech about Northumberland in the Eton midsummer holidays'.

By August 1849 Swinburne was back at East Dene after his first term.
In September the Swinburnes went north to the Lakes. They saw Aira
Force, the waterfall on Aira Beck, and visited the aged Wordsworth at
Rydal Mount. Elizabeth Sewell, who accompanied them, said Algernon
was 'greatly interested at the thought of seeing the great poet' who was
'so very nice' to him that Swinburne cried when they left. In a sonnet of
1887 Swinburne remembered how Wordsworth's 'hand laid blessing on
my head'. Several years later he was to meet another ageing poet,
Samuel Rogers, who prophesied great things in poetry for the boy. Not
all the holidays were spent in Northumberland or the Isle of Wight; at
Ashburnham Place, Sussex, wrote Gosse, 'Algernon adopted airs of
chivalrous protection to his little cousin and playfellow, Lady Katherine
(1841–85), with whom, each mounted on a robust pony, he took endless rides in the forest'. Surrounded by so many female relatives of a

similar age (such as Mary Gordon), it is hard to believe Swinburne escaped the usual adolescent crushes and attractions.

Gosse claimed that Swinburne looked back on his Eton years with 'unfailing happiness', and Francis Warre Cornish was 'particularly anxious to repel the assumption that Swinburne was not happy at Eton'. Given Cornish was Vice-Provost of Eton this anxiety is predictable. With his physical appearance, his mannerisms, his absorption in books, and his shyness, it would have been incredible if Swinburne had not been bullied. Redesdale wrote that 'other boys would watch him with amazement, looking upon him as a sort of inspired elfin – something belonging to another sphere. None dreamt of interfering with him – as for bullying there was none of it. ' Gosse wrote of Swinburne as a 'fairy child' leading a 'charmed life', 'over whose bliss no shadow of a cloud had yet passed'. But whatever Eton did for Swinburne's intellectual and poetic sensibilities, there is no doubt that it played a significant role in nurturing his masochism. The combination of his peculiar sensibility and the school's tradition of birching was fatal for Swinburne's sexual life.

William Sewell had tried to persuade the Swinburnes to send Algernon to Radley College, near Oxford, believing 'I could shelter him . . . lead him on gently to manliness of character', whereas 'Eton would be his ruin'. The first time Sewell saw Lady Jane after Swinburne had gone to Eton she 'told me a charming trait of him':

> He was of course bullied, bullied fearfully. You might as well give a cockchafer to a boy in the street, and tell him not to spin it, as to put Algernon Swinburne down in the playground of any school, and think he will escape being tormented and baited. They wanted to make him swear and say bad words. And he would not. He refused and no cruelty (O the cruelty of boys!) could induce him to speak.

What comes across from this anecdote is the complacency of maternal price that has no understanding of the damage such treatment might be causing. This side of Swinburne's school experience is further supported by an old Etonian who remembered the head boy pointing out the 'little fellow with curly red hair' with the words, 'Kick him if you are near enough, and if you are not near enough throw a stone at him.' His 'outsider' status is signalled by the fact that he acquired the epithet 'mad' Swinburne.

Henry Salt countered Gosse's anodyne version of Algernon's schooldays in 1919 with no less an authority than Joynes, who used to tell how Swinburne 'once came to him before school and begged to be allowed to "stay out", because he was afraid to face some bigger boys who were temporarily attached to his Division – "those dreadful boys," he called them. "Oh, sir, they wear tail coats! Sir, they are men!" The request was not granted.' Joynes's response was to read Swinburne the 23rd psalm. 'Thus fortified he underwent the ordeal.' The bullying may have had a bearing on the strong religious feelings Swinburne told William Rossetti he had between the ages of fifteen and eighteen.

Bullying was rife at Eton. A. D. Coleridge witnessed one battering of a friend that was so savage

> the poor lad was kept in bed for days, until his bruises were healed. I was a witness of that performance, and shall not forget it to my dying days. I marvelled at the sixth-form boys at their supper-table, conscious of all the brutality going on, and never lifting a finger to interfere with their comrade's all-licensed cruelty.

Apart from the bullies, there was the birch. Through much of his adult life Swinburne entertained himself and a few select friends with descriptions of schoolboys being flogged by their masters. At the same time as he composed the impeccably decorous 'Eton: An Ode', Swinburne produced 'Eton: Another Ode':

> Dawn smiles sweet on the fields of Eton, wakes from slumber her youthful flock,
> Lad by lad, whether good or bad: alas for those who at nine o'clock
> Seek the room of disgraceful doom, to smart like fun on the flogging-block!

Sadly, 'Eton: Another Ode' has a perverse energy quite lacking in its official counterpart. Swinburne's flagellant writings, still largely unpublished, are considerable. They include 'The Flogging Block. An Heroic Poem by Rufus Rodworthy (Algernon Clavering) with annotations by Barebum Birchingham' (written c. 1862–87), 'The End of a Half', 'The Schoolboy's Tragedy', prose and poetry held at Worcester College, Oxford, written during the 1870s and 1890s, amongst them 'Redgie's Return', 'The Swimmer's Tragedy', 'Redgie's Luck' – 'A tragicomedy in 3 acts, 4 double acrostics, 16 scenes and 4 floggings' – and 'Cuckoo Weir' (probably written at the same time as 'Eton: Another Ode'). Some of his flagellant writings, by means as yet unknown, were published: 'Arthur's Flogging', 'Reginald's Flogging' and (probably) 'A Boy's First Flogging', in *The Whippingham Papers* (1887), 'Charlie Collingwood's Flogging' in *The Pearl* (no. 3, Sept. 1879), and 'Frank Fane. A Ballad' (no. 11, May 1880) and an obscene parody of the National Anthem (no. 18, Dec. 1880). Numerous references to flogging in Swinburne's fiction and letters demonstrate the grip it had on his imagination.

Swinburne's flagellant writings circle repetitively around a few motifs. A schoolboy is caught for a minor misdemeanour, endures the fearful anticipation of being beaten, pleads for mercy where there is none, undergoes the shame of exposing his bottom before the master and the other boys, and is beaten. The damage inflicted by the birch is described in lurid detail. There are no obscene words, and no sexual activity takes place, though there is a diffuse sexual anxiety and fear of the body. Swinburne obviously enjoyed the comic juxtaposition of the subject with a mock-heroic style, with its parodic invocatory opening 'I sing the Flogging Block. Thou, red-cheek'd Muse' and explicatory note. The comedy was a way of controlling this anxiety and fear.

The poems have frequent references to 'crimson ridges . . . beaded with gouts of blood' and 'bloody weals'; in 'Percy's Flogging' Frank says to Leonard, 'Oh, look at his bum!/What red ridges! what weals! what sore places! what great cuts!'. Swinburne was sometimes so carried away that whole pages are punctuated with the word 'swish'; folio 13 alone contains 37. It is a world in which punishment is commonplace, inevitable, self-perpetuating. In folios 8–9 Algernon Clavering is beaten seven times in a day, one of these beatings being inflicted because he went to bathe in the river 'there to cool the smart of his stripes' and another because he consequently cannot concentrate on his work. Boys are beaten for crying out, and beaten for not crying out. The black humour of such perverted causality obviously owes much to Swinburne's obsession with de Sade. The adult world is in collusion against the victim. When Reginald of Eclogue II complains to his father about being beaten on his first day at school, the father replies to the boy's tutor, 'You have flogged my boy well, sir, it seems; flog him better/Next time, and still better the next time: the pain may improve him.' Jerome McGann has suggested that 'The Flogging Block' can be seen as an ironic protest against the iniquities of the school system, or a way of laughing at adversity in which 'the impulse to play is seized as the human alternative to a situation as grotesque as it is unalterable'.

The motifs of shameful exposure, adult authority, voyeurism, pleading for mercy, and sadism are all present in these stanzas from 'Frank Fane. A Ballad':

> 'Now loosen your braces,
>   And lower your breeks,
> And show your companions
>   Your bare nether cheeks.
> Make haste to the closet
>   And bring a good rod,
> Or I'll cut you to ribands
>   You shuffler, by God!'
>
> O Master! dear Master!
>   Have pity for once!'
> 'What, pity for a truant,
>   A thief and a dunce!

> For once, and at once,
>   You shall smart for all three;
> A three-fold example
>   Your bottom shall be. '

The boy's consciousness of being exposed before the others and the treatment of flogging as a trial of manhood are evoked in the 'Prologue' to 'The Flogging Block':

> Hard as the hard old wooden Flogging-Block
> The Faces are, that meet my Face and mock:
> My Cousin chuckles, and my Brother grins,
> To see their Junior suffering for his sins:
> At each fresh Birchen Stroke they smile afresh
> To see 'the young one' suffer in the Flesh.
> Each time the Twigs bend round across my Bum
> Pain bids 'Cry out', but Honour bids 'Be dumb'.

Similar scenes, presented without humour, occur in Swinburne's fiction. In *Lesbia Brandon*, Herbert Seyton is punished by his tutor Denham, to their mutual benefit: Herbert 'fearless enough of risk, had a natural fear of pain, which lessened as he grew familiar with it', and Denham thus 'eased himself of much superfluous discomfort and fretful energy':

> The boy sobbed and flinched at each cut, feeling his eyes fill and blushing at his tears; but the cuts stung like fire, and burning with shame and pain alike, he pressed his hot wet face down on his hands, bit his sleeve, his fingers, anything; his teeth drew blood as well as the birch; he chewed the flesh of his hands rather than cry out, till Denham glittered with passion. A fresh rod was applied and he sang out sharply.

Afterwards, Herbert's eyes are said to be 'full of light . . . that comes into the eyes of one still fighting against pain, hot with fever and brilliant with rebellion'. For Swinburne the extremity of these mixed sensations of pain, shame and indomitability was exhilarating. Similarly, in the Prologue to *A Year's Letters*, where young Frank Cheyne is treated to a disquisition on the horrors of flagellation by Reginald Harewood:

> You'll sing out – by Jove! won't you sing out the first time you catch it? I used to. I do sometimes now. For it hurts most awfully. But I can stand a good lot of it. There were bits cut right out of me yesterday on one side. Here. And one twig stuck in the cut and I couldn't get it out for half an hour . . . At school, if you kick, or if you wince even, or if you make the least bit of row, you get six cuts over. I always did . . . The big fellows used to call me all manner of chaffy names: Pepperbottom . . . and the Wagtail; because I used to wriggle about on the block: between each cut . . .

Many of Swinburne's flagellant writings refer to Eton. In an untitled drama of four sons and four fathers, Sir William Bellingham says, 'Come here, Master Bertram. How often last half did they flog you at Eton, my lad?', to which the boy replies 'Two or three times a week, father':

Mr Clavering: 'And how often have you had it hot on the flogging-block, Algernon?'
Algernon: 'Four times a week about. '
Mr Clavering: 'And the master lays into you smartly, sir, eh?'
Algernon: 'Pretty well, sir?'
Mr Clavering: 'Oh! nothing to speak about?'
Algernon: 'Well, he gives it me hot – but a swishing is not, sir, a thing for a fellow to squeak about – we don't think so at Eton, at least, you know, father. '

'Redgie's Luck' and 'The Swimmer's Tragedy' are set at Eton; and 'The Three Degrees of Punishment' takes pride in the severity of Eton floggings. Similarly, in another untitled prose sketch where Arthur is beaten by a tutor 'B.', 'I had held out for about as long as an Eton flogging usually lasts, but then I gave in.' Occasionally Swinburne varied the content by introducing a dominant female figure, as Arthur encounters the housekeeper's niece, Miss Rhoda Carter. At first she watches, encouraging B. Then she beats Arthur herself, asking him how he likes it. The boy's response is revealing:

If I could have spoken, though the pain was cruel, and my voice was stifled with sobs, I had never been whipped by a woman before since I left the nursery, and I began to taste, in the midst of the torture she inflicted at each stroke on my tender flesh, the [?] thrill of pleasure that mingles with the voluptuous agony of the rod.

In 'The Wentworth Flogging Lists' Swinburne wrote of Algy and Charlie that 'pain and punishment were inseparably connected in either little boy's mind with the idea of their dreaded governess: a remarkably tall, strong, big-boned young woman, dark, high-complexioned, and rather handsome'. 'Frank's Flogging' tells how 'this boy's flagellations began in the nursery':

'Twas a sight for the others,
Frank's sisters and brothers,
To see how the nurse as she dressed him and stripped him
Turned him over and held him face downwards and whipped him
Till the horny hard palm of her hand would become
As hot with the work as the little boy's bum
And at every fresh slap
As he lay on her lap
She would moisten and wet it afresh with her tongue
Ere she smacked him again – and by Jove how it stung!

Does the nursery setting suggest Swinburne's Eton floggings revived earlier childhood memories?

To correspondents such as Charles Augustus Howell, Richard Monckton Milnes, John Camden Hotten, George Powell (who was at Eton 1855–60), and Simeon Solomon, Swinburne could indulge his obsession. He thought flogging a preferable punishment to the tedium of copying out passages, being 'manlier and wholesomer'. He told Powell the two things at Eton he would like to see again were the river and the block. After Powell had obtained a picture of the block Swinburne replied, 'I would give anything for a good photograph taken at the right minute – say the tenth cut or so – and doing justice to all sides of the question . . . I don't think I ever more dreaded the entrance of the swishing room than I now desire a sight of it. To assist at the holy ceremony some after twelve I would give any of my poems.' But what are we to make of a letter of February 1863 to Milnes, in which Swinburne, 'really speaking now in my own person', says that a tutor he knew would perfume the flogging room with incense or 'choose a sweet place out of doors with smell of firwood'?:

> This I call real delicate torment . . . Once, before giving me a swishing that I had the marks of for more than a month, . . . he let me saturate my face with eau-de-Cologne. I conjecture now that, counting on the pungency of the perfume and its power over the nerves, he meant to stimulate and excite the senses by that prelimi-nary pleasure so as to inflict the acuter pain afterwards on their awakened and intensified susceptibility. If he did, I am still grati-fied to reflect that I beat him; the poor dear old beggar overreached himself, for the pleasure of smell is so excessive and intense with me that even if the smart of birching had been unmixed pain, I could have borne it all the better for that previous indulgence . . . You must excuse my scribbling at this rate when I once begin for the sake of that autobiographical fact about perfume and pain, which you can now vouch for as the experience of a real live boy.

How far can we trust Swinburne here? Ian Gibson, whose chapter on 'Eton, the Birch and Swinburne' in *The English Vice* (1978) is the most detailed discussion yet of this topic, feels Swinburne was beaten, and that the 'villain of the piece' was Joynes, whom he describes as 'some-thing of a dilettante flagellant'. Donald Thomas dismissed this letter as fantasy, 'another of what Cecil Y. Lang aptly calls "Algernonic hoaxes"'. However, according to Gosse, Swinburne told him that 'the taste for this punishment had come to him at Eton'.

The account of an Etonian who was at the school in the 1840s suggests beating was frequent, public and unregulated:

> It was, in my time, so far from being a punishment administered on special occasions only, or with any degree of solemnity, that some half-dozen to a dozen boys were flogged every day. It was entirely public; any one who chose might drop in. I have sometimes been

one of three spectators, and sometimes one of a hundred. These latter large assemblages were collected, of course, only on occasions of very great interest, either as to quantity or quality – a member of the eight, or the eleven, to be 'swished', as they used to term it, or a number of culprits to catch it for doing something or other particularly heinous ... The crowd on these occasions (always swollen by the culprits' particular friends and associates, who came to see how they 'stood it') would throng the staircase leading up to the headmaster's room ... Then, sometimes after an interval of a quarter of an hour, the door would be thrown open from within, and spectators and victims, in one confused mass, poured into the execution chamber.

Members of the school as old as eighteen or nineteen were punished in this way. Gibson has a number of similar contemporary reports.

Put in this historical context, even allowing for the embroidering impulse of fantasy, the conclusion that Swinburne both suffered and witnessed such beatings seems to me difficult to resist. But the letter to Milnes shows that distinguishing fact from fantasy requires us to be vigilant. How could an Eton tutor punish a boy out of doors? If Joynes was only in his mid-twenties, what of Swinburne's 'poor dear old beggar'? And what of the passive construction '*he let me* saturate my face with eau-de-Cologne'? 'Let' turns Swinburne from victim into willing participant. That he derived pleasure from the experience is clear when he admits '*even* if the smart of birching had been *unmixed* pain', and his 'I beat him' is triumphant, the psychological reward of defiance. The flogging is a contest wherein manliness, 'pluck' in schoolboy parlance, may be proved.

Equally problematic is the note of a talk with Swinburne written by Milnes in November 1862. Swinburne had described how a tutor had:

> ... flogged him over the fallen trunk of a tree, till the grass was stained with his blood and another time when wet out of the water after bathing: the last much more painful! His dreadful disappointment at seeing the big boys at Eton getting off with a few unimpressive switches. Tutor telling him he had no pleasure in flogging boys who were not gentlemen: the better the family the more he enjoyed it. The tutor once flogging him in 3 different positions till he was quite flayed. A. S. very fair, the tutor often flogging a very dark boy by way of contrast, making them hold (?) each other. Using different rods – sometimes made of the lower (?) twigs of fir with the buds on. Calling A. S. Pepperbottom.

The detail of two boys, one light, one dark, seems quite fantastic, and the gruesome grass stained with blood has the ring of Swinburne the apostle of de Sade in full anecdotal flight after dinner. Other details are more believable. As Gibson points out, in *Lesbia Brandon* Herbert Seyton is beaten after bathing and Reginald in *The Sisters* recalls being

flogged for bathing at Cuckoo Weir; the name 'Pepperbottom' occurs in
A Year's Letters and 'The Flogging Block'. Perhaps the tutor in question
was Fenwick at Brooke Rectory or one of Swinburne's two post-Eton
tutors.

One passage in Swinburne's flagellant *oeuvre* establishes that he did
draw on his own experience and suggests there may be others. In
'Redgie's Luck' (Act III, sc. ii) Redgie is half out of a window in a
storm. The tutor Mr Roddam enters:

> Mr Roddam: 'What on earth are you doing up there at the window
>   – or out of it?'
>   (Pulls him down by the leg with a violent jerk)
> Redgie: 'O, sir, I say, how jolly it is.'
> Mr Roddam: 'What, the thunder and lightning? Why, doesn't it
>   frighten you? Eh?'
> Redgie: 'It's no nice, sir – just look at it!'
> Mr Roddam: 'Nice! Why, it's awful. '

Compare this with a letter to his cousin Mary, in which Swinburne
remembers how 'my tutor caught me . . . two-thirds out of a window on
the top storey and jerked me down violently by one leg when I was
bathing in storm. '*What* on *earth* are you doing?' 'Oh, sir, *isn't* it *nice*'
. . . 'NICE!' said Mr Joynes, in large capitals, 'It's *awful*'. '

Faced with the sheer bulk and compulsion of Swinburne's flagellant
writings, is it harder to believe that he was beaten as a youth than to
deny this and search for an arcane psychological trigger for his obsession? Whatever the cause, Swinburne's fixation should not be reduced
to a simple formula. The experience of being beaten fired his imagination because it stimulated more than just his body. He got some pleasure from it – the pain was not 'unmixed' – and that pleasure was partly
erotic. As Gosse wrote, 'I cannot help believing that these scourgings
were in some extraordinary way a mode by which the excessive tension
of Swinburne's nerves were relieved'. It was an adolescent rite of passage that gave him the chance to prove his manhood. As he writes of
Reginald in *A Year's Letters*, 'the boy was immeasurably proud of his
floggings . . . A flogging was an affair of honour to him; if he came off
without tears, although with loss of blood, he regarded the master with
chivalrous pity, as a brave enemy worsted.' Swinburne's relationship
with the world in general was problematically extreme, oscillating between homage and rejection, enthusiasm and hatred, and it was as
though a barrier often descended between himself and the environment.
It seems as though he could only cross it either by being violently
transported out of himself or by being violently invaded, or both at
once, 'mingled and mastering and mastered'. Flogging seems to have
achieved this, partly through pain and by putting him at another's

mercy. Such an interpretation links it with the rest of his life rather than seeing it as an unrelated sexual quirk. His idolatry, his love of the sea and storm, of galloping horses over moors, of getting drunk, of reciting verse, and the energy of his poetry can be seen as expressions of the same impulse. If so, Gosse was incorrect to say that alcoholism and flagellation 'had no more to do with the inner character of Swinburne than the laudanum had to do with the inner character of De Quincey'.

Swinburne told Sir Charles Dilke in the 1870s that the last time he was properly flogged at Eton it was for reading *The Scarlet Letter* instead of his Greek. According to Blanche Warre Cornish, Swinburne left Eton sometime in February 1854. He said it was 'near the end of his seventeenth year', and that he spent five years at Eton. The letter to Milnes quoted above refers to swishings 'had up to seventeen and over'. It is unclear why Swinburne left. His academic performance had been creditable; in 1852 he had won the Prince Consort's Prize for Modern Languages. Swinburne recalled that languages were 'the only thing I had any turn for as a schoolboy' and that he was in 'perpetual disgrace' for his failings in mechanics, geography and arithmetic, 'till at last they gave up expecting me to do a decent sum or a decent map'. Ober conjectured that 'the masters at Eton recognized his erotic response to flagellation and were unwilling or unable to cope with it'. Gosse stated that 'a certain change took place in Swinburne's character at the opening of his last year at school. He became less amenable to discipline and idler at his work', and that there was 'increasing trouble with Joynes of a rebellious kind'. During Swinburne's Eton years William Sewell 'heard little of him, only I had reason to believe that the bullying still went on. And then he was removed to a Private Tutor'.

Swinburne's prizes are mentioned in the only surviving letter written to him by his sister Edith, who was thirteen. It is dated 5 October 1853 from Capheaton:

> My darling Hadji,
> I am so very glad that you have got both prizes you darling Boy! how very delightful IT is! I hope you will get dreadfully lovely books; . . . I wonder what the books will be; when shall you have them? I wish you were here that I might give a real hug but as I can't, I send you a very hard one by post. I'm sure if all the cats and the ponies etc knew about it they would send their congratulations to you! I hope you are quite well and able to enjoy your grand success!!! . . . It is a very foggy evening here; is it fine at Eton? I send 99990000000000 of loves and kisses to you darling and I remain ever your very affectionate sister Edie

The tutor Charles O. Goodford gave Swinburne a copy of W. Whewell's *Astronomy and General Physics* in 1853 and he received Hallam's *Introduction to the Literature of Europe* the same year as a prize.

Joynes presented him with *Household of Sir Thomas More* in November 1853, and on 5 December Edward Coleridge gave him Scott's *Lady of the Lake*. W. S. Lascelles gave him a three-volume set of Cowper inscribed 'on his leaving Eton' but unfortunately with no date! It was a good year for his bookshelf. On 23 March Swinburne's parents gave him *The Book of Common Prayer* and Bishop Ken's *Approach to the Holy Altar* for his confirmation, and on 31 December his grandfather gave him an edition of Milton.

Swinburne had two tutors who prepared him for Oxford. The first was the Revd John Wilkinson, curate of Cambo, a village near Capheaton in Northumberland, who complained he could not get his charge to study. The distractions of Swinburne's favourite countryside were too much. On rides with his sister Alice, he related stories of Cesare Borgia, garnered from R. W. Church's *Essays and Reviews* which his parents gave him in 1854. The painter William Bell Scott allegedly saw Swinburne 'riding a little long-tailed pony at a good pace towards the village': 'he had the appearance of a boy, but for a certain mature expression on his handsome high-bred face ... On his saddle was strapped a bundle of books like those of a schoolboy.' It would have been around this time that Swinburne was befriended by Lady Pauline Trevelyan, an intelligent and artistic woman who lived at Wallington, nearby, with her husband Sir Walter. He evidently had less time and patience for Swinburne but his wife exercised a steadying influence until her death in 1866. She was one of the first people to encourage Swinburne's writing and the Trevelyans' house was an important cultural centre.

Swinburne was then tutored by James Russell Woodford (1820–85, afterwards Bishop of Ely) at Lower Easton near Bristol; the poet later fondly remembered him for taking him carefully through Juvenal. Swinburne said he had read Middleton in 1855. One of Swinburne's fellow tutees, Thomas Snow, recalled the future poet as 'a gentle and delightful man, but we, his fellow pupils, were not capable of appreciating him!', and often heard him declaiming Greek poetry to a late hour of the night. Sewell recorded that Woodford had brought the boy to Radley in the years before Oxford:

> I kept him to stay with me some days. But he was odd. I made up a little dinner party with ladies on purpose to see how he got on. And to my astonishment when we met in the drawing room he was not dressed, his shoes dirty, and his morning coat. And I made him go and change. I observed also a great tendency to sarcasm. He was fond of quizzing people. And I suspect the exclusive way in which he had been brought up at East Dene was at the bottom of this.

In Bonchurch he met Signora Annunziata Fronduti, who was 'greatly impressed with the simplicity of the boy'. She read him Italian poetry and he sat 'gazing into space, absolutely transfigured and absorbed by the magic and music of the classic Italian verse'. If the recitation was not to his taste, the consequences could be alarming. At Eton, during an illness, he was once left in the company of a maid by his mother. Her task was to continue reading Shakespeare to him while he had his tea. Algernon did not like her performance and emptied a jar of water over her head.

His parents hoped Swinburne might enter the Church. But when news of the Balaclava charge broke in October 1854 the idea of becoming a cavalry officer and taking part in some similarly brave (he might have said *ripping*) action (involving galloping horses) became paramount. He told his cousin Mary Gordon, 'the Balaclava Charge eclipsed all other visions. To be prepared for such a chance as that, instead of being prepared for Oxford, was the one dream' of his life. The family deliberated. After three days the answer came in the negative. Swinburne was mortified. Walking on the beach at Shanklin, just north of Bonchurch, during the Christmas holidays, he impetuously decided to prove his courage:

> I went for a good hard tramp by the sea till I found myself at the foot of Culver Cliff; and then all at once it came upon me that it was all very well to fancy or dream of 'deadly danger' and forlorn hopes and cavalry charges, when I had never run any greater risk than a football 'rouge'; but there was a chance of testing my nerve in face of death which could not be surpassed . . . It wasn't so hard as it looked, most of the way, for a light weight with a sure foot and a good steady hand; but as I got near the top I remember thinking I should not like to have to climb down again.

As he neared the top he realized the final ascent would not be possible at that point, so he descended a little to find a better approach. He disturbed a flock of seagulls that flew out of a hollow; for a moment he was surrounded by a tumult of white and grey, rising 'all about me in a heaving cloud'. He then lost his footing and only just managed to swing himself to safety:

> There was a projection of rock to the left at which I flung out my feet sideways and just reached it; this enabled me to get breath and crawl at full speed . . . up the remaining bit of cliff. At the top I had not strength enough left to turn or stir; I lay on my right side helpless, and just had time to think what a sell (and what an inevitable one) it would be if I were to roll back over the edge after all, when I became unconscious . . . On returning to conscious life I found a sheep's nose just over mine . . . I couldn't help bursting into such a shout of laughter . . . that the sheep scuttled off like a boy out of bounds at sight of one of the masters.

When he told his mother why he had risked his life, she said, '"Nobody ever thought you were a coward, my boy". I said that was all very well: but how could I tell till I tried?'

In July and August 1855 Swinburne visited France and Germany with his uncle, Major-General Thomas Ashburnham. He was impressed with Cologne Cathedral, and his enjoyment of religious ritual was still intact. He wrote fine descriptions of the countryside near Wiesbaden. But the most memorable incident was a storm in the Channel as they crossed back to England on the night of 23 August. Some 45 years later he described the experience in 'A Channel Passage', 'Three glad hours, and it seemed not an hour of supreme and supernal joy,/Filled full with delight that revives in remembrance a sea-bird's heart in a boy.' It also became a metaphor for the genius of Victor Hugo in an essay on *L'Homme qui Rit*:

> About midnight the thundercloud was right over head, full of incessant sound and fire, lightening and darkening so rapidly that it seemed to have life, and a delight in its life. At the same hour the sky was clear to the west, and all along the sea-line there sprang and sank as to music a restless dance or chase of summer lightenings across the lower sky; a race and riot of lights, beautiful and rapid as a course of shining Oceanides along the tremulous floor of the sea. Eastward at the same moment the space of clear sky was higher and wider, a splendid semi-circle of too intense purity to be called blue; it was of no colour nameable by man; and midway in it between the storm and the sea hung the motionless full moon . . . Underneath and about us the sea was paved with flame; the whole water trembled and hissed with phosphoric fire; even through the wind and thunder I could hear the crackling and sputtering of the water-sparks. In the same heaven and in the same hour there shone at once the three contrasted glories, golden and fiery and white, of moonlight and of the double lightnings, forked and sheet; and under all this miraculous heaven lay a flaming floor of water.

As a metaphor it would have served equally well to describe his own genius.

CHAPTER THREE

Commoner Swinburne

It had been decided that Algernon was to attend Balliol College, Oxford. In the winter of 1855 he made a number of visits to Radley College, a few miles outside the city, where Sewell was Warden. Swinburne was there with his tutor J. R. Woodford on 29 November and may have remained for much of December. The Sub-Warden William Wood noted in his diary on 8 December, 'in afternoon walked with Owen, West and Swinburne by Sunningwell round to top of Bagley Hill. Swinburne most mad about Tennyson. "To think (he said) that this time last year the world was without *Maud!*"' On 17 December Wood, Forbes and Swinburne walked to Oxford.

Swinburne matriculated at Balliol College on 24 January 1856, aged eighteen. He quickly took a dislike to what he later described as the enervating 'foggy damp of Oxonian atmosphere'. The theological atmosphere, still tense with the conflicts and divisions surrounding the Oxford Movement, soon became equally oppressive. The Mastership of Balliol had been contested by Robert Scott and Benjamin Jowett (1817–93), and Jowett had lost, for having too liberal a religious outlook. An appointment as Regius Professor of Greek in 1855 had not, in his mind, atoned for this. Swinburne found himself with Jowett as his tutor. 'Not the tutor I had selected for him, and hoped he would have been with', said Charles Henry Swinburne. In fact, Jowett became one of the chaster influences in Swinburne's adult life, though it was only after Swinburne had left Oxford that their friendship really developed. Jowett described Swinburne as:

> ... in some respects the most singular young man I have ever known ... He has extraordinary powers of imitation in writing and he composes (as I am told) Latin medieval hymns, French vaudevilles, as well as endless English poems, with the greatest facility.

On more than one occasion, after listening to Swinburne read him an essay, Jowett would drily observe, 'Mr Swinburne, I do not see that you have been pursuing any particular line of thought.' After monitoring Swinburne's progress for a year or so, Jowett decided his talented charge would achieve little academically 'unless he can be hindered from writing poetry'. This was, of course, impossible.

Swinburne's first-term work in Divinity, Greek, Latin, Mathematics, and Logic was commended by the Master Robert Scott as 'very good'.

3.1 Balliol College in the 1860s

3.2 Benjamin Jowett

His studies included St Mark, the Acts of the Apostles, Aeschylus, Thucydides, Cicero, Tacitus and Euclid. James Riddell marked essays such as 'On the Source of False Impressions', 'Sources of Greek History', and 'De Scriptoribus Antiquis'. For the summer term of 1856 Scott's comment was 'industrious but eccentric' and then 'very respectable but peculiar'. Swinburne's undergraduate career began as it was to end, with a fall. The later fall was from a horse. The earlier was a

tumble at the first academic fence. In his second term Swinburne failed
'Responsions' (nicknamed 'Smalls'), which was looked upon as something of a schoolboys' examination, apparently because he was im-
mersed in Browning's *Sordello*. Balliol, proud of its high academic
standing, was not amused. He re-sat it and passed on 10 December.

Initially, his social life was quiet. His father gave him an introduction
to Manuel John Johnson, Keeper of the Radcliffe Observatory, and his
wife, with whom Swinburne remained on good terms. Johnson was of
the same High Church outlook as the Swinburnes, with a fine collection
of prints, drawings and illuminated manuscripts. It was at the Observatory, on 19 May, that Swinburne, in the company of his father, met
George Birkbeck Hill, who later told a friend:

> ... he is the most enthusiastic fellow I ever met, and one of the
> cleverest. He wanted me to read some poems he had written and
> have my opinion. They are really very good, and he read them with
> such an earnestness, so truly feeling everything he had written, that
> I for the first time in my life enjoyed hearing the poetry of an
> amateur.

Hill was part of the Pembroke set that included Edwin Hatch and R. W.
Dixon, and knew Edward Burne-Jones, though at Easter Burne-Jones
had moved to London.

During the summer Swinburne spent a few weeks at Radley College.
Sewell found that 'the Sarcastic Spirit was strong upon him'. When he
heard on the grapevine that young Algernon was poking fun at Radley
and its boys, his chagrin found vent in a half-hour lecture during
Swinburne's next visit. Nevertheless, Swinburne was elected an honorary member of the prefect's common room, and ate at 'high table'
with the masters. Woodgate recalled that Swinburne 'did not go in for
games but was enthusiastic about poetry'. When Radley's Debating
Society passed a motion that 'Maud' was a blot on the reputation of
Tennyson, an indignant Swinburne declared they were all a bunch of
philistines and stormed out. If Swinburne's parents hoped that Radley's
influence might steer their son toward a career in the Church, they
were mistaken. Sometime toward the end of 1856 or early in 1857,
Sewell told the Sixth Form that Swinburne would no longer be coming
to Radley. He feared Algernon might 'inoculate boys with his sinister
tenets'.

A fellow Balliol undergraduate, Donald Crawford, who met Swinburne
in the autumn, noted he 'took no part in the ordinary outdoor amuse-
ments, and never appeared at wine-parties or at breakfasts; he remained
much in his rooms'. Crawford, like many others, was struck by
Swinburne's appearance:

3.3 Swinburne as a young man

> A slight girlish figure, below the middle height, with a great shock
> of red hair, which seemed almost to touch his narrow sloping
> shoulders. He had the pallor which often goes with red hair. There
> was a dainty grace about his appearance, but it was disappointing
> that, like some figure in a Pre-Raphaelite canvas, where he would
> not have been out of place, there was a want of youthful freshness
> in his face. He walked delicately ... with a mounting gait, as if
> picking his steps. He had a pleasant musical voice, and his manner
> and address, slightly shy and reserved, had a particular charm of
> refinement and good breeding.

Apart from his academic work and his own writing, Swinburne had
plenty to brood over. In 1856 Edith Swinburne, then sixteen, had been
examined by a doctor for her chest complaint. The family's worst fears
were confirmed: she had consumption. There had been cases in the
village, not all of them confined to the ranks of the poor. They could
only guess what course the disease would take.

Whatever Sewell's later impression, Birkbeck Hill saw Swinburne as
still having a High Church outlook and in need of being 'plucked out of
the fire'. The main instrument for his redemption was the Old Mortality
Society and in particular John Nichol (1833–94), one of its founders in
November 1856, along with Swinburne, Algernon Grenfell, G. R. Luke,
A. V. Dicey and Hill. The Society's name was a comic allusion to the
fact that they all felt under the weather (illness forcing Nichol to withdraw from Oxford until May 1857). The group photograph suggests an
audition for Hamlet, each man competing to evoke a sea of troubles
before his gaze – with the exception of Swinburne, who looks debonair
and tetchy. Old Mortality aimed to stimulate thought 'on the more
general questions of literature, philosophy, science, as well as the diffu-
sion of a correct knowledge and critical appreciation of our Standard
English Authors'. It was unashamedly radical in its outlook. The second
meeting, at which a constitution was established and minutes taken,
was on 2 May 1857, and thereafter it met on Saturday evenings during
term-time. There was an annual excursion. On 3 May Hill wrote, 'to-
morrow I believe the Old Mortality intends to take a picnic up the river
and make merry. We shall go to Godstow and dream of Fair Rosamond
there, I suppose, and the days of the nunnery.' 'Fair Rosamond' was the
subject of a play by Swinburne.

Swinburne chaired some of the meetings and read the most papers.
He talked on *Wuthering Heights*, Marlowe and Webster, poetry by
Browning and Morris, and from George Sala's *Household Words* delivered the character of Colonel Quagg 'with full effect in the best American manner, and received by the society with shouts of laughter'. He
was commended for having 'varied the usual style of subjects by introducing the humorous element'. Swinburne was not so keen on some of

the more staid contributions. T. H. Green was reading a paper on the history of Christian dogma when, glancing up, he 'nearly burst out laughing at the sight of Swinburne, whose face wore an expression compounded of unutterable ennui and naif astonishment that a man whom he respected could take an interest in such a subject'. By then, Swinburne had rejected his religious upbringing.

Swinburne's involvement with Old Mortality was a turning point in his intellectual development. While the weekly academic essays continued, he gave papers to the Society, wrote a paragraph on Congreve for the *Imperial Dictionary of Universal Biography* (1857), and composed 'Church Imperialism' and the republican 'Ode To Mazzini' which he read to Birkbeck Hill in March. His passion for republican Rome fuelled 'The Temple of Janus', unsuccessfully entered for the Newdigate Prize in Trinity term 1857. Lafourcade has memorably described the poem as exhibiting 'the rushing stream of Shelley's influence . . . carrying along with it small fragments of Keatsian rock'. It is at least as readable as some of Swinburne's later republican odes. His political passions did not make for his best poems; the strongest in his most agitative volume, *Songs before Sunrise*, succeed inspite of, rather than because of, their political themes. If, to adapt Yeats's famous dictum, poetry is what Swinburne made out of the quarrel with himself, rhetoric was what he often made out of the quarrel with priests and kings.

For Swinburne, the most significant member of Old Mortality was John Nichol, a Scot of radical politics and later Professor of English Literature at Glasgow. Swinburne said Nichol gave him 'valuable help in the study of logic', praised his 'steady grasp . . . of all matters connected with Mental Science' and called him the 'guide of my boyhood in the paths of free thought and republican faith'. Whether or not it is true Nichol introduced Swinburne to alcohol, he strengthened the poet's republicanism and hastened his break with Christianity. Swinburne's rejection of Christianity can be dated roughly to his first two years at Balliol. To others, perhaps to Swinburne himself, it would have seemed a sudden event. Swinburne's beliefs behaved like geological fault-lines. The gradual build-up of animosity and antipathy went on largely unseen. The subterranean pressure increased until the fault slipped and a whole citadel of belief and emotion subsided into the abyss. When it happened, it was irrevocable.

Nichol's credibility as a republican was enhanced by his acquaintance with the Italian patriot Mazzini. According to A. V. Dicey, Old Mortality was interested in 'the cause of foreign nationalities, and especially of Italy, the crimes of Louis Napoleon, and the abolition of University Tests, as well as all restrictions on the freedom of opinion'. This influence may have inspired the 'Ode to Mazzini'. William Rossetti

described Nichol as 'a keen fine-witted man' who 'seems a good hater . . .
Both he and his wife are very free in religious matters.' Nichol's father
took to Swinburne and prophesied great things for him, and Nichol is
said to have told Lord Bryce that Swinburne 'is the one among us who
certainly has genius'. The two men shared literary passions, such as
Browning, and visited the Western Isles of Scotland in the late summer
of 1857. Afterwards Nichol reported: 'Swinburne says we ran a Muck
once or twice, and were like to have made a Mull of the affair, but on
the whole it was a Rum go!' They were the first to climb Blaven, 3200
feet high, on Skye. A. C. Bradley told Gosse in 1916 that during their
holiday Nichol had left a tired Swinburne at an inn. On his return he
found Swinburne incapacitated from sampling its supply of spirits.

Association with Old Mortality encouraged Swinburne to attend debates at the Oxford Union. On May 18 and 25 he spoke in the affirma-
tive with Nichol and Green for a motion 'that the despotism of Louis
Napoleon as at present exercised over France is both prejudicial to the
progress of that country and to the true interests of Europe'. Napoleon
III was Swinburne's *bête noire*. In addition to a portrait of Mazzini,
Swinburne bought one of Felice Orsini, who threw a bomb at the
Emperor in January 1858 and was guillotined. Swinburne's small, dap-
per red-haired figure, shrilly denouncing the policy of Napoleon III, or
opposing capital punishment (except for Napoleon III, whom he wished
to see 'kick heels in a rope') would have been a not infrequent sight at
the Union.

On 31 November 1857 Old Mortality met in Swinburne's room to
celebrate the first issue of its magazine, *Undergraduate Papers*, which
was taken over by the Society at the invitation of the publisher. Nichol
went out to fetch copies from the printer but they, and he, failed to
appear. Hill remembered, 'we still managed to drink its health in very
good claret as well as the health of each contributor, and the absent
editor also. So we made very merry indeed.' Although it only ran to
three numbers, expiring in April 1858, the magazine included five
pieces by Swinburne. 'The Early English Dramatists' discussed Marlowe
and Webster with some panache for a 20-year-old, Swinburne 'relishing
those dramatists with the palate of a connoisseur, rendering his responses with the pen of a poet'. There was a criticism of Matthew
Arnold's 1857 lectures as Professor of Poetry at Oxford, 'Modern Hellenism' and 'Church Imperialism', which Swinburne later ironically
described as a 'terrific onslaught on the French Empire and its Clerical
supporters – which must no doubt have contributed in no inconsider-
able degree to bring about its ultimate collapse'. Finally there was a
burlesque review of *The Monomaniac's Tragedy* by the non-existent
spasmodic poet Ernest Wheldrake. 'Nothing is so tenacious of life as a

bad poet,' began Swinburne; 'The opossum, we are credibly informed, survives for hours after its brains are blown out by a pistol. The author of "The Monomaniac's Tragedy" lives, writes, and finds a publisher.' Swinburne's poetry was represented by the tercets of 'Queen Yseult' (canto one), his first attempt at an Arthurian story and the immediate result of meeting the Pre-Raphaelites who were painting the Oxford Union from September 1857.

It was Edwin Hatch who introduced Swinburne to William Morris on 1 November at Hill's. Meetings with the other artists – Dante Gabriel Rossetti, Edward Burne-Jones, Val Prinsep, J. H. Pollen and Arthur Hughes – soon followed. They were painting Arthurian murals amid much 'jollity, noise, cork-popping, paint-sloshing, and general larking about'. When a pot of expensive lapis lazuli was knocked into another of ultramarine, Rossetti would say to his anxious patrons, 'Oh, that's nothing, we often do that.' Their love for all things medieval, their sensuous and colourful treatment of subjects like 'The Death of Merlin', 'Sir Tristram and Lady Iseult' and 'Sir Lancelot's Vision of the Holy Grail', and the carefree, irreverent atmosphere in which they worked, captivated Swinburne. Burne-Jones ('Ned'), Rossetti (Gabriel) and Morris ('Topsy') soon regarded 'dear little Carrots' as one of them. Rossetti was immediately taken with Swinburne's hair and wanted to use him as a model. Their talk was often racy. Swinburne related how

> One evening . . . Jones and I had a great talk. Stanhope and Swan attacked, and we defended, our idea of Heaven, viz, a rose-garden full of stunners. Atrocities of an appalling nature were uttered on the other side. We became so fierce that two respectable members of the University – entering to see the pictures – stood mute and looked at us. We spoke just then of kisses in Paradise, and expounded our ideas on the celestial development of that necessity of life; and after listening five minutes to our language, they literally fled from the room! Conceive our mutual ecstasy of delight.

For the rest of his undergraduate career Swinburne idolized Morris, Rossetti and Burne-Jones. At a stroke he made three friends for life. In 1859 Scott said, 'at present there seem only two people in the world to him, Topsy and Rossetti, and only those books or things they admire or appropriate will he entertain'.

Reading Morris's first book of poems, *The Defence of Guenevere*, in February 1858, Swinburne wrote, 'I would fain be worthy to sit down at his feet' – a typical reaction when he found a hero to worship. Nine days after meeting Morris Swinburne was reading Hill parts of 'Queen Yseult' and Hill wrote, 'he is already a true poet, I say it without exaggeration':

> For no crown the maiden had,
> But with tresses golden-glad
> Was her perfect body clad.
>
> And no gems the maiden wore
> But the bright hair evermore
> All her warm white hands before.

'Queen Yseult' has some colourful, concise description and some terse narration, as when Tristram parts from Iseult: 'Ere a leaf had left its tree,/Sailed he all the blowing sea/Till he came to Brittany.' But over six cantos the style suffered from monotony. Swinburne soon realized the danger of 'Topsification', of writing too much in Morris's shadow.

Swinburne became something of a medievalist for the rest of his time in Oxford. A large number of compositions had medieval orientations: 'Rudel in Paradise,', 'Lancelot', 'Southwards', 'The Day before the Trial', 'The Queen's Tragedy', 'Joyeuse Garde', 'King Ban', 'A Lay of Lilies', 'The Dream By The River' and 'The Masque of Queen Bersabe'. Swinburne plunged into a detailed reading of medieval authors, pored over manuscripts in his uncle's library at Ashburnham Place during the vacations, planned an epic titled 'The Albigenses', and started the play 'Rosamond', which became part of his first book in 1860. Otherwise he imitated Browning, Shakespeare (the 'Undergraduate Sonnets'), wrote poems with a modern setting and a play 'The Laws of Corinth'. His reading of John Fletcher inspired the dramas 'Laugh and Lie Down' and 'The Loyal Servant'. 'The Travelling of Thor', an unfinished poem of over a hundred lines, is based on Norse myth:

> So with great fear and wonder all they were
>   Astonied as a voyager in strange lands:
> But Freya loosened all the heavy hair
>   Over her face and wept between her hands
> Praying aloud; but Odin heard not her;
>   For standing as a lone sea-eagle stands
> In thunder and the wash of winter streams
>   Rolled round him, and the noise of blowing wind
> From valley on to valley, when it seems
>   That a great mist has made the daylight blind,
> So rose he as a man perplext with dreams,
>   Perplext with dreams and altered in his mind,
> And spake not; and they watching him spake not.

Swinburne's fond but volatile friendship with Edwin Hatch (1835–89), a leading light at Pembroke College, was more important than previous biographies have realized. Hatch's training for his ordination (in 1858) and Swinburne's rapid and probably vocal apostasy put their relationship on a short fuse from the start. How did Hatch take letters with the postscript 'greetings in the name of the devil'? But initially the friendship burned brightly. Hatch was invited to stay at East Dene from 2–12 January 1858. He was 'delighted with the first look of the place – and with the exceeding kindness of the Swinburnes'. His room overlooked the lawns and trees to the Channel. On the Sunday Hatch's diary records 'at home with Swinburne: very pleasant talk both morning, noon, eve and night'. The next day they walked to Shanklin Chine, 'growing into Brotherhood'; at night 'spent glorious hours in hearing Swinburne's poetry – as almost every night this week'. They rode to Sandown, walked to Ventnor, climbed the downs, rode by the sea and visited Luccombe. The climax was a trip west to Freshwater, where they had 'a glorious night together in the Hotel: read and talked and poured soul into soul'. On 12 January they visited Tennyson, 'first in morning when we talked not much, he being busy with his poem. Then at dinner with him and Mrs. Tennyson; stayed till long after midnight.' Tennyson told a correspondent, 'young Swinburne called here the other day with a college friend of his, and we asked him to dinner, and I thought him a very modest and intelligent fellow ... what I particularly admired in him was that he did not press upon me any verses of his own'. They talked of Virgil, and Swinburne found the evening 'very pleasant and hospitable'.

Hatch's friendship with Swinburne soon gained another facet. On 5 January Hatch exclaimed 'Oh God! for another such walk at the downs and for such another beginning to the love of her: DIES MEMORABILIS.' Two days later he wrote, 'went to a stupid lecture in the evening with Lady Jane Swinburne and E', the 'E' being emphasized. It seems Hatch fell in love with Edith, now seventeen, and in the time-honoured way, lent her a book. A month later, Swinburne wrote to Hatch,

> I have a message to you from Edith, which I enclose in her own words. Of course if you like I will write for your book, and she can get another copy; you must not let her interfere between you and what you value. She would be in a great state of mind at the idea.

Further confirmation comes in a letter about Jane Morris:

> All my people desire to be remembered to you. I had a long letter from Edith the other day: *I know you will be glad to hear this, as I am to think of Morris's having that wonderful and most perfect stunner of his to – look at or speak to.* The idea of his marrying her is insane. To kiss her feet is the utmost man should dream of doing. [Italics added]

The Morris/Jane Burden parallel clearly implies Hatch had a romantic interest in Edith. When Swinburne wrote from Capheaton in September 1858 expressing his pleasure that Hatch had taken up Hugo, he added, 'my sisters are already among his faithful worshippers – Edith above all.

Get her to speak of him some day, and see the effect of my training.'
Hatch's interest in Edith could only have deepened his friendship with
her brother.

After a week apart, Swinburne and Hatch met in London on 20
January, the latter noting 'a glorious walk alone with Swinburne in the
parks'. They visited the National Gallery and returned to Oxford on 23
January. Swinburne forgot a dinner date arranged for the following day,
but all was remedied with a walk to Woodstock and an evening in
Swinburne's rooms. There were further meetings on 27 and 28 January
before Hatch left Oxford to work as a curate in the East End. When he
returned in April they met on four days in succession. On 20 April
Hatch observed, 'Poor Swinburne fearfully depressed – seemingly knowing little of trouble – even the slight one of having to read what is
disagreeable:– pleasant walk with him down the High at night.' They
met again in June, October and November. Swinburne often sent Hatch
new poems. A letter of 17 February came with 'two of my latest grinds':

> Lose not the priceless uniques lest the world demand the account
> thereof at your hands. 'The Golden House' is of course 'Rudel in
> Paradise'. The other I can only describe as a dramatico-lyrico-
> phantas-magorico-spasmodic sermon on the grievous sin of flirta-
> tion. It was written off one evening and has never been corrected
> ... It is of course meant for a picture of exceptional weakness;
> inaction of man, impulsive irresolution of the woman; mutual
> ignorance of each other and themselves, with an extra dash of
> sensuous impulse; finally with no ostensible cause, rupture and
> spiflication. Pray abuse it if you feel inclined; I am not (as you
> know) over-delicate and timid concerning my scribbles, and I have
> no tenderness for this; and if it is not what it ought to be, it is a
> decided failure ... I long to be with you by firelight between the
> sunset and the sea to have talk of *Sordello*; it is one of my canoni-
> cal scriptures.

Old Mortality, the Pre-Raphaelites and his own passionate devotion to
writing had a deleterious effect on Swinburne's academic progress.
Through 1857 Robert Scott had summarized his performance as 'highly
respectable', 'very creditable' and 'good but wanting energy'. For Hilary term 1858 he wrote 'well-disposed but very irregular in his habits'.
Admittedly there were successes: on 5 June 1858 he took a second-class
pass in Moderations and on 14 June won the Taylorian Prize for French
and Italian. The Taylorian Institute Library became his means of famil-
iarizing himself with French authors such as Stendhal, Dumas, Janin,
Ronsard and Balzac, and possibly Gautier, whose *Mademoiselle de
Maupin*, with its lesbian theme, became Swinburne's 'golden book of
spirit and sense'. His love of Italy was further stoked by his attendance
at lectures given by Aurelio Saffi (1819–90), in exile since 1851 and a

friend of Mazzini. Rather than continue his studies in the School of Classical Greats, Swinburne elected to read for Honours in Law and Modern History, with a 'minor' in the Pass School of Classics. Lafourcade suggests that this decision, which entailed reading medieval history, may have been influenced by his new Pre-Raphaelite contacts.

But things were not so good at Balliol. On 17 June Swinburne was given a formal warning before the Master and Dean 'on account of persistently neglecting his studies'. He was ill in the summer of 1858; he told Hatch that doctors had considered him 'pulled down and seedy in general' so he was sent home. 'I indulged at East Dene in rhymes, Boccaccio, Chaucer, and general stagnation. The place was in a very jolly condition and I soon "assimilated". Sea-bathing all through July left me rather Herculean than otherwise.' The work from Boccaccio was probably 'The White Hind' which evolved into 'The Two Dreams' (published in 1866). His enjoyment of East Dene was tempered by 'seclusion and Tories'. The replacement of Christianity with republican-ism made home less congenial. On 17 August Swinburne visited Wallington for a few days, and again a little later for four weeks. One of Lady Trevelyan's guests told a friend Swinburne 'is clever and writes quaint ballads. And he reads his poems, which are very nice.'

By the close of 1858 Swinburne may have felt less interested in Oxford. The painting of the Union murals was over, the company of artists had dispersed, Morris returning from time to time to see Jane Burden until their marriage in April 1859. He may have attended Union debates in late October and early November for a motion 'that the ends resulting to France from the Usurpation and Despotic Government of Louis Napoleon can only be remedied by the return of the Bourbons'. A second warning from Balliol came on 16 December, 'on the grounds that by the end of term and after a first warning he in no way improved himself, but continued to neglect College studies'. In January 1858 Swinburne moved out of Balliol and went to live at Rose's, 10 Broad Street, a few minutes' walk away. With the Pre-Raphaelites gone from Oxford there were fewer distractions. On 10 February he spoke at the Union in favour of a motion 'that French interference in Italy is not only objectionable in itself, but prejudicial to the cause of liberty in Italy'. He spoke against a motion criticizing the Reform Bill as 'too sweeping' on 17 March, and a week later in favour of a motion 'that Capital Punishment is objectionable on the grounds both of Justice and Expediency'.

The Master noted 'some improvement apparent' in Hilary term 1859 and that Swinburne was 'still irregular: but rather improved' in the summer term. His studies included Samuel I, II, the first Book of Kings, Plato's *Republic*, Ennius, Livy, Hallam's *Middle Ages* and Gibbon. By

now the 8.00 a.m. litany was anathema to him. Lord Bryce told Gosse
that in 1859:

> ... he had been gated by the Dean, old Mr. Woolcombe, for non-
> attendance, repeated after many admonitions, at chapel, and how
> consequently he could not accompany us on the annual excursion
> which the Old Mortality used to make to some place of interest or
> beauty within reach of Oxford. When we returned in the evening
> ... some one said, 'Let us condole with poor Swinburne,' and so
> we went to his rooms to cheer him up. He launched into a wonder-
> ful display of vituperative eloquence. He was not really angry, but
> he enjoyed the opportunity, and the resources of his imagination in
> metaphor and the amazing richness of his vocabulary had never, I
> think, struck us so much before.

By late July Swinburne was in Northumberland, visiting Wallington on
28 July, 10–11 August, and with Scott on 5–6 September. Swinburne
would lounge on the grass reading French novels or go walking on the
moors with Walter Trevelyan. He and Scott visited the Longships Lighthouse. From the boat, while Scott was being sea-sick, Swinburne saw
three herons on a rock ledge and stored the detail for thirty years, using
it in his Arthurian epic *Tristram of Lyonesse*. It was during this period
that Scott began the small oil portrait of Swinburne that now hangs in
Balliol College.

For part of September Swinburne was at Capheaton. His friendship
with Hatch, who became an object of derision among the Pre-Raphaelite
set, now ruptured. Nothing had come of Hatch's feelings for Edith. On
2 September, about to take up the position of Professor of Classics at
Trinity College Toronto, Hatch wrote from Haverfordwest:

> I cannot leave England without writing to bid you goodbye; but I
> fear that the chain which once bound us together is somehow
> snapped asunder. I don't know that I shall ever see you again – and
> perhaps it may be well if I do not – but I shall never forget how I
> loved you once – and in spite of all the mistaken things which you
> have thought or said of me there will be ever in that old memory
> something to make me continually glad. God forbid that I should
> think blame of you for walking in whatever path you will – only
> take care how you trifle with friendship. Goodbye – God bless you.

Across the foot of the page Swinburne scrawled 'for the matter of that,
rot!'. His reply two days later is an epistle of acid rejection worthy of
his character Lady Midhurst:

> Having received your farewell note I have great pleasure in writing
> to congratulate you on your professional prospects, which I am not
> surprised to hear of as brilliant. It is a further pleasure to me to be
> able to meet you on another point – viz. that, in your own words,
> 'it may perhaps be well that I should never see you again.' As, to
> the best of my remembrance, my protestations of 'love' were never

so enthusiastic as to require a formal recantation, – I am unhappily disqualified from sympathizing in the rupture of a golden 'bond' of whose existence I was first made aware by your own assertions; after which it was of course impossible to doubt of it. That its memory should make you 'continually glad' is nevertheless a matter to me of sincere satisfaction. The mistaken things which, as you further inform me, I have thought and said of you, I commend to the charitable correction [?] of your own friendly and consistent candour . . . .

Perhaps Swinburne had justification for replying so coldly. But he always found it hard to find the middle ground. In March 1859 George Boyce had dined with Swinburne and Morris, both 'mad and deafening with excitement . . . the chaff and row continued with great spirit and cleverness. Swinburne, a man of great reading, memory, and intellectual . . . accomplishment, seemed to be wanting in human feeling. '

By 1859 Swinburne had familiarized himself with the Taylorian's collection of French literature. In the early autumn he had the 'rapture' of getting the first two volumes of Hugo's *Légende des Siècles* and reading Balzac. He read Walt Whitman's *Leaves of Grass* and George Eliot's *Adam Bede*, maintaining in the face of Old Mortality's scepticism that the author was a woman.

The circumstances surrounding Swinburne's departure from Oxford in November 1859 have hitherto been unclear. It has often been said that a consultation between Jowett and the Admiral resulted in a decision to remove Swinburne to avoid more damaging clashes with the College. Bryce told Gosse in March 1915 that Swinburne 'transgressed every college regulation, but we didn't hear of anything graver – I never saw him intoxicated in those days'. Yet as Lafourcade once enquired:

if . . . Swinburne 'left without taking a degree' why should he write of his autobiographical hero, Reginald Harewood, in a passage of *A Year's Letters* which occurs in the manuscript alone, that 'he had got himself twice plucked and once rusticated'? Why should he repeatedly have stated that he had been 'rusticated and all but expelled'?

The formal warnings he received in June and December 1858 clearly explain 'twice plucked'. Swinburne's case came for a third time before the College authorities on 16 and 18 November after he failed his Classics Pass School:

Commoner Swinburne, who had not satisfied the examiners in the School of Literae Humaniores, was reprimanded before the College, since this had evidently not happened without himself being greatly to blame. For he had once been affected by the same disgrace in doing his Responses on account of similar neglect; and besides, now having been warned twice (first time 17 June 1858,

second time 16 December same year) he evidently with the same
persistence as ever showed contempt for the authority of the College. Therefore as a punishment he was ordered to depart to the
country forthwith and not to return to the University before the
day appointed for the public examination. In addition, on his
departure he was given written work to do; with the additional
decree that for a whole year after the completion of the last examination, he should be suspended from the degree of B. A.

He wrote to his mother, from the Union, sometime in November:

> I have myself been rather busy . . . in working (unhappily too late)
> for my first examination in Classics – which turns out a failure. I
> *had* hoped to get it done, and have my way way clear to work for
> honours in the spring. As it is, I shall have them both on my hands
> at once, and I need not add, feel ashamed of myself.

The family had high hopes of Swinburne distinguishing himself at Oxford, so this must have been a disappointment; his 'shame' was meant
to mollify this.

Swinburne packed his bags and left Oxford, having a 'jolly fortnight'
in London, where he visited Rossetti and was much taken with a
portrait of Fanny Cornforth as 'Bocca Baciata' – 'she is more stunning
than can be decently expressed'. He visited the Hogarth Club and met
R. B. Martineau. From there he went to Pierceford in Essex, to stay
with William Stubbs (1825–1901) at Navestock Parsonage, for tutoring
in history and law. The amount of work ahead did not deter him from
his own literary productions, as he told Scott on 16 December:

> I have written a new ballad so indecent that it beats all the rest and
> is nearly up to Blake's Klopstock. N.B. I have got Blake's 'Dante' –
> seven plates – stunners. Also his 'Job'. I shall bring them north next
> year. I wish to goodness I was going up this winter but I shan't be
> let, with that blessed Oxford ahead. Have you read Victor Hugo's
> *Légende des Siècles*? – It's the grandest book that has been pub-
> lished there or here for years. The medieval poems in it – for
> instance – 'Ratbert' – simply whip creation into mush and molasses
> . . . Don't you think a good dramatic subject would be Mary Stuart's
> amour with Chatelet? one might end with cutting off his head on
> the stage. I want to find facts about it; do you know of any?

Swinburne read Blake in the manuscript notebook owned by Rossetti
and his admiration of the then largely unknown artist/prophet eventually flowered in his 1868 study of Blake, and the drama of Mary Stuart
and Chatelet forms the first part of a trilogy about her. He was also
working at this time on a fragment of a drama on Lucrece Borgia, and
the two plays *Rosamond* and *The Queen Mother*, known at this time as
'Catherine'. The latter were ready for publication by February 1860
and Swinburne negotiated a publisher by the summer.

Swinburne's other poetry of this time included pieces showing the influence of Shelley and Keats, such as the 'Fall of Hyperion', 'The Nightingale', 'Echo' and 'Ode to the Night', and more modern poems such as 'From the Boat' and 'By the Sea-side', and 'An Epistle in Verse', erroneously thought to be written for Lady Trevelyan. His enthusiasm for Northumbrian ballads had probably led him to try his hand at that form of narrative verse. He was proud when he managed to pass one of his ballads off as the real article when he read it at Capheaton. The very earliest of the 1866 *Poems and Ballads* date to these years, for example an early draft of 'The Leper' entitled 'A Vigil'. Many of his abiding themes – failed love, sorrow, political rebellion, the necessity to endure, eroticism, beauty over morality and the protest against God – were emerging.

Swinburne went north during the Christmas holidays to spend time at Capheaton and Wallington, where he stayed from 16 to 23 January. He read Pauline scenes from 'Rosamond' and Walter Trevelyan showed him books about Mary Stuart. He visited Scott in Newcastle before returning south by sea to resume his academic labours. One further distraction was *The Guardian*'s announcement on 8 February that a prize would be awarded to 'the writer of the best English poem on "The Life, the Character and the Death of the heroic seaman, Sir John Franklin, with special reference to the time, place, and discovery of his death"'. Franklin's ill-fated expedition set out to find the Northwest passage in 1845 and after contact had been lost, its members were presumed dead. Their remains were found early in 1859 after a search mission had been organized (to which Swinburne's father had contributed £30). Swinburne wrote his entry in two mornings; with its description of the icy northern territory, it is one of his best undergraduate poems:

> Among the thousand colours and gaunt shapes
> Of the strong ice cloven with breach of sea,
> Where the waste sullen shadow of steep capes
> Narrows across the cloudy-coloured brine,
> And by strong jets the angered foam escapes;
> And a sad touch of sun scores the sea-line
> Right at the middle motion of the noon
> And then fades sharply back, and the cliffs shine
> Fierce with keen snows against a kindled moon
> In the hard purple of the bitter sky.

Swinburne is sensitive to the pathos of the men's plight, doomed in such a barren domain, recalling the seasons at home: 'all the branches' tender over-growth,/Where the quick birds took sudden heart to sing/ ... Mere recollection of all dearer things.' The reiteration of 'England' shows the patriotic seed in Swinburne's verse that engulfed the poetry he wrote from his mid-forties. Despite its merits, the poem did not win and Swinburne went back to his medieval law.

It is said that Swinburne read Stubbs and his wife some of 'Rosamond'. Finishing the recitation, which had steadily increased in passion, he sat back, eyes shining, feet tapping, and awaited their commendation. Stubbs and his wife glanced at each other. It was very good, said Stubbs, though perhaps some of the lines were a little . . . well, warm? Swinburne was suddenly still, a shocked look freezing his pale features. Then, with a scream, he rushed upstairs to his room and slammed the door, locking it. His hosts bustled upstairs but could not draw him out. During the night strange noises emanated from the room, and a faint glow was shed from under the door. Next morning, a conciliatory Stubbs expressed the hope that Algernon had not taken the criticism too much to heart. A tired-looking Swinburne replied he had burnt the manuscript in the grate. But it was all right after all – because he sat up the whole night writing it all out again from memory.

Swinburne's stay at Navestock came to an end in April 1860. Stubbs remembered Swinburne fondly as 'the most singular young man I have ever known'. On his return to Oxford Swinburne passed at his second attempt the Literae Humaniores examination on 5 May. His preparation for Finals was terminally interrupted when disaster struck in typically Algernonic fashion. On 5 June he wrote to his mother:

> About the beginning of last week I had a bad fall from a horse in leaping a gate. It was in the end lucky that I alighted full on my chin and the lower part of my face – but as some teeth were splintered, the jaw sprained and the lips cut up it was not pleasant. For a week nearly I have been kept in bed and fed on liquids, and still I can eat nothing but crumb of bread and such like . . . The Dr. *did* last week prohibit ideas of trying to bring my ill-fated work through to some end or other (certainly the Fates *are* against my reading for honours in history), but I must stay a day or two longer to try. If I really *cannot* do enough to get fairly through and take a decent place in the list – then of course I shall not try but come up to you in London this week.

Two days later he walked to Cumnor with Nichol. Swinburne apparently decided that he was not sufficiently prepared for the examination ('Greats') and did not take it. He later embellished this by saying that his Oxford career ended in 'complete and scandalous failure'. He was fond of drawing a parallel with the academic fate of Shelley. On one occasion, returning to Balliol to meet Arnold in the 1870s, he wrote, 'I am to meet him next month at our Common College (which on a time cast me out even as another Shelley, but is now a penitent Mother Magdalen).' Similarly in 1871 when he invited Jowett to stay at the family home in Shiplake, he wrote, 'Times are changed: imagine Shelley within ten years of his expulsion (or say as in my case 'permanent rustication') receiving the Master of his College at his father's house.' Although Swinburne developed a good relationship with Jowett, he had no fond memories of Oxford, and when the University offered him an honorary degree in 1907 he turned it down.

On 25 August the Chiswick Press started typesetting his first book. By September 1860 Swinburne was back at East Dene, writing to Nichol cursing a would-be assassin of Napoleon III – 'Why could not he shoot straight, and rid the world of – Decency forbids me to pursue the subject.' The family planned to go to Italy. But on 21 September news reached the Admiral that his father Sir John was very ill. He dashed north on 26 September, arriving at 7 p.m. to find 'poor Papy' had died at 1 p.m. His diary notes that 'Hadji' (Algernon) arrived the next day. Swinburne was deeply upset. He intensely admired his grandfather and had no liking for his grandfather's successor at Capheaton, Sir John Swinburne, whom he described in later life as 'a terrible bore and a nuisance' and 'Sir Jackass'. He preferred Bertram, the fifth Earl of Ashburnham, 'papist or no papist'. With the death of his grandfather and the loss of Capheaton, a door closed on Swinburne's past.

CHAPTER FOUR

'Such Fair Green Seasons'

After their bereavement, the Swinburnes went to Italy for the winter. Algernon remained behind with an allowance from his father of £400 a year. Committed to being a writer, Swinburne found rooms at 16 Fitzroy Street, Grafton Square, a convenient address for the British Museum. Proof copies of his first book *The Queen Mother and Rosamond* (published by Basil Montagu Pickering) were ready by November. Though it has been said the Admiral financed its publication, in 1872 Swinburne recalled, 'my first boyish book of '60–61 was paid for out of my own pocket, and cost me I remember something under £40 or £50: of which of course it never repaid me a penny'.

The *Queen Mother and Rosamond* did not ignite literary London. *The Spectator* commented on the author's choice of 'two painful subjects, the Massacre of St. Bartholomew and the Murder of Rosamond Clifford by Queen Eleanor', judging Swinburne's language 'painfully distorted, vague, elliptical, and bristling with harsh words'. *The Athenaeum* observed, 'we should have conceived it hardly possible to make the crimes of Catherine de Medici dull, howsoever they were presented. Mr Swinburne, however, has done so ... having had such ill-luck with one wicked Queen, we were unable to cope with a second one.'

Despite some impressive speeches both plays subordinate character and action to a pastiche Jacobean style. But they do shed light on Swinburne's preoccupations, with his desire to shock, his fascination with unnatural death and sensual experience, as he returns to images of hair, eyes, wrists, necks, mouths, and the vulnerability of skin to bruising. Rosamond is a early example of Swinburne's many *femme fatales*; he declares how as Helen, Cressida, Guenevere, she had 'So kissed men's mouths that they went sick or mad,/Stung right at brain with me'. Rossetti (the dedicatee) told the poet William Allingham that although there were 'real beauties' in it, 'he is much better suited to balladwriting and such like'. Swinburne's father thought it 'altogether far worse than useless – most pernicious'. The book was no sooner out than Swinburne acknowledged its faults to friends such as Scott.

Swinburne joined his family in Italy early in 1861. A letter to Lady Trevelyan expresses his dislike for Mentone in terms that evoke Browning's 'Childe Roland'. It was 'a calcined, scalped, rasped, scraped, flayed, broiled, powdered, leprous, blotched, mangy, grimy, parboiled country, *without* trees, water, grass, fields – *with* blank, beastly, senseless olives and orange-trees like a mad cabbage gone indigestible; it is infinitely liker hell than earth, and one looks for tails among the people'. During February Swinburne travelled to Genoa, Turin, Milan, Brescia, Verona, Vicenze, Padua and Venice, delighted not only by many of the galleries and churches, but also by the female population:

> As to women, I saw in Venice one of the three most beautiful I ever saw (the other two were one at Genoa, the other at Ventimiglia in the Riviera); by her gaze I thought I might have addressed her, but did not, considering that we could not have understood each other (verbally at least); so caution and chastity, or mauvaise honte and sense of embarrassment, prevailed. – But I must not begin on Italian things or people, or I shall never stop.

Many years later he recorded how their beauty 'overcame/My sight with rapture of reiterate awe'.

By the spring of 1861 Swinburne had enough poems for a book and was still adding to them. When in January he wrote to thank Scott for a letter which made 'a green and gushing spot in the dullest of lives', Swinburne enclosed 'A Song in Time of Revolution'. It is notable for the long anapaestic lines of Swinburne's authentic poetic voice:

> The wind has the sound of a laugh in the clamour of days and of deeds:
> The priests are scattered like chaff, and the rulers broken like reeds.

Along with 'St. Dorothy', also composed about this period, it would be included in *Poems and Ballads* (1866).

Swinburne had a number of writing projects on hand. An early draft of *Chastelard* was three-quarters done by January 1861 and there is a play fragment featuring Count Giorando dating roughly to this period. He told Lady Trevelyan he was trying to write prose, 'which is very hard, but I want to make a few stories each about three or six pages long. Likewise a big one about my blessedest pet which her initials is Lucrezia Estense Borgia.' The stories were to be called 'The Triameron' and Swinburne made a list of nineteen titles. It seems that 'Dead Love' (published 1862), 'The Marriage of Monna Lisa', 'A Criminal Case', 'The Portrait', 'A Nine Days Wonder' and 'The Chronicle of Queen Fredegond' were the only ones he finished. Lafourcade argued that 'Sans Merci' may be the story incorporated in Chapter 20 of *A Year's Letters*. For 'Queen Fredegond' Swinburne had the advantage of being able to use a rare sixteenth-century history of France in the library of his Uncle Bertram, the Earl of Ashburnham. The medieval and early French sections of the Earl's collection had fascinated Swinburne since he was a boy.

'A Nine Days Wonder' (written *c.* 1865–66) is fairly typical of these stories. Lescombat is married to a woman who likes him less as his passion intensifies. Madame Lescombat is an emotional vampire able to 'strengthen herself upon the health and vigour' of her husband: 'her beauty grew more complete, fuller of blood, more splendid in shape and colour, as if she sucked the life out of his lean laborious body and worried face to nourish it'. She is imperious and coldly voluptuous. She takes a lover, taunts her husband with him and persuades the lover to kill him. Afterwards Madame Lescombat and Mongeot, the lover, are apprehended, tortured and executed. Swinburne lingers over the sad and bitter last talk of the lovers in prison. The final twist is that the execution is witnessed by the five-year-old Marquis de Sade, who enjoys the spectacle of the woman's end.

The longer story about Lucretia Borgia to which Swinburne alludes was published in 1942 as *Lucretia Borgia; or The Chronicle of Tebaldeo Tebaldei*. Chapter IV ('Of the gift of amorous mercy') celebrates earthly love as the best possible heaven, directly challenging the orthodox division of life into the 'spiritual' and the 'physical':

> But of the pleasure ensuing who shall ever be worthy to speak? for before the face of that supreme sweetness are the faces of the very gods made pale and the lips of Delight too harsh to make songs of it. Yea, of the paradise of heaven itself let no man conceive as of a greater thing than this. For by no reach of wit and by no strength of spirit can one in any wise imagine or suppose that God has ever been able to think of anything better; except indeed he were minded to destroy and blot out at one stroke soul and body through the excess of a mortal and deadly pleasure; seeing that hardly sometimes can the human life in us endure to bear up against this extremity, the joy whereof devours us like a fierce and ravenous disease. And of what pleasure can anything alive be capable beyond this of having his soul made part of the soul of another and his body made part of another body through the marvellous work of the pleasure of love? but especially when the body and soul enjoyed by him are so infinitely more beautiful and noble than his own that he is actually and naturally received into a very present heaven, the which may be touched and handled and understood of all the fleshly senses?

The thought of a pleasure so strong it could wipe out consciousness in an instant exposes the impulse in Swinburne to self-transcendence. In some ways anticipating Arthur Symons, D. H. Lawrence and Eric Gill, this attempt to oppose puritanical attitudes to sex was one of Swinburne's main gifts to an age notorious for denying the body. The value of having 'held fair love in the life upon earth' is a constant theme in his work and, as much of *Poems and Ballads* and *Tristram of Lyonesse* show, where he is often at his best.

By the spring of 1861 Swinburne resumed his social life in London. He saw Rossetti and his wife Elizabeth Siddal at Chatham Place,

Blackfriars; Ford Madox Brown at Fortess Terrace; and William and Jane Morris at Upton in Kent. May Morris recalled how Swinburne lay in the orchard 'with his red hair spread abroad, while her baby sister and she scattered rose-leaves over his laughing face'. Living in Russell Place close by, Ned and Georgie Burne-Jones saw him frequently:

> ... sometimes twice or three times a day he would come in, bringing his poems hot from his heart and certain of a welcome and a hearing at any hour. His appearance was very unusual and in some ways beautiful, for his hair was glorious in abundance and colour and his eyes indescribably fine. When repeating poetry he had a perfectly natural way of lifting them in a rapt, unconscious gaze, and their clear green colour softened by thick brown eyelashes was unforgettable. 'Looks commencing with the skies' expresses it without exaggeration. He was restless beyond words, scarcely standing still at all and almost dancing as he walked, while even in sitting he moved continually, seeming to keep time, by a swift movement of the hands at the wrists, and sometimes of the feet also, with some inner rhythm of excitement. He was courteous and affectionate and unsuspicious, and faithful beyond most people to those he really loved. The biting wit which filled his talk so as at times to leave his hearers dumb with amazement always spared one thing, and that was an absent friend.

Such a unique and gifted individual could hardly fail to be noticed among the network of writers, painters and critics in Victorian London. Through Dante Gabriel, Swinburne met William, Christina and other members of the Rossetti family. William remained a life-long friend and wise counsellor. On 5 May 1861 he met Richard Monckton Milnes (1809–85), later Lord Houghton, the politician, writer, poet, collector, bibliophile and socialite who by the age of 50 had travelled widely, read widely, and dined widely. Milnes opened doors for Swinburne, both literal (to his library) and figurative. Milnes had a manor at Fryston, Yorkshire, and a town house off Park Lane where he entertained colourful gatherings; he was a self-effacing, genial, observant host with a droll sense of humour. On one occasion, 'an elderly lady, bewailing the lack of respect shown by the young, remarked that when she was a girl all the young men in London were "at my feet". Milnes, with an expression of weary amazement, confessed that he had no idea there were so many chiropodists in the London of her youth.'

Swinburne's life in the early 1860s has often been caricatured as a cross between a farce and a morality play, where Gifted Innocence is led astray by the malign influence of Corrupt Age. Milnes is usually cast as Mephistopheles to Swinburne's Faustus, a 'sinister Virgil ... guiding Swinburne through the Inferno of his library', who, if he had 'deliberately planned to ruin Swinburne's character and reputation ... could hardly have done a more thorough piece of work'. But Swinburne's elemental energies needed no human agent to go astray. Though their relationship was never particularly warm, Milnes gave Swinburne confidence in his writing and encouraged him to write only the poetry he could create rather than pastiche medieval lyrics and border ballads, even if this involved more obviously sado-masochistic content. Milnes introduced him to books and people, enabling Swinburne to publish in *The Spectator* in 1862. Milnes's library at Fryston, nicknamed Aphrodisiopolis, had an impressive range of books on European literature, the French Revolution, magic and witchcraft, and crime, together with French and Italian erotica, and works by de Sade.

It was at a breakfast party hosted by Milnes on 6 June 1861 that Swinburne met Captain Richard Burton and both felt 'a curious fancy, an absolute fascination, for one another'. Burton was 40, an ex-soldier of the Crimea and a famous explorer, a man of daring and courage. While the undergraduate Swinburne had befuddled Jowett with his essays, Burton and Speke were seeking the source of the Nile. Burton was six foot tall, powerfully built, with a scar on both cheeks caused by a spear wound, which, along with his intense gaze and pendulous moustache, gave him a slightly satanic demeanour. But to see Burton and Swinburne as the man of action and the man of dreams, the 'Herculean explorer' and the 'frail Pre-Raphaelite poet', both admiring 'what the other possessed and he himself lacked', obscures what they had in common.

Though perhaps exaggerated, Burton had a reputation as a sexual as well as a geographical explorer. As Fawn Brodie wrote, 'Burton was a man of great passions, but they were for the most part translated into curiosity and scholarship. His aggressive impulses, too, were transmuted and made safe by this scholarship, though they burst out now and then in the form of literary quarrels and personal truculence.' This is almost as true of Swinburne. Similarly, Burton's talent for riveting stories has a parallel with Swinburne's inspired recitations. Swinburne's flagellation obsessions were paralleled in Burton's interest in the sexual practices of other cultures. Burton was formally expelled from Trinity College, so Swinburne was fond of remarking that 'my connection with Oxford is something like Shelley's or my friend Sir Richard Burton'. Both were sceptical in religious matters and loved disguise (Burton literally and Swinburne in the form of his many literary aliases – Mrs Horace Manners, Ernest Wheldrake, Ernest Clouët, Félicien Cossu *et al.*) As Byron Farwell put it, 'both men had the same curious desire to shock and to make themselves out to be worse than they were'. They both published books that transgressed Victorian propriety, the former with his translations of the *Kama Sutra* and the *Arabian Nights*, the latter with *Poems and Ballads*. They both loved the freakish and unusual.

In 1863 Swinburne wrote three sonnets, 'Hermaphroditus'; on 17 April 1866 Burton read a paper to the Anthropological Society titled 'Notes on a Hermaphrodite'. There was much to attract them to each other, and their friendship lasted until Burton's death in 1890.

Burton was often abroad as a diplomat but when home he and Swinburne were rowdy drinking companions. When Burton left for Brazil in May 1865 Swinburne wrote to Milnes:

> As my tempter and favourite audience has gone to Santos I may hope to be a good boy again, after such a 'jolly good swishing' as Rodin alone can and dare administer. The Rugby purists (I am told) tax Eton generally with Maenadism during June and July, so perhaps some old school habits return upon us unawares – to be fitly expiated by old school punishment. That once I remember and admit. The Captain was too many for me; and I may have shaken the thyrsus in your face. But after this half I mean to be no end good.

Was the swishing literal? Or was this just banter? At Dr George Bird's, Burton and Swinburne would retire to another room. As Gosse describes it, 'the rest of the company would be tantalized to hear proceeding roars and shrieks of laughter, followed by earnest rapid talk of a quieter description'. Burton's wife Isabel came from a staunch Catholic family. Once when Swinburne was expressing himself rather freely her father collared Swinburne and said, 'Young sir, if you talk like that, you will die like a dog! Speechless only for a second, Swinburne replied, 'Oh don't say "like a dog!". Do say, like a cat!'

In August 1861 Swinburne made his first stay at Milnes's house in Yorkshire; the company included the Burtons, Carlyle, Froude and Kingsley. When he returned to London Swinburne continued writing *Chastelard* and wrote a preface to Charles Wells's play *Joseph and His Brethren*. In October he saw a production of *Othello* and concluded that since mere mortals could never adequately act Shakespeare he would never attend a performance of the Bard again.

Swinburne saw a good deal of the Rossettis. His relationship with Dante Gabriel had continued beyond the Balliol years and steadily deepened. In the early 1860s it was probably his closest friendship outside of his family. Rossetti recognized Swinburne's genius without being swept away by it. He attempted to nurture and stimulate it by the example of his own art and through introducing Swinburne to books he had not read. He also realized that Swinburne's artistic energy at times needed tempering. Feeling that in Rossetti he had found a friend and a sensitive critic, Swinburne enjoyed 'the sweet and sudden passion of youth towards greatness in its elder'. Rossetti was charismatic, intense, funny and depressive by turns, the focus of his art on female beauty and

medieval subjects of obvious appeal to Swinburne. Dante Rossetti drew
Swinburne embracing Fanny Cornforth for a planned frontispiece to the
artist's *The Early Italian Poets* (1861), and he collaborated with
Swinburne in writing border ballads such as 'The Laird of Waristoun'.
Swinburne wrote a number of these poems, collating differing versions
and inventing where necessary, though a planned collection never materialized. Border ballads were also an interest of Rossetti's wife Elizabeth
Siddal (1829–62) with whom Swinburne formed an affectionate tie.
Artistically gifted, her delicate constitution and red hair may have reminded Swinburne of his sister Edith. His courteous playfulness often
lightened her spirits. When her health permitted, he would come to
Chatham Place and read to her, and they laughed over Fletcher's comedy *The Spanish Curate*.

On the night of 10 February 1862 Swinburne dined with the Rossettis
at the Hotel Sablonière in Leicester Square. Dante Gabriel and Lizzie
were home by about 8.00 p.m. An hour later Rossetti went out for a
walk. When he returned at 11.30 he found Lizzie unconscious. By her
bed was an empty two-ounce bottle of laudanum. She had taken ten
times the lethal dose. According to William Rossetti, 'all the efforts of 4
doctors for 7 hours or more availed nothing' and she died at 7.20 a.m.
Calling later that morning to sit for a portrait, Swinburne was con-
fronted by a distraught Rossetti. During the inquest at Bridewell Hospi-
tal on 13 February, Swinburne stated that he had seen 'nothing particular
in the deceased except that she appeared a little weaker than usual'. The
Coroner recorded a verdict of accidental death. Swinburne wrote to his
mother the next day:

> I would rather not write yet about what has happened – I suppose
> none of the papers gave a full report, so that you do not know that
> I was almost the last person who saw her (except her husband and
> a servant) and had to give evidence at the inquest. Happily there
> was no difficulty in proving that illness had quite deranged her
> mind, so that the worst chance of all was escaped . . .

The 'worst chance of all' presumably meant her death would be regis-
tered as suicide. In later life Swinburne paid eloquent tribute to 'her
unique and indescribable personal charm', speaking of her 'as I should
a sister' and of the 'deeper and sadder side of my brotherly affection for
her'. Except for Lady Trevelyan, 'I never knew so brilliant and appreciative a woman . . . She was a wonderful as well as a most loveable
creature', possessed of 'matchless grace, loveliness, courage, endurance,
wit, humour, heroism, and sweetness'.

Rossetti had no desire to remain at Chatham Place. Swinburne com-
forted him as much as he could, and so, as Swinburne told his mother:

> Rossetti and I are going to live together as soon as we move – of course he could not stay in the old house, and asked me to come with him . . . In the autumn we get into a house at Chelsea – in Cheyne Walk, facing the trees and the river – with an old garden. The house is taken (like every other nice one) for the Exhibition season, so we must make shift somewhere till then . . .

William Rossetti told Scott that though Swinburne had not been involved with the 'preparations', 'the project entirely meets his own liking . . . no-one could possibly behave with more freedom from self-obstrusion in such a case than he has done. Of course he will live to himself (in 2 rooms) and quite independently of the family.' Whatever his capacity for excess at other times, Swinburne could be tactful when those he cared for were in distress. The household was to have included Rossetti's mother and sister, but it was decided their piety and Swinburne's high spirits would not be compatible.

March saw Swinburne travel to Paris and then to the Pyrenees. His family may have gone hoping the mountain air would help Edith's consumption. Twenty-one years later he enthused about the change of seasons from winter to spring: 'when I was there . . . I thought I had never seen flowers before. And I always back the Lac de Gaube against Switzerland.' The memory of the 'mountain lake shut in by solitary highlands, without visible outlet or inlet, seen fitlier by starlight than sunlight . . . steel-blue and sombre, with a strange attraction for the swimmer in its cold smooth reticence and breathless calm' inspired his last great poem, 'The Lake of Gaube' in 1899. In the summer Swinburne was observed by the diarist A. L. Munby as 'that strange incarnation of PreRaphaelitism'. Munby met Swinburne in June at Rossetti's temporary lodgings in Lincoln's Inn Fields, describing him less charitably as 'the intolerable little prig'. Two days later they met again at a dinner party for Munby's friend Stokes who was about to leave for India: 'Stokes Rossetti Swinburne and I had a good deal of talk about old French literature, with which, in spite of his priggishness, Swinburne seems to have a considerable acquaintance, though not always of a reputable kind.' When the party broke up in the early hours of the morning at Middle Temple Gate, the poet, discovering that Stokes did not have one of Swinburne's canonical texts, ran off to fetch a copy, exclaiming, 'What – go to India without *Sordello*!'.

On 11 July Swinburne held a house-warming party at 77 Newman Street, where he lived until the house at Cheyne Walk was available. Rossetti, Meredith and the painter Frederick Sandys were among those present. Swinburne 'recited much from his own poems and compositions, to the frantic delight of his guests'. There must have been many such readings to startled and excited gatherings. Edward Lear heard of Swinburne as a 'Spasmodic' poet 'who seems to amaze small circles'.

In 1862 Swinburne contributed a number of poems and articles to various periodicals. Meredith's magazine *Once a Week* took a border ballad, 'The Fratricide' (later 'The Bloody Son'), and the story 'Dead Love'. Milnes introduced Swinburne to Richard H. Hutton, editor of *The Spectator*, which took seven poems: 'A Song in Time of Order', 'Before Parting', 'After Death', 'Faustine', 'A Song in Time of Revolution', 'The Sundew' and 'August'. All would be collected in 1866 but aroused no controversy in 1862, even the exultantly cruel 'Faustine':

> Even he who cast seven devils out
>   Of Magdalene
> Could hardly do as much, I doubt,
>   For you, Faustine.
>
> Did Satan make you to spite God?
>   Or did God mean
> To scourge with scorpions for a rod
>   Our sins, Faustine?

The quintessential Swinburne theme of failed love is expressed in 'Before Parting', where the speaker laments, 'I know not how love is gone out of this,/Seeing that all was his'. 'The Sundew', one of Swinburne's most pleasing shorter lyrics, closely observed from nature, concludes like a riddle:

> O red-lipped mouth of marsh-flower
> I have a secret halved with thee.
> The name that is love's name to me
> Thou knowest, and the face of her
> Who is my festival to see.
>
> The hard sun, as thy petals knew,
> Coloured the heavy moss-water:
> Thou wert not worth green midsummer
> Nor fit to live to August blue,
> O sundew, not remembering her.

The plant is rare in the United Kingdom but can be found on the Isle of Wight.

The critical articles in *The Spectator* comprised three on Victor Hugo's *Les Misérables*, praising Hugo's craftsmanship but less comfortable with his overt engagement with social questions, arguing 'any book above a certain pitch of writing must be taken first of all to be a work of pure art ... All the excellence of moral purpose in the world will never serve for salt to a thing born rotten.' Swinburne took the same aesthetic line in September, defending Baudelaire's *Les Fleurs du Mal*, stating that 'a poet's business is presumably to write good verses, and by no means to redeem the age and remould society'. This was one of the first favourable reviews Baudelaire received in any language. Swinburne reveals his own poetic ideals when he describes how Baudelaire's rhythm 'suggests colour and perfume':

> ... his perfect workmanship makes every subject admirable and respectable. Throughout the chief part of the book he has chosen to dwell mainly upon sad and strange things – the weariness of pain and the bitterness of pleasure – the perverse happiness and wayward sorrows of exceptional people. It has the languid, lurid beauty of close and threatening weather – a heavy heated temperature, with dangerous hothouse scents in it ... a natural leaning to obscure and sorrowful things. Failure and sorrow, next to physical beauty and perfection of sound or scent, seem to have an infinite attraction for him.

Baudelaire's poems made 'noble use ... even of the loathsomest bodily putrescence and decay ... pluck out its meaning and secret, even its beauty, in a certain way, from actual carrion'. Swinburne did the same in 'The Leper', where the speaker gazes lovingly on the corpse of his beloved. Swinburne embraced *Les Fleurs du Mal*, as he was to embrace de Sade's *La Nouvelle Justine, ou les Malheurs de la Vertu*, as forbidden books, anti-gospels of pleasure and beauty. *Poems and Ballads* and *Lesbia Brandon* would be the same. Swinburne sent a copy of the review to Paris, but Baudelaire was too unwell to acknowledge it until 10 October 1863, after a reminder from their mutual friend James Whistler. This ill-starred missive, given to a friend to take to London, was put in a drawer and not delivered.

At the end of August William Rossetti told Scott that 'after introducing into his review imaginary quotations from phantasmal French poets of the dishevelled class', Swinburne 'has now actually taken to writing entire reviews of these nonentities, much to his present chuckling, and, I should fear, future confusion'. The two phantoms were Félicien Cossu and Ernest Clouët. The mischief commenced in May when Swinburne appended a note to 'After Death' stating it was from the *Reçueil de Chants Bretons*, edited by Cossu. Several of the Hugo articles cited both Cossu and Clouët and 'those writing formulas peculiar to ... their school'. Parodying the moralistic tone of Victorian reviews, Swinburne wrote of Cossu's volume *Les Amours Étiques*, 'we must warn the British reader that not one of the poems in question is fit to be read aloud in the hearing of Englishwomen. Many it is hardly possible to transcribe; some few it is hardly possible to allude to ... From the poem "Christus" we dare not quote a single verse.' Then he went on: 'nevertheless it might perhaps be well to give some specimens of this foul thing as a warning sign of the unimaginable excess to which the corruption of French literature is now carried' – and he duly obliged. With suave irony Swinburne concludes, 'Surely, whatever our short-comings may be, we may at least congratulate ourselves that no English writer could for an instant dream of putting forth such a book.' The second review, *Les Abîmes. Par Ernest Clouet,* contained a similar mixture of obscenity and mock outrage.

Hutton decided not to use the reviews, for 'the subject seems to me to deserve no more criticism than a Hollywell Street publication, nor could I speak of it in *The Spectator* without more real disgust than your article inspires. There is a tone of raillery about it which I think one should hardly use to pure obscenity.' Swinburne was soon disaffected with *The Spectator.* Early in 1863 he told Milnes, 'I don't want to send any more . . . I don't approve of their behaviour (e. g. never sending one one's own articles and taking back books sent for review . . .) and their principles offend my moral sense.'

With his wide reading, prodigious memory and skill at mimicry and general irreverence, Swinburne was frequently breaking off from serious writing to scribble ideas and sketches for parodies and burlesque. There was his satire on the French novel, 'La Fille du Policeman', and the play 'La Soeur de la Reine', portions of which have survived. In the early 1870s W. H. Mallock heard Swinburne relate 'a sort of parody of what Victor Hugo might have written had he dramatized English events at the opening of the reign of Queen Victoria':

> The first act, he said, showed England on the verge of a revolution, which was due to the frightful orgies of the Queen at 'Buckingham's Palace'. The Queen, with unblushing effrontery, had taken to herself a lover, in the person of Lord John Russell . . . In a later act it appeared that the Queen and Lord John Russell had between them given the world a daughter, who, having been left to her own devices, or, in other words, to the streets, reappears as 'Miss Kitty', and is accorded some respectable rank. Under these conditions she becomes the object of much princely devotion; but the moral hypocrisy of England has branded her as a public scandal. With regard to her so-called depravities, nobody entertains a doubt, but one princely admirer, of broader mind than the rest, declares that in spite of these she really is the embodiment of everything that is divine in women. 'She may', he says, 'have done everything which might have made a Messalina blush, but whenever she looked at the sky she murmured "God" and whenever she looked at a flower she murmured "Mother". '

On a more serious note Swinburne wrote to *The Spectator* for 7 June 1862, to defend George Meredith's *Modern Love.* Hutton attacked it as 'without any vestige of original thought or purpose which could excuse so unpleasant a subject [adultery and the breakdown of a marriage] on which he has no convictions to express'. Swinburne complained that as an established writer Meredith deserved more respect, and pounced on Hutton's use of 'convictions'. 'The business of verse-writing is hardly to express convictions', argued Swinburne,

> and if some poetry ... has at times dealt in dogmatic morality, it is all the worse and all the weaker for that. As to subject, it is too much to expect that all schools of poetry are to be for ever subordinate to the one just now so much in request with us, whose scope of sight is bounded by the nursery walls; that all Muses are to bow down before her who babbles, with lips yet warm from their pristine pap, after the dangling delights of a child's coral ... We have not too many writers capable of duly handling a subject worth the serious interest of men.

Though shortly to become strained, relations between Swinburne and Meredith in 1862 were good. In the same month, Meredith was telling a correspondent about the arrangement at Cheyne Walk, 'a strange, quaint, grand old place, with an immense garden, magnificent panelled staircases and rooms ... I am to have a bedroom for my once-a-week visits. We shall have nice evenings there.' In mid-June Swinburne and Rossetti visited him at Copsham, where Swinburne, freshly inspired by Fitzgerald's *Omar Khayyám*, had written some of 'Laus Veneris'. Swinburne and Rossetti had bought several copies of Fitzgerald's poem after finding it remaindered on a street stall. Swinburne described it as a 'leading chapter in my canon of scripture'.

Swinburne and Dante Gabriel declined an invitation to go to Italy with William Rossetti and Scott in early July. Swinburne's summer was to be memorable for his reading. For some time he had been badgering Milnes to show him 'the mystic pages of the martyred marquis de Sade', that 'illustrious and ill-requited benefactor of humanity', and was sufficiently excited by the thought of the Marquis to write a poem in French called 'Charenton' (dated 27 October 1861) describing de Sade's incarceration in the asylum there. De Sade was a favourite topic of Swinburne's conversation, as William Hardman noted after a meeting at Rossetti's:

> Swinburne is strongly sensual; although almost a boy, he upholds the Marquis de Sade as the acme and apostle of perfection, without (as he says) having read a word of his works ... The assembled company evidently received Swinburne's tirades with ill-concealed disgust, but they behaved to him like a spoiled child. He has a curious kind of nervous twitching, resembling or approaching St. Vitus' Dance.

On 16 August Boyce noted in his diary, 'joined Rossetti at Swinburne's rooms, where they were looking over *Justine* ... recent acquisition of the latter'. Two days later Swinburne wrote a very long and unintentionally revealing letter to Milnes, to give a 'candid record' or his reaction to *La Nouvelle Justine, ou les Malheurs de la Vertu*:

> At first, I quite expected to add another to the gifted author's list of victims; I really thought I must have died or split open or choked with laughing. I never laughed so much in my life. I went from text to illustrations and back again, till I literally doubled up and fell down with laughter – I regret to add that all the friends to whom I have lent or shown the book were affected in just the same way. One scene between M. de Verneuil and Mme. d'Esterval I never thought to survive. I read it out and the auditors rolled and roared. Then Rossetti read out the dissection of the interesting Rosalie and her infant, and the rest of that refreshing episode: and I wonder to this minute that we did not raise the whole house by our screams of laughter.

A disappointed Swinburne invited Milnes to 'weep with me over a shattered idol'. De Sade, he complained, was crude and clumsy in his presentation; he mistook 'bulk and number for greatness'; he gave long lists of horrors without adequate description of any single incident. Whatever the sincerity of these objections, Swinburne was affected by what he had read, and these criticisms, however just, were a rationalization and a defence against the feelings de Sade aroused. As objectivity gives way to Swinburne's intense response, the letter changes to a direct address to de Sade. Even as he tries to have done with the Marquis, Swinburne's creativity is stirred:

> You take yourself for a great pagan physiologist and philosopher – you are a Christian ascetic bent on earning the salvation of the soul through the mortification of the flesh. You are one of the family of St. Simeon Stylites. You are a hermit of the Thebaid turned inside out. You, a Roman of the later empire? Nero knows nothing of you; Heliogabalus turns his back on you; Caracalla sniffs contemptuously at the sight of you, Cotytto veils her face . . . Venus Cloacina dips down into her gutter, and Priapus turns to a mere fig tree stump. Paganism washes its hands of you . . .

And so it goes on until Swinburne concludes, 'I drop my apostrophe to M. de Sade, having relieved my mind for good and all of its final judgement on a matter of some curiosity and interest to me.' But if Swinburne seriously thought he had finished with the 'divine' Marquis, de Sade had not finished with him.

Swinburne's reaction – 'is this all?' – was predictable. To have reacted otherwise would have meant a loss of face. He had cultivated the persona of being unshockable, and wanted to be seen by Milnes as a fellow connoisseur of the erotic and the immoral. Perhaps there was also an element of masculine bravado. De Sade's impact was soon apparent. In a letter to William Allingham several months later, Boyce observed that de Sade and *Justine* was still Swinburne's 'most eloquent vomit'. In his next extant letter to Milnes Swinburne alludes to a character in the novel and for many years Sadeian allusions are common in his correspondence. During his next visit to Fryston, Swinburne wrote to Rossetti explaining that he had been assisting Milnes to decipher 'a priceless autograph letter of the Marquis de Sade', and added that he flattered himself on the handwriting being 'not unlike that of this note'. A letter to Milnes of 27 December begins 'Salus in X Priapo et Ecclesia Sub invocatione Beatissimi Donatiani de Sade' ('Salvation in Christ Priapus and His Church by the intercession of the most Blessed Donatien de Sade'). All the stylistic crudities of de Sade meant nothing. Swinburne had found in de Sade an inverted patron saint, from whom he could spin black comedy and whose dark shadow he could invoke in the minds of his contemporaries. As Lafourcade remarked, it was not that de Sade taught Swinburne anything, since sadistic passages occur in manuscripts that predate the reading of *Justine*, 'but de Sade confirmed Swinburne in some of his instincts. He learnt from them not to be afraid or ashamed at the tendencies of his own nature.'

Lafourcade also saw Swinburne's enthusiasm for de Sade as a partial reaction to a deep romantic disappointment, since 'vice was an obvious remedy to his grief', fulfilling the threat in 'The Triumph of Time' 'to find a sin to do before I die/That will set you higher in heaven'. Swinburne did suffer a crushing disappointment in love. The identity of the woman in question has been the most puzzling aspect of his life and at one time this event was dated to 1862. Gosse's story of Swinburne proposing to Jane Faulkner, the adopted daughter of Dr John Simon, was exploded in 1953 when it was discovered that she would have been only ten or eleven. Swinburne may have had romantic disappointments by the age of 25, but the crisis was yet to come. That Swinburne had an intense appreciation of the beauty of women is unquestioned, as well as a tendency to keep his feelings to himself. Moving in artistic circles, he met many beautiful women and was stirred by them just as they were fascinated by him, especially after he became famous. Once, seeing Christine Spartali walking across a lawn in a white dress decorated with coloured ribbon, Swinburne murmured, 'She is so beautiful that I want to sit down and cry.'

Swinburne was 'in the country' in September 1862. He and Rossetti moved into Tudor House, Cheyne Walk on 24 October. It had a Queen Anne front, elaborate scrollwork gates and spacious gardens. Rossetti used the pillared dining room as a studio. The drawing room was 40 feet long with seven windows, the central one a bay-window looking out on the river. Rossetti filled the place with antique furniture. Munby said it was

so utterly unlike the commonplace comfort or splendour of London houses, that I was never wearied of walking up and down it,
absorbing as it were the aroma of its manifold romance. Tea, too,
was served there (absolutely with thick cream!) in antique china
cups, upon a carven table and by the light of massive Elizabethan
candlesticks.

Swinburne's two rooms were on left on the ground floor. But Cecil
Lang believed that 'the duration of Swinburne's stay, which was irregular (in all senses), seems to have been much exaggerated'.

Sometime in 1862 Swinburne completed his novel *A Year's Letters*.
As its editor Francis Sypher has pointed out, many of its elements
express Swinburne's passions, though in a more disciplined form than
in *Lesbia Brandon*. As we have seen, Swinburne admitted Reginald
Harewood was 'a coloured photograph' of himself. Romantic and im-
pulsive, Reginald discourses freely on flagellation, writes sonnets on the
sea, becomes obsessed with Italian nationalism, and his academic career
at Oxford ends in failure. More importantly for the plot he falls in love
with a married cousin, Clara Radworth, with whom he shares horse-
rides along the shoreline. Clara is described as 'quite Elizabethan, weakened by a dash of Mary Stuart . . . at once excitable and cold'. He wants
her to leave her loveless marriage but she refuses. He says admiringly of
her, 'She has in her the royal scornful secret of a great silence' and his
attitude to love can be summarized as 'we have counted all and found
nothing better than love'.

The novel's other dominant character is the 60-year-old Lady Midhurst,
an arch gossip, matchmaker and cool observer of human behaviour.
The overall ironic tone is felt most powerfully in her letters, which are
judiciously sprinkled with such comments as this of Amicia Cheyne:
'She is past all medicine of mine. I dare say she will begin to develop a
spiritual tendency: she reads the unwholesomest books.' For Lady
Midhurst life is black comedy endurable only with wit and stoicism,
where to act on feeling is ruinous. In advice such as 'bear what you have
to bear steadily, with locked teeth', 'endure as much as you can; repent
of as little as you can, and hope for as little as you can', or 'liberty and
courage of spirit are better worth keeping than any indulgence in hope
and penitence', Lady Midhurst gives us an insight into the faith Swinburne
evolved to replace his Christian upbringing.

The prose is taut and precise, less given to rhapsody than *Lesbia
Brandon*. The epistolary form makes the plot difficult to follow. But *A
Year's Letters* challenges the reader to take an active role in not only
working out what is going on in these upper-class marriages but also
tempts and frustrates any attempt at judgement. Swinburne's avoidance
of a third-person narrator denies the book (and the reader) a reliable,

absolute moral guide. Lacking such a moral framework, the irony cuts indiscriminately, like a sword without a handle. Certain targets – the institution of marriage, Christian forbearance and resignation, didactic art – are obvious. But the novel provides no other stable moral view to replace those it attacks. Morality is linked to individual perspective: Reginald has his romantic idealism; Lady Midhurst her cynicism. The novel gives no way of evaluating them, except perhaps the pragmatic one of results and survival. Various characters dissect and comment on each other's letters. The novel is difficult because it leads the reader into a moral quicksand. In the panoply of Victorian fiction *A Year's Letters* deserves to be much better known and in Swinburne's *œuvre* it is his first mature piece. Swinburne's efforts to find a publisher from 1863 onwards fell on stony ground. Those who read it found it beyond the pale. Their negative judgement may well have inspired Swinburne later to give the story a prefatory letter addressed 'to the author', in which a publisher advises the book be suppressed or destroyed since 'it is a false picture of domestic life in England': 'A long sojourn in France, it appears to me, has vitiated your principles and confused your judgement. Whatever may be the case abroad, you must know that in England marriages are usually prosperous; that among us divorces are unknown, and infidelities incomprehensible. '

In October Swinburne decided to write an essay on William Blake. His interest in Blake had been developing since 1859. The Rossettis were corresponding with Anne Gilchrist, widow of Alexander Gilchrist, Blake's biographer, and checking his proofs. Rossetti informed her that Swinburne had read the chapter on the Prophetic Books and 'found a good deal which he thought might be improved by rearrangement, addition, and even omission'. Rossetti went on, 'Swinburne would be glad to take any pains in connexion with them ... He is far more competent for this than I am.' Swinburne told William Rossetti he felt patching up the book would be a waste of time. Instead, 'what I now want to do, and mean to set about this year if I can, is the making of a distinct small commentary of a running kind, but as full and satisfactory as it could well be made, on Blake's work'. By the time it was published in 1868, Swinburne's commentary on Blake had grown into a sizeable book and one of his finest pieces of criticism.

In October 1862 Swinburne inadvertently found himself accused of having been overheard saying of Gabriel Rossetti 'that procuring abortions was an every day amusement to him'. Rossetti remonstrated with Swinburne who vehemently denied it and became 'painfully excited'. Rossetti let the matter rest but Swinburne remained agitated. Letters passed back and forth between Ford Madox Brown and Holman Hunt and Swinburne's innocence was established. Brown wrote to Hunt on

13 October 'while admiring his great genius and regarding him with affection his extraordinary way of talking does at times dismay one and it is gratifying that it turns out not to be his blame this time'.

In late November Swinburne travelled north to stay with Milnes at Fryston. He was there five or six weeks, save a brief absence for the funeral of his maternal grandmother the Countess of Ashburnham, who died on 26 November. Another of Milnes's guests was the American writer Henry Adams, to whom Swinburne seemed 'a tropical bird, high-crested, long-beaked, quick-moving, with rapid utterance and screams of humour, quite unlike any English lark or nightingale. One could hardly call him a crimson macaw among owls, and yet no ordinary contrast availed ... '. Milnes told Adams that Swinburne had written unpublished poetry 'of really extraordinary merit'. Once the dinner was underway Milnes encouraged Swinburne to talk, and Adams, along with the rest of the company, was astonished at what he heard. The remainder of the evening was a monologue – 'original, wildly eccentric, astonishingly gifted, and convulsively droll' – in which Swinburne held his listeners spellbound:

> They could not believe his incredible memory and knowledge of literature, classic, medieval, and modern; his faculty of reciting a play of Sophocles or a play of Shakespeare, forward or backward, from end to beginning; or Dante, or Villon, or Victor Hugo. They knew not what to make of his rhetorical recitation of his own unpublished ballads ...

On 13 December Swinburne left Fryston for Wallington. There was a hiatus of some sort because two days later he wrote to Lady Trevelyan from the Turf Hotel in Newcastle, sounding slightly peeved:

> I hope you are prepared for one thing, the natural consequence of your unnatural conduct, viz., to come and bail me out when the hired minions of oppressive law have hailed me to a loathsome dungeon for inability to pay a fortnight's unlooked for hotel expenses. Nothing on earth is likelier, and all because I relied with filial shortsightedness on that fallacious letter of invitation which carried me off from Fryston. If I had but heard in time, I should have run down to London, and come up later. As it is I see Destitution and Despair ahead of me, and have begun an epitaph in the Micawber style for my future grave in the precincts of my native County's jail.

Evidently Swinburne was short of 'tin'. By 27 December he was at Wallington writing a letter to Milnes, 'Mon Cher Rodin', after a character in de Sade.

On 5 January 1863 Swinburne left Wallington and turned up unexpectedly at the house of Bell Scott. His host wrote later, 'why so early? he could not well explain; just thought he had been there long enough;

he wanted letters at the post but had not given his address! I could inquire no further; there seemed to be some mystery he did not wish to explain.' Perhaps this was the occasion Walter Trevelyan threw Swinburne's copy of Balzac into the fire, disgusted at finding such an immoral book under his roof. Raleigh Trevelyan narrates how

> The Scotts, who were just off in Tynemouth for a holiday, found themselves accompanied therefore by Swinburne. As they walked along the beach he declaimed his 'Hymn to Proserpine' and 'Laus Veneris', two of his most lovely performances, never to be forgotten when recited in his strange intonation which truly represented the white heat of the enthusiasm that produced them.

Swinburne may have then returned to Wallington. If there had been some kind of argument it was soon resolved, for he travelled down to London with Lord and Lady Trevelyan on 14 January. Then events plunged him into gloom and apprehension.

A week later Swinburne wrote to Milnes from Bournemouth, 'having had to come down hither in something of a hurry owing to sickness in the family'. His sister Edith had been taken seriously ill. This sickness could not have been unexpected, as earlier biographies have it, because Edith's illness was identified in 1856. She may have been in Bournemouth seeking treatment and had probably had an episode of haemoptysis or blood-spitting, caused by a rupture of blood-vessels in the lung. In mid-Victorian England tuberculosis accounted for roughly half of all deaths in women aged fifteen to 35 and from 1851 to 1863 the greatest incidence of the disease was in women. Unpredictable, it could take the form of 'galloping' consumption and be fatal within months. More often it waxed and waned, was initially mistaken for bronchitis and allowed the sufferer several years of intermittent if fragile health before the final stage. The family fully expected her to die in Bournemouth. In 1875 Swinburne described the resort as having 'sad associations', for 'several of the last hopeless months of my dear sister's illness were spent there by us in weary expectation of the end'.

But a 'sickness in the family' was a private matter not to be discussed. His letter to Milnes continues 'have you read Salammbô? I have just written Lady Trevelyan a brilliant account of it. The tortures, battles, massacres, and Moloch-sacrifices are stunning.' He wrote several more letters to Milnes from Bournemouth during February 1863, full of flagellation and de Sade but little else. Edith rallied enough to be moved, so some time in the spring the family returned to East Dene.

In March Swinburne went to Paris with Whistler, met Manet and Fantin-Latour and wrote four sonnets titled 'Hermaphroditus', inspired by a statue in the Louvre. He was fascinated by the way it united opposites, 'Turning the fruitful feud of hers and his/To the waste

wedlock of a sterile kiss'. It was around this time that Whistler gave
Swinburne the first version of 'La Mère Gérard'. It is said that Whistler
'could sometimes talk Swinburne out of excessive drinking if he could
provide something to occupy his mind'. Boyce saw Swinburne at
Cheyne Walk on 13 March and dined there on 30 April. Much of
Poems and Ballads was written by this time for in April Meredith
wrote that Swinburne 'has ready a volume of poems of a kind to
attract notice'.

The same month Swinburne was once more a guest of Milnes at
Fryston Hall. He arrived one afternoon, advancing 'up the sloping
lawn, swinging his hat in his hand, and letting the sunshine flood the
bush of his red-gold hair'. His witty conversation immediately engaged
the interest of Thackeray, whose daughters were taken with Swinburne's
playfulness. On the Sunday evening he was invited to read some of his
poems. Mischievously, Swinburne chose 'The Leper', with its necrophiliac
theme, and 'Les Noyades' in which a man and a woman are tied
together naked and drowned:

> At this the Archbishop of York made so shocked a face that
> Thackeray smiled and whispered to Lord Houghton, while the two
> young ladies, who had never heard such sentiments expressed be-
> fore, giggled aloud in their excitement. Their laughter offended the
> poet, who, however, was soothed by Lady Houghton's tactfully
> saying, 'Well, Mr. Swinburne, if you *will* read such extraordinary
> things, you must expect us to laugh.' 'Les Noyades' was then
> proceeding on its amazing course, and the Archbishop was looking
> more and more horrified, when suddenly the butler – 'like an
> avenging angel', as Lady Ritchie says – threw open the door and
> announced, 'Prayers! my Lord!'.

During May, June and July 1863, Swinburne attended five breakfast
parties at Milnes's London address. There he met Matthew Arnold,
whose initial reaction was to find Swinburne 'a sort of pseudo-Shelley'.
When Munby visited Cheyne Walk in May he found Rossetti 'much
injured by the constant toadying of that clever little prig Algernon
Swinburne, who was present, echoing all his master said'.

In the early 1860s Swinburne suffered intermittent convulsive fits, 'in
which, generally after a period of very great cerebral excitement, he
would suddenly fall unconscious. These fits were excessively distressing
to witness, and produced a shock of alarm, all the more acute because
of the deathlike appearance of the patient.' It was Gosse's impression
that Swinburne's real danger in these attacks was hitting himself in
falling. One such fit in 1864 occurred in Whistler's studio and Swinburne
was nursed by the artist's mother. This condition, which may be another sign of brain damage at birth, seems to have ceased in middle age.
The drinking was another matter.

It had probably started after Swinburne left Oxford and Burton's company may have encouraged it. By 1863 it was getting out of control. Assessments of Swinburne's capacity for drink vary. It is usually said that he only needed a moderate amount of alcohol to become excited until either his body, or the patience of those he was with, gave way. However on one occasion Ruskin saw him drink three bottles of port. Mr and Mrs Hungerford Pollen, who had met Swinburne in Oxford in 1859, arrived at Rossetti's one day to find the painter looking exhausted:

> At 3 a.m. he had been wakened by a tremendous knocking, and on looking out of the window, he saw Algernon being held up in the arms of a policeman, with a whole bevy of gutter-boys accompanying; he had been out on the spree, and no one knew where. Rossetti went out and let him in, and had a fearful time with him, 'screaming and splashing about', before he got him to bed. Mrs. Pollen made a curious observation that, when Swinburne was angry, he used to collapse at once upon the floor, as though his legs had suddenly given way, and sometimes he bumped down so hard that he hurt himself . . . Once at the Pollens' own house, having drunk some sherry, Swinburne became so violent and so blasphemous, that Mrs. Pollen told her husband that Swinburne must never come again. Mr. Pollen answered, 'Oh! my dear, we must never be unkind to him; he is just a child!' This was before 1866. Mrs. Pollen commented, 'he was just a very, very *spoilt* child', and she never liked him. She says, when he was not in the least drunk, his 'one idea of rational conversation was to dance and skip all over the room, reciting poetry at the top of his voice, and going on and on with it'.

During his twenties, and especially during the years of his initial fame, Swinburne's drinking was tolerated by those who knew him, but in the 1870s it led to his increasing social isolation.

The original domestic arrangement at Cheyne Walk broke up in the summer of 1863, though Swinburne retained his room there until the summer of 1864. Images of a happy Pre-Raphaelite menagerie of artists, models and animals have often exaggerated the cohesion of the household. Swinburne, it is alleged, got on Rossetti's nerves, and whilst it may not be true that he slid down the bannisters or chased Simeon Solomon naked about the house, Lafourcade believed that Swinburne had annoyed Rossetti by passing nude from one room to another. The larking got out of hand, people were pushed against cupboards and valued china got smashed. Loyal to the memory of Lizzie Siddal, Swinburne resented the presence of Rossetti's model Fanny Cornforth. Toward the end of his life he exclaimed acerbically that Fanny was to Lizzie 'as a clot of dung in the gutter at nightfall to the splendour of the evening star'. William Rossetti was hardly ever there, and Meredith 'slept at the house only once', his relationship with Rossetti quickly becoming strained. Soon after June 1863 Meredith gave up his room, perhaps after some irreverent words about Hugo had caused Swinburne to reply by throwing a poached egg. A letter of Rossetti's to Anne Gilchrist in 1863 confirms that 'our household consists of four men, two of whom only, myself and Mr. Swinburne, are at all constantly inmates'. In August he told Allingham, 'I see hardly anyone. Swinburne is away. Meredith has evaporated for good, and my brother is seldom here.'

Looking for a publisher for Swinburne's poems, Milnes approached Chapman and Hall who in turn asked Browning, one of their authors, for his opinion. Browning had heard Swinburne read his work at one of Milnes's gatherings and wrote in July:

> I know next to nothing of Swinburne, and like him much: I have received courtesy from him, and been told he feels kindly to me . . . Of his works, since his first volume, I know not a line, except a poem which he recited the other night which I looked over a long while ago at Rossetti's, and the pieces he recited the other night: I could only have an opinion, therefore, on these. I thought them moral mistakes, redeemed by much intellectual ability. They may be a sample of the forthcoming book, – or just the exceptional instances – I hope so.
>
> When I was abruptly appealed to, some days after, for my estimate of Mr. Swinburne's powers, – I don't know what I could do but say 'that he had genius, and wrote verses in which to my mind there was no good at all'.

Chapman and Hall decided not to take up Swinburne. His poems would have to wait another three years. Some of his friends were relieved. Ruskin confessed he would be 'sorry if he published these poems for they would win him a dark reputation'. Swinburne was undeterred.

CHAPTER FIVE

'And None be Grievous as This to Me'

By August Swinburne was at East Dene working on Blake. 'I am half living in the sea here, rough or smooth', he told William Michael, 'and generally swimming riding and croquetting myself into a rampant state of muscular Christianity.' But he was hiding the unfolding tragedy. He went to see William Sewell who was at Bonchurch when 'his sister was dying at East Dene':

> . . . he came up to see me one day, and we had a talk. I thought him looking very ill, and altogether in an unhappy state. He spoke of Poetry, of the duty and pleasure of creating beauty. And I said yes – creating beauty which you know is Truth and which you hope will bless mankind. But he seemed to have no idea except of blowing soap bubbles. We parted kindly. I told him if he was ever unhappy and I could be of the least use to him to remember that he had a friend who would never forget him . . . Poor fellow.

Outside East Dene, the summer-flowering jasmine planted in 1860 decorated the village-facing wall with its gold. In one of the rooms overlooking the sea, Edith was in the last weeks of her life. The stereotypical image of the wan, decorously ill female consumptive of nineteenth-century art was far from the truth. Around 200 BC the Greek physician Aretaeus wrote this classic description of the consumptive patient:

> Voice hoarse; neck slightly bent, tender, not flexible, somewhat extended; fingers slender but joints thick; of the bones alone the figure remains, for the fleshy parts are wasted; the nails of the fingers crooked, their pulps are shrivelled and flat . . . Nose sharp, slender; cheeks prominent and red; eyes hollow, brilliant and glittering; swollen, pale, or livid in the countenance; the slender parts of the jaws rest upon the teeth, as if smiling; otherwise of a cadaverous aspect. So also in all other respects; slender, without flesh; the muscles of the arms imperceptible; not a vestige of the mammae, the nipples only to be seen; one may not only count the ribs themselves, but also easily trace them to their terminations . . . the whole shoulder-blades apparent like the wings of birds.

Lesbia Brandon has often been analysed for its autobiographical elements, the heroine variously identified with Christina Rossetti and Mary Gordon. But the chapter 'Leucadia', which describes Lesbia's suicide, seems to draw on Swinburne's experience of his sister's death. Lesbia's symptoms are close to accounts of consumption, with the proviso that Swinburne suppressed those details that would spoil the aesthetic effect.

In 'Leucadia' the dying Lesbia summons Herbert Seyton to her rooms, having poisoned herself with opium and eau de Cologne. Swinburne subverts the stock Victorian death-bed scene. There is nothing pious or morally edifying about Lesbia's death, and in contrast to the death of a consumptive, hers is self-willed, an elegantly perverse gesture of life-denial. But with consumption in mind, her appearance is striking:

> Along her sofa, propped by cushions and with limbs drawn up like a tired child's, lay or leant a woman like a ghost; the living corpse of Lesbia. She was white, with grey lips; her long shapely hands were pale and faded, and the dark tender warmth of her even colour had changed into a hot and haggard hue like fever ... She looked like one whom death was as visibly devouring limb-meal as though fire had caught hold of her bound at a stake: like one whose life had been long sapped and undermined from the roots by some quiet fiery poison. Her eyes and hair alone had a look of life: they were brilliant and soft yet, as she reached out her worn hot hands.

Whatever Swinburne says about poisoning, all the imagery here points to the wasting, the haggard appearance, the fever, the brilliant eyes, of phthisis, 'the name given by the Greeks to the individual shrivelling up under intense heat' (from the Greek verb 'to decay'). The only incongruity is a phrase marked by the ellipsis: 'her beauty of form was unimpaired; she retained the distinction of noble and graceful features and attitudes'. Lesbia must die a beauty, as befits a *femme fatale*. The treatment is romantic and amoral, rather than religious and edifying. So we are left with the tell-tale paradox that Lesbia is a 'living corpse', yet still beautiful. The text proceeds to describe how Herbert

> came to her with a sense of pressure at his heart, and something like horror and fear mixed with the bitterness of natural pain. The figure and the place were lurid in his eyes, and less fit to make one weep than to make him kindle and tremble. There was an attraction in them which shot heat into his veins instead of the chill and heaviness of terror or grief.

The same sentiment is expressed a little further on:

> The morbid and obscure fascination of obscure disease began to tell upon her listener: his nerves trembled in harmony with hers: he felt a cruel impersonal displeasure, compound of fear and pain, in the study of her last symptoms. Then by way of reaction came a warm sudden reflux of tenderness; and he clasped one pale restless hand with a sweet acute pang of physical pity.

Herbert is profoundly disturbed at being excited by her suffering. If Swinburne is drawing upon his experience of watching Edith die of consumption, perhaps these were his own feelings. As often in his writings, it is the physical body that becomes the focus of a power struggle, in this case between health and decay, life and death. It is not hard to imagine such a reaction in a disciple of de Sade who had already written the first draft of 'The Leper' in which 'Love bites and stings me through, to see/Her keen face made of sunken bones,/Her worn-off eyelids madden me'. Bertie feels 'a cruel impersonal displeasure . . . in the study of her last symptoms'.

Nor is this all the evidence, for

> Throughout medical history there runs this suggestion . . . that the same fire which wastes the body in consumption also makes the mind shine with a brighter light. In fact, so much were Greek physicians impressed with the peculiar nervous force displayed at times by consumptive patients that they invented a word for it. They characterized *spes phthisica* by a perpetual hope of recovery even in the face of devastating disease, and by a feverish urge for accomplishment.

The *spes phthisica* was never a universal feature of consumption, but it contributed to a myth of the disease as peculiarly spiritual, a purification of the self by an inner fire. The consumptive Swiss philosopher Henri-Frédéric Amiel wrote in 1880, 'it seems to me that with the decline of my physical strength, I am becoming more purely spirit'. Compare this with Lesbia's 'I'm dying upwards. My head is as clear as my voice', 'I feel inclined to die talking', 'Here I am going out by inches, and every minute I feel more alive here, in the head, and less in the body', and her poetic vision of Proserpine.

Chapter XVI is written on paper watermarked 1863 and it is unlikely the novel was started before 1864. Herbert's vigil during Lesbia's last night of life may reflect Swinburne's own feelings in the last days of Edith's illness:

> The watcher felt sad and sick and half afraid; his mind was full of dim and bitter things. He was not in heart to pray; if indeed prayer could have undone things past, he might have believed it could break and remould the inevitable future growing minute by minute into the irrevocable present. The moments as they went seemed to touch him like falling drops of sand or water: as though the hourglass or the waterclock were indeed emptied by grains or gouts upon his head: a clock measuring its minutes by blood or tears instead of water or sand. He seemed in the dim hours to hear her pulses and his own. That night, as hope and trust fell away from under him, he first learnt the reality of fate: inevitable, not to be cajoled by resignation, not to be averted by intercession: unlike a God, incapable of wrath as of pity, not given to preference of evil or good, not liable to repentance or to change.

This takes us into the spiritual darkness from which *Atalanta* and some of *Poems and Ballads* were forged. The experience of profound power-lessness and injustice confirmed Swinburne's anti-theism, expressed in the anger against God of many of the poems published in 1866. He seems to have started *Atalanta in Calydon* around the time of Edith's death, with its central image of Meleager consumed by an invisible fire as the brand burns:

> And all this body a broken barren tree
> That was so strong, and all this flower of life
> Disbranched and desecrated miserably,
> And minished all that god-like muscle and might
> And lesser than a man's: for all my veins
> Fail me, and all mine ashen life burns down.

Charles Henry's promotion to Vice-Admiral on 12 September must have seemed a bitter irony as he sat at the bedside of his daughter. Edith died on 25 September and was buried five days later, in the grounds of the new church the Swinburnes had helped to fund. When the south transept was added in 1873 the family commemorated her with the St Edith window. As Swinburne wrote in *Atalanta*, 'Yea, son for son the gods may give and take,/But never a brother or sister any more'.

After Edith's death the Swinburnes went to Italy to be away from East Dene for a time. Algernon chose to remain on the Isle of Wight and stayed with the Gordons at Northcourt, Shorwell. On 11 October, he told William Rossetti he would be in London in two or three weeks. Two months later he was still at Northcourt, writing he would be up 'in a week or two'. He did not arrive in London until early February 1864. The brief stay extended to four months, the longest continuous time he ever spent at Northcourt. Swinburne explained:

> ... the truth is having settled down here for quiet with no com-pany but some of my nearest relations and older intimates I have shrunk from moving week after week, perhaps not wisely. But I think after being hard hit one is more afraid of any change than any monotony: and so I let myself be kept beyond the date I had thought of, readily and rather thankfully: especially as one can neither do nothing, or *retremper* oneself with riding and walking, only one's choice in a place like this. I wish I could send Gabriel a photograph of it; the old gardens and hall would be in his style; and of all such houses it is about the quietest.

Northcourt had more to hold him than just its hall, library, gardens, or familial attention of his aunt and uncle. Swinburne had the daily com-pany of his cousin Mary, now a young woman of 23. His emotions in turmoil, grieving for Edith and desperate for consolation, it would not

5.1   Edith Swinburne

be surprising if their relationship now flowered and his feelings toward her intensified. Behind them were years of friendship, a wealth of common interests and a shared grief, since Mary was probably close to Edith. Because she was an only child, the Swinburne children were almost Mary's own brothers and sisters, and Edith was the same age. Is it a coincidence that Mary's first daughter, born in 1871, was christened Edith?

Apart from writing his essay on Blake, Swinburne assisted Mary with a story, *Trusty in Fight,* and her second novel, *The Children of the*

Chapel. They had 'great amusement over the story, which I may almost call a joint production':

> ... from the first conception of my story he took the greatest interest in it, finding historical details for me, correcting anachronisms, suggesting or amending names, costumes, and incidents. In short, not a sentence was written out without being read by him, not an episode worked out without his advice. Finally he proposed, since the 'Children' were to act a play, that he should himself write a Morality for them. Hence the origin of 'The Pilgrimage of Pleasure'.

Swinburne's part in the writing was not publicly acknowledged until 1910, though he gave George Powell a copy in 1868. The musical theme expresses one of Mary's passions; the number of floggings inflicted on the boys one of Swinburne's. The central character, Arthur Savile, shares Swinburne's initials and his being sent to Eton at the end may be a touch of black humour on Swinburne's part.

At Northcourt Swinburne also worked on *Atalanta in Calydon*. Into this tragedy he poured all his grief and anger at Edith's death, and an exultant energy fired by Mary's company, as his heart was tormented by a bitter-sweet mixture of loss and love, sorrow and pleasure. One day as they rode north toward Newport, Swinburne recited the famous chorus 'When the hounds of spring are on winter's traces'. Mary described how

> In our library, often alone with my mother and myself, much of the work was written out, and the table would be strewn with the big sheets of manuscript. But I think none of those who have since read and delighted in 'Atalanta' would believe the amount of 'nonsense' which was going on side by side with the famous work. We were both devoted to the game of *bouts rimés*, and used to set each other pages and pages of *bouts*, always of a comic nature; and then he used to read them aloud when completed, in the evening.

Mary's company was a powerful stimulus to Swinburne's creativity. In December he wrote to Alice:

> My greatest pleasure just now is when Mary practises Handel on the organ; but I can hardly *behave* for delight at some of the choruses. I care hardly more than I ever did for any minor music; but *that* is an enjoyment which wants special language to describe it, being so unlike all others. It crams and crowds me with old and new verses, half-remembered and half-made, which new ones will hardly come straight afterwards: but under their influence I have done some more of my Atalanta which will be among my great doings if it keeps up with its own last scenes throughout.
>   I repay Mary to the best of my ability but cheaply, by blundering over Greek verbs with her. She keeps her energy fresh by her versatility. I wish you were here, and as quiet as I have happily

been all this time, thanks to their kindness, instead of being pestered by strangers on a foreign coast.

This sounds like the tone of someone in love.

Towards the end of his stay Swinburne rode across the island to visit Tennyson but, because of the illness of his wife, the Laureate was not receiving visitors. Shortly before his return to London in February 1864 Swinburne wrote to William Rossetti that his work on Blake was almost complete:

> Coming after you and Gabriel, I wanted to do something durable also for Blake, if of less direct value than your own work and his; I have for once taken the same pains in arranging and designing the parts of this essay as if I had been dealing with a poem. It is about as good a memorial now as I can make it; I have worked into it with real care, and sometimes not without much labour, all the elucidations and expressions of thought or feeling on the matter that I could put into reasonable form or coherent shape.

Scott saw Swinburne at Rossetti's and wrote to Lady Trevelyan that 'Algernon is not much different, only developing some singular conditions of vanity, and otherwise interlarding his discourse with ferocious invectives against Browning. '

In the spring of 1864 Swinburne went to Paris with Milnes (who had been created Lord Houghton in 1863) where they visited the latter's friend Sir Charles MacCarthy, who was dying. Swinburne's poetry reading evidently so excited MacCarthy that 'he had quite a bad night: he thought them wonderful and they quite haunted him'. By late March, Swinburne had arrived in Italy, presumably to see his family, but also to seek out two men with a special significance to him. After a day in Genoa looking at pictures, Swinburne went to Florence to meet the aged poet Walter Savage Landor, a literary idol since his Eton days. Swinburne wrote a long account to Lord Houghton of this visit, Houghton having provided the introduction. Landor had been too ill when Swinburne made his first call, causing Swinburne to come away 'in a grievous state of disappointment and depression . . . fearing I was really too late'. Eventually Landor responded to Swinburne's letter of explanation and admiration. Swinburne set off immediately and found the old man 'as alert, brilliant and altogether delicious as I suppose others may have found him twenty years since':

> I have got the one thing I wanted with all my heart. If both or either of us die to-morrow, at least to-day he has told me that my presence here had made him happy . . . There is no other man living from whom I should so much have prized any expression of acceptance or goodwill in return for my homage . . . I should like to throw up all other things on earth and devote myself to playing valet to him for the rest of his days. I should black his boots if he

wore any – moi. He has given me the shock of adoration which one
feels at thirteen towards great men. I am not sure that any other
emotion is so durable and persistently delicious as that of worship,
when your god is indubitable and incarnate before your eyes.

Landor insisted that Swinburne take a Correggio from his wall as a gift.
Years later he discovered it was a fake. Swinburne much preferred
Landor's Greek poems to 'such magnificent hashes and stews of old and
new with a sharp sauce of personality as "Oenone" and "Ulysses" . . .
not that I am disloyal to Tennyson, into whose church we were all in
my time born and baptized as far back as we can remember at all; but
he is not a Greek nor a heathen; and I imagine does not want to be.'

With or without a religion, Swinburne needed to worship, to feel the
ecstatic loss of self in adoration. Spending days in the Uffizi, Swinburne
wrote that Michelangelo's pictures 'fill and exalt the mind with a strange
and violent pleasure which is the highest mood of worship; reverence
intensified to the last endurable degree. The mind, if then it enjoys at all
or wonders at all, knows little of its own wonder or its own enjoyment
. . . ' As for Titian's statue, the Venus of Urbino: 'Sappho and Anactoria
in one – four lazy fingers buried dans les fleurs de son jardin – how any
creature can be decently virtuous within thirty square miles of its passes
my comprehension. I think with her Tannhauser need not have been
bored – even till the end of the world: but who knows?'

Swinburne visited Fiesole, Majano, Siena, Pisa and San Gimignano,
and enjoyed the company of Elizabeth Gaskell, who was 'the only
person who sympathized with his raptures over the "Medusa" of
Leonardo da Vinci'. At Fiesole in May Swinburne read Carlyle 'in a
huge garden' with nightingales and roses, and wrote 'Itylus'.

Swinburne's other important meeting was with Seymour Kirkup (1788–
1880), the English painter who had known Blake and went to live in
Italy in 1817. Lady Jane Swinburne had spent some of her early life in
Tuscany and Kirkup had painted her as a young woman. In his famous
house on the Ponte Vecchio, Kirkup thrilled Swinburne with his personal recollections of Blake. 'We all envy you the privilege of having
known a man so great in so many ways', wrote Swinburne, who had
not only Kirkup's age to venerate but also his little daughter Imogen
with whom to run round the Boboli Gardens. Imogen remembered the
red-haired poet who played with her as 'Il Signor di Boboli'. Swinburne's
letters to Kirkup revolve mainly round Blake, for he could never sympathize with Kirkup's passion for spiritualism. His invocation of the devil
in letters was a turn of phrase, not an incipient satanism. Swinburne
seems to have been uninterested by the occult section of Lord Houghton's
library. Recalling this visit in 1873, Kirkup told Swinburne he was a
'powerful magnetizer'. As Gosse writes, 'Swinburne, though then, as

always, a relentless disbeliever in "psychic phenomena", had, with his usual good nature, taken part, in 1864, in manifestations at the Ponte Vecchio.' Was Swinburne teasing Kirkup when he wrote on the subject of reincarnation, 'I certainly do not remember having been another man before my birth into this present life, but I have often felt that I have been once upon a time a cat, and worried by a dog. I cannot see a cat without caressing it, or a dog, without feeling its fangs in my flanks.'?

By May 1864 he was in London, 'beaten back by the Italian sun and starved out by the want of companionship' but still enthusing over his meeting with Landor, 'the greatest thing achieved by me in Italy in the way of great things seen'. In his next letter to Nichol in June Swinburne debating the merits of Browning, whose poetry had sunk somewhat in his estimate since the heady days of reading *Sordello* with Hatch. Browning had just published *Dramatis Personae*. Swinburne praised 'Caliban upon Setebos' and 'Mr Sludge the Medium' but 'in all the rest of the book I see much that is clever and nothing that is good – much that is ingenious and nothing that is right'. Allingham heard Swinburne recite a parody of Browning at the Rossettis on 27 June.

Swinburne's domestic arrangements at this time were unsettled. While Swinburne was at Northcourt, Rossetti had decided that he wanted the house in Cheyne Walk to himself. Meredith had never lived there much and William Michael was often away. Possibly Swinburne failed to keep up with the rent. Rossetti informed him of his decision. Swinburne's hackles rose:

> It was not without surprise that after a separation of many months spent by me in the country I received from my friend a letter, couched in language as affectionate and cordial as had been the terms in which we parted when an impending domestic affliction had summoned me from London, but intimating with all possible apology that he wished to have the house at Chelsea to himself . . . My reply was brief and clear, to the effect . . . that I had not understood our common agreement to be so terminable at the caprice of either party that one could desire the other to give place to him without further reason alleged than his own will and pleasure: but the ultimate result could only be an amicable separation.

This was the first rift in their friendship.

After leaving Cheyne Walk, Swinburne moved several times, in July going to 124 Mount Street, Grosvenor Square. He told Nichol:

> For eight hours on end I have been unpacking, blaspheming, arranging, losing, finding, swearing, stamping, blessing Satan, and cursing. The villains who have mismanaged for me have half ruined some of my choicest books, and mislaid endless things, for which may they descend into Gehenna long before I pay their bill on earth.

5.2 John William Inchbold

During August Swinburne stayed at Fryston with Lord Houghton until the 22nd. He then travelled to Cornwall at the invitation of the Leeds-born painter John William Inchbold (1830–88) who was lodging at an old schoolhouse in Tintagel, six miles from Camelford and about 25 miles from the nearest railway station. Swinburne had acknowledged Inchbold's invitation earlier that month, saying how eager he was to enjoy the sea. Inchbold had painted in Cornwall at least as early as 1860 and exhibited several Cornish pictures in 1862. It is not known when or how the two men met, though either Ruskin or Rossetti is the obvious link. Swinburne described Inchbold as

> a very religious man and a strong Churchman, but most charitable and liberal-minded (as you may infer from the cordiality of our friendship) to men of different views or leanings. And I don't know where you could beat – or perhaps match – his finest studies of landscape, since the days of Turner . . . one thinks . . . of his inexhaustible kindness and goodness, and his beautiful sincerity and simplicity of character. He had not many friends, being very shy and rather brusque in manner, so that people were apt to think him odd; but you could not come to know him really without loving and honouring him truly and deeply.

Inchbold became a friend of Coventry Patmore and later published a book of poetry, *Annus Amoris* (1876). To William Rossetti he seemed 'partly shy and partly demonstrative, and not easy to break the ice with'.

These three months in North Cornwall made a lasting impression on Swinburne. In 1899, writing to Sir Arthur Quiller-Couch (who lived in Fowey), Swinburne remarked 'I wish I were dating from your divine county. Of all parts of England I know I love Cornwall best after my own county of Northumberland.' When not engaged in painting or writing, the two friends walked, swam, and borrowed horses from a nearby farm to ride to Boscastle where (Swinburne told Mary), 'as there is no beach or shore of any kind, you can imagine how the sea swings to and fro between the cliffs, foams and swells, beats and baffles itself against the steep faces of rock'. Coming back one evening, he impetuously decided to test the speed of his mount so that 'we tore over the ground in the night at such a rate that we all but banged against late carts in the lanes, and quite electrified the stray population'. What the stray population thought of this is, sadly, unrecorded. Swinburne found the locals 'very hospitable' and joined in a hunt that degenerated into a farce. He noted how the 'treacherous and tiring' sea 'takes it out of one much more than one thinks', regretting the lack of beach and the problems this caused the swimmer but added 'the sea-views are, of course, splendid'. He was obviously impressed by Tintagel itself:

> . . . the double ruin, one half facing the other, of the old castle or palace of the kings of Cornwall. Opposite on a high down is the old church, black with rain and time and storm, black at least in the tower, and grey in the body. The outer half of the castle . . . is on the very edge . . . of the cliff; and has indescribable views of the double bay, broken cliffs, and outer sea.

Only two events interfered with his enjoyment. Since March, Dante Gabriel Rossetti had been corresponding with publisher Alexander

Macmillan, acting as Swinburne's literary agent. Rossetti had written describing Swinburne's poems as 'still unpublished, their author being more apt to write new ones than to think of the old':

> I hardly know how to give you an adequate idea of what not I alone, but many excellent judges who have seen them, think of their astonishing beauty. They inspire a certainty that Swinburne, who is still very young [he was 27], is destined to take in his own generation the acknowledged place that Tennyson holds among *his* contemporaries.

Initially Rossetti sent a manuscript of 'Chastelard'. On 3 June Macmillan replied, saying he thought it 'a work of genius, but some parts of it were very *queer* – very'. He was doubtful whether it would be liked by the public. Years later he confessed that he felt Swinburne's portrayal of Mary was 'carried to characteristically hideous exaggeration'. Macmillan asked for some poems to be sent for his perusal. On 29 June Rossetti requested a decision on 'Chastelard', adding, 'I would also be glad to know from you whether you think that a volume of 'Poems and Ballads' by him would be likely to suit you for publication. They are no less than supremely splendid work.' More were sent in early September, but Macmillan decided not to publish anything by Swinburne. On 15 September Rossetti relayed the bad news: 'Mac has spoken. Don't swear more than you can help . . .'

Further unwelcome tidings came late in the month, this time news of the death of Landor:

> By this white wandering waste of sea,
> 　Far north, I hear
> One face shall never turn to me
> 　As once this year:
>
> Shall never smile and turn and rest
> 　On mine as there,
> Nor one most sacred hand be prest
> 　Upon my hair.

After the deaths of his grandfather and sister and now Landor, small wonder he came to describe September as the 'month of the long decline of the roses'.

One day Swinburne was caught in a cove with a fast incoming tide. Trying to run over rocks to safety around the next point he badly cut his foot. On 26 October he wrote that 'after full three weeks close and often solitary confinement, I enjoy getting out among the downs and cliffs so much that I hardly know if I shall be able to tear myself away from my last chance of the sea this week.' With the noise of the Atlantic in his ears he completed *Atalanta in Calydon*, and memories of this time inspired 'Autumn in Cornwall', parts of *Tristram of Lyonesse* and, when Inchbold died in 1888, one of his greatest elegies. 'In Memory of John William Inchbold' recalled how they had 'Tracked in and out the lines of rolling bays/And banks and gulfs and reaches of the sea':

> Deep dens wherein the wrestling water sobs
>   And pants with restless pain of refluent breach
> Till all the sunless hollow sounds and throbs
>   With ebb and flow of eddies dark as death –
>
> I know not what more glorious world, what waves
>   More bright with life, – if brighter aught may live
> Than those that filled and fled their tidal caves –
>   May now give back the love thou hast to give.
>
> Tintagel, and the long Trebarwith sand,
>   Lone Camelford, and Boscastle divine
> With dower of southern blossom, bright and bland
>   Above the roar of granite-baffled brine,
>
> Shall hear no more by joyous night or day
>   From downs or causeways good to rove and ride
> Or feet of ours or horse-hoofs urge their way
>   That sped us here and there by tower and tide.
>
> The headlands and the hollows and the waves,
>   For all our love, forget us: where I am
> Thou art not: deeper sleeps the shadow on graves
>   Than in the sunless gulf that once we swam.

Sometime in November Swinburne returned to London, consoling Burne-Jones on the loss of his second son Christopher, who was only a few months old. 'The news', wrote Swinburne, 'has struck half my pleasure in anything away for the present.' 'I see just now a good deal of my mother and sisters; they have seen so much of fevers and there is still so much of delicate health in the house.' Of this time Mary Gordon remembered:

> The autumn of that year found us again both in London, and he was a frequent guest at my father's house at Chelsea. I think it was at that time that he wrote some chapters of a novel, which never saw the light, or, as far as I know, was completed. He used to read me bits of the MS. of an afternoon when he happened to come in. I do not know what was the plot of the story, but I recollect some of the characters – one being the bright young lovable schoolboy he delighted in portraying, in constant scrapes, but noble and honourable through all; and a tutor who bid fair to be the 'villain of the piece'.

This was *Lesbia Brandon*, so titled by Randolph Hughes, who edited it in 1952. It was intended to be something of a hybrid work, containing whole poems interspersed amongst the prose, and although the plot is unclear because there are too many gaps, it remains a fascinating work because Swinburne pours so much of his own experience into it. His remark about *Songs before Sunrise* that 'that book was myself' is more true of this, which should have followed *William Blake* in his publications.

Lesbia Brandon opens with the childhood experiences of Herbert Seyton. The first chapter describes Bertie and his older sister Margaret, how like each other they were, with 'the same complexion and skin so thin and fair that it glittered against the light as white silk does, taking sharper and fainter tones of white that shone and melted into each other'. Early in the story their father dies and Bertie goes to live at Ensdon, the house of his sister and her husband Lord Wariston, drawn from Capheaton, Ashburnham Place and possibly East Dene in its proximity to the sea. There Bertie feasts upon the riches of the library and enjoys the countryside and the shore, as we have seen.

His life changes with the introduction of a tutor, Denham, who flogs him often and, in an especially unpleasant episode, after bathing. Denham conceives a passion for Margaret, and as Bertie resembles his sister, Denham is able to alleviate some of his frustration by beating the boy. Further characters are introduced – Mr Linley, Lady Midhurst from *A Year's Letters*, Sir Charles Brandon and his daughter Lesbia, Leonora Harley, and the French and Italian patriots Pierre Sadier and Count Mariani. Lesbia falls in love with Margaret, Bertie falls in love with Lesbia, and the story features two deaths: Lesbia poisons herself and Margaret's lover commits suicide. Most readers have assumed this is Denham but Fuller suggests Swinburne intended it at one time to be Bertie, thus making an incestuous relationship the key to the book. At the end Mr Linley reveals that Denham is the illegitimate child of Fred Seyton, Bertie and Margaret's father, thus their half-brother. Furthermore, Denham's mother married Charles Brandon, making Lesbia his half-sister. The consanguinity is tortuous to say the least, but not wilder than that existing between Swinburne and Mary Gordon.

The text is too incomplete to enable the plot to be reconstructed. Either some of the manuscript has been lost or Swinburne never finished it. However, it contains all of Swinburne's preoccupations: the sea, flogging, incestuous relationships, horse-riding, poetry, Northumberland, ballads, aestheticism, pain, pleasure and doomed love. Balzac was Swinburne's avowed model and Mr Linley remarks, 'reading Balzac is all but eating the fruit of knowledge and seeing men with the eyes and the sense of gods' before advancing the aesthetic position that 'if art is not worth more than virtue, it must be worth less; and in that case may as well go overboard'. De Sade provides the title of Chapter XIV, 'Les Malheurs de la Vertu' and Lady Midhurst, advising Bertie to avoid getting 'any notion of providential justice into your head', remarks 'One must face the misfortunes of virtue in this universe, my dear child, and put up with prosperities of vice.' It gives us a striking picture of the life in aristocratic and upper-class circles in Victorian England, complete with authentic dialogue, especially between the boys.

Much of the work is clearly autobiographical, though any attempt to simply equate characters with people Swinburne knew is not helpful. In *Lesbia Brandon* experiences and feelings can be attributed wherever Swinburne likes. That Bertie Seyton gives us the best document we have of Swinburne's childhood is indisputable. He goes to Eton at almost the same time as Swinburne, and has a best friend (Walter Lunsford) who may be based on Algernon Mitford. Lady Wariston has a son in 1848, the same year as Swinburne's brother Edward was born. Chapter XIII refers to a youth drowned at Oxford, as G. R. Luke, one of Old Mortality had done in 1862, and to a beating at Eton given for bathing in the river – an incident mentioned in several works, including *The Sisters*. As we have seen, Lesbia's death draws upon his experience of the death of Edith, and the romantic disappointments suffered by Denham and Bertie have a basis in his own experience. While Mr Linley has reminded some readers of Lord Houghton, 'a scholar and collector, fond of books, coins, prints, and bric-à-brac of a secret kind, kept under locks and behind curtains', Lady Midhurst – the 'venomous old beauty, who had gone all to brain and tongue ... voluble and virulent with a savour of secret experience' – is hardly Lady Trevelyan, and the fact that Lesbia Brandon is a poet should not immediately equate her with Christina Rossetti! We must allow them to be characters while remaining alert to the possibility of Swinburne's indirectly expressing his life experiences through the fiction.

The themes of *Lesbia Brandon* often parallel Swinburne's poetry. There are fine descriptions of the sea, and Bertie says to Denham, 'I think they were right to put a lot of women in the sea; it's like a woman itself: the right place for sirens to come out of, and sing and kill people', which reminds us of the personification of the sea as the 'great sweet mother' in 'The Triumph of Time'. Another scene includes the kind of horse-ride used in 'Hesperia':

> Both made forward in silence, riding hard, swallowing at every bound of the horsehoofs the delight of the wind as a wine: drinking the cold sweet night with nostril and lip. Overhead the grey ghost of a moon, with sharp edges and hollow cheeks through which you saw the blue horror of remote darkness – the broken glass of the sun – seemed as if hung to move along the torrent of the blowing wind. Rare stars sprang into sight and went out between the bright wan bays of cloven cloud. All the sky seemed a rapid masque of faint colours and mutable forms. Below and beyond the dim windy

world of earth, past the blown moors and swept cliffs, the pale sea
flashed and swelled and sounded.

Bertie is riding with Lunsford. The boys – now young men – chaff each
other and Bertie yells out scraps of verse. The description continues:

> They were in sight of the bay under Wansdale Point in full windy
> moonlight; the waves went racing under the blue night like a
> concourse of flying flowers, matched for speed, and playing at
> white horses, but their breaking and blossoming beauty betrayed
> their floral kind; the edge of sand they kissed, leaving the banks of
> the shingle still dry and hard against the muffled yellow light, was
> one long wavering wreath of visible sighs and kisses, radiant and
> weary and passionate; they saw the thin white line of loving foam
> flicker and fluctuate up and down with tender motion as mutable
> as fire. Above the sky was by this time, as Bertie said, a leopard's
> skin of stars: and the grass of the downs was full of running wind
> and falling light.

It is after this ride that Bertie has a remarkable dream (one of two in the
book, the other being Lesbia's dream of Proserpine):

> He saw the star of Venus, white and flower-like as he had always
> seen it, turn into a white rose and come down out of heaven, with
> a reddening centre that grew as it descended liker and liker a living
> mouth; but instead of desire he felt horror and sickness at the sight
> of it, and averted his lips with an effort to utter some prayer or
> exorcism; vainly, for the dreadful mouth only laughed, and came
> closer. And cheek or chin, eyebrow or eye there was none; only this
> mouth; and about it the starry or flowery beams or petals, that
> smelt sweet and shone clear as ever; which was the worst. Then,
> with a violent revulsion of spirit, he seemed to get quit of it; but
> then his ears instead were vexed with sound. The noise of the sea
> hardened and deepened and grew untunable; soon it sharpened
> into a shrill threatening note without sense or pity, but full of
> vicious design.

The sexual symbolism of the reddening flower about to devour him is
obvious. Does Swinburne mean to indicate in Bertie some fear of the
feminine? Is he attracted to Lesbia precisely because he knows that she
will not be able to return his affections? Is unrequited love therefore a
defence? Does the shift from the seeming purity of the white flower that
comes down out of heaven to the red, living mouth, signify a problem
with matching idealized notions of women – the legacy of Swinburne's
religious upbringing – with a perception of them as desirable and sexually desiring? The association with the sea simply reinforces this fear of
the feminine element in which individuality can be drowned.

The narrator's comment is a valid answer to a question that obviously
perplexed Swinburne throughout his life: 'The torture of the dream was
the fancy that these fairest things, sea and sky, star and flower, light and

music, were all unfruitful and barren; absorbed in their own beauty; consummate in their own life.' Much of Swinburne's writing is essentially a hymn to 'these fairest things' and their beauty, which is why he devotes so much space, in this novel as elsewhere, to description. He perceives the natural world as a dance of life and an organic unity. However, here he seems beset with the fear that this life may be an illusion. In later works such as *Tristram of Lyonesse* he moves beyond this fear to an exultation in the forces of nature. In his early work the deadness of nature in 'The Garden of Proserpine' is more typical.

The romantic colour of the descriptive passages should not obscure the satirical wit of the novel, which is full of sharp observations. Take, for example, the epigrammatic style of his description of Lady Midhurst, 'fond of art and voracious of literature; and knowing somewhat of each had never tried her hand at either' or:

> Lord Charles Brandon was a man endurable but indescribable. His one feat when off the turf had been his marriage; and for this it is said he was indebted to other exertions than his own. The venerable Marquis of Burleigh, twenty years his senior, having married at sixty-five a low-born maiden who brought him by way of dowry good looks, copious ridicule, and a brace of boys within the year, could not but recommend to a younger brother, thus twice cut off from one chance, a prompt and profitable union with some equally ineligible female in the bonds of unholy matrimony.

or this description of Leonora Harley:

> There was afloat in London about this time a lady of aspiring build, handsome beyond the average and stupid below the elect of her profession. She had a superb and seductive beauty, some kindness of nature, and no mind whatever. Tall, white-faced, long-limbed, with melancholy eyes that meant nothing and suggested anything, she had made her way in good time.

At times *Lesbia Brandon* is like a mad tea-party story told in turn by Jane Austen, Emily Brontë, an Eton schoolboy and an anthologist of Northumberland border ballads.

It was probably late in 1864 that Swinburne suffered the great romantic loss of his life. Mary Gordon told Swinburne she was engaged to marry Colonel Robert William Disney Leith, whom she seems to have met in Aberdeenshire in 1864. Mary 'received constant letters' from her cousin when she was in Scotland and he was in Cornwall, which seems hardly likely if he already knew of the engagement. When he returned from Cornwall she tells us Swinburne was often at her father's house in Chelsea.

Cecil Lang wrote, 'the evidence, both internal and external, of an unhappy affair is overwhelming'. The explicit evidence comes from

Swinburne. In August 1875 he wrote to congratulate Gosse on his impending marriage:

> I wish you all the joy and good fortune that can be wished, without admixture of envy of that particular form of happiness which I am now never likely to share. I suppose it must be the best thing that can befall a man to win and keep the woman that he loves while yet young; at any rate I can congratulate my friend on his good hap without any too jealous afterthought of the reverse experience which left my own young manhood 'a barren stock' – if I may cite that phrase without seeming to liken myself to a male Queen Elizabeth.

Our authority for connecting this 'reverse experience' with some of the poetry comes from Swinburne. In 1875 Gosse wrote that when Swinburne returned from Italy, 'a great sorrow came upon him ... After a long pause of bitterness and silence, the anguished spirit found voice in what is, perhaps, the very greatest of all his poems, "The Triumph of Time". ' Gosse misdated the trip to Italy and the meeting with Landor to 1862. If he is right about this sorrow smiting Swinburne *after* the meeting with Landor, that would date it to the second half of 1864. Swinburne personally linked the event with 'The Triumph of Time' but did not name the woman concerned:

> Speaking to me of this incident, in 1876, he assured me that the stanzas of this wonderful lyric represented with the exactest fidelity the emotions which passed through his mind when his anger had died down, and when nothing remained but the infinite pity and the pain ... The whole poem deserves close study as a revelation of the poet's innermost feelings, which he exposes with an equal frankness in no other section of his work.

Swinburne said something similar at a Balliol dinner-party in the 1870s, talking about *Poems and Ballads* and 'explaining their relation to his own experiences':

> There were three poems, he said, which beyond all the rest were biographical – 'The Triumph of Time', 'Dolores', and 'The Garden of Proserpine'. 'The Triumph of Time' was a monument to the sole real love of his life – a love which had been the tragic destruction of all his faith in woman. 'Dolores' expressed the passion with which he had sought relief, in the madnesses of the fleshly Venus, from his ruined dreams of the heavenly. 'The Garden of Proserpine' expressed his revolt against the flesh and its fevers, and his longing to find a refuge from them in a haven of undisturbed rest . . . .

Other poems, including 'A Leave-Taking', 'Satia te Sanguine', 'Hesperia', 'A Wasted Vigil', 'At a Month's End' and 'The Year of the Rose', seem to express various aspects of this experience. These private comments take biographical precedence over the public defence of *Poems and*

Ballads in 1866 when he needed to assert the right of the poems to be treated as art, insisting that 'no utterance of enjoyment or despair, belief or unbelief, can properly be assumed as the assertion of its author's personal feeling or faith'. Likewise in 1904 he wrote:

> There are photographs from life in the book; and there are sketches from imagination. Some which keen-sighted criticism has dismissed with a smile as ideal or imaginary were as real and actual as they well could be; others which have been taken for obvious transcripts from memory were utterly fantastic or dramatic.

One further piece in the jigsaw links his disappointment to the Isle of Wight. In 1873 he wrote to a Balliol friend Edwin Harrison that 'at the risk of realizing the sensations of a damned ghost revisiting earth before my natural date of damnation' he would be soon in the Isle of Wight at The Orchard, one of the Gordon's houses:

> My mother wants me to go, and I think I may as well once for all break through all sentiment of reluctance and association and tread out all sense of old pain and pleasure for ever, if I can, by coming back in this my old age to where I was so happy and unhappy as a child and youth.

The area would have had sad associations because of Edith, but perhaps Swinburne was also alluding to the loss of Mary.

Whatever its status as a biographical document, 'The Triumph of Time' is one of Swinburne's greatest lyrics. Swinburne did not care much for reciting old poems but made an exception of it. Gosse heard him chant fragments 'with extraordinary poignancy. On these occasions his voice took on strange and fife-like notes, extremely moving and disconcerting, since he was visibly moved himself.' It was not the first of his poems to deal with the theme of failed love but remains one of the most impassioned and certainly dramatic, as Swinburne evokes the ebb and flow of the speaker's moods. The opening stanza is crucial:

> Before our lives divide for ever,
>   While time is with us and hands are free,
> (Time, swift to fasten and swift to sever
>   Hand from hand, as we stand by the sea)
> I will say no word that a man might say
> Whose whole life's love goes down in a day;
> For this could never have been; and never,
>   Though the gods and the years relent, shall be.

The poem opens at the moment of crisis: they are about to be separated. The image of the hands is at once specific and symbolic of joining in marriage. The speaker is evidently shocked by a turn of events disastrous to his hopes, for a 'whole life's love' has come to an end 'in a day'. The line 'I will say no word that a man might say' has been interpreted

The Triumph of Time

1

Before our lives divide for ever,
  While time is with us & hands are free,
(Time, swift to fasten & swift to sever
  Hand from hand, as we stand by the sea)
I will say no word that a man might say
Whose whole life's love goes down in a day;
For this could never have been; & never,
  Though the gods & the years relent, shall be.

2

Is it worth a tear, is it worth an hour,
  To think of things that are well outworn?
Of fruitless husk & fugitive flower,
  The dream foregone & the deed forborne?
Though joy be done with & grief be vain,
Time shall not sever us wholly in twain;
Earth is not spoilt for a single shower;
  But the rain has ruined the ungrown corn.

3

It will grow not again, this fruit of my heart,
  Smitten with sunbeams, ruined with rain.
The singing seasons divide & depart,
  Winter & summer depart in twain.
It will grow not again, it is ruined at root,
The bloodlike blossom, the dull red fruit;
Though the heart yet sickens, the lips yet smart,
  With sullen savour of poisonous pain.

4

I have given no man of my fruit to eat;
  I trod the grapes, I have drunken the wine.
Had you eaten & drunken & found it sweet,
  This wild new growth of the corn & vine,
This wine & bread without lees or leaven,
We had grown as gods, as the gods in heaven,
Souls fair to look upon, goodly to greet,
  One splendid spirit, your soul & mine.

5.3 First page of the manuscript of 'The Triumph of Time' to mean that Swinburne did not declare his love to the woman concerned. It might also express a resolve not to say anything in condemnation, anger, sorrow or persuasion.

In stanza two he asks rhetorically if it is worth thinking of the past, of 'The dream foregone and the deed forborne' and finds a grain of consolation in the thought that 'Time shall not sever us wholly in twain' although 'the rain has ruined the ungrown corn'. He predicts 'It will grow not again, this fruit of my heart,/Smitten with sunbeams, ruined with rain' because it is 'ruined at root' by the experience. He believes he has lost the chance of a relationship fulfilling all levels of being, 'one splendid spirit, your soul and mine':

> In the change of years, in the coil of things,
>   In the clamour and rumour of life to be,
> We, drinking love at the furthest springs,
>   Covered with love as a covering tree,
> We had grown as gods, as the gods above,
> Filled from the heart to the lips with love,
> Held fast in his hands, clothed warm with his wings,
>   O love, my love, had you loved but me!
>
> We had stood as the sure stars stand, and moved
>   As the moon moves, loving the world; and seen
> Grief collapse as a thing disproved,
>   Death consume as a thing unclean.
> Twain halves of a perfect heart, made fast
> Soul to soul while the years fell past;
> Had you loved me once, as you have not loved;
>   Had the chance been with us that has not been.

The poem then describes the landscape in which this is taking place, which is certainly consonant with the Isle of Wight:

> The low loose downs lean to the sea; the stream,
>   One loose thin pulseless tremulous vein,
> Rapid and vivid and dumb as a dream,
>   Works downward, sick of the sun and the rain;
> No wind is rough with the rank rare flowers;
> The sweet sea, mother of loves and hours,
> Shudders and shines as the grey winds gleam,
>   Turning her smile to a fugitive pain.

The detail of the stream that runs to the sea occurs in several places in Swinburne's writing. Another important stanza is the thirteenth where he speaks of what would have happened if they were 'once made one for a single hour', a reference to sexual union taken up in a later stanza where Swinburne writes that nothing would have severed them 'were you once sealed mine,/Mine in the blood's beat, mine in the breath,/ Mixed into me as honey in wine'. But she has chosen another man:

> But now, you are twain, you are cloven apart,
> Flesh of his flesh, but heart of my heart;
> And deep in one is the bitter root,
>   And sweet for one is the lifelong flower.

In the extant manuscript (a late draft) Swinburne made this even more pointed by writing 'And deep in me is the bitter root,/And sweet for him is the lifelong flower'. In 'Dolores' Swinburne would refer to how:

> Time turns the old days to derision,
>   Our loves into corpses or wives;
> And marriage and death and division
>   Make barren our lives.

His pain is intensified not only by the longevity of his feelings (which would accord with the length of time Swinburne and Mary had known each other) but also by the insistence that 'Let come what will, there is one thing worth,/To have had fair love in the life upon earth' and by the obscure sense of betrayal which lingers throughout the poem. Gosse mentions Swinburne's bitterness and anger, and the Balliol party had heard Swinburne say the experience had been 'the tragic destruction of all his faith in woman'. For this to be so he must have felt that they should have been together and that her choice was the wrong one for both of them. At one point in 'The Triumph of Time' Swinburne writes half-accusingly, 'You have chosen and clung to the chance they sent you,/Life sweet as perfume and pure as prayer'. The 'they' fits the scenario of a husband chosen by the young woman's parents. A little further on she is cast in the role of potential redeemer: 'But you, had you chosen, had you stretched hand,/Had you seen good such a thing were done,/I too might have stood with the souls that stand in the sun's sight'. There is an allusion to his experience of hearing Mary play the organ at Northcourt, since music is associated with the beloved, when he writes of how 'These were a part of the playing I heard/Once, ere my love and my heart were at strife' and that 'I shall hate sweet music my whole life long'.

Swinburne's emotions for Mary are possibly mirrored by Denham's for Margaret in *Lesbia Brandon*:

> Denham looked her in the face, shaken inwardly and throughout by a sense of inevitable pain. Curiously he seemed to contemplate himself with a quiet scientific wonder; to feel the pulses of his fever, to examine and approve or condemn the play played out on the inner stage of his mind, to count up the acts and scenes of the tragic agony underlying for him all these infinitely little incidents, childish and comical chances of the day. Standing with her hand over Bertie's shoulder, the woman waited half smiling. The glory and the terror of her beauty held down desire and absorbed despair. Rage rose in him again like a returning sea. Furious fancies

woke up and fought inside him, crying out one upon the other. He would have given his life for leave to touch her, his soul for a chance of dying crushed down under her feet: an emotion of extreme tenderness, lashed to fierce insanity by the circumstances, frothed over into a passion of vehement cruelty. Deeply he desired to die by her, if that could be; and more deeply, if this could be, to destroy her: scourge her into swooning and absorb the blood with kisses; caress and lacerate her loveliness, alleviate and heighten her pains; to feel her foot upon his throat, and wound her own with his teeth; submit his body and soul for a little to her lightest will, and satiate upon hers the desperate caprice of his immeasurable desire; to inflict careful torture on limbs too tender to embrace, suck the tears off her laden eyelids, bite through her sweet and shuddering lips.

Such feelings are reminiscent of 'Anactoria'. More direct is Bertie's reaction when Lesbia tells him that she cannot return his love: 'he sat and felt a breakage inside him of all that made up the hopefullest part of his life'. Mrs Hungerford Pollen told Gosse she remembered the affair with the young lady of 'The Triumph of Time', 'and at that period she was "kind" to Algernon, because he was so much "cut up". He inspired pity, but he was not at all sorry for himself.'

Mary denied that they had ever enjoyed anything other than a brother and sister relationship. In 1917 she declared:

> I know it is difficult for the world to understand such friendships as ours without weaving into them a thread of romance, existing only in its imagination. I know that such has been the case even with us, and that a fiction has somehow been built up, and has even got into print. Therefore, especially, I am anxious to say once and for all that there was never, in all our years of friendship, an ounce of sentiment between us. Any idea of the kind would have been an insult to our brother-and-sister footing, and would have destroyed at once and for ever our unfettered intercourse and happy intimacy, which Algernon himself has so beautifully described in the 'Dedication' to me of his tragedy of *Rosamund, Queen of the Lombards*:
> 'Scarce less in love than brother and sister born,
> Even all save brother and sister sealed at birth. '

Given the evidence, it is hard to take this statement at face value. Perhaps Mary did not realize the extent of Swinburne's feelings for her, though this is difficult to believe even allowing for his reticence in such matters. Mildred Leith, one of her grand-daughters, said Swinburne never declared his love to Mary. There would certainly have been family opposition. Swinburne's rejection of Christianity, his drinking, his lack of position in society and the close blood ties between the cousins would all have worked against their marrying. In the first stanza of 'The Triumph of Time', Swinburne fatalistically wrote 'For this could never

5.4 Col. Robert and Mary Disney Leith

have been'. As for his response, in *A Year's Letters* Francis Cheyne says, 'If I can never marry the one woman perfectly pleasant to me and faultlessly fit for me in the whole beautiful nature of her, I will never insult her and my own heart by marrying at all.'

Mary's marriage took place on 14 June 1865 at St Peter's, Shorwell, on the Isle of Wight, the Revd Algernon Wodehouse and the Revd T. Renwick presiding. Swinburne was one of the trustees of the marriage settlement (dated 13 June). Mary's husband Colonel Robert William Disney Leith was born in 1819, making him 21 years older than his bride. The year Swinburne was born Robert Disney Leith entered the army. His military career was short but distinguished. He served in the Persian Gulf and the Punjab and during the siege of Moultan in January 1849 was severely wounded after he had leapt on to the outer wall. His left arm cut off by a sabre, he managed to cleave his assailant to the teeth before being shot in the arm and chest. He left Moultan on 17 February and sailed home. On 20 July, the morning of his homecoming to Glenkindie, Aberdeen, 'flags were displayed from every house in the neighbourhood, while triumphal arches decorated with flowers and evergreens, spanned the roadings' for the local hero. He returned to India in the 1850s, seeing active service in the Indian Mutiny of 1857 and attaining the rank of Lieutenant Colonel in 1862. He succeeded to the ancestral home on the death of his father in 1859 and was placed on half-pay on 29 May 1866. A strong Conservative, he served as a Justice of the Peace, though largely unconcerned with county affairs or politics. He liked shooting and fishing and in later life developed a routine of going to the Isle of Wight each April. The Gordons and the Leiths had been friends for many years and Mary most likely met him at the Gordons' mansion at Knockespock, which they inherited in 1854. Robert Disney Leith was back from India at least by the end of 1863.

Mary Gordon later wrote:

> My marriage in 1865, and subsequent residence for much of the year in Scotland, naturally caused something of a gap in our con-stant correspondence and intercourse, though he was always the same when we did meet. I have been unable to trace the letter he wrote when I announced to him my engagement, and said that as he had always been to me like an elder brother, I should like to feel that I had his approval. I know that he did write most kindly, saying that 'If it was A. or any of my sisters, I could not feel more sincerely interested', or words to that effect.

'Sincerely interested'? The phrase sounds strangely cold. For years 'all my unmarried life – we rode together constantly and without mischance', wrote Mary. She claimed one of her most valued wedding gifts was a copy of *Atalanta*. The inscription says only 'M. C. J. Gordon/from A.

C. Swinburne/May 1865'. It seems rather impersonal, given how long they had known each other.

After her marriage Mary found time between having six children to write (between 1867 and 1893) ten novels and a volume of poetry. F. A. C. Wilson has convincingly demonstrated that in these stories she repeatedly goes over the events leading up to her marriage, her heroine invariably having to choose between a young, romantic but unreliable companion and a more reliable older man.

The poem 'Felise', which Swinburne called 'a personal favourite of mine', dramatizes a situation in which a man rejected by a woman has cut her out of his affections. A year later she regrets her decision and returns. It is a bitterly ironic study:

> What shall be said between us here
>   Among the downs, between the trees,
> In fields that knew our feet last year,
>   In sight of quiet sands and sea,
>   This year, Felise? . . .
>
> I had died for this last year, to know
>   You love me. Who shall turn on fate?
> I care not if love come or go
>   Now, though your love seek mine for mate.
>   It is too late . . .
>
> And these love longer now than men,
>   And larger loves than ours are these.
> No diver brings up love again
>   Dropped once, my beautiful Felise,
>   In such cold seas.

CHAPTER SIX

A Temple of Lizards

In March 1865 Swinburne's *Atalanta in Calydon* appeared in cream buckram covers with three gold roundels designed by Rossetti. The Admiral contributed over £100 to the cost of the first edition, probably of 500 copies, and Swinburne later claimed he had no money from the first or the second edition. Rossetti had suggested that Swinburne publish *Atalanta* before any other of his poems 'as it was calculated to put people in a better humour' for them. Presentation copies were duly sent out to family and friends, drawing a generally warm response. Swinburne was especially pleased *Atalanta* found favour with Lady Trevelyan, to whom he wrote on 15 March:

> ... I think it is the best executed and sustained of my larger poems. It was begun last autumn twelvemonth, when we were all freshly unhappy, and finished just after I got the news in September last, of Mr. Landor's death, which was a considerable trouble to me, as I had hoped against hope or reason that he who in the spring at Florence had accepted the dedication of an unfinished poem would live to receive and read it ... In spite of the funereal circumstances which I suspect have a little deepened the natural colours of Greek fatalism here and there, so as to have already incurred a charge of 'rebellious antagonism' and such like things, I never enjoyed anything more in my life than the composition of this poem, which though a work done by intervals, was very rapid and pleasant. Allowing for a few after insertions, two or three in all, from p.66 to 83 (as far as the Chorus) was the work of two afternoons, and from p.83 to the end was the work of two other afternoons ....

His comments about the ease of writing are borne out by the manuscripts, which are relatively free of emendations. Swinburne felt similar works by Shelley, Goethe and Arnold were unsuccessful, 'so I thought, and still think, the field was clear for me'.

Lafourcade considered that 'a keen sea breeze blows through the lines of *Atalanta*'. Much of the play had been written near Tintagel during the stay with Inchbold. This marine influence is evident in one of the loveliest passages, where Meleager remembers past sea-voyages, 'when the sail':

> First caught between stretched ropes the roaring west,
> And all our oars smote eastward, and the wind
> First flung round faces of seafaring men
> White splendid snow-flakes of the sundering foam,

And the first furrow in virginal green sea
Followed by plunging ploughshare of hewn pine,
And closed, as when deep sleep subdues man's breath
Lips close and heart subsides; and closing, shone
Sunlike with many a Nereid's hair, and moved
Round many a trembling mouth of doubtful gods,
Risen out of sunless and sonorous gulfs
Through waning water and into shallow light,
That watched us; and when flying the dove was snared
As with men's hands, but we shot after and sped
Clear through the irremeable Symplegades;
And chiefliest when hoar beach and herbless cliff
Stood out ahead from Colchis, and we heard
Clefts hoarse with wind, and saw through narrowing reefs
The lightning of the intolerable wave
Flash, and the white wet flame of breakers burn
Far under a kindling south-wind, as a lamp
Burns and bends all its blowing flame one way;
Wild heights untravelled of the wind, and vales
Cloven seaward by their violent streams, and white
With bitter flowers and bright salt scurf of brine;
Heard sweep their sharp swift gales, and bowing birdwise
Shriek with birds' voices, and with furious feet
Tread loose the long skirts of a storm . . . .

Transcending all his influences, Swinburne hymns the elements in a blank verse transformed by trochaic and anapaestic substitution, bunched stresses, alliteration, strong verbs, plural nouns, and inclusive sentences. Rutland argued 'such poetry as *Atalanta* can only be made out of life, and I would go so far as to say that it proves what he lived very much more clearly than it shows what he read'. Swinburne's loss of religious belief and the deaths and disappointments in love he had suffered refute the notion that *Atalanta* is only inspired by other literature. His feelings for Edith, Mary, Northcourt, the seas off East Dene and Tintagel, coupled with the long years of writer's apprenticeship fused to create a masterpiece.

The story centres on Althaea, queen of Calydon, and her son Meleager. A prophetic dream reveals he will always be safe if she saves from destruction a particular 'brand', or piece of firewood. Meleager lives to achieve many heroic exploits, eventually battling the tribes who wage war on his homeland of Aetolia. These tribes are spurred on by the goddess Artemis because the King of Calydon has failed to honour her. Artemis further punishes Calydon by plaguing it with a wild boar. Meleager hunts the boar in the company of the maiden Atalanta, whom he loves. Artemis permits the boar to be slain because of Atalanta's dedication to her. Meleager tries to present the dead boar to Atalanta, provoking the jealous anger of his uncles Toxeus and Plexippus. A fight ensues, and Meleager kills them. Overcome by a desire to avenge her brothers, Althaea casts the brand into the fire, destroying her own son.

Atalanta is mentioned in the 'Hymn to Artemis' in the Eton anthology *Poetae Graeci*, and there are fragments of the 'Meleager' of Euripides in the *Poetarum Scenicorum Graecorum Fabulae Superstites* (1851) given to Swinburne by schoolfriends when he left Eton. His version of the story mainly draws on Ovid and Apollodorus. Love is seen throughout as a destructive force that leads men to pain and death. Althaea calls it 'a thwart sea-wind full of rain and foam', 'an evil thing' that brings no joy 'but grief,/Sharp words and soul's division and fresh tears ... /Pitiful sighs, and much regrafted pain'. Meleager's love for the independent-spirited Atalanta is unhappy and unrequited. The Chief Huntsman calls her 'snowy-souled,/Fair as the snow and footed as the wind', and to the Chorus:

> She is holier than all holy days or things,
> The sprinkled water or fume of perfect fire;
> Chaste, dedicated to pure prayers, and filled
> With higher thoughts than heaven; a maiden clean,
> Pure iron, fashioned for a sword; and man
> She loves not . . . .

But Althaea speaks slightingly of how 'A woman armed makes war upon herself':

> Unwomanlike, and treads down use and wont
> And the sweet common honour that she hath,
> Love, and the cry of children, and the hand
> Trothplight and mutual mouth of marriages.
> This doth she, being unloved; whom if one love,
> Not fire nor iron and the wide-mouthed wars
> Are deadlier than her lips or braided hair.

The second chorus, 'We have seen thee, O Love, thou art fair; thou art goodly, O Love', takes up the theme of Love's nature in describing the birth of Aphrodite, calling love 'an evil blossom ... the seed of it laughter and tears'.

The verse-drama's other major theme is the protest against the higher force responsible for these sufferings. God is inscrutable, a bitter and jealous oppressor who has given us 'ephemeral lips' and unquenchable desire. In the second chorus ('Before the beginning of years') the Chorus raises its voice in protest against 'the supreme evil, God', who has made us 'transitory and hazardous,/Light things and slight' and 'With pain ... filled us full to the eyes and ears'. Part of the fourth Chorus is written on the same sheet of manuscript as some lines from 'Anactoria', suggesting that the theme of 'the mystery of the cruelty of things' links both works and forms one strand of the 'internal centre' which Meredith (having heard some burlesque by Swinburne) mistakenly thought he lacked. Rutland summarized the three strands of *Atalanta* as 'an overwhelming sense of the tragedy of life; a conviction that love produces only agony and ruin; and a tremendous denunciation of the all powerful malignant providence that is responsible for these things'. The word 'god' or 'God' retains a magnetic presence in the poetry. Swinburne's attacks on religion have the force of 'an evangelist turned inside-out', as Gosse put it: 'Swinburne was deeply instructed in the text and teaching of the Bible, and it is noticeable that there is a distinct strain of the religious controversialist running through his poems.' In depicting God as an essentially cruel figure Swinburne was, of course, drawing on Blake's Urizen and de Sade, as he commented to Lord Houghton after the latter had reviewed the verse-drama:

> I only regret that in justly attacking my Antitheism you have wilfully misrepresented its source. I should have bowed to the judicial sentence if instead of 'Byron with a difference' you had said 'de Sade with a difference'. The poet, thinker, and man of the world from whom the theology of my poem is derived was a greater than Byron. He indeed, fatalist or not, saw to the bottom of gods and men.

In 1865 the literary world was more attuned to the domestic and pastoral vision of Tennyson's *Enoch Arden* and the character analyses of Browning's *Dramatis Personae*. *Atalanta*'s music resounded through that world like the crash of an Atlantic roller over the tinkling of a fountain. The reviews were very favourable and elevated Swinburne to the first rank of modern English writers. *Atalanta*'s lyricism and Greek form distracted attention from its antitheistic sentiments. *The London Review*, noting Swinburne's relative youth, called the volume 'extraordinary, not simply for the strength and vividness of imagination, (what is far more remarkable with inexperience) for maturity of power, for completeness of self-control, for absolute mastery over the turbulent forces of adolescent genius'. Ironically, it praised his reproduction of 'the old Greek faith or want of faith' – a sentiment found in a number of the reviews. As *The Examiner* put it, 'he has, with rare artistic feeling, let scarcely a trace appear of modern life. The Poem is all alive with the life of a classic past.' This must have been comforting to the Admiral and Lady Jane. *The Saturday Review* wrote 'a careful study of the Attic dramatists has enabled him to catch their manner, and to reproduce felicitously many of their terms of expression', though it thought the matter 'not really Greek in its essence'. Other journals were more sceptical about the drama's Hellenic qualities. There were predictable comparisons with Shelley. *The Times* wrote, 'he is gifted with no small portion of the all-important divine fire', and *The Sunday Times* judged Swinburne 'a subtle analyst of human motive' with 'imagination of the highest order, wonderful play of fancy, and a complete command over every form of versification'.

Not only did the reviews miss the antagonistic spirit of *Atalanta*; there were even those such as F. D. Maurice, the moral philosopher, who thought it attacked paganism, which prompted Swinburne's ironic remark:

> For myself, I think of addressing a memorial to the government which shall set forth my own claims to a pension as Defender of the Faith and moral teacher of my own generation. Mr. Maurice, you may remember, considers *Atalanta* a complement to the hitherto imperfect Evidences of Christianity. As the second Paley, I expect at least a lay archdiaconate.

Years later Swinburne came to resent its popularity and felt its famous first chorus ('When the hounds of spring are on winter's traces') had been 'reprinted so very much oftener than it deserves that if the public is not tired of it I am'. When Morris printed the beautiful Kelmscott *Atalanta* Swinburne wished *Erechtheus* had been chosen instead. In 1904 he described how:

> My first attempt to do something original in English which might in some degree reproduce for English readers the likeness of a Greek tragedy, with possibly something more of its true poetic life and charm than could have been expected from the authors of 'Caractacus' and 'Merope', was perhaps too exuberant and effusive in its dialogue, as it certainly was too irregular in the occasional licence of its choral verse, to accomplish the design or achieve the success which its author should have aimed at. It may or may not be too long as a poem; it is, I fear, too long for a poem of the kind to which it belongs or aims at belonging.

In the spring of 1865 the Admiral decided to sell East Dene, to Swinburne's 'life-long sorrow'. Capheaton had been lost in September 1860. Now, just as *Atalanta* brought Swinburne fame, his other childhood refuge was taken from him. In March he stayed with his family in London at 36 Wilton Crescent while both they and he searched for new habitations. His parents eventually moved to Holmwood, Shiplake, Henley-on-Thames. His friend Charles Augustus Howell helped with the search for lodgings. The day Swinburne turned 28 he wrote, 'it is the greatest nuisance to me to have this endless hunt going on'. On 10 April he found ground-floor rooms at 22A Dorset Street, just north of Marble Arch, which 'though not light are large and convenient otherwise' and he occupied them until the end of the decade. He complained to Lady Trevelyan he was feeling the effects of the English winter after so many spent abroad, but enthused over Ford Madox Brown's exhibition. On 18 April he met Lewis Carroll, who parodied him in 'Atalanta in Camden Town'.

His social life was enlivened by the Arts Club, which he joined in 1864, and dinners with Richard Burton and others at the Cannibal Club, an offshoot of the Anthropological Society. The Society was founded in January 1863 by Burton and Dr James Hunt, with its avowed aim to 'promote the study of Anthropology in a strictly scientific manner ... to study Man in all his leading aspects, physical, moral and historical; to investigate the laws of his origin and progress; to ascertain his place in nature and his relations to the inferior forms of life ... to establish a de facto science of man.' The Society prided itself on its free-thinking spirit. Papers were read on a variety of exotic subjects, with titles such as 'On Phallic Worship in India' and 'On the Negro's Place in Nature'. On occasions skulls were examined and a skeleton presented. In 'Notes on Certain Matters connected with the Dahoman' (a paper given on 17 November 1863), Burton said,

> I cannot but congratulate ourselves upon the fact, that we find in this room a liberty of thought and a freedom of speech unknown, I may assert, to any other Society in Great Britain. It is well so. Our object of study being MAN in all his relations, physical, moral, psychical, and social, it is impossible to treat the subject adequately without offending in general the *mauvaise honte*, the false delicacy and ingrained prejudices of the age.

As another of the Fellows, Sir Edward Brabrook, put it,. 'O, do not ask me if I can throw/A light on the impiety/The fellows utter at the Anthropological Society'. It is hardly surprising, therefore, that the talks and atmosphere at 4 St Martin's Place would appeal to Swinburne, who was elected a Fellow on 4 April 1865. At that time James Hunt was President, and Burton, Dr Bepthhold Seemann, J. Frederick Collingwood and Thomas Bendyshe were Vice Presidents. Bendyshe was a Fellow of King's College Cambridge, from whom Swinburne may have gleaned information about Eastern religion for his later poem 'Hertha'. The Curator, Librarian and Assistant Secretary was Charles Carter Blake, and members included Winwood Reade, author of *The Martyrdom of Man* (1872) and James Reddie, who Peter Mendes believes was active in the writing of pornographic literature, along with Charles Cameron, another member and friend of Swinburne's in the late 1860s.

According to Brabrook, the Cannibal Club was formed to 'fill up the interval between the Council Meetings of the Society and the evening meetings for the readings of papers'. It met in a suitably Bohemian ambience at Bartolini's Hotel near Leicester Square, and had an ebony mace in the shape of a negro head gnawing an ivory thigh-bone on the table in front of the President. Swinburne apparently dubbed it 'Ecce

Homo' and composed a parody of Christian grace called the 'Cannibal Catechism'. A club member recalled Swinburne's talk as 'spirited and characteristic' and 'accompanied by those fidgety movements which seemed to help it out'.

In the summer of 1865 Swinburne visited Ashburnham Place in Sussex, and there enjoyed 'domestic life, rural gallops with cousins, study of art and illuminated MSS. and Caxton prints'. He wrote 'Dolores' and checked the proofs of a second edition of *Atalanta* and the long-delayed *Chastelard*. Rossetti complained in June that he had not seen Swinburne for some time. In July Swinburne met the French painter Daubigny and Bryan Procter, who wrote poetry as 'Barry Cornwall'. Swinburne's reverence for the aged found expression in 'In Memory of Barry Cornwall' and 'Age and Song'. From 28 August to 4 September Swinburne was with Lord Houghton at Fryston, where Mrs Gaskell noted him as the author of *Atalanta*. From Fryston Swinburne travelled to Wallington to see the Trevelyans and Scott. He then stayed at Shernfold Park, Tunbridge Wells, the seat of his maternal uncle the Hon. Percy Ashburnham. It may have been on this occasion that he met Mary for the first time since her marriage. She remembered that 'though nothing of particular moment occurred' there were 'lively and merry games in the evening with him and the large party of cousins, such games as "consequences" and the like'. What were Swinburne's feelings on seeing her with her husband? On 20 September the painter Frederick Shields was at a party at Burne-Jones's house and saw 'an impenetrably close knot of listeners gathered round some central point of interest ... A mass of rich auburn hair leaped up for a moment, disappeared and reappeared indicative of some excitable being pouring forth unseen. This I afterwards learned was Swinburne'.

In November George E. J. Powell and Eirikr Magnusson dedicated their *Legends of Iceland* to Swinburne, who read several books on Iceland at this time. It was another shared interest with Mary who in later years translated Icelandic poems and made a number of visits to Iceland. George Powell was five years younger than Swinburne, a Welshman and Etonian, whose father owned the Georgian mansion of Nant Eos, near Aberystwyth. They became close friends, stayed at each other's parental homes, and exchanged flagellatory letters. Powell's love of music endeared him to Swinburne's sisters. When in Wales Swinburne and Powell haunted a tavern in Aberystwyth 'kept by a disreputable old woman whose Rabelaisian talk owned a special attraction for Swinburne'.

Like those to Houghton, Solomon and Powell, Swinburne's letters to Howell often contained flagellation allusions, which caused him trouble in the 1880s. Charles Augustus Howell (1840–90) was a hanger-on among the Pre-Raphaelites, known to Rossetti, Burne-Jones, Madox

Brown, Ruskin and Whistler. William Rossetti called him 'a man whom I certainly did not esteem, but did none the less to a certain extent like'. Of mixed Portuguese and English parentage, Howell came to England in his teens and met Rossetti sometime around 1857. After going abroad he returned to England in 1864. Howell was a chain-smoking raconteur often found at dinners wearing the sash of a Knight Commander of the Portuguese Order of Christ. He helped sell Rossetti's pictures and supervised the recovery of his poems from Lizzie Siddal's grave in 1869. He was quick-thinking, adaptable, with enough talent to copy drawings by famous artists. His claim to have known Orsini would have endeared him to Swinburne almost immediately.

Howell read parts of *Lesbia Brandon* and was fond of reciting lines from 'A Reiver's Neck-Verse'. Swinburne wrote a lively letter to Howell from Ashburnham Place in the early summer of 1865 which is quite typical. Addressing Howell as 'Infâme libertin', Swinburne exclaims 'I have added yet four more jets of boiling and gushing infamy to the perennial and poisonous fountain of Dolores', and then adds as a postscript:

> I want you to compose for me a little dialogue (imaginary) between schoolmaster and boy – from the first summons 'Now Arthur (or Frank – or Harry) what does this mean, sir? Come here' – to every lash (and plenty of them) and a shriek of agonized appeal from the boy in reply. I want to see how like real life you will make it. Write me this – and you shall have more of my verses – a fair bargain.

No hard evidence has emerged to support claims that Howell flagellated Swinburne. It is possible that Howell's part in negotiating the republication of *Poems and Ballads* in 1866 with publisher John Camden may have put Swinburne at a disadvantage when he tried to extricate himself from Hotten in the early 1870s.

Swinburne continued seeing Rossetti almost every day he was in London. Other friends included James Whistler, with whom he was to quarrel in old age but whose work at this time he enjoyed. One Sunday morning in April after breakfast, Swinburne improvised some lines on Whistler's picture of his lover Joanna Hiffernan 'Symphony in White, No. 2: The Little White Girl' (1864). He found in the picture 'the notion of sad and glad mystery in the face languidly contemplative of its own phantom and all other things seen by their phantoms'. 'Before the Mirror' views the girl as a seer whose contemplation unveils the mystery of existence:

> Glad, but not flushed with gladness,
>   Since joys go by;
> Sad, but not bent with sadness,
>   Since sorrows die;

Deep in the gleaming glass
She sees all past things pass,
    And all sweet life that was lie down and lie.

Face fallen and white throat lifted,
    With sleepless eye
She sees old loves that drifted,
    She knew not why,
Old loves and faded fears
Float down a stream that hears
    The flowing of all men's tears beneath the sky.

If Rossetti, Whistler or Burne-Jones were engaged, Swinburne could visit Simeon Solomon. Born in 1840, Solomon trained to become a painter from the age of ten. By fifteen he was studying at the Royal Academy school. Late in the 1850s he met Rossetti and started working on the design of stained glass for Morris, Marshall, Faulkner and Co. He illustrated books and magazines and exhibited occasionally at the Royal Academy. One contemporary described Solomon as

> facile and spasmodically intense, sensitive to extreme touchiness, conscious of his great abilities, proud of his race, but with something of the mystic about him which was pagan, not Christian. Quaint was his humour. He touched all subjects lightly, and with so much brilliancy, that the follies he uttered and wrote seemed to be spontaneously wise and witty sayings.

A kindred spirit to Swinburne, it would seem.

Solomon drew a portrait of Swinburne and may have used him as a model for such pictures as 'Shadrach Meshach and Abednego' (1863). Although many of Solomon's pictures have Judaic or Old Testament themes, he created others of obvious interest to Swinburne, for example, a watercolour of Sappho in 1862, 'Sappho and Erinna' (1864) and 'Atalanta' (1866). His 'Damon and Aglae', exhibited at the Academy in 1866, inspired Swinburne's poem 'Erotion'. Swinburne later reviewed Solomon's A Vision of Love Revealed in Sleep and Solomon illustrated Swinburne's 'The End of a Month' (1871). Just as Swinburne has been cast as an innocent corrupted by Houghton and Burton, so in turn Swinburne has been portrayed as the corrupter of innocents like Solomon; it is alleged that

> The influence of Swinburne's unstable character on the all too impressionable Solomon was to prove fatal. The artist's youthful innocence was no match for his mentor's capriciousness. Swinburne's nickname for Solomon, 'The Lamb', was all too apposite. Before long both Solomon and 'Ned' Burne-Jones were drawing illustrations to Swinburne's de Sade-inspired Lesbia Brandon and 'The Flogging Block'.

Solomon had his own fund of instability and his own predelictions. Neither he nor Burne-Jones (with Marie Zambaco) needed a 'mentor' to get them into deep water. A letter of Burne-Jones to Swinburne ('my dear but infamous pote') dates their acquaintance with Solomon to 1861. Burne-Jones had read Swinburne's missive to Solomon and 'our enjoyment was such that we spent a whole morning in making pictures for you, such as Tiberius would have given provinces for'. In one:

> a clergyman of the established church is seen lying in an extatic dream in the foreground – above him a lady is seen plunging from a trap door in the ceiling about to impale herself upon him – how poorly does this describe one of my most successful designs but you shall yet see it . . . .

Solomon had a close relationship with his sister Rebecca (1832–86) who was also an artist. Rebellious and prolific, she exhibited at the Royal Academy from 1852 to 1869 and at other galleries. She was devoted to her Jewish roots but led a Bohemian existence. It has been said that her behaviour was 'equally erratic' as that of her brother and that she had an affair with Swinburne which 'proved as unsatisfactory as might be expected from the poet's physical and emotional inadequacy'. This affair is so far unsubstantiated.

It was at Simeon Solomon's studio in Howland Street that George du Maurier met Swinburne on 12 May 1864 and found him 'without exception the most extraordinary man not that I ever met only, but that I ever read or heard of':

> . . . for three hours he spouted his poetry to us, and it was of a power, beauty and originality unequalled. Everything after seems tame, but the little beast will never I think be acknowledged for he has an utterly perverted moral sense, and ranks Lucrezia Borgia with Jesus Christ; indeed says she's far greater, and very little of his poetry is fit for publication. If you like I will copy one of his very mildest which has been published, namely Faustine, and send it you. These strange creatures all hang in a clique together, and despise everything but themselves; and really I don't wonder. Swinburne's French poetry is almost as fine as his English. The other day at Jones's he was asked to write verses for four pictures of the seasons Jones has just painted, and in *twenty minutes* he had produced four beautiful little Latin poems!

Thomas Armstrong, who accompanied Du Maurier, recollected that there had been a discussion of early French poets, which led to Swinburne demonstrating his astonishing memory:

> A propos of Villon, Swinburne spoke of 'Les Neiges d'Antan', and after asking Rossetti in vain to try and remember it, he himself recited it without hesitation as it is printed in the collection of Rossetti's poems. He afterwards repeated the French original. It

was said that Swinburne had seen and read the manuscript once only, and it must have been several years earlier, for Mrs. Rossetti had died in 1862. These recitations led to others from his manuscript poems, afterwards published in the *Poems and Ballads,* and we both came away very much impressed by what we had heard. It was something like a revelation to us. We both knew the *Atalanta in Calydon,* which had already been published, but in these other poems . . . there were rhythms and metres which were new to us, word music most melodious and fascinating. Neither of us could ever forget that evening.

One of Rossetti's assistants, a young Cornishman Henry Treffry Dunn, described one of Swinburne's visits to Cheyne Walk around this time:

Soon, something I had said anent his last poem set his thoughts loose. Like the storm that had just broken, so he began in low tones to utter lines of poetry. As the storm increased, he got more and more excited and carried away by the impulse of his thoughts, bursting into a torrent of splendid verse that seemed like some grand air with the distant peals of thunder as an intermittent accompaniment. And still the storm waxes more violent, and the vivid flashes of lightning became more frequent. But Swinburne seemed unconscious of it all, and . . . paced up and down the room, pouring out bursts of passionate declamation . . . How long his ecstasy would have lasted I know not. I was wondering, when the sounds of a latchkey and the closing of the hall door were heard. In another minute Rossetti entered the studio, boisterously shaking off the raindrops from his Inverness cape, and with a 'Hullo! old fellow!' welcomed Swinburne.

On 19 November Swinburne told Joseph Knight he had been 'so long in the country at different houses' that his affairs were in chaos. In November his third book, *Chastelard,* was published by Moxon. Swinburne had worked on it for six years, rewriting it many times. In 1904 he described it as 'a play . . . conceived and partly written by a youngster not yet emancipated from servitude to college rule'. Swinburne dedicated his previous books to Rossetti and Landor; *Chastelard* was for Hugo. It is based on an episode of November 1562 in the life of Mary Stuart, who for Swinburne was a prime embodiment of the fatal, powerful woman. Chastelard is aware of her cruelty and knows that loving her will most likely cause his own destruction, but he contrives to die at her hands regardless, tearing up the warrant for his release after being imprisoned for getting caught in her bedchamber. For Chastelard, love is more important than life, and passion more important than love. Swinburne's main sources were John Knox's *History of the Reformation in Scotland* (1584) and Brantôme's *Discours sur Marie Stuart* and, more importantly, feelings for Mary Stuart that went back to his boyhood. He believed that Thomas Swinburne of Capheaton fought for

Mary and fell in love with her. As a child he had visited Roxburgh
Castle, where Mary raced to attend the wounded Bothwell. She was the
'Queen, for whose house my fathers fought,/With hopes that rose and
fell,/Red star of boyhood's fiery thought'.

Chastelard is a play whose essential decadence stubbornly resists any
attempt to interpret it as in any way life-affirming. It celebrates a
perverse and wilful death-wish. Chastelard's desire for Mary is egocen-
tric and masochistic. She is the perfect means of his self-destruction; he
loves her not as a being outside his imagination but as a projection from
himself. As with his first plays, Swinburne is nervily sensitive to the
body, its sensory potential, and its vulnerability to pain. Wearing
Chastelard's sword, Mary says:

> It hurts right sorely. Is it not pitiful
> Our souls should be so bound about with flesh
> Even when they leap and smite with wings and feet,
> The least pain plucks them back, puts out their eyes,
> Turns them to tears and words?

Mary's beauty is seen as dangerous – 'A flower's lip with a snake's lip' –
her breast-clasp 'A Venus crowned, that eats the hearts of men'. As
Chastelard says on his first appearance, 'I know her ways of loving, all
of them:/A sweet soft way the first is; afterward/It burns and bites like
fire; the end of that,/Charred dust, and eyelids bitten through with
smoke.' Chastelard's passion becomes the supreme value and like the
knight in 'Laus Veneris', he exalts it above God, referring to Mary as
'the one thing good as God'. The power of Venus is undefeated by
Christianity, 'For all Christ's work this Venus is not quelled'.

A more immature work than *Atalanta*, *Chastelard*'s antitheism and
sensuality could less easily be attributed to the characters than to the
author. The reviews gave qualified praise to Swinburne's verse but
criticized the emphasis on passion. *The Reader* facetiously described it
as 'redundant with kissings . . . if, after a perusal of this play, the reader
is not adept in the art of osculation, it will be through no fault of Mr.
Swinburne's'. *The Spectator* wrote that 'the want of moral and intellectual relief for the coarseness of passion, and for the deep physical
instincts of tenderness or cruelty on which he delights to employ his rich
imagination, strikes us as a radical deformity of his poetry'. Completing
the book was like escaping from 'a forcing house of sensual appetite'.
The Athenaeum felt readers would be unlikely to sympathize with the
characters:

> Besides being inherently vicious, their language will offend not
> only those who have reverence, but those who have taste. We
> decline to show by quotation how often the Divine Name is
> sported with in scenes which are essentially voluptuous . . . If

Chastelard be remembered at all, it will solely be for its detached beauties of expression. We hope, should we meet Mr. Swinburne again, that he will be able to exhibit Vice without painting a Monster, and to give us a higher type of knightly devotion than an infatuated libertine.

In the *Forthnightly Review* Lord Houghton praised the depiction of Chastelard and the melody of the verse but criticized the role that Mary plays. The reception in America was similar to that in England. The play was complimented as verse but not as a drama, and there were objections to the central characters. The *Boston Daily Advertiser* called Mary 'a beautiful harlot, amorous, heartless, and fickle', and complained that the play dwelt 'too warmly upon scenes which are neither noble, edifying, nor decent'.

Closer to home Mrs Hungerford Pollen

> was extremely indignant with *Chastelard*, and she gave Algernon 'a real talking to' about it. She said he had not the smallest idea of history, and believed all the spiteful tales which were invented about Rizzio and Chastelard. She said he would not take what she said seriously, and added if he felt like that, he had better not come to the house anymore.

Swinburne may have enjoyed the disquiet his play caused among the staid journals of Victorian literary society, but his behaviour was causing another kind of disquiet among his friends. Fame increased his artistic confidence and his waywardness. Madox Brown called one day in November and found Swinburne in bed at 3.30 in the afternoon. Scott wrote to Lady Trevelyan, asking her to intercede:

> The remark you make on his behaviour at Wallington I believe I quite understand, he suffers under a dislike to ladies of late – his knowledge of himself and of them increasing upon him. His success is certainly not improving him, as one might easily suppose with so boundless a vanity.
>
> His new book *Chastelard* is just ready; . . . you will perhaps see certain things there – the total severance of the passion of love from the moral delight of loving or of being loved, so to speak, and the insaneness of the impulses of Chastelard – for example; which may give you a text for writing him. With all his boasting of himself and all his belongings he is very sensitive about society, and I certainly think you will do him the very kindest of actions if you can touch his sensibility on his vanity – a little sharply. Of late he has been much excited, and certainly drinking. Gabriel and William Rossetti think he will not live if he goes on as lately without stopping. He says he is to leave town, however, for a long time, in a few days. and we hope he may quiet down . . .

Scott's comment about Swinburne suffering from a dislike of ladies has a different complexion if we take into account Swinburne's raw feelings of rejection by Mary. The romantic crisis may well have precipitated a phase of extreme mood swings.

At the same time that Lady Trevelyan heard from Scott, she received a letter from Josephine Butler, wife of the Vice-Principal of Cheltenham College, who informed her that someone who often came to Wallington had 'a deplorably vicious reputation; people were talking and she had therefore better be careful'. Mrs Butler meant Swinburne, 'of whom she had heard much that had shocked her about a week ago'. This prompted Lady Trevelyan into warning Swinburne that he was skirting the limits of propriety. Swinburne's response on 5 December was immediate and grateful. He was shocked 'at the infamous wickedness of people who invent in malice or repeat in levity such horrors':

> I can only imagine 1) that the very quietness of my way of living as compared with that of other men of my age exposes me, given up as I almost always am to comparative solitude, to work at my own art, and never seen in fast (hardly in slow) life – to spitefulness and vicious stupidity, 2) that as you say I must have talked very foolishly to make such infamies possible. All I can ever recollect saying which could be perverted was (for instance) that 'the Greeks did not seem to me worse than the moderns because of things considered innocent at one time by one country were not considered so by others.' Far more than this I have heard said by men of the world of the highest character. This sort of thing, I was told afterwards, might be thought wild and offensive by hearers who were bent on malignant commentary, or 4) [sic] I do remember saying, 'if people read the classics, not to speak of the moderns very often, they must see that many qualities called virtues and vices depend on time, climate, and temperament'. The remark may have been false or foolish, but who could have imagined it (until he had proof) capable of being twisted into an avowal that I approved vice and disapproved virtue? Any one who says he has heard me speak personally, as if *I* agreed with other times or disagreed with this, lies. Even when talking thus at random, in an atmosphere of men's chaff and loose hasty words, I was always careful to draw the difference. And now I really have told you all. I was once told before that a friend 'had heard said' that I boasted of distributing indecent books at Oxford. I quite expect soon to learn that at school I committed murder.

Phrases like 'the very quietness of my life' would have had Rossetti, Burne-Jones and Solomon beside themselves with laughter. Perhaps Swinburne was surprised that rumours had travelled so far and was genuinely concerned his image would be damaged in the eyes of a woman he respected.

At the Arts Club later that evening he wrote again, overcome by 'my sense of your goodness to me':

Nobody in my life was ever so good to me as you have been. You must know what pain any man would feel who was conscious that, in however innocent and ignorant a way, he had (I will not say deserved, but) exposed himself through rashness and inexperience to such suffering as I underwent in reading what you wrote . . . For years I have regarded you . . . with a grateful affection which I never could express. Now I can say less than ever how deep and true is my sense of obligation to you. You were always kinder to me (when much younger) than others – now you are kinder than I could have dared to think of. I am amazed beyond words at people's villainy or stupidity – but yet more at people's goodness.

As a P.S. he added, 'I see this is too chaotic – but please excuse it. I never do cry, and never did I think much as boy or man for pain – and this morning when I wrote I never felt less tempted – but this time I have really felt tears coming more than once.'

On 6 December Lady Trevelyan cautioned Swinburne about his poems:

Now do, if it is only for the sake of living down evil reports, do be wise in which of your lyrics you publish. Do let it be a book that can be really loved and read and learned by heart, and become part and parcel of the English language, and be on every one's table without being received under protest by timid people . . . It is not worth while for the sake of two or three poems to risk the widest circulation of the whole. You have sailed near enough to the wind in all conscience in having painted such a character for a hero as your Chastelard, slave to a passion for a woman he despises, whose love (if one can call it love) has no element of chivalry or purity in it; whose devotion to her is much as if a man should set himself to be crushed before Juggernaut, cursing him all the while for a loathsome despicable idol . . . Don't give people a handle against you now.

That some of this advice was in vain was evident from Ruskin's letter to her two days later:

I went to see Swinburne yesterday and heard some of the wickedest and splendidest verses ever written by a human creature. He drank three bottles of porter while I was there. I don't know what to do with him or for him, but he mustn't publish these things. He speaks with immense gratitude of you – please tell him he mustn't.

But she already had, and Swinburne, for all his gratitude to her, never allowed anyone to limit his artistic freedom. On 10 December he thanked her again for defending him against 'the villainy of fools and knaves'. His impression of Ruskin's response to his readings was rather different:

As to my poems, my perplexity is this: that no two friends have ever given me the same advice. Now more than ever I would rather take yours than another's; but I see neither where to begin nor where to stop. I have written nothing to be ashamed or afraid of. I have been advised to suppress *Atalanta*, to cancel *Chastelard*, and so on till not a line of my work would have been left. Two days ago Ruskin called on me and stayed for a long evening, during which he heard a great part of my forthcoming volume of poems, selected with a view to secure his advice as to publication and the verdict of the world of readers or critics. It was impossible to have a fairer judge. I have not known him long or intimately; and he is neither a rival nor a reviewer. I can only say that I was sincerely surprised by the enjoyment he seemed to derive from my work, and the frankness with which he accepted it. Any poem which all my friends for whose opinion I care had advised me to omit, should be omitted. But I have never written such an one. Some for example which you have told me were favourites of yours, such as the Hymn to Proserpine of the 'Last Pagan' – I have been advised to omit as likely to hurt the feeling of a religious public.

At the same time Scott was exchanging letters with Lady Trevelyan, further commenting on Swinburne's responses. She apparently thought she might have made an impression, and Scott felt her news of Swinburne was 'gratifying':

> You know he has been warned in all sorts of ways by Gabriel and myself and has scouted the warnings, and now his collapse into deprecation and denial is only, I fear, through cowardice. He is a craven when it comes to the point . . . You will have done him great good by your writing, but it will not be in Rossetti's power or mine, I fear, to supplement your work. He has for weeks been talking against Rossetti in a very unhappy way after all that has passed, just because R. will not always stand him now and I fear he has parted company with me . . . In the meantime the honours he is receiving from America and at home, are not reducing his egotism.

Swinburne's behaviour was putting a strain on many of his relationships. The artist James Smetham met him twice in early December, recording that Swinburne was drunk on one occasion and blaspheming on the other. On 13 December he and Lord Houghton met Tennyson at a party probably organized by Moxon to bring together some of their authors. Swinburne, who once rode across the Isle of Wight to dine with Tennyson, now apparently snubbed him. Houghton rebuked Swinburne for ill manners and for jeopardizing the publication of *Poems and Ballads*. Swinburne refused to concede an inch. 'My dear Lord Houghton':

> As I do not doubt your kind intention, I will only ask – Why? where? and how? Last time we met I had been spending the soberest of evenings here before starting to pick you up at 11 o'clock, which I understood was the order of the day. You as we returned seemed considerably infuriated with my unpunctuality – which I

did not attribute to any influence of Bacchus on yourself. I am not aware of having retorted by any discourtesy. As the rest of the evening had been spent, after the few words of civility that passed between Mr. Tennyson and me, in discussing Blake and Flaxman in the next room with Palgrave and Lewes, I am at a loss to guess what has called down such an avalanche of advice. I have probably no vocation and doubtless no ambition for the service of Bacchus: in proof of which if you like I will undertake to repeat the conversation of Wednesday evening throughout with the accuracy of a reporter ...

It was the sort of reply that must have exasperated his friends.

Swinburne stayed with his family at Holmwood over Christmas until mid-January 1866. He began the most dramatic year of his life as a writer with a number of projects in hand. Most important were the proofs of *Poems and Ballads*, to be published by Moxon. Swinburne told William Rossetti the book 'must be got out in the spring'. He boasted to Lady Trevelyan of having 'the wildest offers made me for anything I will do; and expect soon to have in effect the control of a magazine which I shall be able to mould and use as I please'. He edited a selection of Byron for Moxon's Miniature Poets series, with further selections from Landor and Keats to follow. Only the Byron came to fruition. Swinburne completed the preface by 5 January. In February relations with Moxon's became tense. Swinburne complained that James Bertrand Payne had broken an agreement not to show the manuscript of *A Year's Letters* to anyone in order to preserve its anonymity. Payne had also seen the essay on Blake, and Swinburne had understood that Moxon intended to publish both, but Moxon was now withdrawing that offer. From now on, insisted Swinburne, terms would have to be put in writing.

Once back in London Swinburne resumed imitating a loose cannon on one of the Admiral's ships. Madox Brown made the terse entry in his diary for 27 January, 'Swinburne wasted my evening'. Swinburne badgered Howell:

> Pig!
> Why do you make and break promises? Come and see me if you can. That you are alive I know from others who have met you abroad. And I have expected you (being but young and foolish) ever since we last met in Cheyne Walk. And in three or four days must be out of TOWN (which I write big that it may impressive). Write! and come! and if you won't, be ———
>
> Yours affectionately (if you come),
> A.C. Swinburne

And if you don't come BE D ——— D.
Oh! Monsieur

Boyce saw Swinburne at the Arts Club, 'in a very excited state, using fearful language' on 16 February. Ruskin told Lady Trevelyan on 25 February, 'I have not seen Algernon again. I was hopeless about him in his present phase, but I mean to have another try soon.' This 'other try' has not survived. Perhaps Swinburne screwed it up and hurled it across the room before penning this spirited reply. He was glad Ruskin liked the essay on Byron that prefaced the selections,

> But I do not (honestly) understand the gist of what you say about myself. What's the matter with me that I should cause you sorrow or suggest the idea of a ruin? I don't feel at all ruinous as yet. I do feel awfully old, and well may – for in April I believe I shall be twenty-five [sic] which is 'a horror to think of'. Mais ————! what have I done or said, to be likened to such terrific things?
>
> You speak of not being able to hope enough for me. Don't you think we had better leave hope and faith to infants, adult or ungrown! You and I and all men will probably do and endure what we are destined for, as well as we can. I for one am quite content to know this, without any ulterior belief or conjecture. I don't want more praise and success than I deserve, more suffering and failure than I can avoid; but I take what comes as well and as quietly as I can; and this seems to me a man's real business and only duty. You compare my work to a temple where the lizards have supplanted the gods; I prefer an indubitable and living lizard to a dead or doubtful god.

The letter expresses Swinburne's stoicism and its link with his sense of masculinity.

Moxon published Swinburne's selections from Byron in March 1866. Swinburne was attracted to Byron as an aristocrat as well as a revolutionary, and was fond of allusions to Byron's incest with his half-sister, much to the eventual exasperation of Rossetti. The essay is a good example of Swinburne's impressionistic criticism, ever ready to surf his literary judgements on the crest of a wave. He wrote that between *Childe Harold* and *Don Juan* 'the same difference exists which a swimmer feels between lake-water and sea-water: the one is fluent, yielding, invariable; the other has in it a life and pulse, a sting and a swell, which touch and excite the nerves like fire or like music. Across the stanzas of *Don Juan* we swim forward as over "the broad backs of the sea".' Swinburne castigated Byron's reviewers:

> At the first chance given or taken, every obscure and obscene thing that lurks for pay or prey among the fouler shallows and thickets of literature flew against him; every hound and every hireling lavished upon him the loathsome tribute of their abuse; all nameless creatures that nibble and prowl, upon whom the serpent's curse has fallen, to go upon his belly and eat dust all the days of his life, assailed him with their foulest venom and their keenest fangs.

Swinburne had experienced a little of this with *Chastelard* but it became ironic after the publication of *Poems and Ballads*. Not only
Ruskin praised the selections from Byron; there was commendation
from Meredith and Lady Trevelyan. Even Lady Jane was delighted with
the book, despite Byron being one of the authors she had black-listed
when Swinburne was younger.

Meanwhile, Swinburne's wild behaviour continued, bringing him into
conflict with the Arts Club, where he was often drunk, using ribald
language and shattering the peace. The last straw was an incident
involving members' top hats in the cloakroom. There are several versions of this story. An inebriated Swinburne, trying to find his hat,
samples all for size and stamps them flat when they don't fit. A variant
has himself and a partner in crime making two lines of hats before
pancaking them all in a one-legged race. A third version states Swinburne
perpetrated this destruction, having gone to the Club without any hat at
all. William Rossetti stepped in to protect Swinburne from the wrath of
the Committee, and in late March wrote of the allegations against him.
'This is the first I have heard of the matter', replied Swinburne,

> I have certainly objurgated more than one waiter, and remember
> bending double one fork in an energetic mood at dinner. I had
> already thought of withdrawing at or before the end of my present
> year of subscription. As to freedom of voice or tone – I am stunned
> daily by more noise at that place than I ever heard (or, you suggest,
> made) in my life. If I damaged a valuable article belonging to them,
> why did they not send in a bill? I have remained in order more
> frequently to meet a few intimates, who relieve if they cannot
> redeem the moral squalor of the place. I know but few members,
> and never knowingly cut or 'ignored' any.

Swinburne's membership of the Arts Club just survived this crisis. In the
spring of 1866 he wrote a substantial amount of *Lesbia Brandon*.

On 2 May Swinburne made the only public speech of his adult life.
Lord Houghton provided the opportunity by chairing the Royal Literary Fund dinner. Charles Kingsley proposed a toast to 'The Historical
and Imaginative Literature of England', and seconded George Stovin
Venables when he praised Swinburne as 'the representative of that
future generation ... he alone, of his age, has shown his power to
succeed in the highest walks of poetry'. A contemporary newspaper
account said:

> After Mr. Kingsley arose Mr. Swinburne. He spoke in such a low
> voice that I could only see his lips move, and hear no word. But it
> was enough to see Swinburne's face – especially with his cheek and
> eye kindled – and I shall never forget it. A small, young, even,
> boyish man, with handsome, regular features and smooth skin;
> with eyes that glitter; with thin, flexible lips, whose coldness is in

strange contrast to the passionate intensity of his eyes; with a great
deal of reddish hair that surrounds his face like a halo. He seemed
to me like some wild bird of rare and beautiful plumage, which has
alighted in our uncongenial climate, and who is likely to die before
it is acclimatised. No one who has ever looked upon his face would
doubt for a moment that he is a man of genius.

Swinburne took as his theme for the speech the influence of England
and France on each other, a literary exchange which went back to the
Middle Ages. He spoke of Dante, Chaucer and Villon, praising Chaucer's
'Troilus and Criseyde' for its 'bitter absorption of life' derived from 'the
heathenish love of Provençal fighters and singers' and the virtues of
Hugo and Baudelaire.

On 8 May Munby met Swinburne for coffee, and 'with all his flighty
restless manner, he talked without his old pretentiousness and paradox,
and showed simply such pure enthusiasm as a poet ought to have; which
pleased me, after all one has heard of his "bumptiousness" of late'. On
13 May Lady Trevelyan, who had been ill for some time, died in Neuchâtel,
Switzerland. Nine hours before her death she asked anxiously after
Swinburne. Ruskin reassured her 'that she need not be in pain about him
– the abuse she heard of him was dreadful – but not – in the deep sense,
moral evil at all, but mentally-physically and ungovernable by his will, –
and that finally, God never made such good fruits of human work, to
grow on an evil tree'. The task of telling Swinburne of her death fell to
Scott, who told Alice Boyd, 'we broke down together'. In later life
Swinburne memorialized Lady Trevelyan in 'A Study from Memory' and
'After Sunset'. George Otto Trevelyan described this loss as 'a very real
and permanent misfortune to him'. She had been a positive influence,
probably of wider sympathies and a more liberal outlook than his mother.

Although Moxon had published *Atalanta*, Swinburne considered a
number of publishers for *Poems and Ballads*, the study of Blake and his
novel *A Year's Letters*. He told Joseph Knight on 21 November that
others had made offers for the poems and for a selection from Landor.
By 4 March Murray turned down the opportunity to publish Swinburne's
poems. Swinburne considered John Camden Hotten but on 20 March
wrote to Knight that,

> On second thought I have made up my mind *not* to put any MS. of
> mine, anonymous or pseudonymous or signed into the hands of
> Hotten, under any circumstances. Through Ld Houghton I have
> found out such an instance of his audacious rascality that I would
> not trust him with anything of mine – a conclusive sort of matter. If
> you like I will give you the detail and evidence when we meet.

In the end *Poems and Ballads* was brought out by Moxon. The first
copies were sent out at the beginning of July. On 31 July William

Allingham visited Rossetti and noticed on a table the small green book that was to cause a sensation almost unequalled in English poetry.

CHAPTER SEVEN

The Libidinous Laureate

Poems and Ballads, First Series marks the turning point of Swinburne's career. Had he published nothing else, his fame as a poet would have been assured, for the notoriety it created lasted to the very end of his life. In the 'Dedication' (1865) Swinburne described these poems as 'scattered in seven years' traces/As they fell from the boy that was then', indicating that the earliest dated to 1858 when Swinburne was at Balliol. *Poems and Ballads* was a tempestuous synthesis of all his poetic labours during those seven years, in which the darker side of Swinburne's vision is only too apparent.

The collection employed a dazzling range of poetic forms: dramatic monologue, couplets, sapphics, ballads, quintains, rondels, sonnets, odes, dramatic verse, border ballads; a variety of metres; translations from Greek, French, Breton, Finnish; parodies and imitations. The verse fluted or trumpeted Swinburne's distinctive metrical signature, from the six-beat lines of 'Hesperia':

> By the sands where sorrow has trodden, the salt
>   pools bitter and sterile,
>   By the thundering reef and the low sea-wall and
>   the channel of years,
> Our wild steeds press on the night, strain hard
>   through pleasure and peril,
>   Labour and listen and pant not or pause for the
>   peril that nears;
> And the sound of them trampling the way cleaves
>   night as an arrow asunder . . .

to the subtle cadences of 'Anima Anceps':

> Grief, when days alter,
> Like joy shall falter;
> Song-book and psalter,
>   Mourning and mirth.
> Live like the swallow;
> Seek not to follow
> Where earth is hollow
>   Under the earth.

Swinburne's poetry should never be read only attending to its metrical pulse. Despite the rhythmic allure of his anapaests and dactyls, reinforced by alliteration and other sound-patterning devices, some of the most satisfying moments in his verse come when sentence and metre are pitted against each other through enjambement, as in these lines from 'The Triumph of Time':

> To have died if you cared I should die for you, clung
>   To my life if you bade me, played my part
> As it pleased you – these were the thoughts that stung,
>   The dreams that smote with a keener dart
> Than shafts of love or arrows of death;
> These were but as fire is, dust, or breath,
> Or poisonous foam on the tender tongue
>   Of the little snakes that eat my heart.

In 1902 Swinburne described the volume as 'lyrical and dramatic and elegiac and generally heterogeneous'. Poems such as 'A Ballad of Life', 'A Ballad of Death', 'In the Orchard', 'A Ballad of Burdens', 'The Two Dreams' and 'April' had medieval settings. In 'Laus Veneris', a knight exults in choosing Venus over Christ:

> Yea, for my sin I had great store of bliss:
> Rise up, make answer for me, let thy kiss
>   Seal my lips hard from speaking of my sin,
> Lest one go mad to hear how sweet it is.

Swinburne challenged the sexual taboos of Victorian literature by writing poems not only about heterosexual love but lesbianism, hermaphroditism, necrophilia and sado-masochism. In 'Dolores' he invoked the anti-Madonna of some symbolist nightmare whose kiss causes men to change 'in a trice/The lilies and languors of virtue/For the roses and raptures of vice'. 'Phaedra', 'Itylus', 'Sapphics', 'Anactoria', 'At Eleusis', 'Faustine' and 'Hymn to Proserpine' looked back to classical Greece and Rome. 'A Litany' and 'Aholibah' were Hebraic in influence. There were also poems in a contemporary setting, such as 'The Triumph of Time', 'The Sundew', 'Felise', 'August' and 'Before Dawn'.

Like *Lesbia Brandon*, *Poems and Ballads* presents almost all of Swinburne's passions. His republicanism is caught in 'A Song in Time of Order' and 'A Song in Time of Revolution'; he pays homage to two of his literary idols in the elegy for Walter Savage Landor and 'To Victor Hugo'; he translates 'Song before Death' from de Sade; his Northumbrian roots are celebrated in several border ballads; his antipathy to Christianity is given full expression in 'Laus Veneris' and in the 'Hymn to Proserpine', with its image of Christ as the 'pale Galilean' and the famous lines of pagan defiance:

> O lips that the live blood faints in, the leavings of racks and rods,
> O ghastly glories of saints, dead limbs of gibbeted Gods!
> Though all men abase them before you in spirit, and
>   all knees bend,
> I kneel not neither adore you, but standing, look to the end.

Poems and Ballads denounces the cruelty of fate and the gods (or God) for creating the tragedy of human existence where life is hazardous, 'Grief a fixed star, and joy a vane that veers' and where pain and pleasure are indissolubly linked. Sappho – Swinburne's 'supreme head of song' – is the presiding muse of *Poems and Ballads*, appearing in 'Satia te Sanguine' and 'Sapphics', and it is she who focuses this vision most powerfully in 'Anactoria', an extended dramatic lyric racked by frustrated passion:

> My life is bitter with thy love; thine eyes
> Blind me, thy tresses burn me, thy sharp sighs
> Divide my flesh and spirit with soft sound,
> And my blood strengthens, and my veins abound.
> I pray thee sigh not, speak not, draw not breath;
> Let life burn down, and dream it is not death.
> I would the sea had hidden us, the fire
> (Wilt thou fear that, and fear not my desire?)
> Severed the bones that bleach, the flesh that cleaves,
> And let our sifted ashes drop like leaves.
> I feel thy blood against my blood: my pain
> Pains thee, and lips bruise lips, and vein stings vein.
> Let fruit be crushed on fruit, let flower on flower,
> Breast kindle breast, and either burn one hour.

The emphasis on physical beauty, desire that is mixed up with pain and frustration, the bitterness of love, the agony of separation ('divide ... severed ... cleaves'), the longing for obliteration of the self ('I would the sea had hidden us') are all chords struck from Swinburne's internal centre. Sappho's abandon is the more remarkable for being evoked in heroic couplets, which through Swinburne's artistry resonate with a music not usually associated with the form.

'Anactoria' develops into a powerful indictment of the forces responsible for the human condition:

> For who shall change with prayers or thanksgivings
> The mystery of the cruelty of things?
> Or say what God above all gods and years
> With offering and blood-sacrifice of tears,
> With lamentation from strange lands, from graves
> Where the snake pastures, from scarred mouths of slaves,
> From prison, and from plunging prows of ships
> Through flamelike foam of the sea's closing lips –
> With thwartings of strange signs, and wind-blown hair
> Of comets, desolating the dim air,
> When darkness is made fast with seals and bars,
> And fierce reluctance of disastrous stars,
> Eclipse, and sound of shaken hills, and wings
> Darkening, and blind inexpiable things –
> With sorrow of labouring moons, and altering light

> And travail of the planets of the night,
> And weeping of the weary Pleiads seven,
> Feeds the mute melancholy lust of heaven?

Lesbian desire functions as a metaphor for the frustration of all love, for humankind being 'cursed' with longings that cannot be satisfied. From its lustful, feverish beginning, 'Anactoria' evolves into one of Swinburne's noblest protests against the way of things. That the 'God' that Swinburne attacks in 'Anactoria' and *Atalanta in Calydon* owes something to Blake's Urizen is clear from a passage in *William Blake*, where Swinburne describes Blake's Creator as 'a divine daemon, liable to error, subduable by and through this very created nature of his invention, which he for the present imprisons and torments' and where he writes of the 'radical significance of Christianity' being 'a divine revolt against divine law; an evidence that man must become as God only by resistance to God'.

In 'Dolores', 'Faustine', and 'The Masque of Queen Bersabe', *femmes fatales* personify desire, pain and cosmic cruelty. Others poems, such as 'Felise', capture the perverse ebb and flow of romantic feeling in a manner reminiscent of Hardy. Like 'Anactoria', though in a different key, 'Felise' is a protest against the God 'who slays our souls alive' but cannot 'make dead things thrive'. It is one of a number of lyrics that show Swinburne's vocabulary is not as luxuriant as often thought. Some of his most memorable poetry is created with what John Rosenberg called 'the bleak beauty of little words':

> Let this be said between us here,
>   One love grows green when one grows grey;
> This year knows nothing of last year;
>   Tomorrow has no more to say
>   To yesterday.

The cultural impact of *Poems and Ballads* was immense. Not only did it strike Victorian poetry with the force of a tidal wave; it sent ripples of sexual and religious rebellion far and wide. It confirmed and darkened the literary reputation Swinburne had gained with *Atalanta*. It made him an international figurehead for sexual, religious and political radicalism. Despite Swinburne's inability to escape from the shadow of the Church, typified in his retention of the concept of 'sin', it challenged Victorian culture's repressive attitudes to the body, to sex, to the value of sensual life, and struck a blow for artistic expression. That Swinburne had kindled its fire in part from a sexual sensibility the majority of his readers would never share made no difference to the potency of its example. His very name was now a flame of inspiration even to those who never read him and a beacon for change among liberal-minded people, just as it became charged with a satanic aura for the timid and conservative.

On 4 August 1866 the first reviews appeared. The rumblings that had greeted *Chastelard* now thundered denunciation. In *The Saturday Review* John Morley attacked Swinburne's choice of subjects, objected to 'an attitude of revolt against the current notions of decency and dignity and social duty', and the portrayal of the 'animal side of human nature'. In language that could only further excite public interest, Morley wrote hysterically of the 'nameless shameless abominations which inspire him' while trying to belittle a Swinburne who showed the 'feverish carnality of a schoolboy over the dirtiest passages in Lemprière'. *Poems and Ballads* was crammed 'with pieces which many a professional vendor of filthy prints might blush to sell if only he knew what they meant'. Swinburne's poetry offered only a vision of lust or despair.

In *The Athenaeum*, Robert Buchanan judged Swinburne's style monotonous, and his poems inferior because essentially derivative of other writers such as Musset, Sand, Hugo, Ovid or Boccaccio. Buchanan's attack was more personalized than Morley's; too juvenile to be immoral, Swinburne's verse was immoral, insincere, effeminate, unmanly, 'unclean for the sake of uncleanness'. Swinburne's poems paraded sensuality as the end of life, and were blasphemous. For Buchanan the glory of 'our modern poetry' was its 'transcendent purity', which Swinburne had blatantly violated. By 1866 Swinburne had already formed a low opinion of Buchanan. If word of this reached the author of *London Lyrics*, there may have been a personal animus behind this review.

Other journals echoed these sentiments. *The London Review* wrote, 'we do not know when we have read a volume so depressing and misbegotten – in many of its constituents so utterly revolting'. It conceded some of the poems had beauty and power, and praised the 'beauty and lyrical sweetness' of 'Itylus' and the 'Ballad of Burdens'. Otherwise it was the product of 'a diseased state of mind'. Swinburne was criticized for choosing depraved classical stories – 'Anactoria' and 'Dolores' being found especially horrible – and for advancing as philosophy a 'hopeless way of looking at life'.

The day these papers hit the London news-stands, Swinburne and Payne, of Moxon and Co., were walking down Dover Street when Swinburne stopped to buy a copy of *The Saturday Review*. As he read, he became livid, and burst forth in a torrent of vituperation. Payne was obliged to lead him off the street into a restaurant, and then to plead with the poet to continue, if he must, in French. Swinburne gave a different account of his reaction to correspondents, telling Joseph Knight, 'I have exhausted myself with a quasi-venereal enjoyment of the incomparable article in the Athenaeum' which had given him 'delicious and exquisite amusement'. Both Knight and Lord Lytton were among friends

who expressed their support. Swinburne was willing and able to weather
the storm.

However, his publisher was not. On 5 August Moxon withdrew the
book. Swinburne immediately called on Lord Houghton, who was about
to leave for France. On 6 August Swinburne scrawled to Knight, 'that
damned hound Payne writes me word that he "cannot continue the
issue of my Poems". What am I to do with him or them? Pray write to
me at once and give me some hint.' On 10 August Swinburne explained
to Lord Lytton that because

> of the abusive reviews of my book, the publisher (without consult-
> ing me, without warning, and without compensation) has actually
> withdrawn it from circulation.
> I have no right to trouble you with my affairs, but I cannot resist
> the temptation to trespass so far upon your kindness as to ask
> what course you would recommend me to take in such a case. I am
> resolved to cancel nothing, and (of course) to transfer my books to
> any other publisher I can find. I am told by lawyers that I might
> claim legal redress for a distinct violation of contract on Messrs.
> Moxon's part, but I do not wish to drag the matter before a law
> court.

A rumour had reached Payne that a forthcoming article in *The Times*
would call for the prosecution of poet and publisher alike; the book had
been withdrawn from Mudie's Circulating Library, and J. M. Ludlow,
one of the leaders of the Christian Socialist movement, demanded that
the Attorney-General prosecute. Payne feared a repetition of the fine
Moxon had incurred in 1841 for publishing Shelley's *Queen Mab*. As
one Victorian publisher wrote, the name of Moxon 'on the title-page,
and on the well-known green covers, is a guarantee for the propriety of
any book and ensures its admission into the most respectable families'.
Rossetti and Sandys went to negotiate with Payne but found him unwilling to change his mind.

Swinburne turned to his friends for their advice. Whistler and Burton
were abroad. His family no doubt were offended by the poems and
irritated at having their name scandalized. The option of self-censor-
ship was broached with Payne but this was unacceptable to Swinburne.
On 13 August he told Lytton, 'as to the suppression of separate
passages or poems, it could not be done without injuring the whole
structure of the book, where every part has been as carefully considered and arranged as I could manage . . . I have no choice but to break
off my connection with the publisher'. Swinburne sent Lytton's letters
on to his family, hoping the favourable comments contained therein
would mollify them.

After being delayed by an unspecified illness for a day or two, on 17
August Swinburne went to Knebworth, near Stevenage in Hertford-

shire, the home of the Lyttons. On 20 August Lord Lytton told his son of the guest 'whose poems are rousing a storm of moral censure'. Lytton thought Swinburne should 'purgate his volume of certain pruriences' and described him as looking sixteen (Swinburne evidently claimed to be 26 and not 29), 'a pale, sickly boy, with some nervous complaint like St. Vitus' Dance':

> He has read more than most reading men twice his age, brooded and theorised over what he has read, and has an artist's critical perceptions. I think he must have read and studied and thought and felt much more than Tennyson; perhaps he has over-informed his tenement of clay. But there is plenty of stuff in him. His volume of poems is infested with sensualities, often disagreeable in themselves, as well as offensive to all pure and manly taste. But the beauty of diction and masterpiece of craft in melodies really at first so dazzled me, that I did not see the naughtiness till pointed out. He certainly ought to become a considerable poet of the artistic order ... On the other hand, he may end prematurely both in repute and in life. The first is nearly wrecked now, and the 2nd seems very shaky. He inspires one with sadness; but he is not so sad himself, and his self-esteem is solid as a rock.

While Swinburne was at Knebworth, Howell negotiated with the publisher John Camden Hotten, Swinburne having decided to override the reservations he had expressed in March about Hotten's trustworthiness. After discussing how Hotten might buy up unsold copies of Swinburne's works to date, together with the unpublished study of Blake, Swinburne told Howell, 'it is very jolly here, people, place and weather. The furniture would at once cause Gabriel to attempt murder of the owner through envy' before adding a private postscript: 'If you *have* heard of any boy being *swished* lately in our schools, let me hear of the distressing circumstances. Ecris-moi quelque chose de piquant, by way of *salt* to all this business.' Rossetti observed Swinburne, returned from Knebworth on 24 August, 'in high feather, delighted with Lytton who really appears to give him a friend's advice – which I needn't say he doesn't take'. The advice was presumably that Swinburne should 'purgate his volume of certain pruriences'.

Hotten was of the same opinion, since outlets such as Mudie, W. H. Smith, Simpkin and Marshall, and Hamilton and Co. did not want to stock *Poems and Ballads*. On 29 August he told Powell, 'if Mr. Swinburne would only modify (or omit) a very few lines, the whole trade would take up a second edition, and at least £200 additional would result to Mr. Swinburne ... I'm not afraid, but I think it would be discreet to throw at least one or two small rabbits to the great public boa constrictor.' Hotten obtained a letter from a Police magistrate whose opinion was that the book was neither seizable nor indictable.

From his shop in Piccadilly, Hotten sold a wide variety of books. He specialized in contemporary American literature, and erotic titles such as *An Exhibition of Female Flagellants* and *Lady Bumtickler's Revels: A Comic Opera*, given a spurious respectability as 'The Library Illustrative of Social Progress'. The agreement with Hotten meant Swinburne would receive £200 for 1000 copies of *Poems and Ballads*, and Hotten would immediately buy up Moxon's stock, 'that there may be no delay in the reappearance of the book'. When Hotten checked, he estimated Moxon had about 700 copies of *Poems and Ballads*, and 'fair stocks of the other works'.

Swinburne was back in London 'after a very pleasant week's visit' by the end of August, predicting the book would be out in a few days. He was forced to delay visiting Powell in Wales by the illness of his mother. His friends discussed the situation. Ruskin acknowledged a copy of *Poems and Ballads* on 9 September, saying that 'their power is so great, and their influence so depressing' that he could not read very much at a time. But his final verdict was magnanimous:

> For the matter of it – I consent to much – I regret much – I blame or reject nothing. I should as soon think of finding fault with you as with a thundercloud or a nightshade blossom. All I can say of you, or them – is that God made you, and that you are very wonderful and beautiful. To me it may be dreadful or deadly – it may be in a deeper sense, or in certain relations, helpful and medicinal. There is assuredly something wrong with you – awful in proportion to the great power it affects, and renders (nationally) at present useless ... I'm glad to have the book at any rate. I cannot help you, nor understand you, or I would come to see you. But I shall always rejoice that you are at work, and shall hope some day to see a change in the method and spirit of what you do.

From Eton the Revd. Edward Coleridge asked Ruskin to exert a moral influence on the poet. Ruskin demurred, saying, 'he is so boundlessly beyond me in all power and knowledge that the only good I *can* do him is to soothe him by giving him a more faithful – though not a less sorrowful, admiration than others do'. Like Lytton, Ruskin was unsure whether Swinburne would live very long, and,

> As for criticising the poems – that is a wholly unnecessary piece of business – and would only irritate him. I don't see anything to criticise in *Atalanta* – and if there be – he will find it out himself – he will not listen to me or anyone; and *ought* not, except to know what we enjoy and what we don't. (I've got the original MS of the 'Hymn to Proserpine', and wouldn't part with it for much more than leaf gold.) Say to his people that there are many who much more want praying for than he. We all want it alike I fancy – but he's worth a good many sparrows and won't be lost sight of.

This letter was passed on to Swinburne's family, prompting Admiral Swinburne to thank Ruskin on 17 September for expressing 'so truly the thoughts and feelings that his Mother and I have long had about him':

> We all care for sympathy, but he is so far beyond us that it is not easy in his case to give it, at least with reference to his writings: and they contain passages that give us great pain and sorrow, and check the longing desire to be pleased. But we see him changing, and I have a strong trust that if it please God to spare his life he will leave those blemishes behind and do good in his day.

If the family hoped Swinburne would return to the High Anglicanism of his youth they hoped in vain. Ruskin replied on 18 September to further reassure, though his hesitancy reveals how difficult this was:

> Even now – you ought not – none of us ought – to be pained grievously by anything in these poems ... The more I read it – the nobler I think it is. It *is* diseased – no question – but – as the blight is most on the moss-rose – and does not touch – however terrible – the inner nature of the flower ...
>
> Cannot you enjoy (for one out of many instances of noblest work in these poems) the three last stanzas of the ode to Victor Hugo without any bye-fear or pain?

A new Swinburne poem, 'Cleopatra', in *The Cornhill Magazine*, written to illustrate a picture by Sandys, went unnoticed as the controversy raged on. Buchanan published a satirical poem, 'The Session of the Poets', in *The Spectator*. In it Swinburne jumps up among the gathered poets 'and squeal'd, glaring out thro' his hair,/"All Virtue is bosh! Hallelujah for Landor!/I disbelieve wholly in everything! There!"' Order is restored when, 'flaming and red as a gipsy,' Tennyson

> Struck his fist on the table and utter'd a shout:
> 'To the door with the boy! Call a cab! He is tipsy!'
> And they carried the naughty young gentleman out.

Swinburne's propensity for drink was now public knowledge. He called Buchanan's satire 'the last thing out in blackguardism'.

There were voices raised in Swinburne's defence. Professor Henry Morley of University College London defended the book on moral grounds in *The Examiner*. Of *Poems and Ballads* and *Chastelard* he wrote, 'there is a terrible earnestness about these books'. Morley claimed to see in the former the inspiration of the Old Testament: 'He sings of Lust as Sin, its portion Pain and its end Death'; he said that although Swinburne painted the outward beauty of sensuality, 'the beauty drops away and shows the grinning skeleton beneath with fires of hell below'. Such a defence would have amused Swinburne, as did stray letters from clergymen who believed *Poems and Ballads* to be a warning of the wages of sin, and nuns who mistook 'Anactoria' for a hymn to the Virgin Mary. James Douglas took a similar view when he called 'Dolores' 'the despairing cry of the baffled voluptuary'. The poet James Thomson was more outspoken. Admitting he had not read *Poems and Ballads*, he considered thoughtful men would 'rejoice in the advent of any really able book which outrages propriety and shocks Bumbledom ... for the condition of our literature in these days is disgraceful to a nation of men ... Our literature should be the clear and faithful mirror of our whole world of life.' Thomas Hardy remembered how as a young man he had walked and read 'with a quick glad surprise/New words, in classic guise': 'It was as though a garland of red roses/Had fallen about the hood of some smug nun.'

Swinburne was proud of resisting pressure to change any of the poems. In 1877, hearing of a bookdealer selling a first edition and claiming it contained poems later suppressed, Swinburne categorically stated, 'there is not one "piece", there is not one line, there is not one word, there is not one syllable in any one copy ever printed of that book which has ever been changed or cancelled since the day of publication'. By mid-September *Poems and Ballads* was once more on sale, undergraduates chanted the poems in the streets of Oxford and Cambridge, and indecent epigrams about Swinburne were exchanged over port in the gentlemen's clubs. In October the historian W. H. E. Lecky wrote to his cousin,

> A very great poet has arisen in England – Algernon Swinburne – who stands apart from all his predecessors, and is probably destined to exercise a most profound influence on the ways of thought of Englishmen for many years to come. All literary London is now ringing with the genius, the blasphemies and indecencies of his last book.

Hotten asked Swinburne to reply to the press criticism. Swinburne obliged with a pamphlet, *Notes on Poems and Reviews*, of which, as Gosse says, 'there is much more of the red flag than the white sheet about it'. On 20 September Swinburne told Hotten it would be ready 'in a day or two', adding that contractual matters were in the hands of his solicitors, having consulted his father, 'a better man of business than myself'. On 10 October Swinburne explained to Hotten:

> I am, you will understand, particularly reluctant to be classed (even by the lowest scribbler in the 'Star') among the literary small fry of people who write in answer to their reviewers. Also, it is not exactly a reply to any critic or critics that I have written, but rather a casual set of notes on my poems, such as Coleridge and Byron (under other circumstances) did on theirs.

Writing to Powell he referred to 'my defensive and offensive pamphlet – Laus Diabolo'. William Rossetti corrected the text, persuading Swinburne to make changes, and sending a proof to Hotten on 4 October. Swinburne left London mid-month for Wales and returned to Holmwood on 30 October to find a copy of the pamphlet waiting for him. To an American correspondent he wrote that day, 'I fear the Philistines are very strong – but one must give them battle if only with so small a sling as this of mine.'

Notes on Poems and Reviews is a fine piece of ironic commentary: 'I am compelled to look sharply into [*Poems and Ballads*], and inquire what passage, what allusion, or what phrase can have drawn down such sudden thunder from the serene heavens of public virtue.' Before discussing specific poems singled out by the reviewers, Swinburne argued that the poetry should be read as art and that no necessary inference should be made from it to his own beliefs: 'The book is dramatic, many-faced, multifarious; and no utterance of enjoyment or despair, belief or unbelief, can properly be assumed as the assertion of its author's personal feeling or faith.'

Swinburne defended 'Anactoria' as an attempt to render 'that violence of affection between one and another which hardens into rage and deepens into despair', reminding readers that the fragments of Sappho included in it were part of the classical syllabus of boys in England's leading public schools, those fragments, he acidly remarked, 'which the Fates and the Christians have spared us'. Any blasphemy was the speaker's, not the author's. As for the charge of unmanliness, Swinburne picked up the tenor of his defence of Meredith in 1862, protesting, 'our time has room only for such as are content to write for children and girls' and that he had no desire to be one of the many 'moral milkmen . . . crying their ware about the streets and by-ways'. There were plenty of satirical asides, as when he refers to 'Faustine', 'the reverie of a man gazing on the bitter and vicious loveliness of a face as common and as cheap as the morality of reviewers'. Like *Poems and Ballads*, *Notes on Poems and Reviews* is both mischievous and a healthy protest against stifling hypocrisies, for 'nothing is so favourable to the undergrowth of real indecency as this overshadowing foliage of fictions, this artificial network of improprieties':

> If literature is not to deal with the full life of man and the whole nature of things, let it be cast aside with the rods and rattles of childhood . . . the office of adult art is neither puerile nor feminine, but virile; that its purity is not that of the cloister or the harem; that all things are good in its sight, out of which good work may be produced . . . Literature, to be worthy of men, must be large, liberal, sincere; and cannot be chaste if it be prudish.

Swinburne was pleased with the pamphlet, feeling he had 'proved "Dolores" to be little less than a second Sermon on the Mount, and

"Anactoria" . . . an archdeacon's charge'. To Lord Houghton he wrote, 'I thought the sharper, shorter, and singler in tone it was, the better. My motto is either to spare or strike hard. Mere titillation is lost on porcine hides.' William Rossetti's verdict was that *Notes* was 'vigorously written, and I think calculated to lighten the odium against the poems; though it goes (as I told Swinburne some weeks ago) beyond what I think effective or candid in repudiating the imputations of "immoral and blasphemous" matter'.

As early in the controversy as 12 August William Rossetti decided to write his own comments on *Poems and Ballads*, at first as a journal article, though it eventually became a small book. Rossetti told Charles Eliot Norton that the book had been 'ferociously assaulted here on moral etc. grounds, and not unreasonably' but he was determined to write out of a sense of 'the glorious poetic qualities of the book and the writer, my personal friendship for him, and my redoubled wish to stand up for him in my small way now that he is on his defence against fairly and unfairly aimed attacks'. In a letter of 2 September he wrote:

> Swinburne's superiority over his contemporary poets, with the sole *possible* exception of Tennyson, appears to me to lie in his mastery of all the *literary* or *artistic* resources of poetry – versification, language, harmony, vividness of expression, etc.: there are *other* qualities in which Tennyson and Browning, at any rate, may be preferred . . . As to blasphemy, Swinburne is certainly a pronounced antichristian, and something very closely resembling an atheist: I consider that he is right in entertaining these or any other speculative opinions which commend themselves to his own mind, and in expressing them as freely as Christians, Mohammedans, etc., express *their* speculative or traditional opinions. As to indecency . . . nor do I think his writings are likely to do any practical harm to anybody fitted by taste and training to admire them . . .

On 7 October, while suggesting revisions to *Notes on Poems and Reviews*, Rossetti approved Swinburne's comments on 'Dolores', 'Garden of Proserpine' and 'Hesperia', and thought Swinburne might want to group them as 'A Trilogy of Desire'. This drew Swinburne's revealing linkage of the latter poems with 'The Triumph of Time' and his statement, 'were I to rechristen these three as a trilogy, I should have to rename many earlier poems as acts in the same play'. But Swinburne showed good judgement in not yielding to advice from several quarters that *Notes on Poems and Reviews* should form a part of *Poems and Ballads* itself – 'It would in my opinion be making far too much of an ephemeral and contemptible subject. If the poems are fit to live they must outlive the memory of this'.

William Rossetti's *Swinburne's Poems and Ballads* was published in November 1866, a judicious mixture of criticism, explanation and praise.

It criticized Swinburne for publishing 'Dolores' and the sadistic over-tones in 'Anactoria', and thought the 'passionate sensuousness' in the poetry rather factitious. It undermined Swinburne's insistence that the poems were dramatic by arguing 'he ... dramatizes certain opinions, and not their contraries, so continually, because he sympathizes with them, and rejoices in giving them words', and observed that a lack of common sympathies would prevent him holding the mass of poetic readers, for 'he is radically indifferent, and indeed hostile, to what most persons care for; and he poetizes, for the greater part, from a point of view which they will neither adopt nor understand'. From a stylistic angle, Rossetti found an 'excess of emphasis' and length, monotony, repetition of words and images, and over-use of alliteration. But he praised Swinburne's 'deep and eager sense of beauty', 'fervour and intensity', 'eloquence', a 'wonderful charm of metric melody' and a pervading sublimity: 'we find in him an impulse, a majesty, a spontan-eity, a superiority to common standards of conception, perception, and treatment, an absoluteness ... of poetic incitement and subject-matter'. Rossetti's diary records that Swinburne spoke of the pamphlet 'with great satisfaction'.

Meanwhile Dante Gabriel Rossetti wrote to Tennyson on 6 October that he had heard the Laureate had been 'speaking of the qualities which displease you in Swinburne's poetry' and that they might partly be due to the poet's friendship with the painter. Dante Gabriel was quick to correct this false impression, saying, 'as no one delights more keenly in his genius than I do, I also have a right to say that no one has more strenuously combatted its wayward exercise in certain instances, to the extent of having repeatedly begged him not to read me such portions of his writings when in ms.'. So much for the abandon of earlier days, the circle of intimates roaring with laughter over de Sade.

Swinburne spent much of September and early October with his mother, who had a serious illness. Around 15 October he went to Aberystwyth to stay with Powell for two weeks, reading him parts of 'Child's Song in Winter' (reprinted as 'Winter in Northumberland') and

> fighting the tides as a swimmer on the west coast of Wales ... for after twenty minutes profane swearing at the keepers of the shore, I did last week frighten them into giving me entrance to the sea, which they thought too fierce to be met and swum through; and the result of my swim, I am told, is that I have 'won their hearts for ever'.

Otherwise Swinburne read Whitman's *Drum-taps* enthusiastically ('I always smelt the sea in that man's books'), corresponded with Hotten about his study of Blake and drew comparisons between the two poets. Swinburne was already being firm with Hotten: 'I will say plainly that *any* suggestion made about my affairs to a third party is officious and *useless* – I take unasked advice from no one, friend or not – especially not at second hand.'

The attacks on *Poems and Ballads* continued in the press and Buchanan reviewed Swinburne's pamphlet in *The Athenaeum*. Fame brought a strange variety of letters, including a poem from a lady in Florence about himself and his critics, 'in which it is stated that the seven leading angels of heaven are now occupied in singing my praises before God and returning thanks to him for my existence'. G. W. Carleton and Co. published *Poems and Ballads* in America under the title *Laus Veneris and Other Poems and Ballads*. Carleton told Swinburne on 24 November that since publication he had had 'a rough time of it' – but it was selling well (6000 copies by early December) and attracting the same attention as in England.

In October Swinburne turned his mind to other themes than those which had dominated *Poems and Ballads*:

> I have begun verse again after many months of enforced inaction through worry and weariness. I am writing a little song of gratulation for Venice with due reserves and anticipations; and hope to wind up the scheme of the poem by some not quite inadequate expression of reverence towards Mazzini ... After all in spite of jokes and perversities ... it is nice to have something to love and to believe in as I do in Italy. It was only Gabriel and his followers in art (L'art pour l'art) who for a time frightened me from speaking out; for ever since I was fifteen I have been equally and unalterably mad ... about this article of faith; you may ask any tutor or schoolfellow. I know the result will be a poem more declamatory than imaginative; but I'd rather be an Italian stump-orator than an English prophet.

The poem in question was *A Song of Italy*, and for the next eight years Swinburne's published poetry would centre on Italy and republican politics. Lafourcade thought there was 'nothing more remarkable in the whole life of Swinburne than this sudden and spontaneous change of attitude'. In fact it was neither spontaneous nor sudden. Swinburne's interest in Italy went back to his Balliol days and the 'Ode to Mazzini', and *Poems and Ballads* included several pieces which would not have looked out of place in *Songs before Sunrise* (1871). But there was a narrowing of theme and a consequent increase in rhetoric. By contrast there was the 137-line fragment 'Pasiphae' which tells the story of Pasiphae's passion for a bull and how she satisfied her desire through the contrivance of a hollowed-out wooden cow, the issue of their coition being the minotaur. Its imagery is as sexually explicit as anything in *Poems and Ballads*. Swinburne was still working on *Lesbia Brandon*.

Reports of Swinburne's behaviour at this time are conflicting. William Rossetti gave him a 'screed of friendly counsel concerning Bacchus ... I own the soft impeachment – now and then – notamment when we met last. It's the fault of good conversation – never so good as tête-à-tête of a night – and that means – Bacchus.' Scott told Walter Trevelyan on 3 December, 'Algernon Swinburne is now in town again, and as far as I have seen has given up the peculiarities of speech and action that frightened his friends, and quite as much as his poems themselves, brought down upon his book so much criticism.' The previous day Munby had had a different impression:

> I found Swinburne, and had some talk with him about Poe's Raven, Walt Whitman (whom of course he frantically praised) and Bourdelaire, a certain ribald French poet, whom he declared to be '15 million times' better than Tennyson. He spoke of 'my unfortunate book' and its resemblance to Walt Whitman. He was obviously drunk: he sat waving his arms and writhing his little legs after his manner, and talking loud and wild. He ordered a cab'; counter-manded it; jumped up and down, shook hands with me, with glazed eyes, and tottered out of the room, saying he 'must make a call'. Presently ... Walter Severn came in, crying 'What a sad business! Here is Swinburne come into the club again, dead drunk!' and he described the scene downstairs; and every one looked grave and sorrowful, but hardly a word was said. Truly it is sad enough ... to see this young poet ... belching out blasphemy and bawdry and prostrated by drink.

Boyce wrote in his diary for 14 December that he dined at Rossetti's and Swinburne had been drunk. On 12 December Swinburne was reporting that he had been 'bedridden or helpless upwards of a week with another of those damned bilious attacks which prove the malevolence of the Deity, and his ability to excel in ingenious cruelty that illustrious work of his hands, the Marquis de Sade'.

He went to Holmwood to be with his family for Christmas and remained there until late February 1867. Relations must have been strained; he had made his difference of beliefs public, and attacked their religious and political principles. Rossetti's defence of his poems was not mentioned to his mother 'as it acknowledges [Swinburne's] practical atheism etc., which matters, it seems, he never troubles her with'. Inviting George Powell to Holmwood, Swinburne referred to his brother Edward's presence in the New Year and mentioned that he shared Powell's enthusiasm for music: 'my art is at a discount here, but yours idolized'. During the winter Swinburne composed 'Regret', published September 1867. When it was reprinted in book form in 1878 he made a number of changes which effectively depersonalized it. The earlier version is more revealing of his frame of mind, inwardly mourning Capheaton and East Dene:

Now the days are all gone over
Of our singing, love by lover,
Days of summer-coloured seas,
Days of many melodies.

Now the nights are all past over
Of our dreaming, where dreams hover
In a mist of fair false things,
Nights with quiet folded wings.

Now the kiss of child and mother,
Now the speech of sister and brother,
Are but with us as strange words,
Or old songs of last year's birds.

Now all good that comes or goes is
As the smell of last year's roses,
As the shining in our eyes
Of dead summer in past skies.

In 'Pastiche', lines 9–10 became 'Now the loves with faith for mother,/ Now the fears with hope for brother', an alteration which makes the literal family relationships of stanza 3 purely figurative. The first version is unusually personal in tone. 'Regret' shows that the notion that Swinburne switched from the erotic blasphemy of 1866 through the political fervour of *Songs before Sunrise* to the wistful elegiacs of *Poems and Ballads, Second Series* (1878), as though these were discrete stages, is too simple. These three books are facets of a poetic sensibility constant in Swinburne; merely the emphasis changed from time to time.

Swinburne's Christmas was vexed by the news that 'Moxon, after violating their agreement to sell my Poems ... after advertising in all the literary papers that they had withdrawn the book and had nothing to do with it ... are now secretly selling copies withheld or rather stolen at one guinea each', and sending his post to the Dead Letter Office. Creatively, he was still at work on what he called 'a hymn of triumph for Italy'. By January he was snowed in at Holmwood, 'unable to get to and fro, but the twilight and frost make fine weather of it by day'. There were proofs of the much-delayed study of Blake to correct. On 12 January 1867 William Rossetti arrived for a couple of days:

> The old gentleman is kindly and conversible, and has seen and observed a number of things. Lady J. Swinburne has an attaching air and manner, and seems very agreeable in home-life – simple, dignified, and clever. There are three daughters at home, all sensible and agreeable; the second (Charlotte) with a handsome sprightly face, and the youngest evidently talented. The younger son was unwell, and has not shown. Swinburne shows well at home, being affectionate in his manner with all the family, and ready in conversing ... The Swinburne family generally have Algernon's passion for cats.

Early in January Swinburne was asked to write something for the refugees of the troubles in Crete. On 12 January Ford Madox Brown wrote that 'Mr Spartali the Greek consul thinks a poem on the unhappy Cretans would rouse public attention ... if there is only one English man with a soul left, be that one'. Brown added that there was the reward of pleasing Spartali's beautiful daughter Marie. Fame was bringing its own poetic imperatives. On 13 January William Rossetti noted, 'Swinburne read me at night his poem, approaching completion, on Italy; yesterday, one which he has written for the Candiote refugees, to give them the profits.'

Swinburne met William Rossetti in London on 16 January at the British Museum to look for designs from Blake to reproduce in his forthcoming book. Powell came to Holmwood early in February. There was increasing irritation with Hotten, as on 18 February, when Swinburne penned a splendidly impatient letter:

> You must really speak to the people you employ to send papers. If I cannot be supplied regularly with what I want, I had rather be told so. This is the *third* week since I left town, and now at last I receive, *not* the *Saturday Review* and *Spectator* of yesterday – but a set of *old* weekly papers, some three weeks old – *Athenaeums* (which I didn't order) and so on. Now I can be much better served if necessary at the next town. You also send me *duplicates* of Trollope's last numbers which I have received already in regular order. This is a waste of time, money, and patience. Pray give them a good 'rowing' and let me know if I am to expect things *regularly* henceforward.

On 22 February Swinburne finished *A Song of Italy*. The 'Ode on the Insurrection in Candia' was published in the *Fortnightly Review* in March 1867. Meredith wrote from Kingston-upon-Thames to describe it as 'the most nobly sustained lyric in our language ... Broader, fuller verse I do not know.' The tension between them in 1863–64 (exacerbated by Meredith's portrait of Swinburne as Tracy Runningbrook in his novel *Sandra Belloni*) had eased. As for the controversy over *Poems and Ballads*, Meredith commented, 'it will do you no harm, and you have partly deserved it; and it has done the critical world good by making men look boldly at the restrictions imposed upon art by our dominating damnable bourgeoisie'.

Whether by the design of his friends, or by more innocent social arrangements, it was in the spring of 1867 that Swinburne met the Italian exile Guiseppe Mazzini, who had long been one of his heroes. This meeting, which had a profound impact on Swinburne, did not, as has previously been suggested, suddenly change the direction of his writing, for Swinburne was writing about Italy from the autumn of 1866. But the meeting did confirm the concentration on political poetry.

Mazzini had written to Swinburne on 10 March, congratulating him on the 'Ode on the Insurrection in Candia', and making an appeal to the side of the poet that relished fervent speech on behalf of a cause:

> Don't lull us to sleep with songs of egotistical love and idolatry of physical beauty: shake us, reproach, encourage, insult, brand the cowards, hail the martyrs, tell us all that we have a great Duty to fulfill, and that, before it is fulfilled, Love is an undeserved blessing, Happiness a blasphemy, belief in God a Lie. Give us a series of 'Lyrics for the Crusade'. Have not our praise, but our blessing. You *can* if you choose.

And Swinburne did so choose, once he came under the personal spell of the man he was soon calling 'my Chief'. On 21 March Boyce dined at Solferino's restaurant, and remarked that Swinburne 'was quite thrown off his equilibrium, if he may be said to have any, by a commendatory letter from Mazzini'.

CHAPTER EIGHT

The Church of Rebels

On Sunday 31 March 1867 Swinburne was writing excitedly to his mother:

> All last evening and late into the night I was with Mazzini. They say a man's highest hopes are usually disappointed: mine were not. I had never dared to dream of such a reception as he gave me. At his desire, I read him my verses on Italy straight through; of course I felt awfully shy and nervous when I came to the part about him personally, but when I looked up at him I saw such a look on his face as set me all right again at once. . . . I am not going to try and tell you what he did me the honour to say about my poetry and the use of my devotion and belief to his cause . . . He has asked me to go and see him whenever I like. The minute he came into the room, which was full of people, he walked straight up to me . . . and said 'I know *you*', and I did as I always thought I should and really meant not to do if I could help – went down on my knees and kissed his hand . . . I know, now I have seen him, what I guessed before, why, whenever he has said to anyone, 'Go and be killed because I tell you', they have gone and been killed because he told them. Who wouldn't, I should like to know?

Mazzini was 61, and for Swinburne the meeting with the man 'who from my boyhood has been to me the incarnate figure of all that is great and good', matched that with Landor in 1864. Mazzini personally reinforced his call for some 'Lyrics for the Crusade'. The poem Swinburne refers to was *A Song of Italy*, published in the spring of 1867, which includes a long eulogy of Mazzini as 'our prophet, O our priest'. Eager to do away with priests of other persuasions, Swinburne was reluctant to be without one of his own.

His enthusiasm for Mazzini was not shared by his parents. On 10 April Swinburne asked his sister Alice to reassure Lady Jane about 'my Chief and myself', and that 'he is not at all likely to despatch me on a deadly errand to Rome or Paris, nor have we Republicans any immediate intention of laying powder-mines under Windsor Castle . . . I love her and him too much to write to the one about the other when I see it is hopeless to make the one share my love for the other.' Swinburne nonetheless enumerated the virtues and public reputation of Mazzini, before describing an evening spent with the blind poet Philip Bourke Marston. Marston was sixteen, had written some enthusiastic verses to Swinburne and thought almost as much of him as Swinburne did of Mazzini:

I gave him chocolate bon-bons, etc., and read to the company unpublished things of mine – among others the little old Jacobite song that you and A. liked so much when I read it you at Holmwood. It was really very touching to see the face that could just see where I was across the table looking at me ... And he did seem to enjoy himself so much that I really felt it was worth living, to give so much pleasure to a poor boy afflicted as he is from his birth.

The writer Bayard Taylor met Swinburne in April 1867 and compared him to the young Shelley, 'a wilful, perverse, unreasonable spoilt child':

> ... a clear headed and hearted woman could cure him of his morbid relish for the atrocious forms of passion. He has a weak moral sense, but his offences arise from a colossal unbalanced affectation. This, or something like it, is the disorganizing element in his nature, which quite obscures the organizing (that is artistic) sense. What I admire in him – yet admire with a feeling of pain – is the mad, unrestrained preponderance of the imagination. It is a god-like quality, but he sometimes uses it like a devil ... The preponderance of some disorganizing force in him gave me a constant keen sense of pain ... He is now, with all his wonderful gifts the most wretched man I ever saw ... One thing is certain – his aberration of ideas is horrible. He told me some things, unspeakably shocking, which he had omitted from his last volume. I very freely expressed my opinion and he took it with a gentle sort of wonder! He is sensitive, hugely ambitious and utterly self-absorbed ...

Swinburne struck Mrs Taylor differently; she recalled how his appearance had arrested her attention:

> his slender form, the reddish hair that curled thickly over his head, his fine and mobile features, high forehead, bright brown eyes, and a thin moustache above the sensitive mouth – all were combined to give him the air of an unusual personality. He was very excitable, impulsive in speech and gesture. He teased our little daughter, romped with her and hid under the long folds of the tablecloth.

Through April and May, Swinburne's letters continued to be full of Mazzini, who was 'more divine the more one sees him'; he told William Rossetti, 'we are quite on familiar terms now and what a delight this is to me I needn't tell *you*'. But he knew the limits of his dedication. On 7 May he told his mother:

> As to my chief, if you are really anxious about his influence upon me, you may be quite at rest. I do not expect you to regard him with my eyes, but you must take my word for it that nothing but good can come from the great honour and delight of being admitted to see and talk with him. He is always immensely kind and good to me, but all he wants is that I should dedicate and consecrate my writing power to do good and serve others exclusively, which I can't. If I tried I should lose my faculty of verse even.

> When I can, I do; witness my last book, which I hope you have
> received at last . . .

William Rossetti noted the same day, 'Mazzini urges him much to
write poems with a directly democratic or humanitarian aim: which
Swinburne finds it difficult to shirk, at the same time he feels conscious that is not exactly his line, and would not promote his true
poetic development.'

In May a rumour that Charles Baudelaire had died inspired Swinburne
to compose 'Ave Atque Vale', which Peter Sacks has called 'one of the
finest and least understood elegies in the language'. The first stanza
typifies, in Jerome McGann's words, its 'elusive beauty and enigmatic
greatness':

> Shall I strew on thee rose or rue or laurel,
>   Brother, on this that was the veil of thee?
>   Or quiet sea-flower moulded by the sea,
> Or simplest growth of meadow-sweet or sorrel,
>   Such as the summer-sleepy Dryads weave,
>   Waked up by snow-soft sudden rains at eve?
> Or wilt thou rather, as on earth before,
>   Half-faded fiery blossoms, pale with heat
>   And full of bitter summer, but more sweet
> To thee than gleanings of a northern shore
>   Trod by no tropic feet?

Swinburne retains many of the characteristic features of his verse but
states them in a minor key, mournful and restrained, his rhythmic
energy held in check, carefully balancing exquisitely contrasted images
like 'half-faded fiery blossoms, pale with heat' and incorporating a
translation of Baudelaire's 'La Géante'. Swinburne weaves his own
variations on the pastoral elegy and its traditional formulas, to close
with a haunting stoicism:

> For thee, O now a silent soul, my brother,
>   Take at my hands this garland, and farewell.
>   Thin is the leaf, and chill the wintry smell,
> And chill the solemn earth, a fatal mother,
>   With sadder than the Niobean womb,
>   And in the hollow of her breasts a tomb.
> Content thee, howse'er, whose days are done;
>   There lies not any troublous thing before,
>   Nor sight nor sound to war against thee more,
> For whom all winds are quiet as the sun,
>   All waters as the shore.

'I wrote it with very sincere feelings of regret for the poor fellow's
untimely loss', Swinburne recalled in 1874, saying he would be content
'if it may be allowed to take its stand below the lowest of them or to sit

meekly at their feet' – referring to 'Lycidas', 'Adonais' and 'Thyrsis'. But 'Ave Atque Vale' is one among equals in their company.

Swinburne was 'seedy' at this time, joking to Powell that 'I have been myself a prominent instance des *malheurs* de la *vertu*, for I never lived more carefully and chastely and soberly and never had such a bad fit of bilious influenza'. G. F. Watts started a portrait of him, which Swinburne regarded as an honour, 'but he won't let me crop my hair, whose curls the British public (unlike Titian's) reviles aloud in the streets'.

In early July he declined an invitation to a dinner party with Lord Houghton due to 'a severe bilious attack, which came on suddenly this morning'. A few days later he had recovered sufficiently to meet, through Karl Blind, Louis Blanc, a radical French politician in exile who may have influenced the character of Pierre Sadier in *Lesbia Brandon*. Swinburne was 'much struck and delighted' by the meeting. The meeting with Mazzini led Swinburne into a new social circle of Italian expatriates, chief among them Mazzini's friend Emilie Venturi.

It may have been this visit to Blind on 5 July at which Swinburne had an attack of some sort, followed by another more serious on 13 July. Lord Houghton told his wife, 'We were sitting after breakfast, when Swinburne fell down in a fit. Tweed was out, but I got Dr. Williams in a few minutes and there is no immediate danger.' Thomas Woolner, also present, told Sir Walter Trevelyan, 'poor little Swinburne had a dreadful fit yesterday at Lord Houghton's. From all accounts he seems to lead a sadly wild and unwholesome life. He made a great commotion, as you may imagine, at the breakfast table among the assembled guests.' William Rossetti described it as 'an attack of insensibility, more perhaps in the nature of a fit than a faint. He remained insensible some long while: the Doctor called in absolutely prohibited his continuing to use any brandy or the like stimulant, but considered it necessary to allow him Champagne.' The Admiral was telegraphed and took Swinburne home the next day, hoping 'that care and more regular hours and diet will do him good'.

On 18 July Swinburne explained to Lord Houghton that the doctors 'have together prescribed for me a course of diet and tonic medicine and advise country air; since my arrival I have felt not a moment's pain or sickness, and am now really quite well, though rather tired and weakened'. It is interesting that to Howell, from whom he presumably had no reason to hide any of his excesses, Swinburne called it 'a sudden and *unprovoked* fainting fit' – presumably meaning unprovoked by drink. On 26 July the Admiral reported to Houghton, 'my Son's health appears at present to be very good':

> He recovered his appetite as soon as he got home, and fell willingly into regular hours and habits, as he always does when he is with us. He is tractable and willing to do every thing that is required of

him. It cannot be expected, and therefore is not insisted upon, that his mental faculties should lie fallow, but we do all we can to keep them tranquil.

We feel him to be safe while he is here; the trial and test of his firmness will come when he shall return to the temptations to which he has been hitherto exposed.

In July the *Fortnightly Review* published his appreciation of Morris's *Life and Death of Jason*. At Holmwood Swinburne wrote 'A Wasted Vigil', which he sent to Powell. Wishing for diversion, he asked for news of Eton and the block: 'can you tell me any news of the latter institution or any of its present habitues among our successors? the topic is always most tenderly interesting – with an interest, I may say, based upon a common bottom of sympathy.' August passed with 'no return of fainting or any discomfort here beyond a strained knee' and the writing of more flagellant letters to Powell. When Powell sent a photograph of the Eton block, Swinburne was pleased but sighed, 'if I were but a painter – ! I would do dozens of different fellows diversely suffering. There can be no subject fuller of incident, character, interest – realistic, modern, dramatic, intense, and vividly pictorial.'

Swinburne was eager to go to Wales, but his parents forbade him moving. 'You see my last attack was, they say, of a really dangerous kind, and I am prescribed a *torpor* of mind and body for months.' So he stayed until mid-September. His fame now brought him the attention of budding poets who wrote to ask his opinion of their verses. Among them were W. E. Henley and Edmund Gosse, who became a friend and his first biographer. Swinburne's reply shows another application of his creed of self-reliance:

> I understand the impulse to write of which you speak and the pain of checking or suppressing it; nor do I tell you to suppress or check it; only not to build upon it overmuch. To fret yourself in the meantime with alternations of hope and fear is useless if you are to succeed, and more than useless if you are not: I always thought so for myself, before I had sent anything to press. One wishes of course for success as for other pleasant things; but the readier we hold ourselves to dispense with it if necessary, the better.

When Gosse's father found out that his son had been in contact with the author of *Poems and Ballads* he said, 'How could you, as a Christian, seek his acquaintance?'

On 17 September Swinburne wrote to William Rossetti, asking him to get some information from Hotten as to the state of the printing of the essay on Blake, and his royalties. Hotten had held up Swinburne's Blake because he was busy producing some facsimiles of Blake's illustrated books. Rossetti shared Swinburne's suspicion that Hotten was reprinting *Poems and Ballads* without paying the author. The sales of *A*

Song of Italy had been disappointing. Swinburne wrote 'Siena' and 'The Halt before Rome', and thought of tackling the subject of Bothwell as the next stage in the life of Mary Stuart.

Swinburne was now sufficiently famous to be the topic of other writers' texts. He read Catherine A. Simpson Wynne's novel *Catherine's Engagement*, 'in which I am bodily introduced with only a difference of height etc. but my ways and looks reproduced unblushingly. C'est un peu fort; but it has amused too much to irritate me.' Swinburne's surrogate is Collingwood Fernleigh, entering houses with 'a peal of uproarious laughter', with eyes 'which were for ever sparkling restlessly round, seldom seeming to dwell upon any object, but flashing quick keen glances upon everybody and everything ... the uncontrollable vivacity, the overflowing vitality, that spoke in Collingwood's every gesture ... made it impossible for him to remain quiet a moment'. Chapter 16 is a fictionalized version of the controversy surrounding *Poems and Ballads*, even quoting 'Itylus'. In a scene played out for real in pious homes across the country, Collingwood's brother confronts him, demanding 'How dare you bring into English homes a book that can be placed in no woman's hands?', to which Collingwood answers, 'I write for scholars, for men of letters, not for a pack of girls.'

By October the concept of *Songs before Sunrise* was taking shape, 'a book of political and national poems as complete and coherent in its way as the Châtiments or Drum Taps', such as Mazzini had requested:

> There is I think room for a book of songs of the European revolution, and if sung as thoroughly as Hugo or as Whitman would sing them, they ought to ring for some time to some distance of echo. The only fear is that one may be disabled by one's desire – made impotent by excess of strain.

His essay on Matthew Arnold's new poems appeared, in which he urged Arnold to restore a number of early poems to his canon. In a revealing passage Swinburne wrote that 'the lord of our spirit and our song, the god of all singers and all seers, is an intolerable and severe god, dividing and secluding his elect from full enjoyment of what others enjoy', and rejected the assumption that nature was humanity's to do with as it pleased. Humanity must learn to submit, 'not by ceasing to attempt and achieve the best we can, but by ceasing to expect subservience to our own ends from all forces and influences of existing things; it is no reason or excuse for living basely instead of nobly, that we must live as the sons and not as the lords of nature'.

In October Swinburne met Henry Kingsley at Holmwood, and liked him, 'especially as in a minute's talk on Italy I found him of one mind with me'. When staying at his family home, Swinburne would often visit the Kingsleys at Wargrave close by. By November Swinburne was in London, seeing Meredith and Powell, and making himself ill. The case of the condemned Fenians, Allen, Larkin and O'Brien, who were due to be hanged for the shooting – apparently accidental – of a police sergeant, stirred him to write 'An Appeal to England' on their behalf, which was published on 22 November through the offices of the *Morning Star*. By November Swinburne's plans for a trilogy of plays about Mary Stuart had been formalized and he had started *Bothwell*, as well as writing more poems of a political nature. A long poem on the legend of Tristram and Iseult was also in his thoughts.

On 2 December Munby saw Swinburne at the Arts Club. They talked of Shakespeare's sonnets, 'he upholding that hateful theory of their meaning, and talking of them with an air of high moral indignation':

> After dinner, when I was alone in the back drawing room, he came to me, and kept up a long and earnest talk, or rather declamation, about the merits of Walt Whitman and W. B. Scott. Having taken a little wine – not much more than a pint – at dinner, he was off his balance at once, and absolutely raved with excitement; leaping about the room, flinging up his arms, blowing kisses to me, and swearing great oaths between whiles. He would hardly let me go
> . . .

Meeting him on the 14th, Munby noted that, 'being perfectly sober, he was as agreeable and kindly and rational as could be'.

In late November or early December Swinburne started an affair with a world-famous American theatre performer, Adah Isaacs Menken. He wrote to Thomas Purnell, a journalist friend: 'If you see Dolores before I do, tell her with my love that I would not shew myself sick and disfigured in her eyes. I was spilt last week out of a hansom, and my nose and forehead cut to rags – was seedy for four days, and hideous.' Born in New Orleans in 1838, Menken led a thoroughly turbulent life, marrying five times, having a son who died in infancy, performing on the stages of America, England and the Continent, and writing poetry in the style of Whitman. Her most famous role was an adaptation of Byron's 'Mazeppa', which climaxed with her riding bareback on a horse in an outfit that gave the illusion of nudity. It was a role that provoked similar outraged feelings to those drawn by *Poems and Ballads*. One reviewer wrote of her performance that 'the attraction . . . lies undoubtedly in its impurity'. She invented many stories about herself and adopted various personae. Menken transgressed many Victorian conventions of what women should say and do, her most recent biographer describing her as 'a true revolutionary, a female libertarian'.

She had associated with literary men before Swinburne: Mark Twain, Dickens, D. G. Rossetti and Gautier had alike fallen under her spell. On first arriving in England in April 1864, she set up court at the Westminster Palace Hotel, entertaining the literati and journalists as preparations for 'Mazeppa' were made at Astley's Theatre. 'Mazeppa' opened in October 1864, when Swinburne was in Cornwall. She is said to have invited Rossetti to Astley's on more than one occasion. In March 1866 she left England, returning in the late summer of 1867. She was anxious to see her poems published and had contacted John Camden Hotten.

There are conflicting stories of how Menken and Swinburne started their affair. The legend that Rossetti and Burton gave her £10 to seduce Swinburne sounds like a chauvinistic invention. Menken was earning a considerable sum each week, hardly needed the money, and had more than enough pride to reject it. Another version states that Rossetti and Mazzini arranged a meeting because they wanted a woman to exert a positive sexual and domestic influence on the increasing chaos of Swinburne's life. Gosse was told that it was John Thomson who introduced Menken to Swinburne. Mazzini knew Swinburne was an endangered species – mostly endangered by himself – observing, 'he will not last two years unless he changes his habits . . . I wish very much, that he would, before vanishing, write something.' Not long after their first meeting Mazzini had said, 'he might be transformed, but only by some man or woman – better a woman of course – who would like him very much and assert a moral superiority on him'. Mazzini had tried to encourage more contact between Swinburne and Emilie Venturi (who was widowed in 1867), writing to her on one occasion, 'I should like a certain degree of intercourse between you and him: it might do good, in your sense, to him' (June 1867). Neither this nor Mathilde Blind's alleged romantic interest in Swinburne came to anything.

Intelligent and independent, looking for editorial help with her poems, Menken had good reasons of her own for seeking out Swinburne. Her third husband, Robert H. Newell, said she 'had the keenest mind I ever encountered in a member of her sex. Indeed, few men were her mental equals, and she could discourse fluently on matters pertaining to literature, the sciences and the latest news of the world in which we live.' Swinburne's fame as a poet of daring verse would have attracted her; as a woman of considerable sexual experience she may well have assumed the same in the author of *Poems and Ballads*. They were both rebels against a society which had lambasted them for offending public decency. She showed her interest in Swinburne's poetry by using four lines from 'Dolores' for an epigraph to *Infelicia*. On Swinburne's side, the man who had written so much in praise of female beauty could hardly have been insensitive to hers.

Swinburne told Julian Osgood Field 'all about Menken calling . . . and telling him bluntly she had come to sleep with him'. Her only fault was waking early in the morning and reciting her verse, swinging her legs as she sat on the bed; Swinburne said a woman with such beautiful legs shouldn't worry herself with poetry. The gossip percolated to William Rossetti who wrote on 15 March 1868:

> Swinburne has a liaison with her. I am told by A., who has it from B., who has it from C., who has it from Swinburne's landlady, that, Miss Menken having one evening visited Swinburne at his lodgings, he besought her to stay into or through the night; and that, she declining this favour, he seized her, pulled her to the ground, and was throttling her, and a policeman had to be called in. A small *gentillesse* of excited and thwarted affection: Miss Menken was verily obliged to run for it. About 'sucking her real blood' and so on I know absolutely nothing . . .

On 4 December 1867 the journalist Thomas Purnell wrote to Swinburne:

> To-day I have had such a letter from Dolores – such a letter! She fears you are ill; she is unable to think of anything but you; she wishes me to telegraph to her if you are in danger, and she will fly on the wings of the wind to nurse you. She has become a soft-throated serpent, strangling prayers on her white lips to kiss the poet, whose absence leaves her with ghosts and shadows. She concludes:
> 'Tell him all – say out my despairing nature to him – take care of his precious life. Write at once; believe in me and my holy love for him. Let him write one word in your letter. He will, for he is so good.'
> What do you think of this? It is Cleopatra over again.

The fact that one of Adah's many names was 'Dolores' became a private joke between them. Swinburne's 'Dolores' had been written in the summer of 1865, so there is no truth in assertions that it was written about her and their relationship.

Rumours of the affair quickly spread, along with quips that the author of 'Unchastelard' was about to publish a new work called 'Adalanta in California'. Journalist Shirley Brooks, who had slandered Swinburne with epigrams in the clubs since *Poems and Ballads*, met Menken in February 1868 and became besotted with her, telling William Hardman, 'I am my own no longer, *nor my wife's neither* . . . I am Ada's . . . She lives at No. 26, Norfolk Street . . . Swinburne is the only rival I dread – he knew her first. But I shall sit upon his corpse. He boasts – but he lies!' Swinburne's friends teased him. Burne-Jones drew eleven cartoons relating 'Ye Treue and Pitifulle Historie of ye Poet and ye Ancient Dame'. Swinburne told Lord Houghton on 21 December he was enjoying 'the bonds of a somewhat riotous concubinage. I don't know many *husbands* who could exact or expect from a *wife* such indulgences as are hourly laid at my feet!' Further scandal was caused by Menken and Swinburne sitting for some photographs, as Swinburne mentions to Powell on 26 January 1868:

> I am ashamed to have left your last note so long unanswered – but
> I have been so worried of late with influenza, love-making, and
> other unwholesome things – such as business, money, etc. – that I
> have 'left undone all that I should have done.' I must send you in a
> day or two a photograph of my present possessor – known to
> Britannia as Miss Menken, to me as Dolores (her real Christian
> name) – and myself taken together. We both come out very well.
> Of course it's *private*. I hope you are better than I am, or you are
> not much in the way of health.

The most famous of these photographs shows Swinburne standing and
Menken sitting. Another has a slightly stunned-looking Menken seated,
while Swinburne stands holding her hand, gazing at the camera with
proprietorial complacency. Unsurprisingly, given their celebrity status,
the pictures were soon visible in London shop windows. In modern
terms, the liaison could only be paralleled by Arthur Miller and Marilyn
Monroe, or Madonna photographed on the lap of a dissolute Booker
Prize novelist. One or two of the pictures found their way back to
Holmwood, where the Admiral and Lady Jane were horrified to learn
that their errant son was consorting with a woman of the theatre. On
17 April Swinburne told Powell:

> There has been a *damned* row about it; paper after paper has flung
> pellets of dirt at me, assuming or asserting the falsehood that its
> publication and sale all over London were things authorized or
> permitted or even foreseen by the sitters: whereas of course it was a
> private affair, to be known (or shewn) to friends only. The circula-
> tion has of course been stopped as far as possible, but not without
> much irritating worry. The one *signed* I think good – the other not,
> except for the pose of her shoulder and bosom.

The affair lasted about six months. We do not know why they parted or
whether it was amicable. Scott heard at the beginning of April 1868
that 'Woolner has been entertaining friends with an account of a quarrel between Swinburne and Menken'. In May or June Menken left
London for Paris, where she died on 10 August 1868, not much more
than 30. When the news reached Swinburne he told Powell, 'I am sure
you were sorry on my account to hear of the death of my poor dear
Menken – it was a great shock to me and a real grief – I was ill for some
days. She was most lovable as a friend as well as a mistress.' Shortly
after her death, *Infelicia* was published by Hotten, though he withheld
his name from the title-page. Menken's fame was sufficient to carry it
through a number of editions. Whether or not Swinburne had any hand
in either revising the poems or checking the proofs is unclear.

During the winter of 1867–68 Swinburne continued working on the
poems for Mazzini. On 3 December Mazzini told Emilie Venturi, 'Do
write yourself to Swinburne that I am ill, *cannot* write, but read, mark

each step of his, feel grateful and admiring and touched.' Swinburne alludes to this in a letter to William Rossetti on 12 December, saying 'I have received a message from Mazzini of which I cannot trust myself to write.' He seems to have been unaware of the way he was being manipulated.

It was in December 1867 that Swinburne was at last able to send friends *William Blake. A Critical Essay*, the study begun almost six years before. Hotten advertised it in *The Bookseller* for 1 February 1868 as 'ready this day'. It has an honourable place in the history of Blake scholarship, the first book systematically to examine Blake's *oeuvre*, and to recognize that 'the text is an integral part of the design and the design an integral part of the text. Divide them, and you kill them; at least you mutilate and stultify them.' Swinburne was prepared to labour on the longer 'Prophecies' and used insights from them to illumine the shorter lyrics. Blake was the one man, apart from Shelley, who had lived earlier in the century, whom Swinburne would have 'most liked to see and speak to in person'. The *Critical Essay* also tells us a good deal about Swinburne and his self-definition as an artist during the 1860s in the way it remakes Blake in his own image. Swinburne's is a creative and fruitful misreading – but a misreading nonetheless. Swinburne writes of Blake as 'born and baptized into the church of rebels', writes of his 'republican passion', and of his ability to worship: 'like all men great enough to enjoy greatness, Blake was born with the gift of admiration'. He writes too how 'Liberty and religion, taken in a large and subtle sense of the words were alike credible and adorable to him'. He even writes of one period in Blake's life when a 'first daily communion with the sea wrought upon him at once within and without'.

Swinburne saw Blake as a defender of life who attacked the 'old ascetic assumption that the body is of its nature base and the soul of its nature noble, and that between the two there is a great gulf fixed ... Blake, as a mystic of the higher and subtler kind, would have denied this superior separate vitality of the spirit', Blake's faith being based on 'an equal reverence for spirit and flesh as the two sides or halves of a completed creature'. In the course of the study Swinburne draws an erroneous parallel between Blake and de Sade, and a more appropriate one between Blake and Whitman, the 'passionate preacher of sexual or political freedom'. Section II opens with a digression about art for art's sake, which Swinburne argues was Blake's position. Art cannot be the 'handmaid of religion, exponent of duty, servant of fact, pioneer of morality', for:

> ... if the artist does his work with an eye to such results or for the sake of bringing about such improvements, he will probably fail even of them. Art for art's sake first of all, and afterwards we may

suppose all the rest shall be added to her ... but from the man who falls to artistic work with a moral purpose, shall be taken away even that which he has – whatever of capacity for doing well in either way he may have at starting.

In many of the poems that made up *Songs before Sunrise* and *Songs of Two Nations*, Swinburne transgressed his own doctrine.

The study of Blake is full of passages of fine prose, as when Swinburne describes the 'Songs of Innocence', or Blake's 'twofold vision':

He walked and laboured under other heavens, on another earth, than the earth and the heaven of material life ... To him the veil of outer things seemed always to tremble with some breath behind it: seemed at times to be rent in sunder with clamour and sudden lightning. All the void of earth and air seemed to quiver with the passage of sentient wings and palpitate under the pressure of con-scious feet. Flowers and weeds, stars and stones, spoke with articu-late lips and gazed with living eyes. Hands were stretched towards him from beyond the darkness of material nature, to tempt or to support, to guide or to restrain. His hardest facts were the vaguest allegories of other men. To him all symbolic things were literal, all literal things symbolic. About his path and about his bed, around his ears and under his eyes, an infinite play of spiritual life seethed and swarmed or shone and sang.

In 1882, Swinburne called the essay 'the most unlucky and despised of all my brain-children', remembering how

I spent days in the print-room of the British Museum scribbling in pencil the analysis of Blake's 'prophetic books', and hours at Lord Houghton's in the same labour with pen and ink – to produce a book which was received with general contumely, ridicule, and neglect, and has never yet, I believe, paid half its expenses, or struggled into a second edition.

The reviews were mixed. Blake's mysticism and unorthodox morality, filtered through Swinburne's lyrical prose, was too much for periodicals like *The Saturday Review* to accept.

Swinburne spent Christmas 1867 and the New Year in London, laid up with influenza. He saw Mazzini in early February 1868 when his Chief returned from abroad. At a meeting of the Anthropological So-ciety on 17 March, Swinburne spoke in response to J. McGrigor Allan's paper, 'Europeans, and their Descendants in North America'. He felt he must protest against the view that there was no real difference between the literary men of America and England:

In his opinion there was a marked difference; and if there were any similarity between the writers mentioned and those of our own country, he thought it was to this extent – that Washington Irving's compositions were Addison and water, and those of H. W. Longfellow, Tennyson and water. But there was one American poet, who, at least in his opinion, exhibited a special peculiarity not taken from any European model; namely, Edgar Allan Poe, whose works he had always admired as poetical and having an intellectual expression of their own. There might be many better writers in Europe, but he knew of none; and, at any rate, there was undeniably a peculiarity in Poe. So much for the south, of which Poe was an example. And with regard to the north, there was Walt Whitman, whose compositions were undoubtedly superior. There was something quite fresh and new in them, whether for praise or dispraise, and a decided originality. His writings had received a slow acceptance even in America; but they were slowly and surely making their way in Europe, and would in time be fairly recognised. America was not so sterile as the author had endeavoured to make out; but, on the contrary, she appeared to have, nay, she had, a new spring of intellectual power.

Swinburne's ill-health, compounded by toothache and money worries, continued into the spring. He wrote more poems for *Songs before Sunrise*, the idea for 'Tiresias' coming in April. Rossetti held a party on 2 April, writing 'I hear bye the bye that little Swinburne is considering himself neglected, and am almost inclined to ask him . . . but am rather afraid of the results.' On 18 April Swinburne was seen 'frantically joining in' political discussions at the Arts Club. Even if the bouts of influenza were real, his drinking led to the breaking of more than just social engagements. On 28 April he had 'what might have been a dangerous accident which has laid me up ever since':

> I was carrying my lamp (unlit) in the dark (having already in looking for it smashed a looking glass to begin with) when I fell over something, smashed the lamp (it was very dark and the curtains close drawn) and cut open my head, my right knee and (in rising barefoot) my left foot. I could get no help or plaster till morning and by then had lost a lot of blood . . . Dr. Bird has been with me, dressed, and prescribed etc. I am going on very well, quite strong and healthy otherwise, but of course disabled from locomotion as yet . . . I assure you the bed and floor of my room next morning looked as if M. de Sade had had a few friends to a small and select supper party the night before, and had enjoyed himself thoroughly on the festive occasion.

That he was drunk at the time is confirmed by a letter of 12 May from his doctor to Mazzini, saying that 'for five days past Mr. Swinburne has avoided "the perilous stuff" and is consequently very much improved in body and mind', and that his family should not be written to at present. In June a small advertisement was placed in the papers, asking for the return of some manuscript: 'May have been left in a cab. Of no use to anybody but the owner. Small REWARD will be given upon restoration by Mr. Hotten, 74 Piccadilly, W.' Swinburne had lost between ten and twenty sheets of *Bothwell* and 'Tristram and Yseult'. On 11 May Arnold had sent the second edition of his *New Poems* 'to one who has been so splendidly their friend'. On 3 July Swinburne asked when he would be writing more poetry: 'I, and my betters, are athirst for a larger and clearer draught in these Tennysonian times (*the* Laureate is of course delicious at his best – but one can't live, even chez Tortoni, on sorbets – it isn't digestible without bread and wine).'

In June and July Swinburne published his 'Notes on the Designs of the Old Masters at Florence' in the *Fortnightly Review* and *Notes on the Royal Academy Exhibition of 1868* (with William Rossetti). The latter showed Swinburne still stressing 'the love of beauty for very beauty's sake, the faith and trust in it as a god indeed', despite the creative energy he was directing into republican poetry. Writing of Albert Moore's 'Azaleas', Swinburne remarks, 'the melody of colour, the symphony of form is complete: one more beautiful thing is achieved, one more delight is born into the world; and its meaning is beauty; and its reason for being is to be.' One thing which conspicuously lacked 'symphony of form' was his account at Hotten, which was causing anxiety as a difference in understanding about what had been agreed in September 1866 surfaced. Hotten was still prepared to talk about new titles, on 25 July reminding Swinburne of his idea to write introductions to a collected edition of George Chapman's plays.

On 10 July Swinburne had 'a fainting fit brought on by the damnable unventilated air of the Museum'. He told Nichol:

> I went early to the Brit. Mus. to look up certain references ... began to feel giddy and faint in an hour or so ... but thought I would hold out and keep my promise, and consequently after some twenty minutes' struggle fainted right out, and in falling cut my forehead slightly.

Edmund Gosse was a witness to Swinburne being carried out, his first encounter with the poet:

> I was walking along a corridor when I was passed by a couple of silent attendants rapidly carrying along in a chair what seemed to be a dead man. I recognised him instantly from his photographs which now filled the shop windows. His hanging hands, closed eyelids, corpse-white face, and red hair dabbled in blood presented an appearance of the utmost horror, but I learned a few days later that his recovery was rapid and complete.

In his diary Gosse wrote that Swinburne had hit his head 'so violently as to make a gash 1½ inches long and penetrating to the bone'. Mary Mohl, who had met Swinburne at Fryston in August 1861 and 1864, told Lady Augusta Stanley on 21 July:

> Mr Milnes made me go to lunch with him the day I saw you that I might see and talk to that unfortunate rag of a man Swinburne – I

> believe he is murdering himself with drink. He was there at Mr
> Milnes's and had fell down in a fit at the British Museum. He sent
> him away, the poor creature is really pitiable. After he was gone I
> expressed this pity and . . . Mr Milnes's eyes filled with tears, his
> face coloured up and he covered it with his hands.

A few days after, William Rossetti found Swinburne 'in capital spirits,
with health apparently to correspond: a little plaistering on his forehead'. Browning called to show his concern. Jowett wrote 'a really kind
and friendly letter, on the hypothesis that I have been injuring my
natural health by intemperate and irregular ways'. Jowett's influence
with Swinburne steadily increased over the next few years.

A letter of 28 July to Powell adds, 'My life has been enlivened of late
by a fair friend who keeps a maison de supplices à la Rodin – There is
occasional balm in Gilead!' This is an allusion to a brothel which
catered for flagellant tastes. He referred to it again in November, telling
Lord Houghton, 'Our fair friend of the grove of the Beloved Disciple
has also returned from France and is in high feather. I always find her
delicious dans son genre.' It was John Thomson, whom Swinburne had
met through the journalist Savile Clarke, who introduced Swinburne to
what Gosse termed

> a mysterious house in St. John's Wood where two golden-haired
> and rouge-cheeked ladies received, in luxuriously furnished rooms,
> gentlemen whom they consented to chastise for large sums . . .
> There was an elder lady, very respectable, who welcomed the guests
> and took the money. Swinburne much impoverished himself in
> these games, which also must have been very bad for his health.

The house at 7 Circus Road was called 'Verbena Lodge'. Late in 1868
or 1869 Swinburne quarrelled with the women about money – Gosse
found no evidence of Swinburne going to them after 1869. So it was
that,

> . . . in 1868, on mornings when Swinburne was on his way from
> his lodgings in Dorset Street to the brothel, he used to pause in the
> Regent's Park, at a particular bench, and write down the verses he
> had been composing in his head. Several of the *Songs before Sun-
> rise* were so written.

This fact was noted by 'a friendly and intelligent park-keeper, who
knew who the poet was, and who often conversed with him'. It was said
that this brothel had 'two very young girls, who pretend to be school-
masters and whip fearfully severely, belabouring their clients across
their knees like children'. Fuller points out that in July 1865 a letter to
Lord Houghton contains the phrase 'old school habits return upon us
unawares', so Swinburne could have discovered the brothel earlier. Ian
Gibson has argued that in Swinburne's case flagellation was the neces-

sary prelude to heterosexual activity. On 2 December Swinburne told Powell that if he could he would celebrate the fifty-fourth anniversary of the death of the Marquis de Sade 'by a partial reproduction (with female aid) of the rites of Artemis Orthia, mixed with those of the Europian Cotytto and the Asiatic Aphrodite of Aphaca'. A similar reference occurs in a letter of July 1872:

> In these shades might the learned M. Rodin and the venerated Père Severino revel unchecked in the infliction of the most exquisite torture on the loveliest limbs of blooming boyhood – of the most burning shame, the most intolerable suffering, on blushing and writhing adolescence – while Naiads and Oreads, maidens of the mountain and the stream, stood not far off, to repay the labours and allay the pangs with kisses. Here Pain and Pleasure, twin sisters, might dance hand in hand round the blood red and rose red altar of Love.

And on 9 November he wrote, 'I have found far from dry or chilling the Sadice-Paphian spring of St. John's Wood whereof I once spoke to you.' De Sade and Venus, blood-red and rose-red. The images imply both masochistic and heterosexual activity.

In August the Reform League invited him to stand for Parliament 'for some place in or near the Isle of Wight' with all his expenses paid. 'Most of my friends have been day after day urging and pressing me to accept. Still I don't think it is my line.' Brown told William Rossetti that Swinburne eventually declined on the advice of Mazzini.

In September Swinburne had a vacation in Normandy with George Powell. Writing to his mother from Étretât on 14 September, he said

> I am here safe and *so* well and fresh, thanks to the mere sight and smell of sea. *Such* a lovely passage on Saturday – hard due east wind, alternate roll sideways, and plunge forward and splashing – that I was wild with pleasure and others with sickness – *I had left that behind on shore. I must* hail the Flying Dutchman and get taken on board in some capacity – then, never stopping or landing, I shall always be well and happy . . . Powell has got the sweetest little old farmhouse fitted up inside with music, books, drawings, etc. . . . There is a wild little garden all uphill, and avenues of trees about. The sea is splendid, and the cliffs very like the Isle of Wight . . .

The stay lasted for about three or four weeks, and included 'a real sea adventure' when he was swept two miles out. Swinburne explained, 'I was all right though very tired, and the result was I made immense friends with all the fishermen and sailors about'. At 10 o'clock on a Friday morning, he had gone to the eastern side of the Porte d'Amont, taken his clothes off and dived in. Powell had seen Swinburne:

> carried out to sea through a rocky archway, and entirely out of my sight, by one of the treacherous undercurrents so prevalent and so

dreaded on that dangerous coast. After I had lost sight of him for about 10 minutes, I heard shouts on the cliffs above me to the effect that 'a man was drowning'. Guessing what had occurred, I gathered up Mr. Swinburne's clothes by which I had been sitting, and running with them through the ankle-deep shingle to where some boats lay, sent them off to the rescue. In but a few minutes, however, a boat coming *from* the point at which I feared a catastrophe had taken place, brought us the welcome news that my friend had been picked up by a fishing smack bound for Yport, a few miles distant. I therefore took a carriage and galloped off at fullest speed, with the clothes of the rescued man to the village of Yport, whence we returned to Étretât, in the smack which had picked up Mr. Swinburne, he declining to use the carriage.

Swinburne told Gosse that when he 'set himself to shout and yell . . . the sound of his own voice struck him as very strange and dreadful', and that he was filled with annoyance at the fact that he had not completed *Songs before Sunrise*. Swinburne described the experience in 'Ex-Voto', seeing another parallel with Shelley:

When thy salt lips wellnigh
Sucked in my mouth's last sigh,
Grudged I so much to die
    This death as others?
Was it no ease to think
The chalice from whose brink
Fate gave me death to drink
    Was thine – my mother's?

Swinburne kept the outsize garments the French fishermen dressed him in for the rest of his life. The young Guy de Maupassant, who waded in after the poet (whom he claimed was drunk), was thanked by Powell and invited to lunch the next day. The young Frenchman's impression was of 'A strange house, a sort of cottage, containing some very beautiful pictures . . . and a great monkey gambolling about inside'. Swinburne was 'a little man, quite short, with a pointed face, a hydrocephalous forehead, pigeon-chested, agitated by a trembling which affected his glass with St Vitus' dance, and incessantly talking like a madman'. The two Englishmen had pornographic pictures of men, and Swinburne talked of snakes and translated some of his poems into French. Powell later named the cottage La Chaumière de Dolmance, after de Sade's *La Philosophie dans le boudoir*, and a walk in the garden 'Avenue de Sade'. The cottage had a number of youths acting as domestic servants. In 1891 Maupassant described Swinburne as 'perhaps . . . the most extravagantly artistic person alive in the world today':

He was very cordial and hospitable; and the extraordinary charm of his intelligence captivated me at once. During the whole of lunch we talked about art, literature, humanity, and the opinions of those two friends cast over everything a kind of disturbing, macabre light, for they had a way of seeing and understanding that made them seem like diseased visionaries, drunken with a poetry magical and perverse ... They recounted Icelandic legends, translated by Mr Powell, of a griping and terrible novelty. Swinburne spoke of Victor Hugo with boundless enthusiasm.

Wild stories about sex with the boys and the monkey, and the monkey being killed and served up for dinner, which later circulated on the Continent, show how Swinburne had become the mythic English pervert for all seasons.

By November Swinburne was back at Holmwood suffering from 'the usual November influenza': 'I am hardly let out of bed, *or* to write.' He read with pleasure the first part of Browning's *The Ring and the Book*, rejoiced over reports of Mazzini's improved health, and spent Christmas at King's College, Cambridge as a guest of Thomas Bendyshe, a senior Fellow. Swinburne described Bendyshe, a fellow Etonian and member of the Cannibal Club, as 'a raging and devoted atheist, at whose talk God trembles on his tottering throne'. Bendyshe directed Swinburne to a French translation of the Hindu classic the 'Mahabharata', about which William Rossetti noted he was 'excessively enthusiastic'. Religious questions became a major part of the thinking that fermented *Songs before Sunrise*. In part it was not just about the struggle in Italy, but Swinburne's attempt to deal with his loss of faith and fill the void Christianity had left.

For Swinburne, 1869 was a largely uneventful year. In February he wrote to Karl Blind: 'I have been the last two or three days ill in bed – and ought – medically and domestically ought – to be off to my father's.' In March Swinburne sent what would be the dedication of *Songs before Sunrise* to the dedicatee, 'Mazzini'. He told Emilie Venturi to tell Swinburne he considered it 'a splendid piece of poetry'. His prefatory note and selections from Coleridge, commissioned in 1868 by James Hain Friswell, were published. He had told Friswell, 'in my eyes his good poems have no fault, his bad poems no merit; and to disengage these from those will be a pleasure to me'. Friswell's daughter Laura remembered meeting Swinburne in her home. She had been ill and was unsuccessfully trying to get the grown-ups to reveal the identity of 'Our Lady of Pain' in 'Dolores'. Since her head ached so much, perhaps *she* was, 'at which my governess looked shocked, and advised me not to say so to my father or mother'.

Much of Swinburne's correspondence at this time was directed at assisting William Rossetti with the text of Shelley's poems. He published an essay, 'Notes on the Text of Shelley', in May. By the summer he was engaged on a review of Hugo's *L'Homme qui Rit*, which drew an admiring letter from Hugo hailing Byron, Shelley and Swinburne as 'trois republicans, trois aristocrates'. Then Swinburne was again in trouble at the Arts Club. On 24 May Munby saw him totter into the drawing room, 'drunk and childish, yet capable of brilliant incoherence' and heard on 2 June that Swinburne had invited Charles Cameron there to dine, leading to further trouble. Cameron had joined the Anthropological Society in May 1863, though he had been abroad as a diplomat for much of the 1860s. He returned from Abyssinia in July 1868, after a prolonged period of captivity. In his diary for 29 May William Rossetti noted,

> ... in the evening we went round to Brown's where were Scott, Gabriel and Swinburne who had brought round Consul Cameron ... who he has got to know through Consul Burton and for whom he seems to have conceived an excessive affection. The consul is a man of large physique, but still suffering considerably from the effects of his tethers, etc., and there is something strange and inconclusive in his demeanour, which Brown thought must arise from his having been drinking, but I should rather be inclined to attribute to his strange experiences and sufferings.

Of events at the Arts Club Munby wrote, 'Cameron, it appears is a disreputable fellow; and he and Swinburne both got drunk, made a scandalous noise in the dining room and hall, and actually – incredible dictu – embraced one another in some indecent fashion. The Committee have called on Swinburne to resign.' While Swinburne was in France in August Whistler interceded on behalf of the poet, telling the Committee, 'You accuse him of drunkenness – Well, that's his defence.' Ezra Pound's version has Whistler saying, 'You ought to be proud that there is in London a club where the greatest poet of your time *can* get drunk if he wants to, otherwise he might lie in the gutter.' Swinburne thanked Whistler 'for all your kindness, and the way in which you have got me out of the row without loss of dignity'.

In July Swinburne went on holiday to Vichy with Burton. Travelling from Paris on a hot day 'with my back to the engine, I got to feel sick as anything', but Burton's attentiveness made Swinburne feel he knew 'for the first time what it was to have an elder brother'. They arrived on 24 July. On 29 July Swinburne wrote to Powell from the Hotel de France that 'the place suits me splendidly for health' and that he was 'better than I have been for five months'. With its famous waters, Vichy was celebrated as a health resort. Swinburne enthused over a meeting with Frederick Hankey, who had assisted Lord Houghton to build his erotic library, calling him 'the Sadique collector of European fame':

> His erotic collection of books, engravings, etc, is unrivalled upon earth – unequalled, I should imagine, in heaven ... There is a

Sapphic group by Pradier of two girls in the very act – one has her tongue up où vous savez, her head and massive hair buried, plunging, diving between the other's thighs. It was the sculptor's last work before he left this world of vulgar copulation for the Lesbian Hades. May we be found as fit to depart – and may our last works be like this. Remember me 'de coeur' to my sailors.

The friends did plenty of walking, drove to Thiers – 'perched like a bird and clinging as with claws among the gorges of the mountain'. On 9 August they scaled 5000 feet of the Puy de Dôme, the summit 'wrapt in a rolling and rushing sea of mist', where Swinburne gathered flowers to send to his sister Alice. The Auvergne country impressed him as 'splendid and singular – a barren and broken land so laboriously cultivated that not an inch was left waste, and the whole stretch of it from left to right looked like a carpet of many colours'. On 13 August he wrote to his mother, praising Burton:

> if you had seen him, when the heat and the climb and the bothers of travelling were too much for me – in the very hot weather – nursing, helping, waiting on me – going out to get me books to read in bed . . . I feel sure you would like him (you remember you said you didn't and then, love him, as I do . . .)

The evenings were enlivened by Lord Leighton, and the operatic soprano of Mrs Sartoris (Adelaide Kemble), who 'plays and sings to me in private by the hour', an experience memorialized in 'An Evening at Vichy'. The detailed descriptions that fill his letters from Vichy suggest Swinburne could have written some fine travel essays. The only mishap occurred on 20 August when 'I strained or jarred my right foot in jumping from rock to rock of the Sichon at its little falls, so that yesterday I was quite disabled and had to lay it up'. Swinburne praised the cathedral of Le Puy, calling the town 'a smaller Siena – the highest praise I can give'. The abiding memories of this holiday inspired 'Auvergne in Summer' and 'Elegy 1869–91':

> Auvergne, Auvergne, O wild and woful land,
>   O glorious land and gracious, white as gleam
> The stairs of heaven, black as a flameless brand,
>   Strange even as life, and stranger than a dream . . .
>
> Thy steep small Siena, splendid and content
>   As shines the mightier city's Tuscan pride
> Which here its face reflects in radiance, pent
>   By narrower bounds from towering side to side,
>
> Set fast between the ridged and foamless waves
>   Of earth more fierce and fluctuant than the sea,
> The fearless town of towers that hails and braves
>   The heights that gird, the sun that brands Le Puy;

The huddled churches clinging on the cliffs
   As birds alighting might for storm's sake sling,
Moored to the rocks as tempest-harried skiffs
   To perilous refuge from the loud wind's wing . . .

By 31 August he was back in Paris, and spent some of September with Powell at Étretât, where he was 'rather astounded at finding myself rushed at, seized by arms and legs, hoisted and cheered, and carried all down the street with shouts of welcome, by the fisher folk and sailors who knew me again at once'. Many years later, he memorialized in 'Past Days' the two holidays where:

Above the sea and sea-washed town we dwelt,
We twain together, two brief summers, free
From heed of hours as light as clouds that melt
   Above the sea . . .

CHAPTER NINE

'Glory to Man in the Highest!'

By the end of September 1869 Swinburne had returned to London. He translated a speech of Mazzini's and wrote to Simeon Solomon, who replied, 'I wept at the recital of the boyish agonies you depicted in your last, I was doubled up with grief at the idea of so many tender posteriors quivering under the pitiless strokes of the rod, swayed, doubtless, by a man not wholly free from faults himself, but enough of a subject from which I avert my mental and physical eyes.'

Safely ensconced at Holmwood in early October, Swinburne turned his thoughts to Italy and the Anti-Catholic Council of Naples. He drafted a letter with William Rossetti supporting the Council's atheist opposition to the Oecumenical Council of Rome. On 15 October Swinburne declared, 'I feel it my mission as an evangelist and apostle (whenever necessary) to atheize the republicans and republicanize the atheists of my acquaintance.' William Rossetti asked Swinburne to modify the first draft because 'I never have professed myself, and never have been nor am, an atheist.' Two days later Swinburne replied,

> as to atheism I do not 'affirm' it in one sense any more than you do. I think that theism is simply an assumption superimposed upon a mystery, but how far (if at all) grounded it is impossible to say. What I do think is that to uphold it as indispensable to full and noble development of life is a pernicious immorality. In the absolute mystery as far as it confronts us there is at least no incoherence, no shock of moral inconsistency, as there is in theism.

The final draft, finished on 10 November, characterized the Pope as 'a poor old Italian man ... congregating at Rome the powers of darkness'. With its talk of 'the Church of priests and the Republic' being 'natural and internecine enemies' and the 'creeds or miscreeds which inflict ... upon the souls of men, the hideous and twofold penalty of blindness and eviration', it would have made an apt preface for *Songs before Sunrise*. Swinburne was inspired to write a poem in support of the Council:

> I have in my head a sort of Hymn for this Congress – as it were a 'Te Hominem Laudamus', to sing the human triumph over 'things' – the opposing forces of life and nature – and over the God of his own creation, till he attain truth, self-sufficiency, and freedom. It might end somehow thus with a cry of triumph over the decadence of a receding Deity:

> 'And the love-song of earth as thou diest sounds
>   over the graves of her Kings;
> Glory to Man in the highest! for man is the
>   master of things.'

It is interesting that the last lines came first to Swinburne, for the 'Hymn to Man' never quite shakes off the feeling it came into existence to lead up to the rhetorical flourish of the last line. However, impressive in parts, it exhibits a new philosophical strain in Swinburne's poetry:

> Thou and I and he are not gods made men for a
>   span,
> But God, if a God there be, is the substance of men
>   which is man.
> Our lives are as pulses or pores of his manifold body
>   and breath;
> As waves of his sea on the shores where birth is the
>   beacon of death.
> We men, the multiform features of man, whatsoever
>   we be,
> Recreate him of whom we are creatures, and all we
>   only are he.
> Not each man of all men is God, but God is the fruit
>   of the whole; . . .

The effort to forge a philosophy to replace the despair and nihilism of *Poems and Ballads* sparked a phase of considerable inspiration. By the end of November Swinburne had started two of the finest of *Songs before Sunrise*, 'Hertha' and 'Before a Crucifix', 'addressed to the Galilean (Ben Joseph) in a tone of mild and modified hostility which I fear and hope will exasperate his sectaries more than any abuse'. His concentration on religion led him to read articles on Islam in the *Quarterly Review* with 'intense interest as well as illumination'.

In early October Dante Gabriel Rossetti obtained a permit from the Home Office to open Lizzie Siddal's grave and recover the manuscript of his poems. On 26 October he expressed the hope that Swinburne would 'think none the worse of my feeling for the memory of one for whom I know you had a true regard'. 'I cannot tell you how rejoiced I am at the news you send me. None could have given me a truer or deeper pleasure,' replied Swinburne two days later. They renewed their correspondence, discussing in detail the text of the poems.

In November the *Fortnightly Review* published four sonnets entitled 'Intercessions' which Swinburne had written in Paris in September with 'a cold bitterness of venom which may be palatable to some tastes'. These were directed at his *bête noire* Napoleon III. William Rossetti described them as '*creepy* sort of stuff that one wouldn't even like to hear rumoured as being written of one'. Though enjoying them, he said

'I sincerely deprecate the publication, and consider that Mrs. Grundy and M. Prudhomme will be nearest the right.' Swinburne's republican ardour often produced poetry too unrelentingly bitter.

Although the religious and political poems of *Songs before Sunrise* were uppermost in Swinburne's mind during the winter of 1869, he had other projects simmering. A letter of 4 November to Edward Burne-Jones discusses possible source material for *Tristram of Lyonesse*:

> I want my version to be based on notorious facts, and to be acceptable for its orthodoxy and fidelity to the dear old story: so that Tristram may not be mistaken for his late Royal Highness the Duke of Kent, or Iseult for Queen Charlotte, or Palomydes for Mr. Gladstone ... I want to have in everything *pretty* that is of any importance, and is in keeping with the tone and spirit of the story – not burlesque or dissonant or inconsistent.

Having quit 22A Dorset Street Swinburne needed to find new lodgings. He wanted to leave Hotten, and asked William and Dante Rossetti to advise him how best to do this. F. S. Ellis was approached to take on the publication of Swinburne's next volume of poetry, though the legality of this move was uncertain. An article by Walter Pater on Leonardo da Vinci in the *Fortnightly Review* gave Swinburne the satisfaction of seeing his prose imitated. Pater later told Swinburne 'he considered them as owing their inspiration entirely to the example of my own work in the same line'.

In December he hit upon the title for his poems which had hitherto eluded him. To William Rossetti he wrote,

> I must settle on a name for my progressing book; 'Songs of the Republic' is not generally liked, and seems to myself presumptuous for any man but Hugo to take by way of title; 'Songs of the Crusade', Mazzini's proposed name, is ambiguous, and suggests by derivation the Galilean gallows. I think of calling them 'Songs before Sunrise': will you tell me how you like that – and 'before Dawn' or 'Morning'?

On 12 December Swinburne visited Jowett in Oxford. Thereafter he was at Holmwood, corresponding on Dante Gabriel's poems and his brother's text of Shelley. Swinburne anticipated the lavish praise of his 1870 review of Dante Gabriel's poems by calling 'Eden Bower' 'the most altogether triumphant poem you ever wrote ... the greatest thing done in English since Shelley's 'West Wind' in its different way – and that I think on the whole the supreme lyric of the language'. For Swinburne it was 'a most real pleasure and interest to me to watch the growth and help (if I can) in the arrangement of your poems to ever so small an extent by ever such petty suggestions of detail'. He kept up with the publications of another friend from Pre-Raphaelite Oxford days, William Morris:

I have just received Topsy's book; the Gudrun story is excellently told, I can see, and of keen interest; but I find generally no change in the *trailing* style of work; his Muse is like Homer's Trojan women ... drags her robes as she walks; I really think a Muse (when she is neither resting nor flying) ought to tighten her girdle, tuck up her skirts, and step out. It is better than Tennyson's short-winded and artificial concision – but there is such a thing as swift and spontaneous style. Top's is spontaneous and slow; and especially, my ear hungers for more force and variety of sound in the verse. It looks as if he purposely avoided all strenuous emotion or strength of music in thought and word.

Swinburne's Muse at this period was often stepping out like a fire-breathing dragon. On 16 December Swinburne sent a draft of his sonnet on Shelley 'Cor Cordium' to William Michael, who judged it 'intensely beautiful' but complained

one hears through it frequent echoes of a Galilean serpent-hiss or Jew's-harp twang, which, though perfectly appreciable in their abstract intellectual relation, and also in their conversion from the use of the enemy, do not nevertheless appear to me, I confess, the appropriate treatment.

Swinburne often failed to anticipate the predictable unease bordering on distaste even his friends felt about his parodic use of Christian imagery. He wrote brightly to William Rossetti about an idea for 'a sonnet on the Most Holy Trinity, entitled "Cerberus"', after the three-headed dog of Greek myth. Rossetti thought it sounded 'rather strong, but would depend on the treatment'.

As Christmas approached, Swinburne, spurred into action by reading Tennyson's *The Holy Grail and Other Poems*, 'fell at once tooth and nail upon Tristram and Iseult and wrote at an overture of the poem projected, all yesterday' (that is, 21 December). To Purnell Swinburne commented, 'How admirable is Tennyson's new-style Farmer – and how poor his old style Idyls of the Prince Consort – Morte d'Albert ... My first sustained attempt at a poetic narrative may not be as good as Gudrun – but if it doesn't lick the Morte d'Albert I hope I may not die without extreme unction.' Swinburne had the titles of the opening and closing cantos – 'The Sailing of the Swallow' and 'The Sailing of the Swan' – and explained, 'My poem begins with saying how Love brought these two chosen lovers through "Quanti dolci pensier, quanto disio" to everlasting hell and honour':

As you see, my verse (though the British buffer may say I am following Topsy in the choice of metre for romantic narrative) is modelled not after the Chaucerian cadence of Jason but after my own scheme of movement and modulation in Anactoria, which I consider original in structure and combination. On board ship I mean to make the innocent Iseult ask Tristram about the knights and ladies, and him tell her of Queen Morgause of Orkney and her incest with the 'blameless king', and other larks illustrative of the Alberto-Victorian purity of the Court.

During the holiday Swinburne composed the 'Christmas Antiphones', the first part (an expression of orthodox faith) for his mother. He considered making mischief by publishing it 'and enjoying the remarks of the great Briton on my conversion and return to the fold of faith and resumption of my sullied baptismal robe. There ought to be more joy over me in the Galilean camp than over ninety and nine Topsies who need no repentance.' Pulling in the reins, William Rossetti agreed this would be 'most delightful as a lark, though perhaps hardly worthy of the dignity of "le premier poète vivant de l'Angleterre"'.

On 14 January 1870 Swinburne completed 'Hertha', 'another mystic atheistic democratic anthropologic poem'. William Rossetti saw it in progress and 'admired it exceedingly – and have little doubt that it will prove one of your finest, as it is certainly one of your loftiest poems'. Swinburne believed 'Hertha' struck 'such a blow at the very root of Theism' that *Atalanta* and 'Anactoria' 'might have been written by churchmen':

> I have broken the back (not only of God, but) of the poem in question by this time, having perfected the verses necessary to combine and harmonize the connecting links of the idea; which needed to be done with all distinctness and delicacy at once, as it was not at first evident why the principle of growth, whence and by which all evil not less than all good proceeds and acts should prefer liberty to bondage.

He felt 'Hertha' was the single poem he would choose to be represented by, since 'it has the most in it of my deliberate thought and personal feeling or faith, and I think is as good in execution and impulse of expression as the best of my others'. It shows the influence of his reading of Whitman, Blake, Emerson's 'Brahma', and the 'Mahabharata':

> I am that which began;
>   Out of me the years roll;
> Out of me God and man;
>   I am equal and whole;
> God changes, and man, and the form of them bodily; I am the soul.
>
> Before ever land was,
>   Before ever the sea,
> Or soft hair of the grass,
>   Or fair limbs of the tree,
> Or the flesh-coloured fruit of my branches, I was, and thy soul was
>   in me.

. . .

> Beside or above me
>   Nought is there to go;
> Love or unlove me,
>   Unknow me or know,
> I am that which unloves me and loves; I am stricken, and I am the
>   blow.

Swinburne's intention was to deconstruct the concept of God but his use of the first person, his diction, and the prophetic tone (springing from a frustrated religious impulse) reconstruct the impression of a Supreme Being as fast as Swinburne tries to erase it. As with other poems of *Songs before Sunrise*, there is a resulting internal tension. Out of this tension would eventually come the nature poetry of his later years.

Swinburne delayed coming up to London so as to continue writing undistracted; as for the weather, 'a few more such high winds as that of this day week would make me overflow with poetry. Nothing else has so delicious and fructifying an effect on my system.' By 12 February 1870 the 'prologue or overture to Tristram' was finished:

> I have put as much fancy and light and play of colour into the prologue as possible, to throw out the tragic effect: and by the grace of the Devil I hope to make the copulative passages of the poem more warm and provocative of sinful appetite than anything my chaste Muse has yet attempted. I am much inspirited by observing the traces of my influence on younger men and boys. I trust that my present work may be the means (under Satan) of turning many a heart to perdition. But not to me be the glory.

By mid-February Swinburne had 'all but finished the centre poem and mainspring of my volume – "The Eve of Revolution". I never worked so hard at perfecting a poem into which I had put so much heart – I only hope the result will be answerable to the work I have spent on it.' He asked William Rossetti to overlook the poem to correct 'any tendency . . . to the "didactic-declamatory"'. As he said to Gabriel Rossetti, the book must avoid 'any touch of metrical stump-oratory or spread-eagleism, such as is liable to affect and infect all but the highest political or polemical poetry. I will have nothing of the platform in it if possible.'

Swinburne's letters to Dante Gabriel continued to be a mixture of line-by-line textual criticism on the latter's poems, religious parody – his 'fragment of an address from S. Joseph to S. Mary': 'So *this* is your bloody religion – / To father your kid on a pigeon?' – and bawdy, as when he imagines that Sappho 'might have sung and played to children with the same mouth and the same hand which made music on the Lesbian lyre, and on another feminine organ not necessary to specify'. Rossetti was nervous about the prospect of being reviewed by Swinburne in the *Fortnightly Review*, fearing Swinburne's hyperbole would do more damage than good, and wrote to this effect on 23 February. But Swinburne declared on the 24th, 'I shall not – to speak Topsaically – say a bloody word which is not the blasted fact. You shall see what it is to fall into the hands of a fellow craftsman.' Swinburne was determined to write a laudatory review, for 'you have done more work in more ways of the highest order, as a poet, than we'.

In March Swinburne travelled up to London to see the Old Masters' Exhibition. Dante Gabriel Rossetti lamented,

> It is most annoying to find after all that you are to be in town just after I leave it – you being of all men the one I most want to see at this moment, and indeed so does everyone. all friends are yearning for you after your long absence and hoping that it is not illness which has prolonged it.

These sentiments were echoed by Simeon Solomon, who wrote in late February, 'Are you ever coming to London again?' By 22 March Rossetti said he was vexed to be away from London, 'all the more now that I hear what splendid things you have been reading to our friends in London – the Tristram and Iseult and a poem which is no doubt the Hertha'. At Dorset Street, Swinburne saw Powell, Morris and William Rossetti. Much of *Songs before Sunrise* had now been set up in type by F. S. Ellis, with whom agreement had been reached at the end of 1869. Having completed its 'Prelude', Swinburne enjoyed William Rossetti's praise of 'The Eve of Revolution' and 'Before a Crucifix'. He was delighted to receive appreciative letters from Hugo, who had heard Swinburne described as 'le premier poète actuel de l'Angleterre'.

In London, Swinburne quickly resumed his self-destructive habits. On 25 April he confessed to the Irish poet Denis MacCarthy, 'I have been at once unwell and overwhelmed with business.' He was saddened to hear that one of his maternal cousins, F. G. Vyner, had been kidnapped and killed in Greece. William Rossetti wrote on 1 May generally praising the new poems he had read, only grudging a little

> your frequent use of Galilean machinery: not because it is blasphemous, which is an objection natural and resignable to the professors of that creed themselves, but because it looks as if we 'couldn't do without' this sphere of ideas – as if even those who profess to come out of it must really remain in it.

At the end of April Swinburne's review of Rossetti's poems appeared in the *Fortnightly Review*, claiming that 'the style of Mr. Rossetti excels that of any English poet of our day' and that his sonnets were 'better than Shakespeare in some respects': 'No one till he has read these knows all of majesty and melody, all of energy and emotion, all of supple and significant loveliness, all of tender cunning and exquisite strength, which our language can show at need in proof of its powers and uses.' The essay includes a paean to Sappho and a spirited attack on the notion that the Victorian period was somehow inferior to the past, to which Arnold had given eloquent expression in 'The Scholar-Gypsy', for 'each century has seemed to some of its children an epoch of decadence and decline in national life and spiritual, in moral or material glory; each alike has heard the cry of degeneracy raised against it'.

Swinburne discussed the review with Munby at the Arts Club on 2 May. The subject soon turned to Christianity. Munby expressed frustration at the habit of freethinkers of identifying Christianity with Roman Catholicism. Swinburne said,

> I always find myself an atheist among Christians and a Christian – I mean a philo-Christian – among atheists.' By 'atheists', he in his loose way meant freethinkers ... In the midst of his tirade, a clerical member of the Club came in; but Swinburne went on unheeding, till I turned him (variable and inconsecutive as his flow of talk is, it was easily done) into Shakespeare's sonnets. This however led to worse talk; he expressed a horror of sodomy, yet would go on talking about it; and an actual admiration of Lesbianism, being unable, as he confessed, to see that that is equally loathsome. When I expressed disgust pretty strongly, however, and regret at what he has written thereon, he took it very gently and quietly, instead of blustering, as he used to do ... this man is to me an object of grave and pathetic study: a creature he is so reckless and childish and ungovernable, so far from all sobriety and restraint, from all ordinary moral sanctions and beliefs: and yet so full of genius, of noble enthusiasm for freedom and beauty; and so genuine, and kindly in his way, and unpretending.

In Swinburne's publishing affairs, it fell to William Michael to act as an intermediary of sorts between Swinburne and Hotten. On 3 May he wrote:

> For some while past Swinburne has been impressed with the idea that, while the fame of his writings is very great, and the sale of them presumably in some proportion to correspond, the profits accruing to himself have been but moderate. This no doubt is no news to you: it was the feeling which prompted Swinburne to wish to have a clear and authenticated statement of the accounts between you and himself.

Owing to pressure from Ellis, Swinburne was driving himself to complete the poems, being 'worried about the finishing and perfecting of said book to the last shred of my nerves': 'I am seedy, weary, and crushed by the necessity of finishing some remaining poems "to order" within a given time on pain of the book appearing shorn of some of its best things.' William Rossetti replied, 'tell Ellis that the book shall only come out when it suits you, and when such pieces as you choose to insert are completed at your own discretion'. Rumours circulated about Swinburne's new volume, which as the successor to *Poems and Ballads* must have been eagerly anticipated; *The Athenaeum*'s 'Literary Gossip' column for 21 May carried this notice:

> We believe that Mr. Swinburne, in his new volume of poems, which bears the somewhat mysterious title of 'Songs before Sunrise', deals in a bold manner with the speculative questions of the day. Nearly the whole of the volume is now in type, and it will, in all probability, be published in a week or two.

But some of the poems were making Ellis nervous. As Rossetti noted in his diary on 11 May:

> Gabriel had told me yesterday that two poems of Swinburne's for the forthcoming *Songs before Sunrise* – one raising a comparison between the birth of L. Napoleon and that of Christ, and the other blaspheming the three Persons of the Trinity – are so alarming to the publisher Ellis that, when it comes to the scratch, he will absolutely decline to publish them, or the book with them included. I named this matter to Swinburne and find that he is a little put out by Gabriel's course of action in more than once (as he believes) pressing upon Ellis the objections to the publishing of these poems. Swinburne exhibited considerable excitability on this subject, but still all sorts of cordial goodwill to Gabriel. I heard the poems (among others, mostly sonnets, all very masterly). Swinburne spoke a good deal about the very strong religious Christian feelings he used to have from the age of fifteen to eighteen or so; and attributes partly to this fact the continual use which he makes of Christian or biblical framework in his poems, even when the gist of them is of the most extraneous or conflicting kind.

Gabriel Rossetti wrote to Swinburne on 12 May to remonstrate with him about the sonnets ('The Saviour of Society') in particular and the question of 'Galilean machinery' in general. The letter was sent to Ellis first, Rossetti adding, 'after all, what is to be done when (to enlarge the old saying) *Poeta nascitur non fit* for publication?'

> The supreme nobility of Christ's character should exempt it from being used ... in contact of this kind with anything so utterly ignoble as this ... You have no right to imperil your sacred relation to the minds of many men worthy to profit by your mind, by using one form of metaphor rather than another when its use involves such disproportionately grave issues ... Do, do, my dear Swinburne, withdraw these Sonnets.

Swinburne acceded to the request.

On 26 May Swinburne turned up at Rossetti's and 'an excuse was made for getting him to go away' because 'his intoxicated state menaced serious inconvenience had he been admitted'. Early in June Hotten threatened an injunction if Swinburne allowed any other publisher to bring out his work. Swinburne and William Rossetti consulted lawyers on the matter. On 8 June Meredith wrote to Gabriel Rossetti, 'Swinburne was coming, we expected; but penned a line from bed, which gives me the old uneasiness about him.' Munby saw Swinburne at the Arts Club on 15 June, sitting apart with a book, 'wildly kicking out, after his manner, at any passage that roused him'. On 23 June Swinburne wrote to William Rossetti, 'I hope you have forgiven me for breaking my appointment last week – I was very ill that day and all the week – couldn't write or do any work or business. Gabriel and Fanny have nursed me up again. I am staying here in Cheyne Walk for a few days'. Three days later Swinburne turned up at Cheyne Walk again, 'much muddled' as William Rossetti noted:

> Gabriel remonstrated very sharply with him and seemed to make some faint sort of impression. Gabriel tried (what he has long thought of) to get Swinburne to sign a written pledge for a year to come, but could not prevail on him to do so. Swinburne had recently quitted his lodgings in Dorset Street, but has now returned to them. After innumerable rows and maneouvrings, he has at last ceased to be a member of the Arts Club. The Secretary told him the other day that the question of his compulsory resignation was again about to be mooted, on account of some recent hullabaloo (of which Swinburne professed entire oblivion), and at once withdrew his name from the books of the Club. It was probably the only thing to be done; but I fear this cessation of Club membership will be a daily and serious inconvenience to him. His getting elected elsewhere seems to be most dubious.

On 8 May Whistler had warned William Rossetti that 'something of the sort is again likely to be coming up' at the Arts Club. The end of Swinburne's troubled membership came in August when Munby discovered Swinburne had resigned 'to save himself from expulsion, on account of his gross drunkenness'.

Late in the evening of 5 July William Rossetti was informed that Swinburne had been found 'raving with "delirium tremens" and that he had cut himself in smashing windows, and they do not know what to do with him'. By the time Rossetti reached Dorset Street, Swinburne had been put to bed and Dr Bird arranged for a male nurse to keep an eye on him. Rossetti went to Ford Madox Brown's and debated whether or not to contact the Admiral, 'as it seems the attack is an uncommonly bad one, and his proceedings of late more reckless than ordinary'. The next day Rossetti called again on Swinburne: 'He was again somewhat violent in the course of the day, but was sleeping when I arrived. The attendant says that Dr Bird proposed to write to his father.' The Admiral duly came up to London to retrieve his son.

On 17 July Swinburne wrote to John Thomson asking for various manuscripts and clothes to be sent to Holmwood. He adds:

> ... there was a lot of unfinished burlesque verse about swishing, such as I always amused my idlest minutes with – did you leave them there or confiscate them for Lottie's use? to keep company with Hn's pedagogic rhapsody and my unfinished story. If she likes (she asked me for it once) she is welcome during my absence to the loan of any of my drawings of flagellation, but great care must be taken not to *rub* the pencilled ones. You can take out any you please from the desk for her. I only wish she could send me such another little drawing as she once shewed me (afterwards torn up by the designer because stripes had been added by her and me in black instead of red!) it was charmingly *accurate*, and I should much prize such another with the *names* inscribed by her hand.

Thomson's address was North Lodge, South Bank, Regent's Park. With this letter is a note from F. S. Ellis saying that in 1869 Joseph Knight was aware Swinburne spent much time at this address. In 1875 Frederick Hankey mentioned that the only flagellation house he was aware of 'is in Regent's Park, a lovely little villa presided over by a well-educated lady, well-versed in the birchen mysteries. Her clientele is small but select, consisting of a few persons belonging to the higher order of society ... there come two very young girls who go through all the phases of a schoolmistress and whip fearfully severely.' It seems Lottie may be connected with North Lodge and that Swinburne had found other 'balm in Gilead' after withdrawing his patronage from the ladies in Circus Road.

On 4 August Swinburne wrote from Holmwood, 'being for some time to come under sentence of exile from London'. He read Christina Rossetti's *Commonplace and Other Short Stories*, enjoying 'the delicious description of the babies, which made me purr with pleasure and feel as if my fur was being rubbed the right way', a salutary reminder that life with Watts at The Pines after 1879 did not suddenly infect Swinburne with baby-worship. On 9 August Swinburne admitted, 'I have been far from well, but am now quite right. London and summer together always upset me more or less', and on 28 August told William Rossetti he had revised 'Cor Cordium' since 'you objected to the use of Galilean imagery' and hoped this had removed 'the slimy trail of the Galilean serpent'.

Hotten had threatened to take legal action if Swinburne gave his poems to another publisher. Swinburne felt 'it is utterly out of the question for me to return to Hotten or permit him to continue to act as my publisher after all that has come and gone'. Then news came that Hotten had 'given up the pretension to detain me by force and continue my publisher against my will', being 'ready to part company with me on terms which will leave no stigma on his character'. But Ellis postponed *Songs before Sunrise* until October, causing Swinburne more frustration.

In September 1870 Swinburne tried to find a journal to take 'At a Month's End'. It eventually came out in the *Dark Blue* (April 1871) as 'The End of a Month'. Amid his antitheistic invective, this pastel-coloured elegy for a dead love seems more human. Two lovers about to part, their love blighted, stand by the sea, reflecting on all that has transpired. The opening stanzas are reminiscent of 'The Triumph of Time':

> The night last night was strange and shaken:
>   More strange the change of you and me.
> Once more, for the old love's love forsaken,
>   We went out once more toward the sea.
>
> For the old love's love-sake dead and buried,
>   One last time, one more and no more,
> We watched the waves set in, the serried
>   Spears of the tide storming the shore.
>
> Hardly we saw the high moon hanging,
>   Heard hardly through the windy night
> Far waters ringing, low reefs clanging,
>   Under wan skies and waste white light.
>
> With chafe and change of surges chiming,
>   The clashing channels rocked and rang
> Large music, wave to wild wave timing,
>   And all the choral water sang.
>
> Faint lights fell this way, that way floated,
>   Quick sparks of sea-fire keen like eyes
> From the rolled surf that flashed and noted
>   Shores and faint cliffs and bays and skies.

Alliteration, internal rhyme, and repetition promote a mournful music, the isolation of the lovers in the midst of the elements heightened by the many plural nouns used throughout. Like 'Ave Atque Vale', 'At a Month's End' has something of colours made luminous by twilight. The consolation of the setting is held in check by the feeling of loss and grief:

> Silent we went an hour together,
>   Under grey skies by waters white,
> Our hearts were full of windy weather,
>   Clouds and blown stars and broken light.
>
> Full of cold clouds and moonbeams drifted
>   And streaming storms and straying fires,
> Our souls in us were stirred and shifted
>   By doubts and dreams and foiled desires.

Across, aslant, a scudding sea-mew
   Swam, dipped, and dropped, and grazed the sea:
And one with me I could not dream you;
   And one with you I could not be.

The lovers' feelings are projected on to the seascape. The poem garners a bitter wisdom from painful experience: 'You could not tame your light white sea-mew,/Nor I my sleek black pantheress'. In a private code, Swinburne associates the male speaker with the north and the woman with the south. The closing stanzas are blatantly erotic in their description of two leopards copulating, and images of honey and bees.

The delay of *Songs before Sunrise* was in danger of rendering the book irrelevant to the times. On 5 August William Rossetti commented, 'it is only last night that Gabriel happened to say how disastrous it is that just now – when anything of an excited political tone from you on foreign politics would ring through England and Europe – the book would be shelved'. Mathilde Blind expressed the same sentiment. Early in September Scott said, 'it is a great pity your "Songs" have not been published – a tremendous pity ... And now the tide in the affairs of men and books has set against them, they will be too late.' Scott was right; events on the Continent were to overtake the poems.

The declaration of a French Republic brought a temporary but intense joy to Swinburne early in September: 'I have been in a state of lyric discharge with brief intermission ever since the news came on Monday afternoon. An Ode literally burst out of me, which I have sent to Ellis today to print as a loose sheet or pamphlet.' Swinburne's 'Ode on the Proclamation of the French Republic, September 4th, 1870' was reviewed in *The Athenaeum* by Purnell who wrote, 'this poem shows that Mr. Swinburne is more likely than he at one time seemed to be, to do justice to his great natural powers. His conception is clearer, the expression more matured, and his feeling more regulated: in a word, he is more artistic.' Lady Jane liked it sufficiently to order several copies. As it was printed by Ellis, Hotten was angered and told Howell, 'I thought we were going to settle matters amicably.'

In mid-September Swinburne informed Scott, 'I am going to London at this rural season on business – change of lodging as well as publisher. Wish me better luck in both. I am very well, as I always am in this air.' There he met Karl Blind to discuss the Franco-German war. As the winter deepened he corrected the last proofs of *Songs*, sending the final poem, 'Tiresias', on 13 November and wrote the occasional flagellation missive to Howell. A meeting with Hotten was fixed for mid-November but William Rossetti's diary notes,

> Swinburne having breakfasted with Powell, arrived in such a muddled state that it was found impossible to proceed with the

business, and the affair still hangs over. It seems, however, that the referees agree that Swinburne ought to give Hotten the publishing of his next two books – including ... the *Songs before Sunrise*, now on the eve of publication by Ellis. The latter is said to be quite tired of Swinburne and his affairs and more than willing to resign him.

As it turned out, Ellis published *Songs before Sunrise* and then washed his hands of Swinburne.

Writing on 28 December from the British Hotel, Cockspur Street, Swinburne told John Morley he had 'for days laid up with influenza that held me fast in bed, blind, deaf, exuding, with eyes that could but water and hands that could but blow the lamentable nose'. Swinburne likened his struggle with *Songs before Sunrise* to 'the last agonies of childbirth', while being 'rent in twain between two midwives or publishers – as it might be Mrs. Gamp and Mrs. Prig – contending over me prostrate. Now – thank Something – all that is settled, Mrs. Gamp dismissed as (metaphorically) drunk and incapable – and in ten days I hope a book if not a man "will be born into the world".'

Songs before Sunrise appeared early in January 1871, four and a half years after *Poems and Ballads*. Years later Swinburne commented, 'there is no touch of dramatic impersonation or imaginary emotion. The writer of *Songs before Sunrise*, from the first line to the last, wrote simply in submissive obedience to Sir Philip Sidney's precept – "Look in thine heart, and write".' It was 'my ripest and carefullest – and out of sight my most personal and individual – work'. To the modern reader Swinburne's republican book of common prayer can seem anything but personal. Without a knowledge of mid-nineteenth-century French and Italian politics the context of the poems is lacking. The alternative, to read *Songs before Sunrise* as an allegorical drama of timeless struggle, requires a considerable leap of the imagination.

The two outstanding poems are 'Hertha' and 'Before a Crucifix'. In the second rank come 'Prelude', 'On the Downs', 'Tiresias', 'Siena', 'Hymn of Man', and 'To Walt Whitman in America'. Swinburne's diction is more limited than before, often Biblical in tone and rhythm, as he at once tries to parody and appropriate Christian language. The 'Prelude' sets out a revolutionary programme of poetic metamorphosis, as it looks back to the pagan eroticism of *Poems and Ballads*:

Play then and sing; we too have played,
We likewise, in that subtle shade.
　We too have twisted through our hair
　Such tendrils as the wild Loves wear,

The figure of Youth turns its back on irresponsibility, rejecting 'doubt and faith and fear,/Swift hopes and slow despondencies' for a creed of self-reliance and a soul-communing with 'With the actual earth's equalities,/Air, light, and night, hills, winds, and streams,/And seeks not strength from strengthless dreams.' *Songs before Sunrise* aimed to replace the kingdom of heaven with the kingdom of time. 'On the Downs', for example, evokes a vision of unity in all life:

> A multitudinous monotone
> Of dust and flower and seed and stone,
>   In the deep sea-rock's mid-sea sloth,
> In the live water's trembling zone,
>   In all men love and loathe,
>   One God at growth.

The identity of this 'one forceful nature uncreate/That feeds itself with death and fate' was interpreted by some as the compulsion of evolution in matter; by others as a metaphysical life-force.

The book's onslaught against Christianity is unrelenting. In 'Blessed Among Women', 'Genesis' and 'Hertha' Swinburne writes his own Creation myth. In 'Mater Triumphalis' he refers to Liberty as 'the resurrection and redemption,/The godhead and the manhood and the life'. There is frequent appropriation of the eucharist, as in 'Christmas Antiphonies', where Freedom gives 'her body blest/And the soul's wine shed'. Margot Louis comments that Swinburne's 'negative use of eucharistic imagery . . . was meant to produce that sense of liberation which comes from desecrating old sanctities . . . implicitly criticizes what he perceives as the central expression of Christian devotion . . . and happily exploits the emotional connotations of the Eucharist to sanctify the various deities which he evolves for himself'.

The Church is attacked as the purveyor of beliefs that in Blakeian terms are 'mind-forged manacles'. 'Before a Crucifix' succeeds because of its unifying central image and its specificity:

> Here, down between the dusty trees,
>   At this lank edge of haggard wood,
> Women with labour-loosened knees,
>   With gaunt backs bowed by servitude,
> Stop, shift their loads, and pray, and fare
> Forth with souls easier for the prayer.
>
> The suns have branded black, the rains
>   Striped grey this piteous God of theirs;
> The face is full of prayers and pains,
>   To which they bring their pains and prayers;
> Lean limbs that shew the labouring bones,
> And ghastly mouth that gapes and groans.

In the 1900 years since its founding, Christianity is depicted as having corrupted and betrayed its founder's original message ('Christian creeds

that spit on Christ'), where that Gospel was not in itself a delusion. The
Cross is 'Consumed of rotteness and rust'; Christ can no longer be
loved because it is impossible to divorce Him from His Church, 'because of whom we dare not love thee;/Though hearts reach back and
memories ache'. The poem rises to a powerful, and passionate conclusion of controlled denunciation:

> Nay, if their God and thou be one,
>   If thou and this thing be the same,
> Thou shouldst not look upon the sun;
>   The sun grows haggard at thy name.
> Come down, be done with, cease, give o'er;
> Hide thyself, strive not, be no more.

'Before a Crucifix' is one of the finest responses to the crisis of faith in
Victorian poetry.

Songs before Sunrise did have a personal side. Swinburne's desire for
self-transcendence focused itself on the ideal Republic, sublimating his
longings to a utopian aim – with Mazzini, Italy, and Liberty as figures
before whom he could abase himself. *Poems and Ballads* enacted the
destruction of Swinburne's High Anglicanism and trust in providence.
Songs before Sunrise quests for a philosophy to fill that void, a void not
only of metaphysics but of feeling. No one seems to have commented
on just how angry a book it is, not only on behalf of the oppressed, but
springing from his own sense of betrayal. Swinburne's intellect and
emotional instincts were at war over the question of God. He could
dispense with a personal God, expending that emotion on literary Olym-
pians, but he needed a vision that could spark awe and the loss of self in
the contemplation of some greater sublimity. *Songs before Sunrise* was
Swinburne's personal battleground over the loss of the opportunity for
ecstatic release through religion. In this light *Songs before Sunrise*
appear as an integral part of his own development, not simply lyrics for
the Crusade delivered by request to Mazzini. The poems may have been
left high and dry by the tides of European politics, but not by the
estranging sea of Swinburne's loss of faith.

On 14 January *The Saturday Review* printed a hostile review: 'Much
as he delights in what used in our younger days to be called blasphemy,
he delights still more, if that were possible, in the reddest of Red
Republicanism.' *The Athenaeum* criticized the pantheism and republicanism of poems such as the 'Hymn of Man' and 'Before a Crucifix',
but others, for example, 'Hertha' and 'On the Downs' received some
praise. The book was virtually ignored in America, its focus too European to bridge the Atlantic's divide.

In the early months of 1871 Swinburne lived a vagrant existence. In
February he saw Solomon and Burton, friends 'in the Cannibal faith'.

Rumours of another collapse reached Holmwood. On 9 February his mother told Gabriel Rossetti 'we are in great trouble about Algernon':

> ... his father received a letter this morning telling him that Algernon was again in the state in which he has four times been obliged to go and insist upon his coming home. This time the summons come when neither the Admiral nor myself are able to leave him on account of illness. We sent his old nurse a most trustworthy person hoping she would find him and persuade him to return to us when he heard that we were ill. You know how she has failed ... You know too well what cause we have for anxiety about our son. There is nothing that we have not tried to induce him to remain with us, but after 2 or 3 months it is impossible to keep him and at his age we cannot use force. He has never met with anything but the most affectionate kindness from his father and he had been told most forcibly by medical men both here and in London how fatal such a course must be.

Rossetti advised Swinburne to go home and informed his parents things were not as bad as they feared. The Admiral replied, 'that which you mention respecting my Son's present state is a relief to us, and I hope that the letter you addressed to him may induce him to come home, where he is free from the temptations which he seems to be quite incapable of resisting'. Swinburne answered this letter, explaining that he was staying with John Thomson but withholding the address. On 11 February Lady Jane wrote to Rossetti:

> We do most earnestly wish that he would not take lodgings in Town at all events for the present – and we urged him when he was here to have anything he wanted in the way of furniture and books sent down here. I fear his having his books would not keep him here – it is impossible but a mind like his should require the society of persons with minds and pursuits similar to his own, unless he could make up his mind to remain here as a means of conquering his fearful propensity – for a time he is perfectly happy and his health as good as possible, he says how much better he can work here and how much better he feels.

By 10 March Swinburne was at Holmwood, asking Thomson to send on some Greek classics and the transcript of *A Year's Letters* 'as I shall have more time here than in London to revise it', adding 'I shall be here for some time'. He stayed at home until August 1871, with the occasional trip to London. A dissolute life was by now perceptibly taking its toll even of his seeming indestructable resilience, as William Rossetti noted:

> He looks not well – but still not very particularly ill. His own statement is that he has been much afflicted with influenza that still hangs about him, but not to any serious extent now. His voice is extraordinarily changed; when in a tolerably deep key, has a

> hollow rumbling husky sound: at other times it has a jarring acute
> tone. Whether this indicates the lung-disease that has been talked
> of lately I know not . . . I alluded to the matter in the course of the
> evening, attributing his vocal peculiarity to the influenza; Gabriel
> tells me that the same peculiarity has now existed for some while.

In a letter of 26 April to George Powell, Swinburne writes of having 'a
slightly relaxed throat which has to be nursed. I take twice a day (*not*
together) quinine inside and salt water outside, and am strengthening
thereby.' This letter and those to Solomon contained a certain amount
of ribald humour. Swinburne's review of Solomon's *A Vision of Love
Revealed in Sleep* appeared in the *Dark Blue* for July, and much of April
and May was expended on an essay about John Ford for the *Fortnightly
Review*.

Swinburne told Frederick Locker on 17 May, 'I shall not come to
London just at present, for reasons sanitary, pecuniary, and other.' On 3
June Swinburne attended a dinner at Balliol. Among Jowett's guests
were the French historian Hippolyte Taine, Arnold and Mrs Humphrey
Ward, who noted Swinburne's 'small lower features and slender neck
over-weighed by his thick reddish hair and capacious brow':

> I could not think why he seemed so cross and uncomfortable. He
> was perpetually beckoning to the waiters, then, when they came,
> holding peremptory conversation with them; while I from my side
> of the table could see them going away, with a whisper or a shrug
> to each other, like men asked for the impossible. At last with a
> kind of bound, Swinburne leapt from his chair and seized a copy of
> the *Times*, which he seemed to have persuaded one of the men to
> bring him. As he got up I saw that the fire behind him, and very
> close to him, must indeed have been burning the very marrow out
> of a long-suffering poet. And alack, in that house without a mis-
> tress, the small conveniences of life, such as fire-screens, were often
> overlooked. . . . In a pale exasperation Swinburne folded the *Times*
> over the back of his chair, and sat down again. Vain was the effort!
> The room was narrow, the party large, and the servants pushing
> by, had soon dislodged the *Times*. Again and again did Swinburne
> in a fury replace it; and was soon reduced to sitting silent and wild-
> eyed, his back firmly pressed against the chair and the newspaper,
> in a concentrated struggle with fate.

Gosse states that Swinburne was in Oxford for several days, visiting
Walter Pater at Brasenose and Ingram Bywater at Exeter College.

Later in the month Jowett came to Holmwood. Recalling his
rustification from Oxford in 1859, Swinburne found it ironic that he
was entertaining the Master of Balliol at his father's house. 'If M. de
Sade were now alive, perhaps he might take the chair at a meeting of
the Society for the Protection of Women and Children.' He worked on
Bothwell, the second part of his trilogy about Mary Queen of Scots,

and had the first act set up in type. 'I study Shakespeare constantly, Anthony and Cleopatra especially, to try if I can learn and catch the trick of condensing all this and cramming a great mass of public events into the compass of a few scenes or speeches without deforming or defacing the poem.' He could not; *Bothwell* grew and grew.

Having left Dorset Street, Swinburne took rooms in Salisbury Street for a couple of weeks in July to see the Comédie Française act. While in London Swinburne made himself ill yet again, his father having to come and fetch him. Gabriel Rossetti wrote to Brown,

> I heard of the frightful scenes in Salisbury St. It seems permanent *delirium tremens* became rapidly the order of the day, with constant calls on Urizen père et fils ... These became so fervent that all the old lodgers were packing up and leaving when I heard about it, and the landlady spent her time in blessing the name of Mr. Knight who had brought her such a piece of luck.

Swinburne confessed, 'of course I was very much vexed with my own folly in having made myself ill, and ashamed to think of my friends knowing it was my own fault; but I trust to keep as I now am in good health and sense'. On 20 July Rossetti replied to Brown, 'what you say about Swinburne is deplorable', and he hoped Swinburne's condition 'is not more catastrophic than in previous instances'. William Rossetti stayed out of the picture because he did not want Swinburne to find out about a planned trip to Italy, as 'he might propose to accompany me – with what result to my comfort and peace of mind in travelling I leave you to surmise'.

By mid-August 1871 Swinburne was in Scotland with Jowett and various other Balliol men, including Edwin Harrison, a correspondent of Swinburne's well into the 1890s. Writing to George Powell from Tummel Bridge, Pitlochry, on 24 August, Swinburne said 'I must "purge and live cleanly" like Falstaff, or the devil will have me before his time.' News of Swinburne's attempt at recuperation reached *The Athenaeum* which notified its readers on 26 August that 'Mr Swinburne has gone to Scotland for the benefit of his health'. Swinburne reported, 'there is a good swimming river here and the heights and views are stunning'. Browning, who was nearby, paid them a visit. Swinburne's fame prompted a number of locals to attend the nearby church in the hope of seeing the notorious poet. Some went away thinking they had seen Swinburne, mistaking a young man with dark hair and whiskers 'for me – who was at that sacred hour on the flat of my back reading a novel'.

The walking tour took Swinburne through Glencoe and up the Caledonian Canal to Inverness and thence to the West Highlands, to Loch Maree and Torridon:

the divinest combination of lake, mountains, straits, sea-rocks, bays, gulfs, and open sea ever achieved by the forces of Hertha in her most favourable and fiercely maternal mood. I had a divine day there (the day before yesterday) and swam right out of one bay round a beautiful headland to the next and round again back under shelves of rock shining double in the sun above water and below.

Tummel Bridge he found 'pretty but much defiled by memories and memorials of the royal family':

At the waterfalls, significant of who shall say what other effusions? Her Majesty has set up – I should say erected – a phallic emblem in stone; a genuine Priapic erection like a small obelisk, engraved with her name and the date of the event commemorated, whatever that may have been. It is an object which would assuredly have caused 'our orphan' to blush, and shed a few tears.

Loch Torridon inspired a poem of the same name (dedicated to Edwin Harrison). It describes how they arrived at night from Maree, and Swinburne's ecstasy on seeing the ocean at sunrise:

And the dawn leapt in at my casement: and there,
     as I rose, at my feet
No waves of the landlocked waters, no lake submissive
     and sweet,
Soft slave of the lordly seasons, whose breath may
     loose it or freeze;
But to left and to right and ahead was the ripple
     whose pulse is the sea's.
From the gorge we had travelled by starlight the
     sunrise, winged and aflame,
Shone large on the live wide wavelets that shuddered
     with joy as it came;
As it came and caressed and possessed them, till
     panting and laughing with light
From mountain to mountain the water was kindled
     and stung to delight.

By mid-September he was at his uncle's Sir Henry Gordon at Knockspock, Kinnethmont, Aberdeen, where his family were gathered, and where he may have seen Mary Leith and her husband. Scotland had been a tonic: 'I am grown stout and sunburnt and (for the present) exemplify les prosperités de la vertu. But', added Swinburne, 'I remember the words of wisdom, and keep ever in mind the doom of virtue.'

CHAPTER TEN

'A Rain and Ruin of Roses'

Swinburne returned south with his family on 22 September 1871, saying he would follow them to Holmwood in a day or so after visiting
London. On 29 September he wrote to the Admiral, 'saying he hoped
he would be down on Saturday'. The Admiral told Frederick Locker,
'the note is badly written and this is Monday [that is, three days later].
We cannot help being anxious about him and I should go up to look
after him but that I am not well enough to leave home.' In the event the
Admiral went up to London and on 4 October related how 'with great
difficulty I have persuaded my son to accompany me home'. At
Holmwood later that day, Charles Henry explained that his son had
been 'very unwilling'

> to leave London feeling, and certainly appearing, much better
> than I should have thought possible last night. Yesterday's morn-
> ing post brought a letter warning us of his condition and urging
> his immediate removal, on receipt of which I felt compelled to go
> up to town at once. I do not think that he would have yielded to
> any other person's desire that he should go home this morning
> and I can only hope that he may be persuaded to remain for the
> present at least.

Swinburne's account to Purnell on 10 October was different:

> I was obliged to come down here more hastily than I had expected,
> having been very unwell for a day or two, and some fool and rascal
> having (unknown to me) *again* terrified my people here with news
> that I was risking health etc. in town and must be looked after – so
> my father came up and carried me off, literally out of bed, having a
> doctor's word that I wanted country air. I told him I had business
> (meaning with you) of immediate importance to keep me in town
> or bring me back at once.

Swinburne's version of events to Powell in November suggests his father's concern was justified:

> I have been very seedy since I saw you last, and suffered much in
> mind *and* body. My father came up to town again and was most
> kind – got my things packed up for the warehouse and carried
> away, and brought me finally out of that damned hole where I was
> dying for want of air and light. There were most unpleasant and
> irritating circumstances connected with it which I may tell you
> when we meet.

In October Simeon Solomon patched up a disagreement with Swinburne
that had arisen over his review of *A Vision of Love Revealed in Sleep*.
Solomon felt the review's praise might be incriminating:

> When you sent the M.S. and I read it, I saw and appreciated the
> full beauty of the paper and the great honor that had been done to
> me by the most brilliant of our writers, but I saw that there were
> certain parts which I could not have desired to be omitted but I
> dared not ask you to eliminate or even to modify them, for I
> thought it would have been a liberty, and, as a beggar who had so
> large a boon conferred upon him, I felt it would have been unjusti-
> fiable.

Friends of Solomon's had said they thought it would do him harm, since
'my designs and pictures executed during the last three or four years
have been looked upon with suspicion'. Swinburne had taken offence,
but at the end of the month Solomon wrote, 'I was so pleased and
relieved by your last letter and the kind manner in which you so
completely exonerated me from the charge of ingratitude and ungracious-
ness'.

Early in November Swinburne was annoyed to be once more the
target for a novelist's ridicule, in Mortimer Collins's serial *Two Plunges
for a Pearl*, available as a book in 1872. Swinburne complained that his
alter ego, the 'pigmy poet' Reginald Swynfen, 'with the name and
family connexions and titles of poems given at all but full length, is
made to go through all ludicrous and disgraceful experiences imagin-
able in the brain of a blackguard'. Gabriel Rossetti persuaded Swinburne
to let it pass. Then he found himself under attack.

In October 1871 Robert Buchanan published 'The Fleshly School of
Poetry' in the *Contemporary Review* under the pseudonym of 'Thomas
Maitland'. It was a powerful depreciation of Rossetti, although
Swinburne was also ridiculed. As Christopher Murray said, 'there is a
certain terrible inevitability to the "Fleshly" controversy. Swinburne's
prickly sense of honour and his provocations to the bourgeois found
their answer in Buchanan's dogged fearlessness and sturdy Philistinism.'
The animus between Buchanan and the Pre-Raphaelites went back to
the mid-1860s. Buchanan lost the opportunity to edit a selection from
Keats to William Rossetti, whose defence of Swinburne in 1866 had
referred to 'the advent of so poor and pretentious a poetaster as Robert
Buchanan'. He had attacked *Poems and Ballads* in August 1866 and
Swinburne in 'The Session of the Poets'. Swinburne's 'Matthew Arnold's
New Poems' (1867) criticized the Scottish poet David Gray with whom
Buchanan felt strong personal as well as literary ties. In 1872 Buchanan
admitted, 'when these men, not content with outraging literature, vio-
lated the memory of David Gray, I made a religious vow to have no

mercy'. Buchanan then attacked Swinburne in *The Spectator* article 'Swinburne as Critic' and there were further skirmishes over Whitman in 1868.

Relations between Buchanan and Swinburne were tepid enough in the spring of 1869 for the former to invite Swinburne to a reading of his poetry on 25 January. Swinburne received the invitation too late and dropped Buchanan a polite note to that effect. Swinburne did attend a reading on 3 March. It is probable this was not a success, 'for soon after this Buchanan mentioned to Robert Browning the "intense personal antagonism" between them'. Buchanan caused more annoyance when in January 1870 he criticized William Rossetti's edition of Shelley. Swinburne's review of Rossetti's *Poems* in May 1870 further antagonized Buchanan since it challenged those who think that 'beauty and power of expression can accord with emptiness or sterility of matter' – of which he had been accused – 'or that impotence of articulation must imply depth and wealth of thought' – an allusion to Buchanan's high opinion of David Gray.

In March 1871 Buchanan wrote of the Pre-Raphaelites:

> ... England happens to be infested at present by a school of poetic thought which threatens frightfully to corrupt, demoralise, and render effeminate the rising generation; a plague from Italy and France; a school aesthetic without vitality, and beautiful without health; a school of falsettoes innumerable – false love, false picture, false patriotism, false religion, false life, false death, all lurking palpable or disguised in the poisoned chalice of a false style.

A footnote accused Swinburne of 'vilifying a dead man' (that is, David Gray).

The title of Buchanan's 'The Fleshly School of Poetry' was inspired by Swinburne's half-dozen uses of 'fleshly' in his review of Gabriel Rossetti's poems. Buchanan condemned Rossetti's competence both as a painter and a poet, criticized Swinburne for his 'hysteric tone and over-loaded style' and ridiculed the more offensive poems of 1866 as 'only a little mad boy letting off squibs ... "I *will* be naughty!" screamed the little boy; but, after all, what did it matter?' For several weeks there were rumours and counter-rumours concerning the identity of 'Thomas Maitland'. Sidney Colvin replied for Rossetti in *The Academy* for October 1871. Rossetti, counselled by his brother, abandoned a pamphlet reply, confining himself instead to a letter 'The Stealthy School of Criticism' in *The Athenaeum* for 16 December. By 27 October Swinburne was at work on his own essay *Under the Microscope*, eventually published in the summer of 1872.

Swinburne remained at Holmwood until early December when he went to Oxford to see Jowett. Swinburne joked to his mother, 'I am happy to note a steady progress in the university of sound and thorough Republican feeling among the younger fellows of colleges as well as the undergraduates. A Fellow of Wadham is secretary of a Republican Club just established here; and under these circumstances I find my position and influence properly recognised.' He then went to London where Brown found him a lodging at 12 Upper Woburn Place, Euston Square, near to William Rossetti, to the latter's consternation: 'I am rather afraid this vicinity, combined with Swinburne's unruly habits, will entail some inconveniences upon me at no distant date: for the present evening, Swinburne, though not absolutely unaffected by liquor, was well enough, and perfectly pleasant in demeanour.'

Swinburne was at Woburn Place until the New Year. Brown called and 'found him there in bed in the back kitchen, with all the house bells just above his bed, and constantly on the ring. Apparently he had been transferred to this ineligible site by the people of the house, on some occasion of his being incapable of taking care of himself.' The landlady Mrs Thompson asked Swinburne to leave for causing so much trouble, having, in William Rossetti's words, 'relapsed into his horrible drinking-habits':

> This lady and another younger one who was in the sitting-room with her, had evidently no small liking and regard for Swinburne but had found him impossible as a lodger. It seems he is now with (or *probably* with) Powell – whose acquaintance has, if what I fear is correct, been a very disastrous thing for Swinburne, confirming him in the drinking habits he was already too prone to. The landlady says that a Dr. Duncan ... was in attendance on Swinburne, and got him to give his word of honour that he would drink no more spirits. This was only two or three days ago. Swinburne has now implored the Dr. to release him from his promise, but the Dr. refuses. So much the better – though I am afraid not even such an obligation as this would or could prove a safeguard for long.

In January 1872 he took lodgings at 12 North Crescent, Bedford Square.

This year saw the end of two of Swinburne's significant relationships and the beginning of a third that eventually saved his life. On 10 March Mazzini died. Emilie Venturi wrote to Swinburne the next day, 'the worst sorrow is fallen. Our angel is gone.' On 12 March Swinburne went to a party at Dr Westland Marston's in Chalk Farm; 'overcome by Mazzini's death' he 'arrived inebriated, and had to be concealed down stairs'. The same day he lamented to Lady Jane, 'I have lost the man whom I most loved and honoured of all men on earth. I am not in the humour to write about it, or to think just yet more than I can help ... But of course you and my father will know that it is a great loss to me as it is to the world which was not worthy of the great and good man now removed from it.'

On 6 April the Admiral called on William Rossetti, 'wishing to learn any news of his son'. Swinburne's letters home were becoming infrequent. He had not been at 12 North Crescent the previous evening. 'The Admiral says that the family, as a measure of precaution, drink no wine when Swinburne is with them.' In April Swinburne was at Balliol, writing to ask John Morley if he could review Hugo's new book. He told his mother on 26 April that Jowett was 'the most hospitable of men' and 'I was always welcome for as long as I pleased to stay'.

At this time Swinburne was busy with *Bothwell* and by early May had taken up *Under the Microscope*, reading parts to Gabriel Rossetti. Despite the slightly laboured irony, *Under the Microscope* is an engaging critical essay. He was at pains to establish that 'it was not ... a reply to or an attack on that son of a Scotch bitch who was merely noticed at the end'. Swinburne valued it as a piece of critical prose 'more than I usually do on any other improvisations in that line'. He argued: 'the satirical husk ... is *not* the kernel of it';

> ... the serious part, to which the rest is but mere fringe and drapery, is in the body of the work and consists in the examination of certain critical questions of the day regarding Byron, Tennyson, and Whitman; questions on which I had long been moved to speak my mind and deliver myself of what I believed to be the plain truth as against foes and friends alike of each poet; ... I confess also that I felt some satisfaction in administering to a scurrilous liar and coward such a public castigation (my father calls the pamphlet by the naval name of 'the cat-o'-nine tails') as should make it next to impossible for the dog ever again to hold up his besmired head in sight of other dogs or men.

It was affection for a friend rather than 'personal irritation' that had provoked his savaging of Buchanan:

> To me, who can truthfully say (though evidently the criticasters would rather die than believe or at least admit that they believe it) that no attack ever gave me a quarter of an hour's vexation or deprived me of five minutes rest, it is simply incomprehensible and indeed somewhat provoking to find that others can suffer from the bite of such reptiles as have no sting for me; but (between ourselves) both from what I saw with real pain myself and yet more from what Brown told me I could not but recognize the deplorable truth that the vilest of living scribblers had power to inflict grave annoyance and serious suffering on one of the noblest and to me dearest among men and poets.

This was self-deception. Adverse criticism always roused Swinburne's fury and he could never resist entering the lists. The allusion to Rossetti also explains an insensitive comment in the pamphlet, where Swinburne refers to Carlyle's opinion 'that if any poet or other literary creature could really be "killed off by one critique" or many, the sooner he was so despatched the better; a sentiment in which I for one humbly but heartily concur'.

Under the Microscope deploys a satirical metaphor for the examination of such insignificant creatures as critics, since 'a critic is, at worst, but what Blake once painted the ghost of a flea'. Swinburne argues the relative merits of Tennyson and Byron in the light of an anonymous review in the *Quarterly Review* and Austin's *The Poetry of the Period*, and is especially sarcastic toward those who believe Byron 'the greatest lyric poet of England'. The same critics would be happy to inform us

> that our greatest dramatic poet was Dr. Johnson, our greatest comic poet was Sir Isaac Newton, our best amatory poet was Lord Bacon, our best religious poet was Lord Rochester, our best narrative poet was Joseph Addison, and our greatest epic poet was Tom Moore. Add to these facts that Shakespeare's fame rests on his invention of gunpowder and Milton's on his discovery of vaccination . . .

Swinburne makes wicked fun of Tennyson's Arthurian cycle, re-naming it the Morte d'Albert, and arguing that 'the moral tone of the Arthurian story has been on the whole lowered and degraded by Mr. Tennyson's mode of treatment'. Tennyson had reduced Arthur 'to the level of a wittol, Guenevere to the level of a woman of intrigue, and Launcelot to the level of a "co-respondent"'. As for Vivien, Swinburne had no objection to the portrayal of an 'unchaste woman' provided that she were presented with 'some trace of human or if need be of devilish dignity':

> The Vivien of Mr. Tennyson's idyl seems to me, to speak frankly, about the most base and repulsive person ever set forth in serious literature. Her impurity is actually eclipsed by her incredible and incomparable vulgarity – ('O *ay*,' said Vivien, '*that were likely too*'). She is such a sordid creature as plucks men passing by the sleeve.

With regard to Austin's objection that contemporary poets spent all their time writing verse about women, 'Austin "hardly likes to own sex with" a man who devotes his life to the love of a woman, and is ready to lay down his life and to sacrifice his soul for the chance of preserving her reputation.' Swinburne observed, 'it is probable that the reluctance would be cordially reciprocated'. After a digression on Whitman and an attack on James Russell Lowell, *Under the Microscope* takes the hammer to Buchanan, whom Swinburne castigates for hiding behind a cloak of anonymity, before mentioning 'one David Gray, a poor young poeticule'. *Under the Microscope* did not sell in great numbers and was never reprinted by Swinburne. It was later listed in a German catalogue of the year's scientific publications in Europe.

Initially there had been 'little or no real idea of publishing it'. Events soon changed. On 15 May Gabriel Rossetti went to see his brother with Buchanan's reprint of *The Fleshly School of Poetry and Other Phenomena of the Day* as a pamphlet, disturbed by the use of the word 'cowards' on the first page, which he took as applying to himself, and allusions to his adulterous affair with Jane Morris. William advised him it was 'highly desirable that he should hold utterly aloof from controversy, and leave it to wrangle itself out as best it may'.

As William Rossetti predicted, the pamphlet renewed the controversy and there was no shortage of people coming forward to argue for or against it. Gabriel Rossetti was further upset by the *Echo* review of Buchanan on 18 May, which Buchanan secretly authored. In it he ridiculed his own pamphlet, suggesting that Rossetti and Swinburne must be the 'veriest aestheticised simulacra of humanity' Buchanan thought them if they did not reply to his charges. On 27 May Rossetti told Joseph Knight, 'I have the right to adopt a tone raising me above the question' and that he would hold himself aloof. It was agreed that Swinburne, while avoiding any direct references to Rossetti, should proceed with his own pamphlet. Late in May, ill through drink, his father in Italy, Swinburne was unable to deal with any business. Ellis declined to publish *Under the Microscope*. The final blow for Rossetti came with a piece in *The Saturday Review* which, damning enough of Buchanan, was equally damning of Rossetti and Swinburne. They were attacked for

> sickly self-consciousness, their emasculated delight in brooding over and toying with matters which healthy manly men put out of their thoughts, not by an effort, but unconsciously by a natural and wholesome instinct – it is, in short, their utter unmanliness which is at once so disgusting, and, so far as they exercise any influence, so mischievous.

The next day Rossetti collapsed. On 2 June William Rossetti spent 'all day with Gabriel at Chelsea – a day of extreme distress and anxiety on account of the nervous and depressed condition into which Gabriel has allowed himself to get worked'. On 8 June, gripped with paranoia and depression, Rossetti attempted suicide.

These events led directly to the end of Swinburne's and Rossetti's fifteen-year relationship. Perhaps he could no longer tolerate Swinburne's high-strung temperament and drinking, or blamed Swinburne for having sparked the whole business. It could not have helped that word got round in June that Swinburne and Sandys had been overheard in a restaurant talking loudly about Rossetti's collapse. In July Scott told William Rossetti of his brother's desire not to see Swinburne any more, and William was left to find a tactful way of conveying the news. He wrote on 5 July, 'explaining that, if he should be in the way of meeting Gabriel in Scotland, he ought to avoid rather than seek him. I put the thing in a form which I am satisfied Swinburne will appreciate, and not resent.' Swinburne replied:

> Many thanks for your note – I shall of course take every precaution against a meeting. It is of course a grief to me to be debarred from shewing the same attention and affection as friends who can hardly love him better – as indeed I think no man can love his friend more than I love Gabriel – but I know it can be from no doubt of my attachment that he shrinks from seeing me as yet.

The 'as yet' became forever: they were neither to meet nor correspond again.

The controversy burned itself out, though Buchanan and Swinburne were to clash again in 1876. Buchanan wrote a feeble rhymed response to *Under the Microscope* titled 'The Monkey and the Microscope'. In later years Buchanan drastically revised his opinion of Rossetti's art and poetry, and admitted that he had been wrong and Swinburne's estimate of Rossetti had been essentially right.

In July, Swinburne headed north to Scotland with Jowett, where he remained till 5 August. After a 'very jolly day' in Edinburgh, the party of five Balliol men reached Grantown, 'a small town or village' Swinburne told Powell, 'with a fine rapid river (the Spey) winding under fir-woods between banks clothed with broom and wild roses, and with birch enough at hand for the bottoms of all Eton'. By 18 July Swinburne was at Tummel Bridge, reporting he was 'very well here, with lots of climbing, bathing, and walking . . . I certainly am, and Jowett has remarked it to me, very much stronger and up to far more walking and climbing work than I was last year.' They climbed the Schiehallion, the highest mountain in that part of the Highlands, and Swinburne enthused over some bathing pools he had found. Harrison wrote to his mother from Tummel Bridge:

> Swinburne enlivens the place wonderfully. Elliot and Gillespie are boating men by nature – good pleasant fellows – but somewhat silent at table, so that the burden of talk would fall on me, but for Swinburne, whose paradoxes and extravagances and recitations of Mrs Gamp are a godsend.

Swinburne and Jowett indulged in 'capping quotations from Boswell against each other ad infinitum'. One day Swinburne read a scene from *Bothwell* to Jowett, who thought it needed cutting down. The next morning Swinburne stayed in bed re-working the scene, and appeared at lunch triumphant with the new version – which was three lines longer than it had been. One day Harrison and Swinburne went on a long and demanding walk. Under the effects of tiredness and aching

feet, Swinburne became depressed, but when they chanced upon a
waterfall he forgot his aches and became in an instant ecstatic with
delight. Swinburne helped Jowett revise *The School and Children's
Bible*, the Master observing, 'I wanted you to help me make this book
smaller, and you have persuaded me to make it much larger.' It may
have been on this visit (or in 1871) that Jowett, Swinburne and Harrison
went to a house on Loch Tummel and met Browning and his son for
dinner. After an animated talk Harrison recalled how they journeyed
home by starlight.

In London Powell was finding Swinburne somewhere to live and
dealing with his last landlady, with whom there was a disagreement
over money. A glimpse of what she had to tolerate is given in Swinburne's
allusion to 'any extra trouble in attendance or nursing, and hastiness of
temper in time of illness which I may have shown'. On 20 September
Swinburne wrote, 'I am overwhelmed on all sides with more or less
pressing bills till my power of work is quite interfered with, and my
pleasure in it spoilt by irritation and waste of time temper. I have a
fearful cold too, am stone deaf, and have had three of my few remaining double teeth out at once.' Powell superintended the move of
Swinburne's possessions to 3 Great James Street at the end of October,
after Swinburne had spent ten days in Oxford with Jowett.

Mazzini had died, and Swinburne was estranged from Dante Rossetti.
But in the autumn of 1872 a man who would change the course of
Swinburne's life made contact with the poet. Walter Theodore Watts
was a solicitor with literary ambitions, an intimate of many in the Pre-
Raphaelite circle. The earliest documented meeting between Watts and
Swinburne was 3 October 1872 at a dinner given by Madox Brown.
Their apocryphal first meeting was an unusual one. Watts had rented
rooms at 15 Great James Street. Armed with a letter of introduction
from Rossetti, Watts called at Swinburne's rooms:

> His tappings at the door met with no response, and he entered to
> find an empty sitting room. But from the bedroom (presumably)
> beyond there were sounds of stirring, and after having again tried
> to procure permission to penetrate further, he opened the door. He
> found Swinburne stark naked with his aureole of red hair flying
> round his head, performing a Dionysiac dance, all by himself in
> front of a large looking glass. Swinburne perceived the intruder, he
> rushed at him, and before Mr. Watts-Dunton could offer any ex-
> planation or deliver his letter of introduction, he was flying in
> panic helter-skelter down the stairs, and was driven by the enraged
> Corybant off the premises.

Born in 1832 in St Ives, Huntingdonshire, Watts was the son of a
prosperous country solicitor. After attending a private school in Cambridge, he entered the legal profession, which eventually drew him from

10.1   Theodore Watts-Dunton at 55

St Ives to London. His interest in literature and art, and his ambition to write, led him in time to Gabriel Rossetti. From 1872 Watts was a frequent visitor to Rossetti at Kelmscott Manor. By the mid-1870s he was reviewing regularly for *The Examiner*. His initial service to Swinburne was to sort out the poet's tangled publishing affairs, but before long a strong friendship developed.

From 10 to 20 October Swinburne was in Oxford, reading rare editions of George Chapman in the Bodleian. Joseph Knight invited him to write an essay on Chapman and Swinburne accepted, while admitting that in 1868 or thereabouts he had agreed to write such a piece for Hotten. At a dinner hosted by Jowett on 25 October he spent most of the evening talking with John Addington Symonds who wrote, 'he is more amiable than I expected – very modest yet childishly pleased with his pet works and thoughts; very enthusiastic and not in any way blasé; clearly of a strong brain physically, and at any rate of a memory as yet unimpaired.'

Early in November Swinburne went home to Holmwood, and reviewed John Nichol's dramatic poem *Hannibal* for the *Fortnightly Review*. He was writing elegies for Gautier in French, English, Greek and Latin, which he had been invited to contribute to *Le Tombeau de Théophile Gautier* (Paris 1873). All but the Greek verses appeared in *Poems and Ballads, Second Series* (1878). Of the 'Memorial Verses' and their complicated rhyme scheme, Swinburne noted,

> the metrical effect is, I think, not bad, but the danger of such metres is diffuseness and flaccidity. I perceive this one to have a tendency to the dulcet and luscious form of verbosity which has to be guarded against, lest the poem lose its foothold and be swept off its legs, sense and all, down a flood of effeminate and monotonous music, or lost and split in a maze of what I call draggle-tailed melody.

It was a danger he was not always able to avoid.

In December Swinburne impressed on Watts the necessity for getting a statement of accounts from Hotten. Madox Brown of Tinsleys had expressed a desire to publish Swinburne but the poet was disgusted when Tinsleys purchased Strahan and Co.'s remaindered stock which included 'periodicals which have for some time been persistently and consistently devoted to the defamation of Rossetti and myself not merely by means of insult and reviling but by means also of flat falsehood and calumny' and the collected works of Buchanan. In December it looked as though either Henry King or Chapman and Hall might become Swinburne's publishers. Swinburne said he would 'much rather be connected' to Chapman and Hall 'than any other firm'. They were offering to print a cheap edition of all Swinburne's poems. For Swinburne, this was not only good financial news, but as he explained to Powell,

> imagine me stalking triumphant through the land and displaying on every Hearth and in every Home of my country, naked and *not*

ashamed, the banner of immorality, atheism and revolution! The prospect of the widespread depravation which will ensue in our moral, religious, and hitherto happy land is enough to make God wriggle in heaven and the Marquis stand erect in his grave.

In the meantime on 16 December Swinburne told Morley:

I am working hard and steadily at my gigantic enterprise of *Bothwell* which dilates in bulk and material at every step. If ever accomplished, the drama will certainly be a great work in one sense, for except that translation from the Spanish of an improperly named comedy in 25 acts published in 1631, it will be the biggest I fear in the language. But having made a careful analysis of historical events from the day of Rizzio's murder to that of Mary's flight into England, I find that to cast into dramatic mould the events of those eighteen months it is necessary to omit no detail, drop no link in the chain, if the work is to be either dramatically coherent or historically intelligible . . .

Significantly on 22 December Swinburne asked Hotten to send Watts copies of all his books. It was a sign of the growing friendship between them. Swinburne described Watts as 'most kind and serviceable to me'. He remained at home during the winter. His father had been ill since July and confined to his room for most of November and December.

In January 1873 Watts's patience with Hotten expired, and he threatened legal action if accounts were not forthcoming. Hotten responded immediately. Swinburne needed new publishing opportunities to bring in more money. The vexed question was what exactly had been agreed in the heat of the moment in August 1866 after *Poems and Ballads* had been withdrawn by Moxon. Hotten claimed that Swinburne had by verbal contract given him copyright in perpetuity. Vital notes William Rossetti had made at the time only now surfaced. Swinburne described himself as 'harassed by utter want of money and various unpaid bills – also by legal business and interminable impediments as to publishing affairs'. A letter of February to Howell indicates the delicate nature of these negotiations. 'I am desirous' wrote Swinburne, 'to remain on amicable terms with Hotten in the act of withdrawing from my business connection with him . . . I see no reason why we should part on hostile terms, or why for instance I should cease to deal with him as of old in his bookselling capacity because I see fit to put an end to my relations with him as a publisher.' Swinburne had lent flagellatory writings to Hotten. The fear was that Hotten might use these for blackmail:

Neither Hotten nor for that matter any man alive has in his possession anything from my hand for which I need feel shame or serious regret or apprehension even should it be exposed to public view; but without any such cause for fear or shame we may all agree that we shrink, and that reasonably, from the notion that all our private papers thrown off in moments of chaff or Rabelaisian exchange of burlesque correspondence between friends who understand the fun, and have the watchword as it were under which a jest passes and circulates in the right quarter, should ever be liable to the inspection or the construction of common or unfriendly eyes.

Swinburne explained to Howell that he had, for example, sent Hotten a list of flagellation scenes in school which were to be turned into drawings. But Swinburne was still at this stage willing to contribute to the new *Romance of the Rod* Hotten proposed to publish.

Through the winter of 1872–73 Swinburne remained in solitude in the country, declining even invitations to visit immediate neighbours. On 28 March he wrote to Watts 'and by the by don't you think we might begin mutually to drop the "Mr." in writing as friends?' Hotten advertised *Bothwell* on his list of forthcoming books, causing Swinburne to write on 1 May, 'for this proceeding you have no manner of authority and I think it well to tell you, once for all, that even if I had this or any other poem ready for publication I should use my own discretion as to the publisher to whom I should offer it. I must request that you will immediately remove the announcement of it from your lists.' *Bothwell* continued to monopolize Swinburne's creative energies. He hoped that if it were not 'an utter failure' it would be 'by far the greatest work I have done ... a really great poem and fit to live as a typical and representative piece of work'.

In May Swinburne visited Jowett at Balliol. At Jowett's request Edwin Harrison gave up a day 'to listening to fiendish sonnets against Louis Napoleon, or strolling about Christchurch meadows and discussing Shakespeare, or feeding the poet on tea and strawberry creams and periodical literature at the Union'. The sonnets were the 'Dirae' sequence inspired by the death of Napoleon III, serialized in *The Examiner* since March. *The Spectator* called the sonnets 'a deadly and indecent insult to the faith of the vast majority of Christians'. Swinburne retorted they were intended to express his disgust at the insult 'offered to the name and memory of tradition of Christ by the men who ... bestowed on the most infamous of all public criminals the names till then reserved for one whom they professed to worship as God'. Months at home with his family had not softened Swinburne's antipathy to Christianity. It was merely that his loathing of Louis Napoleon temporarily eclipsed even his antitheism.

The argument over the 'Saviour of Society' sonnets rumbled on into June, with Swinburne sending a long, ironic letter on 2 June to *The Examiner*, explaining that the sonnets were intended to mock the parody of Christianity perpetrated by the supporters of Louis Napoelon. Swinburne had a low opinion of newspapers. Once, at a public dinner to which he had been taken by George Bird his doctor, where a number of journalists were present, Swinburne was asked if he would like to propose a toast to the press. Bird tried to decline the invitation for Swinburne, but the poet rose and cried out, 'The Press is a damnable institution, a horrible institution, a beastly institution!' and then subsided back into his chair.

In May 1873, Swinburne sent the poem 'North and South' to the *Fortnightly Review*, collected in 1878 as 'Relics'. It reveals the melancholy Swinburne often felt and a glimpse of the emotional pain that fuelled his chaotic behaviour:

> This flower that smells of honey and the sea,
> White laurustine, seems in my hand to be
>   A white star made of memory long ago
> Lit in the heaven of dear times dead to me.
>
> A star out of the skies love used to know
> Here held in hand, a stray left yet to show
>   What flowers my heart was full of in the days
> That are long since gone down dead memory's flow

He wrote of past love, gone 'Where the lost Aprils are, and the lost Mays'. It ends with one of Swinburne's most memorable lines:

> This that the winter and the wind made bright,
> And this that lived upon Italian light,
>   Before I throw them and these words away,
> Who knows but I what memories too take flight?

In 1884 he wrote that the laurustine was 'one of the most delightful flowers or shrubs of its kind', and in the poem he had in mind 'the long close range of them above the Channel' – presumably at The Orchard, Niton, one of the Gordon's properties. This links the poem to his feelings for Mary. Occasionally he had letters from her mother, Lady Mary Gordon. On 19 May she wrote to 'my dear Hadji' from Northcourt, adding the postscript 'Mun [Mary] sends her best love'.

A Balliol group, including Edwin Harrison, planned to go to Scotland as in the summers of 1871 and 1872. Swinburne told Harrison he was likely to be in the Isle of Wight instead, 'where I was so happy and unhappy as a child and youth', staying with Lady Gordon. Swinburne's allusion to unhappiness presumably refers to the death of Edith and the loss of Mary Gordon. There is no evidence that Swinburne had visited the Isle of Wight since 1865 when the family left East Dene. In the same letter Swinburne showed the other side of his physical sensitivity to pain when he referred to a case in *The Times* which involved two women in prison with their babies. He wished he had more in him of Burns rather than Shelley:

I thirst with impotent desire to do something – but the mere contemplation of the tyranny and attempt for a moment to realize the suffering is literally intolerable pain to me. I could no more write under its influence than under the influence of neuralgia . . . These things are incredible – and they are next door to us. How is it that the whole countryside has not been driven mad between rage and pity?

Another of Swinburne's relationships foundered at this time. Simeon Solomon was arrested for soliciting outside a public lavatory off Oxford Street on 11 February, and sentenced to six weeks in Clerkenwell House of Correction with a fine of £100, and held over for a further period under police supervision. To George Powell Swinburne wrote on 6 June:

I suppose there is no doubt the poor unhappy little fellow has really been out of his mind and *done* things amenable to law such as done by a sane man would make it impossible for any one to keep up his acquaintance and not be cut by the rest of the world as an accomplice? I have been seriously unhappy about it for I had a real affection and regard for him – and besides his genius he had such genuinely amiable qualities. It is the simple truth that the distress of it has haunted and broken my sleep. It is hideous to lose a friend by madness of any kind, let alone this.

Oscar Browning blamed Solomon's 'wayward behaviour and drunkenness on Swinburne's bad influence'. From this time Swinburne was consistent in expressing his loathing for the idea of homosexual activity, whatever the stance or experience of his younger years. Solomon and Swinburne were not to meet again and hardly to correspond. Solomon ended his days as an alcoholic, alternating between the streets and the workhouse. Swinburne wrote to Powell in December after receiving more news of Solomon in Devon, advising him 'not to be led away by any kindly and generous feeling towards an unfortunate man whom he has been used to regard as a friend, into a renewal of intimacy' with someone who 'has deliberately chosen to do what makes a man and all who associate with him infamous in the eyes of the world':

I do think a man is bound to consider the consequence to all his friends and to every one who cares for him in the world of allowing his name to be mixed up with that of a ———— let us say, a Platonist; the term is at once accurate as a definition and unobjectionable as an euphemism.

That Swinburne's attitude to Solomon quickly hardened is clear from another letter of 2 January 1874, stating he had no wish to encounter 'a Platonist of another sort' than Jowett. There were limits, it would seem, even for the 'libidinous laureate of a pack of satyrs'.

During 1873 *Bothwell* remained interminable, diverting creative energy from other projects. Swinburne planned the prose collection which became *Essays and Studies* (1875). Watts volunteered the view that it should omit discussion of contemporary poets. With aristocratic disdain, Swinburne put Watts in his place: 'The points on which I am undecided are those only on which I asked your advice in my last letter.' And then, on 14 June, John Camden Hotten died. The Fates had saved Swinburne from further delay and litigation over his publishing. On 23 July he received a letter from Andrew Chatto, who was contemplating buying Hotten's firm and wished Swinburne to stay, with 'the business relations with yourself placed upon a more satisfactory footing than has been the case for some time past'.

Instead of the Isle of Wight, Swinburne defied his relations and went to Scotland with the Balliol party. By 10 July he was at Grantown, Inverness-shire, a village with one long street. Harrison wrote, 'the country round is well-wooded, and bright with flowers and flowering bushes; Swinburne says he has seen no place comparable with it for flowers except among the Apennines'. They visited the Findhorn river. Having listened to Swinburne read some of his recent work, Jowett noted,

> I think he begins to be aware of his defects – which are chiefly want of clearness and rhetorical phraseology. I wish he had more of the ideal in him – he is too much an imitator and dramatizer, immensely gifted in language and verse, and learned in poetry to a degree which destroys originality. This leads him constantly to introduce archaisms.

Swinburne remained in Scotland until August.

In the autumn he was in London and then in November left suddenly for Holmwood. He was in dire financial straits, £200 'worse than penniless' and considered publishing the first canto of *Tristram* to raise some cash. By the end of 1873 he had reached the last scene of *Bothwell* but was still undecided whether to take up Chatto's offer of publishing his books. Watts's continued ascendancy was signalled by Swinburne telling Chatto, 'the regulation of my business affairs is now in the hands of my legal adviser Mr. Watts, by whose decision I am prepared to abide'. Negotiations were still going on with Chapman and Hall. On 1 January Chatto sent accounts and a cheque for recent sales of Swinburne's books, adding 'we should be very glad to secure the publishing of Mr Swinburne's "Bothwell" and "Tristan and Iseult"'. On 7 January Watts replied from Putney Hill, nettled that Chatto was assuming Swinburne to be one of their authors and demanding, 'I must know whether you really mean to deny that all the correspondence oral as well as written which has passed between us has been based upon the understanding that Mr. Swinburne and I did not consider you as his publisher whatever might have been your imaginings as to your position as Mr. Hotten's successor.' This proved almost too much for Andrew Chatto who on 20 January wrote to Swinburne: 'the enclosed copy of a letter received from Mr. Watts together with the previous correspondence will shew you that I cannot consistently with my own self respect have any more communications with that gentleman.' Watts had blundered. But somehow things were smoothed over and terms were settled with Chatto on 21 April 1874.

During this heated exchange Swinburne was away. On New Year's day 1874 Jowett told Florence Nightingale that Swinburne 'is coming to Cornwall, on condition that we drink fair and nothing but claret. He is incorrigibly vain and has no religion, but he is devoted to his family (who are certainly charming people) and this may yet save him.' They met up in Plymouth, and visited Penzance, St Michael's Mount, Land's End, the Lizard and Tintagel. Jowett remarked 'by far the finest of the places which we saw is the Lizard, which Swinburne had been especially desirous to see. I never saw anything of the kind as fine as the huge Atlantic waves, with the sun glimmering through the tops of them, in a place called Kynance Cove.' Swinburne was sufficiently impressed to describe it in the eighth canto of *Tristram*:

> And whensoever a strong wave, high in hope,
> Sweeps up some smooth slant breadth of stone aslope,
> That glowed with duskier fire of hues less bright,
> Swift as it sweeps back springs to sudden sight
> The splendour of the moist rock's fervent light,
> Fresh as from dew of birth when time was born
> Out of the world-conceiving womb of morn.
> All its quenched flames and darkling hues divine
> Leap into lustrous life and laugh and shine
> And darken into swift and dim decline
> For one brief breath's space till the next wave run,
> Right up, and ripple down again, undone,
> And leave it to be kissed and kindled of the sun.

Years later he recalled 'the unique and incomparable sublimity of loveliness which distinguishes the serpentine rocks and cliffs and slopes and platforms of Kynance Cove from any other possible presentation of an earthly paradise' and the 'glorious outlook so sturdily and so hardily attained' at Tintagel and St Michael's Mount. In 'Recollections of Professor Jowett' Swinburne wrote, 'twice at least during a week's winter excursion in Cornwall I knew, and had reason to know, what it was to feel nervous:

> ... for he would follow along the broken rampart of a ruined castle, and stand without any touch of support at the edge of a magnificent precipice, as though he had been a younger man bred up from boyhood to the scaling of cliffs and the breasting of breakers.

10.2   Max Beerbohm caricature of Swinburne and Jowett on holiday in
Cornwall, 1874

Swinburne brought back a pair of serpentine candlesticks for giving readings of his poetry. He told Powell that the visit 'has left me in love for life with Kynance Cove where (to use an original expression) I could live and die'. Jowett wrote to Florence Nightingale that Swinburne 'behaved very well and showed no inclination to drink. The worst of him is that his moral nature is swallowed up in vanity and literature. But he is very considerate and affectionate.' When *Bothwell* was published in May, Jowett commented to her, 'it is quite intelligible and it is free from licentiousness. In parts I think it very striking and powerful though I fear that it does not come up to your ideal of the poetry which is only to do good. Still, it is something if he is kept from doing harm . . . He has gone on better during the last four months.'

At the end of January 1874 Powell sent Swinburne an article 'Emerson: A Literary Interview' which quoted Emerson as calling Swinburne 'a perfect leper and a mere sodomite, which criticism recalls Carlyle's scathing description of that poet – as a man standing up to his neck in a cesspool, and adding to its contents'. Swinburne's first impulse was to ignore it, but soon his fury had issue in a letter to the *New York Daily Tribune*. It made a great parade of his being too far above such matters to stoop to reply, and then descended to undignified insults, caricaturing Emerson as 'a gap-toothed and hoary-headed ape, carried at first into notice on the shoulder of Carlyle, and who now in his dotage spits and chatters from a dirtier perch of his own finding and fouling'. Swinburne hypocritically told Powell that the letter was to seem published neither with his wish nor against it, 'in other words that I have no wish to put forth or to withhold either, nor any desire or concern in the matter at all. Any appearance to the contrary would naturally expose me to the degrading charge of having lowered my position with regard to my assailants by seeking an occasion of reply.' Naturally. This from the man who had said 'no attack ever gave me a quarter of an hour's vexation or deprived me of five minutes rest.'!

On 1 March Swinburne informed William Rossetti that *Bothwell* was finished, five acts and 60 scenes chronicling two years, two months and a week in the life of Mary Stuart:

> I have throughout followed history with the most dogged or dog-like fidelity . . . because I do really perceive that 'the events which did actually transact themselves on this God's earth' at that particular time were the most dramatic as well as tragic in their interest that even Shakespeare – usually so much greater and more successful a dramatist than God – could have imagined and arranged.

Early in April he read from it to various groups of friends at 3 Great James Street, sometimes for hours, at night by the illumination thrown from his serpentine candlesticks. To his mother on 12 April he wrote, 'I have had so many readings, and reading to a company is just the most tiring thing I know':

> It leaves you next day hardly up to writing or reading either. It is *very* fascinating, and I don't wonder it killed Dickens. The intoxicating effect of a circle of faces hanging on your words and keeping up your own excitement by theirs which is catching even when your own words on mere paper are stale to you is such that I wonder how actors stand it nightly – though after all it passes off and leaves one all right.

Bothwell was the first of his books to be printed by Chatto and Windus, 'the work to which I have given my best powers and my most earnest labour of many months, during which I have resolutely kept my hand from any other task'. It contains much fine writing but yields its best only to readers steeped in the history of Mary Stuart and Scotland. Swinburne defended its length to John Nichol, arguing that 'the tragedy of Mary's personal life gains half its interest and all its dignity from the great background (not of provincial but) of European history which I have tried throughout to keep steadily before the reader's mind, – the great battle between past and future, death and life, tradition and revolution.'

The reviews, though not wholly complimentary, were free of the animus his earlier books had suffered. His relations were delighted. Swinburne was pleased to hear of 'the unbroken interest with which [the Admiral] had read right through' it. On 5 June his maternal uncle Percy Ashburnham wrote to thank Swinburne for a copy 'of your last great Work ... I hear from your Mother that the whole of the first Edition of it was sold before the day of publication, if this does not prove the extraordinary merit of the Work it surely must prove the estimation in which the Author is held.' Three days later Lady Mary Gordon sent her congratulations from The Orchard, and wrote: 'I am glad to hear you are thinking of coming here again when the rest of your party are settled here.' By the summer there was even talk of staging *Bothwell*, though in the end nothing came of this. Drink was probably the cause of more illness in June and Swinburne went to Holmwood to recover. A while later he found himself sitting in a boat crossing the Solent, watching the summer sun gild the waters as he approached the Isle of Wight, with all its memories.

CHAPTER ELEVEN

The Puppet-Show

On 14 July Swinburne wrote to Watts, 'I am in excellent health here and divide my days between swimming and reading Homer.' He was reading the *Iliad* in its entirety 'for the first time with great comfort and benefit to my spirits', finding that Homer and the sea 'keep time perfectly in my mind's ear'. Despite the trepidation he had expressed the previous summer at returning to the island, ghosts of summers past proved weaker than the spell of sun, sea and country air. 'I swim in among the other seagulls now daily, and feel exactly the same enjoyment and as much of it as I did at thirteen.' He corresponded with Richard Herne Shepherd about the text of George Chapman and read Hugo 'under the right auspices of sea and sun and flowers and solitude'.

On 10 July peace broke out between Swinburne and Alfred Austin, who had attacked each other in *The Poetry of the Period* and *Under the Microscope* respectively. Austin had penned a complimentary review of *Bothwell*. Swinburne wrote that he appreciated 'the tone at once of your article and of your letter; not the less but the more for all past debates and differences of opinion on matters of art or other, which indeed now only serve to heighten my sense of the generosity and frankness of the praise bestowed on my last work'. The friendship with Watts grew, though with due acknowledgement of their differing taste in some things. On 18 July Swinburne teased Watts about the 'incurable blindness and stiff-neckedness as of a new Pharaoh which keeps you still in the gall of prejudice and the bond of decency, and debars you from the just appreciation of a Great Man . . . I cannot but think that God must have hardened your heart . . . and nothing else *could* account for insensibility to the peculiar but surpassing merits of the Marquis', signing himself 'Ever yours (would that I could add, in the Marquis)'.

In the summer of 1874 Swinburne wrote his study of George Chapman. He told George Powell he was 'grinding at old Chapman's obscure and unequal poetry which alternately startles and delights or disgusts and infuriates the student'. Chapman was 'the most difficult and obscure writer I ever tried to tackle'. He also composed more of *Tristram of Lyonesse* and exchanged angry letters with Chatto regarding errors in the proofs of the second edition of *Bothwell*, which took Swinburne 'two days' incessant labour':

> Such incompetence and such neglect as this cannot be guarded against by any care or painstaking on the part of an author, who

> after hours and days of drudgery spent in the revision and rectifica-
> tion of the original blunders finds his time and labour utterly
> wasted. In one case, where a word usually wrong was given for
> once rightly, I find it erased, and the wrong word carefully substi-
> tuted – for no apparent reason but that it *is* palpably wrong and
> conveys no meaning.

Swinburne insisted on 'a *complete* set of all the notices that may appear
of *Bothwell*', an interesting request in the light of his feigned indiffer-
ence to the press.

Swinburne enjoyed the sun and sea well into August. On one occasion, for the second time in his life, Swinburne was nearly drowned.
Expressing sympathy for his ill-health to Edwin Harrison, who was
with Jowett at Malvern, Swinburne wrote, 'I should have hoped that
summer and the sea might have done for you what they have never yet
failed to do for me, whom they always restore (as now) to perfect
strength and enjoyment. I have wanted nothing these eight weeks but a
companion to be as happy as I ever expect to be.' He continued:

> I wish with all my heart we were together daily in the sea where I
> need not tell you I find myself daily alone, and have many times
> held imaginary conversations with you as eloquent and as volumi-
> nous as Landor's while swimming across the bays that divide these
> headlands. The weather has been usually divine, and the Oceanides
> as favourable to me as ever to Prometheus: except one day when I
> went in at a new place after a gale and found myself unable to get
> back to land and violently beaten to and fro between the breakers
> in a furious reflux which flung me back off shore as with the clutch
> of a wild beast every time I tried to get up on the bank of shingle
> where at last by dint of grovelling and digging with hands and feet
> I managed, between swimming, crawling and running, to get out
> ... Since then I have kept to the bays I know to be warranted safe
> within reasonable limits, as I trust you do likewise. On clear days I
> swim across half-a-dozen various belts of reef, rock, and weed-bed
> with broad interspaces of clear sea, and can observe all the forms
> and colours changing and passing beneath me, which is one of the
> supreme delights of the sea.

Two days later Swinburne asked Watts to look into the possibility of
having his works translated into French and mused, 'if I write any more
necrological elegies on deceased poets, I shall be taken for the under-
takers' laureate or the forehorse of a funeral car hired out to trot in
trappings on all such occasions as regularly as Mr. Mould and his merry
men'. On 19 August John Tyndall had given the inaugural address on
the relation between science and theology to the British Association for
the Advancement of Science. Swinburne read an account in *The Times*,
and commented to Watts, 'science so enlarged and harmonized gives me
a sense as much of rest as of light':

No mythology can make its believers feel less afraid or loth to be reabsorbed into the immeasurable harmony with but the change of a single individual note in a single bar of the tune, than does the faintest perception of the lowest chord touched in the whole system of things. Even my technical ignorance does not impair, I think, my power to see accurately and seize firmly the first thread of the great clue, because my habit of mind is not (I hope) unscientific, though my work lies in the field of art instead of science: and when seen and seized even that first perception gives me an indescribable sense as of music and repose. It is Theism which to me seems to introduce an element – happily a factitious element – of doubt, discord, and disorder.

Now 37, Swinburne caught his face in a mirror 'looking yesterday rather as it did twelve or fifteen years ago than it does in London with thinned hair and withered cheeks'.

Returning to Great James Street by the end of September, Swinburne finished the essay on Chapman on 18 October. It included an engaging digression on the topic of obscurity, taking Browning as an example of a poet to whom the charge of obscurity had been 'persistently and perversely' misapplied. Swinburne argued, 'he never thinks but at full speed; and the rate of his thought is to that of another man's as the speed of a railway to that of a waggon or the speed of a telegraph to that of a railway'. Browning was no lyricist, but unsurpassed as an analyst of motive and mind. Nor was *Sordello* obscure, Swinburne added, warming to the subject of a passion from his undergraduate days. By contrast Swinburne saw Chapman as a genuinely obscure writer.

In October the poet Bryan Proctor ('Barry Cornwall') died. Swinburne had celebrated him in *Poems and Ballads* (1866) and on 18 October went to see Proctor's widow Anne, who afterwards wrote, 'I cannot tell you what a pleasure your good company was to me, how you lifted me out of all that has been pressed upon me for the last fortnight'. Swinburne composed 'In Memory of Barry Cornwall', printed in the November *Fortnightly Review*. He rewrote his essay on Charles Wells's verse play *Joseph and His Brethren* and started 'a somewhat elaborate history of Shakespeare's style from Romeo to Timon', which grew into A *Study of Shakespeare*. To Gosse on 30 October he complained, 'these damned proofs of my "Chapman" will drive me mad or blind or both'. In November he heard from his old friend Lorimer Graham in Florence that Seymour Kirkup had 'converted from his spirit-rapping nonsense, and given up "spiritualism" (as those vulgarest of materialists have the impudence to call their nonsense and imposture)'. Swinburne had no sympathy with the age's desire actively to seek tangible evidence of life after death. A letter of 24 November speaks of being laid up 'with a bad bilious attack and influenza' and 'still too weak almost to write'. He remained in London until 29 December and then went to Holmwood.

The year 1875 began with Swinburne seeking a title for the proposed collection of his as yet ungathered political poems and sparring amicably with William Rossetti over the text of Shelley. He spent a week in mid-January with Jowett in West Malvern, and read Milton's *Areopagitica*: 'What godlike eloquence and (which surprised me more) what marvellously advanced views of social as well as political freedom for that age! Why, the mass of our contemporaries have hardly got as far yet, and only a handful of such heretics as ourselves would wish to go but a little further.' He worked on the sequence for the contents of *Essays and Studies*, his first critical miscellany (it would be succeeded by two more), a selection of essays written from the mid-1860s onward. There were chapters on Hugo, D. G. Rossetti, Arnold, Shelley, Byron, Coleridge and Morris, John Ford, and two art essays, 'Designs of Old Masters in Florence' and 'Notes on some Pictures of 1868'.

On 20 January Swinburne wrote to Chatto, fuming about the number of errors introduced into the text of *Essays and Studies*, and complained to Watts of the

> ever-new crop of blunders sown by the ignorant and presumptuous stupidity of printers. I suppose others are not expected to re-revise every word of the text in every fresh edition of every one of their works? It would be a dog's life to lead – worse than a galley-slave's; yet I see no such errors foisted into any reissue of Tennyson or Browning.

Swinburne was increasingly sensitive about the treatment of his own books in comparison with those of his leading contemporaries, for 'no such publisher's list is ever tacked to the tail of a book of Tennyson's or Browning's, and I do not wish to set the fashion of allowing my poems to be bound up with an advertising catalogue', an objection Chatto serenely ignored. Works Swinburne had issued with Hotten were now republished under Chatto's imprint: *Poems and Ballads* (1873, 1875), *Atalanta* (1875), *Chastelard* (1878), and *The Queen Mother and Rosamond* (1896).

Watts returned from a holiday in Italy at the end of January. He reminded Swinburne that the manuscript of 'Tristram' had been promised to him. Watts had met some of Swinburne's acquaintances such as Lorimer Graham and been especially struck by the 'bewildering loveliness of Venice', where 'there are to be met ... three pretty, or handsome, women to one in any other Italian city'. This reminded Swinburne of the three beautiful women he had seen there in 1864. Watts still considered the 'Dirae' sonnets in bad taste, particularly 'The Saviour of Society', 'which does, even to me, seem a painful insult to a name that every lover of moral beauty must hold sacred'. Swinburne confessed, 'I cannot understand how anyone, friend or foe, can see anything in it but an indignant protest against the blasphemous misapplication to Bonaparte of the traditional titles of Christ.' Watts could not prevail. Swinburne included the poems in *Songs of Two Nations* (1875).

On 31 January, writing to Gosse, Swinburne made an unfavourable comparison of his own prose with that of Landor:

> it is always a thorn in my flesh when writing prose, and a check to any satisfaction I might feel in it, to reflect that probably I never have written or shall write a page that Landor might have signed. Nothing of the sort (or of any sort) ever troubles me in writing verse, but this always haunts me when at work on prose.

He mentioned the study of Shakespeare which appeared as 'The Three Stages of Shakespeare' in the *Fortnightly Review* (May 1875 and January 1876): 'I need hardly say that I begin with a massacre of the pedants worthy of celebration in an Icelandic saga – "a murder grim and great". I leave the "finger-counters and finger-casters" without a finger to count on or an (ass's) ear to wag.'

Gosse was present at a dinner Swinburne organized in London on 10 February to mark the centenary of Charles Lamb's birth. '"Leave it to me!" he said, in his grandest manner.' Along with William Minto, Thomas Purnell and Watts, they met in an old-fashioned hotel in Soho:

> The extreme dignity of Swinburne is the feature of the dinner which remains most conspicuously in my memory; he sank so low in his huge arm-chair, and sat so bolt upright in it, that his white face, with its great aureole of red hair, beamed over the table like the rising sun. It was magnificent to see him, when Purnell, who was a reckless speaker, 'went too far', bringing back the conversation into the paths of decorum. He was so severe, so unwontedly and phenomenally severe, that Purnell sulked, and taking out a churchwarden left us at table and smoked in the chimney-corner. Our shock was the bill – portentous! Swinburne, in 'organising', had made no arrangement as to price, and there were five long faces of impecunious men of letters.

In the spring of 1875 Swinburne wrote one of the most revealing letters of his life. Ever sensitive to the charge of egotism, he rarely discussed his personal life in correspondence. E. C. Stedman had written an account of Swinburne's poetry in *Scribner's Monthly* and sent Swinburne a copy. Acknowledging it, Swinburne discussed Whitman and other American poets. While respecting the merits of Bryant's 'Thanatopsis' and Lowell's 'Commemoration Ode', 'I cannot say that either of them leaves in my ear the echo of a single note of song':

> It is excellent good speech but if given us as song its first and last
> duty is to sing. The one is most august meditation, the other a
> noble expression of deep and grave patriotic feeling on a supreme
> national occasion; but the thing more necessary though it may be
> less noble than these is the pulse, the fire, the passion of music –
> the quality of a singer, not of a solitary philosopher . . . Now it is a
> poor thing to have nothing but melody and be unable to rise above
> it into harmony, but one or the other, the less if not the greater, you
> *must* have.

Stedman asked for some personal information, and Swinburne com-
plied, though with a disclaimer: 'I have no love of talking of my own or
other men's personal or family matters, uninvited, but there can hardly
be egotism or self-conceit in complying with the direct request of a
friend.' Swinburne talked at length of his ancestry, with especial reference to his paternal grandfather Sir John. 'My life has been eventless
and monotonous', wrote Swinburne, remembering how when young 'I
never cared for any pursuit, sport, or study, . . . except poetry, riding
and swimming':

> Also being bred by the sea I was a good cragsman, and am vain to
> this day of having scaled a well-known cliff on the South coast,
> ever before and ever since reputed to be inaccessible. Perhaps I may
> be forgiven for referring to such puerilities, having read (in cuttings
> from more than one American journal) bitterly contemptuous re-
> marks on my physical debility and puny proportions. I am afraid
> this looks like an echo of poor great Byron's notorious and very
> natural soreness about his personal defect; but really if I were
> actually of powerless or deformed body I am certain I should not
> care though all men (and women) on earth knew and remarked on
> it. I write all this rubbish because I really don't know what to tell
> you about myself, and having begun to egotize I go on in pure
> stupidity. I suppose you do not require a Rousseau-like record of
> my experiences in spiritual or material emotions; and knowing as
> you do the dates and sequence of my published books you know
> every event of my life.

The following day (21 February 1875) he penned a further five pages,
since 'as you have induced me for the very first time in my life to write
about myself, I am tempted, considering that I have been more be-
written and belied than any man since Byron, to pour myself out to a
sincere and distant friend a little more'. Of his religious experience
Swinburne recalled how when the ecstatic faith of his youth was 'stark
dead and buried':

> . . . it left nothing to me but a turbid nihilism; for a Theist I never
> was . . . *because* no man could by other than apocalyptic means –
> i.e. by other means than a violation of the laws and order of nature
> – *conceive* of any other sort of divine person than man with a
> difference – man with some qualities intensified and some qualities

suppressed – man with the good in him exaggerated and the evil excised. This, I say, I have always seen and avowed since my mind was ripe enough to think freely ... But we who worship no material incarnation of any qualities, no person, may worship the divine humanity, the ideal of human perfection and aspiration, without worshipping any God, any person, any fetish at all. Therefore I might call myself if I wished a kind of Christian (of the Church of Blake and Shelley) but assuredly in no sense a Theist. Perhaps you will think this is only clarified nihilism, but at least it is no longer turbid.

Gosse at this time helped Swinburne regain access to the British Museum, and Swinburne returned the favour by putting Gosse in touch with Chatto, who duly published some of his works. Through March and April 1875 Swinburne continued his study of Shakespeare. In April the *Fortnightly Review* printed 'A Vision of Spring in Winter'. The poem echoes the note Swinburne had first struck with 'Ave Atque Vale' and made a welcome change form the harsh rhetoric of the political poems, with its Keatsian diction and stanza form:

> Where has the greenwood hid thy gracious head?
>   Veiled with what visions while the grey world grieves,
>   Or muffled with what shadows of green leaves,
> What warm intangible green shadows spread
> To sweeten the sweet twilight for thy bed?
>   What sleep enchants thee? what delight deceives?

In winter, the speaker imagines the spring ('I reach my heart out toward the springtime lands') and associates it with the past ('I send my love back to the lovely time'). In a vision, the speaker comes upon the girl-child spring, and envisions how she will 'put at last the deadly days to death/and fill the fields and fire the woods with thee/And seaward hollows where my feet would be'. But Swinburne cannot help remember the flowers that will not revive with the return of spring even as he invokes those that will. The close is full of rhythmic subtlety, attempting to face the past and its losses, the sense of which is ever-present:

> The morning song beneath the stars that fled
>   With twilight through the moonless mountain air,
>   While youth with burning lips and wreathless hair
> Sang toward the sun that was to crown his head,
> Rising; the hopes that triumphed and fell dead,
>   The sweet swift eyes and songs of hours that were;
> These may'st thou not give back for ever; these,
>   As at the sea's heart all her wrecks lie waste,
>   Lie deeper than the sea;
> But flowers thou may'st, and winds, and hours of ease,
>   And all its April to the world thou may'st
>   Give back, and half my April back to me.

In the poignant last line consolation and loss are exquisitely balanced.

In May, London or alcohol brought on another bout of illness. On 20 May Swinburne told Burne-Jones, 'I have been too seedy to write or see *any* visitor for upwards of a month. The Grand Inquisitor, Father God, tortures me with insomnia – and opiates drive me mad and leave me sick (Ah! how inferior in invention was the gentle genius of the Marquis to that of the Maker!).' But he had the satisfaction of seeing *Songs of Two Nations* and *A Study of George Chapman* in print.

Swinburne was not so prostrate as to miss an opportunity for a bit of flyting in the pages of *The Athenaeum*. His target was Charles Hastings Collette's Society for the Suppression of Vice. Collette had been quoted referring to 'the book entitled Rabelais' and how the original could not be as objectionable as a modern translation because the former 'is scarcely understood even by accomplished French scholars . . . by reason of its antiquated phraseology'. Swinburne pounced:

> But it is a sad fact that less obscure and obsolete books than these are by no means unamenable to the ban of this wonderful Society. The book entitled Milton is not so immaculate as the virtuous who have never read it may be fain to believe. Of the book entitled Dryden, the book entitled Pope, and the book entitled Swift, I need hardly speak, and should indeed, in the presence of the Society for the Suppression of Vice, prefer to pass them by with a shudder and a blush. I believe that the book entitled Fielding is still permitted to circulate . . .

Swinburne's letter climaxes with the suggestion that the books entitled Homer, Catullus, Ovid, Horace etc. could also be banned, and Shakespeare and the Bible itself. The humourless Collette, failing to see the irony, assured Swinburne and readers of *The Athenaeum* that the Society had no intention of banning Shakespeare and the Bible – much to Swinburne's further amusement.

By the end of June Swinburne was at Holmwood, 'safe here among woods and gardens'. On 21 June he asked Watts to return some of the manuscript of *Lesbia Brandon*. Watts stalled over this for years, evidently to block Swinburne's attempts to complete and publish it. On 26 June Swinburne sprained a foot 'trying to climb and jump from a garden fence – rather schoolboyish at my grave and reverend time of life', resulting in a week confined to bed. He wrote on Beaumont and Fletcher for the *Encyclopaedia Britannica*, and read Tennyson's new play *Queen Mary* – 'my first and last remark on it was and is that it has a very pretty song in it'. To Joseph Knight on 8 July he posted 'At Parting', an experiment with the rondel form – here with six lines to a stanza – which found fruition in *A Century of Roundels* (1883). The refrain –'For a day and a night Love sang to us' – expresses the theme of the brevity of love. Swinburne commented cynically:

> I pique myself on its moral tone; in an age when all other lyrists, from Tennyson to Rossetti, go in (metrically) for constancy and eternity of attachment and reunion in future lives, etc., etc., I limit love, honestly and candidly, to 24 hours; and quite enough too in all conscience.

On 18 July his aunt Lady Gordon wrote from Chelsea, thanking him for sending *Songs of Two Nations*, and bringing news of Mary Leith's novel *The Incumbent of Axhill*:

> Mun's *modest* little work is selling very well Henry heard at Hayes' the other day so I hope the public don't disapprove as much as I do of the horrors wh[ich] the muddy mind of Blun delights in pourtraying. Her letters are always full of illustrations of the most painful and revolting scenes ... Latterly some rather good things in epitaphs.

That the 'bloody mind of Mun' (to unscramble the cypher) filled her letters with 'revolting scenes' is evidence that Swinburne and Mary had some unusual tastes in common.

His injured foot kept him indoors, and he grew bored. He told Powell on 27 July, 'I want some diversion as much as Nero ever did – and after the manner of that imperial Poet. I would give worlds for something – though it were but a drawing of my favourite school subject – to titillate my weary spirits.' His postbag continued to net a variety of letters from admirers, including requests to set his poems to music:

> Year after year I am inundated with applications of this kind from unknown quarters, and especially from 'the Everlasting Female' (for whom *vide* Blake *passim*) uttering incessantly the same modest request to be allowed to turn a penny or make an effect at my expense. Now really I am very indifferent to the honour of being set to music by the first comer and sung to all the pianos of the Daughters of Albion; so henceforward if they want to publish they must pay, as they do in the Laureate's case.

In August 1875 Swinburne congratulated Gosse on his marriage, reflecting on 'that particular form of happiness which I am now never likely to share' and 'the reverse experience which left my own young manhood "a barren stock" – if I may cite that phrase without seeming to liken myself to a male Queen Elizabeth'. The plaintive 'which I am now never likely to share' speaks volumes. Once he had written 'Let come what will, there is one thing worth,/To have had fair love in the life upon earth'. Now it was only 'that particular form of happiness'. He was 38.

On 9 August Swinburne went to Ashfield Place, West Malvern, to stay with Jowett, where he entertained the party with parodies of

Browning. This visit may be the genesis of Swinburne's second play modelled on Greek tragedy. He hoped *Erechtheus* would be 'a more perfect original example of Greek tragedy' than *Atalanta in Calydon*; 'It is very simple in structure, and deals only with two "elementary" passions – that of child and parent, and that of patriotism': 'Jowett approves my scheme highly, and has helped me with some valuable hints from the classical or scholarly point of view, on which side I want to make this poem impregnable.' To this end, Swinburne promised to refrain from attacks on the 'Supreme Being':

> I am trying to infuse throughout a broader undernote of general and world-wide interest based on the immortality of Greece as the everlasting and universal mother-country of thought and art and action, the exemplar to all times and nations for all patriots and poets. One of these days I must write a paper on Athens and Jerusalem as the two rival fountains of light and darkness, liberty and servitude, for the human race; showing how Aeschylus, the greatest Greek poet, would have been less if he had not been a Greek, while Dante, the greatest Christian poet, would have been greater if he had not been a Christian.)

To Watts on 27 August he explained that Jowett supported his plan with 'the warmest and most encouraging sympathy' – no doubt relieved Swinburne had chosen an uncontroversial subject. Swinburne added:

> It is odd how *much* nearer and more real the prehistoric figures of classical than of medieval legend seem to me. I can hardly screw up my faith to practical belief in Arthur, and hardly reason myself into personal doubt of the existence of Erechtheus.

Swinburne returned to Holmwood from Malvern on 7 September, having completed the second instalment of his essay on Shakespeare and written several lyrics, including 'A Forsaken Garden' and 'A Song in Season'. The former is one of his finest hymns to the forces of change and decay, probably inspired by his stay on the Isle of Wight in the summer of 1874:

> In a coign of the cliff between lowland and highland,
>   At the sea-down's edge between windward and lee,
> Walled round with rocks as an inland island,
>   The ghost of a garden fronts the sea.
> A girdle of brushwood and thorn encloses
>   The steep square slope of the blossomless bed
> Where the weeds that grew green from the graves of its roses
>   Now lie dead.

If the garden of The Orchard at Niton held personal memories for Swinburne, he suppresses them. He introduces lovers who once came to the garden, who laughed and wept 'a hundred sleeping/Years ago'. As so often in his work, there is an impulse to reach into the past and rescue the lovers from oblivion, as with Tristram and Iseult in the Prelude to *Tristram of Lyonesse*. 'A Forsaken Garden' hypothesizes two alternative fates for their love:

> Heart handfast in heart as they stood, 'Look thither,'
>   Did he whisper? 'look forth from the flowers to the sea;
> For the foam-flowers endure when the rose-blossoms wither,
>   And men that love lightly may die – but we?'
> And the same wind sang and the same waves whitened,
>   And or ever the garden's last petals were shed,
> In the lips that had whispered, the eyes that had lightened,
>   Love was dead.
>
> Or they loved their life through, and then went whither?
>   And were one to the end – but what end who knows?
> Love deep as the sea as a rose must wither,
>   As the rose-red seaweed that mocks the rose.
> Shall the dead take thought for the dead to love them?
>   What love was ever as deep as a grave?
> They are loveless now as the grass above them
>   Or the wave.

In the first instance love proves so ephemeral that it does not even outlast the flowers of one season. In the second it is life-long but Swinburne faces it with questions about its ultimate end. Death is stronger than love; the only consolation is the stasis envisaged in the next stanza:

> All are at one now, roses and lovers,
>   Not known of the cliffs and the fields and the sea.
> Not a breath of the time that has been hovers
>   In the air now soft with a summer to be.
> Not a breath shall there sweeten the seasons hereafter
>   Of the flowers or the lovers that laugh now or weep,
> When as they that are free now of weeping and laughter
>   We shall sleep.

Change will finally exhaust itself. The garden cannot be ruined any more than it is until the cliff crumbles into the sea. 'A Forsaken Garden' ends with death personified 'As a god self-slain on his own strange altar'.

From 21 September to mid-October, Swinburne had a three-week holiday with Watts at Southwold, on the east coast. The choice of location was probably Watts's, since he knew the east coast from his childhood and was convinced of 'the stinging saltiness of the sea-water off Yarmouth, Lowestoft, and Cromer, the quality which makes it the best, the most buoyant, the most delightful of all sea-water to swim in'. At first Swinburne thought the coast 'as dull as any place can be to me where I have the sea' but on the first bright day Swinburne observed how 'on the dull yellow foamless floor of dense discoloured sea, so thick with clotted sand that the water looked massive and solid as the shore, the white sails flashed whiter against it and along as they fled'. On the fifth day he 'found a place that would have delighted Shelley':

> a lake of fresh water only parted from the sea by a steep and thick pebble-ridge through which a broad channel has been cut in the middle a little above the level of the lake, to let off the water in flood-time; half encircled to the north and west by an old wood of oaks and ash-trees, with a wide common beyond it sweeping side-ways to the sea. It is so unutterably lonely that I thought instantly how like this now beautiful wood must be in winter to Dante's wood of suicides. I would not break a leafless bough there for anything.

He decided it was 'a wonderful country for flocks of strange birds and for gorgeous churches – whole or ruined', wrote more of *Erechtheus* and 'a good deal of verse', including 'By the North Sea'.

Swinburne returned to London and by 16 October was at Holmwood. He posted 'A Birth Song' for William Rossetti's new-born daughter Olivia Frances, 'the best I can do in default of any reply to my repeated invocations of the Genius of Blake, Hugo, or your sister – the triad of perfect baby-poets'. An allusion in the poem prompted Swinburne to comment,

> ... while thinking or feeling almost exactly as Shelley expressed himself to Trelawney on the question of what is called the immor-tality of the soul – i.e. the survival or renascence of conscious and individual personality after death – I have always thought such transmigration of consciousness an open field for speculation or belief, and even a fair and perhaps not unreasonable (any more than it can be called reasonable) ground for hope to such as are that way given . . . .

On 30 November he travelled to London. *Erechtheus* was in proof by this time and Swinburne was eager to read some of it to friends. Ten days later he told Burne-Jones he had been 'prostrate' for six of the days in town. The reading took place on 18 December; among those present were Watts, Burne-Jones, Gosse, William Rossetti, Scott and Philip Marston.

Before spending Christmas at Holmwood, Swinburne embroiled him-self in another controversy, ignited by an anonymous satirical poem *Jonas Fisher. A Poem in Black and White* (written by the Earl of Southesk), which included an attack on Swinburne. Swinburne was not alone in assuming it was the work of Robert Buchanan. He replied with 'Epitaph on a Slanderer' in *The Examiner* (20 November 1875) and a letter titled 'The Devil's Due' and signed 'Thomas Maitland', the pseudonym Buchanan had used in 1871. Swinburne ridiculed Buchanan's original claim that he had been sailing off the Western Hebrides during the 'Fleshly School' controversy by postmarking the letter 'St Kilda' and adding a footnote:

> The writer of the above being at present away from London, on a cruise among the Phillipine Islands, in his steam yacht (the *Skulk*, Captain Shuffleton master), is as can be proved on the oath or the solemn word of honour of the editor, publisher, and proprietor, responsible neither for an article which might with equal foundation be attributed to Cardinal Manning, or to Mr. Gladstone, or any other writer in the *Contemporary Review*, as to its actual author; nor for the adoption of a signature under which his friends in general, acting not only without his knowledge but against his expressed wishes on the subject, have thought it best and wisest to shelter his personal responsibility from any chance of attack.

Buchanan's response was to take the matter to court. The case was settled on 29 and 30 June 1876. Buchanan claimed £5000 damages and was awarded £150.

There were titanic struggles over the proofs of *Erechtheus*. On 26 December 1875 Swinburne exclaimed:

> Perhaps a week's hard work will enable me to find out all the blunders of those ———— the printers; who have done their utmost to disfigure my book and misuse the good type and paper you have given it . . . I can hardly believe my eyes – and I am doubtless wasting time in taking any more trouble – when I see the lines at p. 43 *still all wrong*. Again, and again, and yet again have I corrected them, and seen you do the same – and these dogs pay no more heed than at first. It is insufferable – no human patience could stand it. Tell the damned curs once more what to do – and *pray* see that they do it. *I will not go* before the world in this fashion after taking an eternity of trouble and toil which if they had been fit for their work wd have been spared me.

Four days later E. A. Clowes wrote to Chatto, 'we are sorry that Mr Swinburne should be annoyed with such *curs* of printers, but we forward the readers [*sic*] explanations'. The printers complained that Swinburne's handwriting was 'obscure' and the indentation of lines on the manuscript ambiguous, in addition to which he had often failed to use the correct technical marks where he marked them at all. So the blame was not theirs entirely.

But at last early in 1876 *Erechtheus* was published, with a dedication to Lady Jane Swinburne. The reviews were generally good, there being nothing in the way of subject-matter to which they could object. *The Athenaeum* infuriated Swinburne by comparing it to Euripides, a dramatist he loathed, 'when a fourth form boy could see that as far as it can be said to be modelled after anybody it is modelled throughout after the earliest style of Aeschylus'. Swinburne had a higher opinion of it than *Atalanta*, thinking it more authentically Greek, both in tone and structure, though for the modern reader, the issue of fidelity to Greek tragedy is irrelevant. Critical opinion has been divided over its worth. Lafourcade called it 'cold, pure, and harmless', whereas Gosse felt even though the play might lack an immediate appeal nevertheless Swinburne 'rises, in an altitude of moral emotion that he reaches nowhere else, to an atmosphere which few modern poets have even attempted to breathe'. To which Henderson retorts, 'one is tempted to say that it is an altitude at which Swinburne could not breathe either, for his genius is not suited to moral altitudes, even though the theme is human sacrifice, the sacrifice of a daughter by a father for the sake of Athens'. The appeal of the story to Swinburne lay in the challenge of imitating Greek drama and in celebrating Athens as the fount of Western civilization. But he was also attracted by the pathos of the sacrifice of Chthonia and the image of the individual in the grip of greater powers, for *Erechtheus* is about submission, death and honour. True to his promise to Jowett, Swinburne does not protest against the gods as he did in Atalanta. Jowett pleased Swinburne by writing to say he found 'no non-Greek touch or allusion in it'. Watts called it 'your greatest poem. No words can express to you how it still astonishes me', and when John Churton Collins read the battle-scene he shouted with delight. Edwin Harrison commented that the play was full of the sea, and that 'in a sense you have the sea always with you'. Presentation copies went to William and Christina Rossetti, Burne-Jones, Morris, Scott, Sandys and Madox Brown; also to Watts, Jowett, Powell, Burton, Edwin Harrison, John Nichol, Browning and Arnold and Leconte de Lisle, the critic A. B. Grosart, the family physician George Bird, Emilie Venturi, Trelawney, and Lady Mary Gordon.

On 1 February he completed 'The Last Oracle', which would be the leading poem in his 1878 collection. It alludes to the 'Hymn to Proserpine' as Swinburne evokes a pagan spirit, beginning with the Delphic oracle's response to Julian 'when he sent to consult the oracle the year of his accession':

> I go on to reinvoke Apollo to reappear in these days when the Galilean too is conquered and Christ has followed Pan to death, not as they called him in Greece, merely son of Zeus the son of Chronos, but older than Time or any God born of Time, the Light and Word incarnate in man, of whom comes the inner sunlight of human thought or imagination and the gift of speech and song whence all Gods or ideas of Gods possible to man take form and fashion – conceived of thought or imagination and born of speech and song. Of this I take the sun-god and the singing-god of the Greeks to be the most perfect type attained, or attainable . . .

Swinburne explained the theology of his poem to several correspondents. It marks a further stage in his attempt to find a way of satisfying
his religious instinct, exalting the role of the poet and sustaining the
attack on Christianity from a pagan perspective. As he would put it to
Harrison on 17 February, 'for how, my beloved brethren, without the
destruction of God, can Man be healed?'.

On 8 February Swinburne praised Watts's 'unfailing friendship' and
complained of having no-one at home to talk to. He was busy translating ballads from Villon and burlesquing the activities of the new Shakespeare Society of F. J. Furnivall. The skirmishes between the two men
over Shakespeare went on for years, with much name-calling of the
'Pigsbrook', 'Brothelsdyke' variety. Swinburne later habitually called his
writing paper 'furnivalscap'.

Eventually Swinburne went to London, with the usual consequences.
His mother wrote to his landlady Mrs Magill on 25 February and sent
him a telegram telling him not to travel home unless he was well enough.
By 4 March Swinburne was back at Holmwood. During March he worked
on *Mary Stuart*. When Nichol used the term 'Pre-Raphaelite' of
Swinburne's writing the poet demurred, thinking it inapplicable 'to anything I have written since I was an undergraduate . . . I do not see one
point in common, as to choice of subject, turn of mind, tone of thought,
trick of speech, aim or method, object or style'. He wrote 'A Song in
Season' and 'A Ballad of Dreamland', poems of private meanings and
self-communing: 'I hid my heart in a nest of roses,/Out of the sun's way,
hidden apart' he wrote, echoing 'The Triumph of Time': 'I will keep my
soul in a place out of sight,/Far off, where the pulse of it is not heard'.
Many of the poems he wrote at this time express the emptiness he felt,
which, in an unguarded moment, he described as 'the rather dull monotonous puppet-show of my life, which often strikes me as too barren of
action or enjoyment to be much worth holding onto'.

A letter of 16 April exposes Swinburne's pretence of feigned indiffer-
ence when it came to insults in the press. He asked Watts to send him a
copy of any printed attack:

> You are well aware that there is no form of cowardice which I hold
> in heartier contempt . . . than that of a man, whatever other and
> higher qualities he may possess of genius or of character, who
> pines and writhes under attack or permits the sting of an enemy to
> rankle in his mind and corrode his inner life . . . I can honestly and
> confidently assert that I know no man more indifferent to the
> opinion of strangers than myself . . .

This is hardly borne out by Swinburne's reactions to reviews.

Swinburne came up to London on 6 May and immediately called in
to see Watts. By 15 May he was writing to his mother from the Victoria

Hotel, Guernsey, where he was on holiday with Nichol, 'my oldest friend'. He enthused over the island of Sark, and how 'everywhere the glory of flowers, and splendour of crags and cliffs and sea defy all words'. He celebrated the island in 'A Ballad of Sark':

> High beyond the granite portal arched across
>   Like the gateway of some godlike giant's hold
> Sweep and swell the billowy breasts of moor and moss
>   East and westward, and the dell their slopes enfold
>   Basks in purple, glows in green, exults in gold.
> Glens that know the dove and fells that hear the lark
> Fill with joy the rapturous island . . .

By 31 May he was at home once more, and remained there on Watts's advice while the court case over *The Examiner* and Buchanan went to trial. Meanwhile Swinburne described himself as figuratively in the clutches of Mary Stuart, and in July proposed to Chatto a new edition of *Poems and Ballads* which would remove the earlier poems so they could be separately issued as a volume of juvenilia 'with additions never before published'. Watts persuaded Swinburne against this plan, and it went the way of an earlier one to separate the early poems from the later in one volume. On 29 July Mary Disney-Leith's father Henry Percy Gordon died in Scotland. Henry Gordon's death was a profound loss to Swinburne's father. It is not known whether Swinburne attended the funeral. He was in London in August, and by mid-September Lady Jane was writing anxious letters to his landlady Mrs Magill.

Swinburne was at Southwold in late September, probably with Watts. By October Watts had the first canto of *Tristram of Lyonesse* to sell. The two men had known each for four years, and Swinburne's letters often include remarks like 'there is no friend to whom I would sooner be obliged than yourself'. It was in the early autumn of 1876 that Swinburne claimed to have been poisoned, having slept in a room with a large India lily in full bloom near the bed, since when 'I have been but a rag of unmanned manhood, barely able to read or write or think consecutively,' To an American correspondent the following March Swinburne spoke of it being a 'dangerous illness'. He recalled 'waking in an hour or two literally poisoned by the perfume, in such agony of brain and stomach as I hope never to feel again'. He was amused by the fact that *The Queen Mother and Rosamond* had included a similar poisoning. The year ended with the *Note of an English Republican on the Muscovite Crusade*, expressing Swinburne's views on the 'Eastern question', which had the approval of old political friends such as Karl Blind.

Early in 1877 Swinburne decided to publish *A Year's Letters* (written 1861–62) in serial form under the pseudonym of Mrs Horace Manners in the *Tatler*, where it duly appeared from 25 August to 29 December.

He sent Mrs Horace Manners, as he liked to refer to the book, to Scotland to be inspected by Nichol. Mrs Manners returned from her Hibernian jaunt bearing glad tidings. Nichol thought the story 'an almost consummate piece of art, among English analytical novels of our age only rivalled by "The Scarlet Letter"', though he advised the excision of some of the passages that referred to flagellation. Word did get out that the novel was by Swinburne, much to his annoyance.

Swinburne's other writing projects of 1877 included translating Villon and writing *A Note on Charlotte Brontë*, which argued against the high standing of George Eliot in favour not only of Charlotte but also of Emily Brontë. Swinburne had recognized the power of *Wuthering Heights* as long ago as his Balliol days when he read a paper on it to Old Mortality. Part of Swinburne's affinity with Charlotte Brontë is revealed in his reference to her as 'our illustrious countrywoman', alluding to her connection with Northumberland. In March canto 1 of *Tristram* was published in the *Gentleman's Magazine* and the *New York Independent*. Swinburne was disappointed at the lack of response to it: 'I must say I think it contains the best bit of description (a sunrise at sea) that I, or perhaps any poet going now (except of course the Master) ever accomplished.'

On 4 March 1877 Charles Henry Swinburne died, only a few weeks short of his eightieth birthday, having been ill for some time. According to Swinburne, he had never recovered from the sudden death of Henry Percy Gordon the previous year, the bond between them being 'more like that between an elder and a younger brother'. The next day Swinburne wrote a short but moving elegy, 'Inferiae'. Spring returned to Holmwood, 'but he/Whose heart fed mine has passed into the past':

> The life, the spirit, and the work were one
> That here – ah, who shall say, that here are done?
> Not I, that know not; father, not thy son,
>   For all the darkness of the night and sea.

Swinburne wrote first to Jowett, then Watts. On 6 March he told Nichol, 'among many points of feeling and character that I like to think we have in common, I doubt if there is any stronger on either side than our northerly disinclination for many or effusive words on matter of this kind'. He received a number of letters of sympathy. The funeral was held at Bonchurch on the Isle of Wight on 12 March, where the Admiral was buried next to Edith, and Swinburne returned to Holmwood on the next day. By his father's will, Swinburne inherited £5000, which must have helped his financial situation considerably.

By June Swinburne was at 3 Great James Street, and resuming his social engagements, visiting Lord Houghton on 26 May. Early in June

Swinburne wrote to *The Athenaeum* protesting against Zola's novel *L'Assommoir* in terms which unfortunately echo his mock-outrage of 1862: 'to transcribe the necessary extracts would for me ... be physically impossible. For the editor of any known publication in England to print them would be morally impossible.' Swinburne objected to the book's realism and passages that dealt with brutality towards a little girl. To Houghton he called it a 'damnable dunghill of a book'. On 11 June Swinburne invited Gosse to a reading of his essay on Charlotte Brontë at Great James Street. When Gosse arrived Swinburne was standing 'alone in the middle of the floor, with one hand in the breast of his coat, and the other jerking at his side. He had an arrangement of chairs, with plates and glasses set on the table, as if for a party. He looked like a conjurer, who was waiting for his audience.' He referred vaguely to 'the others', and while they were waiting Swinburne read Gosse a new poem, 'In the Bay', dedicated to Marlowe. Gosse found it 'very magnificent, but rather difficult to follow, and very long'. Still no-one appeared, and Gosse suggested that perhaps Swinburne should begin reading the essay on Charlotte Brontë. Swinburne replied:

> 'I'm expecting Watts and Ned Burne-Jones and Philip Marston, and – some other men. I hope they'll come soon.' We waited a little while in silence, in the twilight, and then Swinburne said, 'I hope I didn't forget to ask them!' He then trotted or glided into his bedroom, and what he referred to there I don't know, but almost instantly he came out and said cheerfully, 'Ah! I find I didn't ask any of those men, so we'll begin at once.' He lighted his two great candlesticks of serpentine and started. He soon got tired of reading the Essay, and turned to the delights, of which he never wearies, of his unfinished novel. He read two long passages, the one a ride over a moorland by night, the other the death of his heroine, Lesbia Brandon. After reading aloud all these things with his amazing violence, he seemed quite exhausted, and sank in a kind of dream into the corner of his broad sofa ...

Gosse states that Swinburne was 'very solitary at this time'. He dined occasionally at Gosse's home, which had the dual attractions of a cat and a baby. His landlady provided breakfast but he was obliged to go out for other meals, often eating at the London Restaurant. Gosse wrote, 'it was a curious spectacle to see him crossing Holborn' when, 'with hanging hands, and looking straight before him', Swinburne would 'walk across like an automaton between the vans and cabs, and that he was never knocked down seemed extraordinary'. From time to time he went to Walter T. Spencer's bookshop, where Swinburne would enter at midday 'looking pasty-white either from bad temper or a less fleeting complaint, and complaining in his shrillest voice that [Mrs Magill] had wakened him at eleven o'clock although he had expressly told her he must be left undisturbed till twelve'. Spencer described him as 'an extraordinary man, abnormally shy when his excitement had calmed down. He never seemed to desire anyone to speak to him, and certainly he wanted no-one to be told who he was.'

The actor and author W. Lestocq saw Swinburne between 1875 and 1878, usually late at night when Swinburne was drunk and 'generally suffering from abuse from a cabman who could not get his fare, which I would pay, and help him upstairs to his room'. Swinburne would invite Lestocq in, point out bits of attractive furniture and his picture of Orsini, and eventually show his guest out 'with his profuse, somewhat incoherent thanks for my help and the presentation to me of one of his books'. A few days later Swinburne's housekeeper would then call and ask for it back.

In June he complained of influenza and deafness, and was ill again early in August, with diarrhoea. His mother wrote to Mrs Magill on 25 August to ask if Swinburne had left London. After a brief stay at Holmwood he returned to London, where his ill-health persisted through October. On 29 September Swinburne told Howell, 'I have been very seedy and am still shaky tho' just able today to hold a pen.' Howell replied on 2 October, inviting Swinburne to the christening of Howell's daughter: 'You always loved children, and your love for them and the old is proverbial throughout London.' In December he wrote that he had been ill in bed for some weeks. Relations with his family were very poor. His mother sent a letter to him via Mrs Magill on 27 December, to be give him 'when he is well enough to read it. You need not fear to give it him as it is as kind a letter as a Mother can write.'

Early in 1878 he was well enough to visit an exhibition at the Grosvenor Gallery. Despite his loathing of railways, Swinburne went to Glasgow to spend some time with Nichol. He was seen 'marching about the Quadrangle, very fashionably dressed, in a close-fitting long Melton coat of dark blue ... his top hat balanced on his great mop of hair'. There he met the poet John Davidson, and a Balliol contemporary, Donald Crawford, who was 'pained' at Swinburne's physical condition. During the latter part of 1877 Swinburne had asked Chatto to set *Lesbia Brandon* in type, though it was still 'my fragmentary novel', and Swinburne read some of it to Nichol. Watts had parts of the manuscript and Swinburne asked for them back, 'as I certainly mean to complete the book some day'. The sonnets 'The White Czar', 'Rizpah' and 'To Louis Kossuth' were published in the *Glasgow University Magazine* in February. He remained with Nichol until 22 February, on the 16th finalizing the order of his new collection of poems.

CHAPTER TWELVE

'Closer than a Brother'

Poems and Ballads, Second Series appeared in the summer of 1878, dedicated to Richard Burton. It was as different from *Songs before Sunrise* as that had been from *Poems and Ballads* (1866). The earliest of its lyrics were written as far back as 1867 and Gosse had heard Swinburne read half of the book on 10 September 1876. It presented a Swinburne turned from political verse to poetry of memory and regret, occasionally blazing into homage or defiance. It has poems which celebrate the tradition of poetry, elegize poets, friends and family, and there are lyrics that hint at Swinburne's romantic disappointment. Swinburne paid homage to a number of writers in 'Cyril Tourneur', 'In the Bay' (Marlowe), 'Ave Atque Vale' (Baudelaire), 'Memorial Verses' (Gautier) and 'In Memory of Barry Cornwall'; there was a poem for Villon and ten Villon translations. The personal elegies were 'Epicede' for James Lorimer Graham (who died at Florence, 30 April 1876) and 'Inferiae' for his father. The topographical 'Four Songs of Four Seasons' drew on memories of Northumberland, Tuscany, Auvergne and North Cornwall. The defiant invocation of Pan and Apollo in 'The Last Oracle' celebrated the power of the poetic imagination in language which gave the verse the same internal tensions as 'Hertha'.

Among the more personal lyrics were 'A Forsaken Garden', 'Relics', 'At a Month's End', 'Sestina', 'The Year of the Rose', 'A Wasted Vigil', 'Ex-Voto', 'A Ballad of Dreamland', 'Pastiche' and 'A Vision of Spring in Winter'. These poems further echoed the emotional disaster which had left his young manhood 'a barren stock'. In 'Sestina' Swinburne describes his soul as barred from the delight that others know by day, but instead consoled by a vision seen in darkness. 'The Year of the Rose' uses the same north/south polarity as other poems and may draw on memories of the rose-gardens at Northcourt and The Orchard:

> The time of lovers is brief;
> From the fair first joy to the grief
>   That tells when love is grown old,
>   From the warm wild kiss to the cold,
> From the red to the white-rose leaf,
>   They have but a season to seem
>   As roseleaves lost on a stream
> That part not and pass not apart
>   As a spirit from dream to dream,
> As a sorrow from heart to heart.

'A Wasted Vigil' looks back to 'Last year, a brief while since . . . /what friends were we'. He asks, 'With me it is not, is it with thee well?' and remembers the lovers' 'barren grief and glee' ('A Wasted Vigil' had originally been published in 1867). So the 'last year' could refer to 1866 or 1865. Even 'Age and Song' begins 'In vain men tell us time can alter/Old loves or make old memories falter'. In 'Before Sunset' he imagines 'One whole hour of amorous breath,/Time shall die, and love shall be/ Lord as time was over death'. A mournful romanticism, present in the 1866 volume but often drowned out by the more strident poems, is heard in its successor in all its troubled beauty. *Poems and Ballads, Second Series* was generally praised and became one of Swinburne's best-selling volumes.

In April 1878 Swinburne was chilled, 'depriving me for weeks of all natural sleep and appetite' which led to a delay in the correction of the proofs for the poems. On 27 May he wrote to Browning to acknowledge a copy of his new book *La Saisiazz* and to express the hope that he could return the compliment in a fortnight. On 28 May John Ingram visited Swinburne and found him 'charming and cordial':

> To me Swinburne seemed most unrestrainedly self-revealing, although some persons assert they have found him quite otherwise. He had no reserve, nor asked for adulation, and appeared to crave for friendship only, offering his confidence unsought. I have never met a man, apparently more ready to open his heart and mind or more willing to enlarge upon the merits of our mutual friends. Listening to the magical music of his speech it seemed to me that if any man deserved the designation of 'golden-mouthed' it was Swinburne. There appeared no subject he was unable to deal with exhaustively and with the most appropriate language.

He read 'In the Bay' 'sitting down in a low chair opposite . . . in a kind of half-chant, in a musical but somewhat monotonous tone', and then showed Ingram some of his pictures – Byron in an Albanian costume, an engraving of Thackeray's Colonel Newcome. They decided to go out for dinner to the 'London' in Fleet Street. Invited to try on Swinburne's hat, Ingram found 'it came down over my head onto my shoulders . . . Contrasted with his small figure Swinburne's head looked unnaturally large.' Swinburne 'was very particular and deliberated for some time as to what to order, consulting me about the viands'. During the meal the conversation turned to death-bed repentances. 'Swinburne said he had recently attended the funeral of a relative who was a Roman Catholic, and he had been deeply impressed by the apparent sincerity of the priests and the solemnity of their ritual. He declared that if he ever joined any professed faith it would be that of the Catholics. The feeling may only have been a transient one', added Ingram, wisely, considering Swinburne's years of anti-Christian invective.

In the summer of 1878 Swinburne was skirting serious illness as never before. Lord Houghton saw him and wrote of his concern to Lady Jane, who on 23 July referred to 'the sad state in which you found my poor son':

> ... the case is a most grievous one and seems so hopeless. We have done our utmost to make our home a happy one for him and he has at times remained many months together with us ... but it was often with much difficulty (and with much suffering to his Father), that he was induced to leave London. Since his Father's death I have not been able to persuade him to come to me – I have tried in every way to make him do so. In one letter to me he told me that nothing would induce him to come here again, – that he hates the place – and that, can I not be satisfied with seeing him in London? – I answered him that I would not again press his coming here but that should he change his mind he would always meet with an affectionate welcome – latterly I have urged his leaving Town and going to the sea if he would not come here ...
> I do not know what I can do – but if my health will allow me I will endeavour to go to see him – but it is difficult for me to do so, as the last time his Father and I went to him to persuade him to leave Town he threatened if we did so again – he would leave London and never let us know where he had gone to – and this he said when he was in a state perfectly to understand and mean what he said.
> I quite agree with what you say about Medical Supervision, but I have no power to enforce it and persuasion I fear would be useless. It is a heavy grief.

Swinburne moved to 25 Guildford Street sometime in June or July. Watts wrote to reassure Lady Jane. There was a plan for Swinburne to spend time with Jowett in Malvern. Powell wrote to Watts on 29 August asking what had happened to Swinburne and why he had not received any replies to his letters: 'Where is he, and how is he?' In September Swinburne was once more describing himself as a bed-ridden invalid. There is an ominous gap in Swinburne's correspondence at this point. From May 1878 to June 1879 there are only five extant letters, and his contributions to journals cease.

We know that Swinburne spent the evening of 10 October with Richard and Isabel Burton, and Alice and George Bird. He arrived at Welbeck Street looking 'ill and worn, and older. He had a haggard expression as if his nerves were out of tune.' 'He can hear nothing now, unless it is tête-à-tête, slowly and deliberately. He said that deafness was in the family on both sides.' Swinburne enthused about Sark and read several poems from his last collection. Lady Jane seems to have visited him in London in November. He told one correspondent of 'a very tedious and painful attack of illness, which has left me with scarcely strength enough even yet to hold a pen ... for upwards of six weeks and more I have been almost entirely bedridden – always incapable of answering, usually incapable of reading, a letter.'

It was a miserable time, as the months passed by and he found himself 42. He was physically unwell, deaf and often alone, and possibly short of money. He felt alienated from his mother and from Holmwood, and his father was no longer alive to take him away from London. Not for him the children who came crowding to the knees of his cousin Mary. East Dene, Capheaton, Ashburnham Place, moorland, sea and shore, were dreamy images before his eyes as he sat at the table, amid the disorder of his room, with the unanswered letters and unpaid bills, sometimes waiting for inspiration to send the nib scratching across the blue foolscap. Across three continents, his poems were being enjoyed by readers thrilled by the thought of a poet radiant with Apollonic light, a rebellious spirit who had challenged the voices of religious oppression. On the side was a leaf from a journal printed in Budapest with his sonnet to Louis Kossuth translated into Hungarian, letters from France and Germany, requests for autographs from San Francisco and Calcutta, missives asking for his enlightenment on issues of God and life. The wax melted and ran down the serpentine candlesticks as the night wore on. The elemental child, the survivor, was being consumed by his inner demons.

Alarmed by Swinburne's rapidly deteriorating condition, Watts decided to act. Perhaps as a temporary measure, he went to Guildford Street and helped Swinburne into a cab. They made their way to the house Watts shared with his sister in Werther Road, Putney. It is said that Swinburne, when initially told of the plan, said plaintively, 'Can't we go now?' On 9 June Lord Ronald Gower saw Swinburne in Putney, and observed, 'while fully aware of the divine gifts within him, he is as simple and unaffected as a child.' On 24 June William Rossetti noted in his diary:

> Watts gives me a melancholy account of Swinburne, who was lately in such a desperate case that Watts saw nothing for it but to take him down for a while to his house in Putney, and at last, with much ado, he has got Swinburne down to Holmwood, where his mother is still living. There Swinburne now is, and has improved observably. Watts says his memory was almost entirely gone, and he has reached a particular stage of malady, due to his incurable irregularities, which Doctors pronounce to be a very advanced and in fact fatal symptom. I fear his faculties, or his life, will not hold out much longer.

Rumours of his impending death had been circulated for at least ten years. But Swinburne had something of the phoenix about him. By 13 June he was writing letters from Holmwood and soon afterwards

corrected proofs of his forthcoming book on Shakespeare. He asked
Watts to send him proofs of an unfinished story (presumably *Lesbia
Brandon*) and the manuscript of *Tristram and Iseult*. His father's library
was sold. On 26 June Swinburne told Chatto he was 'still far from
strong'. The proofs of *Lesbia Brandon* were 'in a simply scandalous and
disgraceful state of confusion. Everything is out of order, and some of
the most important parts, apparently, at first sight, missing alike in
proof and manuscript.'

On 11 July Lady Jane wrote to Lord Houghton, 'I am thankful to say
that Algernon's illness is now a thing of the past – he has been here
nearly a month and is really quite well – happy cheerful and busy with
his writing.' Swinburne's account of his illness shows that he did not
realize how ill he had been: 'I was very unwell for weeks together before
I left London, and a good deal reduced in strength by prolonged insomnia and consequent loss of appetite and exhaustion; but a day or two at
a friend's house near Putney Heath, with plenty of walking exercise
thereon and thereabouts, sufficed to set me up.' During the summer
Watts and Lady Jane conferred. Holmwood was to be sold, and
Swinburne could not be allowed to return to London to live alone. By
13 July Lady Jane and Watts had agreed Swinburne should live with
him from now on. Swinburne was 'perfectly well, working steadily and
is in very good spirits' and seemingly unaware of the negotiations going
on between Watts and Lady Jane.

On 30 July Swinburne invited Watts to Holmwood and mentioned a
new poem, 'On the Cliffs', only a few lines short of 400, 'longer (I will
not say better, whether I think so or not) than any (except the ever
edifying "Dolores") in either of my collections. "Anactoria" which is
next longest is ninety-four lines short of this new-born one . . . You will
regret to hear that in subject-matter and treatment it is not akin to
either of the above-named.' No scandal could be expected from the
song of a nightingale by the sea, the bird in Swinburne's mind being the
spirit of Sappho.

In late July or early August 1879 E. C. Stedman visited Swinburne at
Holmwood shortly before his family left:

> I found it a spacious white mansion of the Georgian type, with a
> garden divided from the carriageway by a wall, against which
> peach-trees and apricot were trailed to face the sun. In the en-
> trance-hall was a quaint collection of old china, heirlooms of the
> family. The poet was working in his bedroom, a chamber plainly
> furnished, but with a glorious view from the windows – the
> Swinburne lawn, with fine old trees sloping from the foreground.
> A wooden table was covered with the manuscript sheets of a poem
> which he had been writing with the speed that is transferred to his
> galloping anapaests. It was the long, melodious, haunting piece,

'On the Cliffs', consecrate to the memory and Muse of Sappho. Although I had heard of Mr. Swinburne's ill-health, and that he was then in great retirement, it seemed that I met him at an auspicious time. Except for a chronic nervousness, or what I should call overpossession of his body by his mind, he was in health, voice, and spirits, and he read me what was then completed of his poem. It grew out of a night in Italy – where he was kept awake by the singing of the nightingales, and fancied their song bore a resemblance to a famous line of Sappho's ... He read his lyrical rhapsody with a free chanting cadence ...

His conversation is as noteworthy as his written text – a flood of wit, humour, learning, often enthusiastic, more rich with epigram and pithy comment than the speech of other men.

On 13 August Swinburne wrote the section on Hamlet for *A Study of Shakespeare*, 'the best piece of prose as well as the subtlest and most accurate work of thought I ever achieved'. Watts's next visit was smoothed by Swinburne revealing that Lady Jane had 'a really cordial liking ... and sincere regard for you – as well she may, considering all you have been and are to her troublesome first-born'. On 27 August, 'this morning before breakfast about eight I put the very last touch in the very last sentence of the very last paragraph of my book on Shakespeare – Glory be to all of us of the true faith; and woe unto the Sham Shakespeareans!' The next day Edward Swinburne wrote to Watts about financial arrangements for looking after Swinburne. Watts was to receive £200 a year. Swinburne's other money was invested in two £1000 bonds 'which I thought might be an advantage in case Algernon should be taken with a paroxysm of extravagance and want suddenly to spend £200 or so, on some book ... but I think these precautions are rather superfluous as being quite beyond his ken'. Edward's exasperation with his brother is apparent.

After a holiday on the coast in September, Watts and Swinburne moved into a large detached house at the foot of Putney Hill toward the end of September. On 27 September Swinburne informed his mother,

You will see that our flitting has been in the main accomplished – into a large double block of building, of which we inhabit the left house (looked at from the street) till the right – our own domicile – is ready. Meantime we are gypsying here with furniture enough for sleep, meals and a sitting room ... The part we live in, as we all agree, is exactly like the outlying (and prettiest) parts of Oxford, where there are (or were) little gardens with large trees overhanging them and little old walls round a 'grass-plat'. And we are within an easy walk of Richmond Park, in which I have already made two longish excursions – and also within an hour of Piccadilly ...

Putney has long been absorbed into London's metropolitan sprawl and choked with its fumes but in 1879 it was far less urban – even allowing

12.1   Swinburne's room at The Pines

for Swinburneian hyperbole. He liked to think of himself as living as Tennyson, 'Close to the edge of a noble down', telling his friends 'our house is in the neighbourhood of such noble woodlands and moorlands that we might fancy ourselves, after a short walk, 100 miles from the nearest town.' For Swinburne, living in Putney was to be 'practically in the country, on the verge of a great moor or down, and within an easy walk of some of the loveliest woodland and meadow scenery in England'. To be fair, one Victorian writer stated that in the 1880s 'Wimbledon Common, at the eastern edge of which is Putney Hill, was a place of unbelievable beauty and wildness to be so near Charing Cross. In some of its birch-crested, heather-and-gorse-clad ravines you might believe yourself in Scotland.'

On 9 October 1879 a van was duly despatched to 25 Guildford Street and his books and few bits of furniture were loaded up for their last migration. Watts and Swinburne had taken on The Pines as equals, as he reminded Gosse, saying, 'you need not put Watts's name on my address any more than mine on his, as we have both moved in together.'

For Swinburne it was a new life. Within a month the occupants of The Pines had increased to five. Watts's sisters Theresa and Mrs Miranda Mason, with her five-year-old son Bertie, moved in. Swinburne had gained an extended family and took to Bertie immediately. The child was 'a sweet thing in infants', despite playing up on the first afternoon he and Theresa had custody of him. Preparations to move into the other side of the building slowly advanced. Swinburne wrote to Houghton,

> I have begun housekeeping in common with a friend, on such terms that we can receive the ladies of our own respective families at any time, our house-hold at all points as respectable as the whitest of white sepulchres. If either of us should ever want a change he can go off without warning given or expected for a day (or night) or so.

Nothing could be more different from the misery of his bachelor rooms in the city. Just before Christmas he told Houghton, 'I was never fresher or stronger or happier at twenty than now and for many weeks back.'

Amid the upheaval Swinburne managed work on a number of books. His correspondence with Nichol at this time shows he wanted to find a publisher for *Lesbia Brandon* and he was commissioned to write articles on Collins and Landor. He corrected the proofs of his *Study of Shakespeare* and composed some new poems, including 'Thalassius'. This originated in an idea for 'a symbolical quasi-autobiographical poem after the fashion of Shelley or of Hugo, concerning the generation, birth and rearing of a by-blow of Amphitrite's . . . reared like Ion in the temple-service of Apollo. It would be a pretty subject, but when should I hear the last of my implied arrogance and self-conceit?' The poem opens with a baby found on a beach taken into care by an elder who teaches the child about liberty, love and hatred of oppression. As a youth he meets Love itself who at first seems unthreatening but is suddenly transformed: 'And in his blind eyes burned/Hard light and heat of laughter . . . /And all his stature waxed immeasurable', saying:

I am he that was thy lord before thy birth,
I am he that is thy lord till thou turn earth:
I make the night more dark, and all the morrow
Dark as the night whose darkness was my breath:
O fool, my name is sorrow;
Thou fool, my name is death.

After a time of grief, Thalassius has a period of frenzied hedonism and eventually finds a new life and a new identity, rediscovering his childhood joy in the elements: 'Being now no more a singer, but a song'. It ends with Apollo as God of Poetry acknowledging the sacrifice that Thalassius has made. By 17 October 'On the Cliffs' was finished. Watts said what he was to say of many of Swinburne's later poems: that it was the best poem Swinburne had ever written. Like 'Anactoria' it incorporates fragments of Sappho as Swinburne hymns the 'supreme head of song' symbolically present in the song of the nightingale.

The only dark cloud on the horizon came in October when news reached Swinburne that Simeon Solomon, now in dire financial straits, had been selling letters Swinburne had written, and that Howell was entertaining people with stories about him. Swinburne responded as usual by pretending he was unperturbed:

> As long as I can feel that I may count, and have a right to count, on the steady friendship and fidelity of honourable gentlemen, I will not for very shame's sake so far forget or forego my own claim to a sense of self-respect as to fret my heartstrings by day or by night over such disgusting facts as that I hear of one person who was once my friend and is yet my debtor habitually amusing mixed companies of total strangers by obscene false anecdotes about my private eccentricities of indecent indulgence as exhibited in real or imaginary lupanaria, and of another, who is now a thing unmentionable alike by men and women, as equally abhorrent to either – nay, to the very beasts – raising money by the sale of my letters to him in past years, which must doubtless contain much foolish burlesque and now regrettable nonsense never meant for any stranger's eye who would not understand the mere childishness of the silly chaff indulged in long ago.

Watts boasted that from 1879 Swinburne's contact with Bohemian London had ceased. This was in part Swinburne's choosing.

In 1880 Swinburne's profile as a writer was raised by the publication of three books (a fourth was anonymous): *Songs of the Springtides*, *A Study of Shakespeare* (out by February 1880), *Studies in Song* (in the autumn) and the anonymous *The Heptalogia*. The appeal of the two poetry collections was limited by the sheer length of the poems they contained. *Studies in Song* was not reprinted until 1896 and *Songs of the Springtides* reached a third edition only in 1891. The latter had only five main poems, of which 'Thalassius' and 'On the Cliffs' are now accepted as important later works. Swinburne said 'Off-Shore' was intended to repeat the metrical effect of 'Hertha'; 'The Garden of Cymodoce' was 'an attempt to supersede Murray by a simple and complete "handbook" in rhyme'. The Landor ode was started in May and finished 6 June. It was 800 lines long, and 'Watts deliberately pronounces it the finest thing I ever wrote.' The enormous panegyrics on Landor and Hugo were of little interest. These books represented a shift in his poetry away from the elegiac lyrics published in 1878. At their worst they have a hard, abstract quality; at best a new breadth of vision. Much of Swinburne's best later poetry is inspired by the sea and landscape enjoyed on his annual holidays on the east and south coast; 'By the North Sea', for example, by the 'dead cathedral city' of Dunwich, Suffolk. Swinburne said, 'the whole picture is from life – salt marshes, ruins, and bones protruding through the soil of the crumbling sand-banks':

> A land that is thirstier than ruin;
>   A sea that is hungrier than death,
> Heaped hills that a tree never grew in;
>   Wide sands where the wave draws breath;
> All solace is here for the spirit
>   That ever for ever may be
> For the soul of thy son to inherit,
>   My mother, my sea.

Swinburne dedicated 'By the North Sea' to Watts because 'Watts likes it better than anything I ever did (and in metrical and antiphonal effects I prefer it myself to all my others).' The dedicatory poem for Watts hailed him as a fellow Thalassian: 'Brother, to whom our Mother as to me/ Is dearer than all dreams of days undone.' The sea is dearer than the past: that was Swinburne's consolation.

The Heptalogia was testimony to his gifts as a parodist, as he mimicked Tennyson, Browning, Elizabeth Browning, Coventry Patmore, Lord Robert Lytton, Dante Gabriel Rossetti and himself – although 'Nephelidia' is not as good a self-parody as 'The Ghost of It'. The poems had been written over a period of 20 years. Never separately reprinted by Chatto, *The Heptalogia* was revised in 1904 when it appeared as part of Swinburne's *Collected Poems*.

A Study of Shakespeare was spoilt by the Bardolatry that runs throughout but Swinburne has interesting things to say about most of the plays. In the 1880s he repeatedly clashed with F. J. Furnivall, President of the New Shakespeare Society. Swinburne complained that Furnivall 'has repeatedly made me the object of such rancorous ribaldry and such foul personal insult in public as well as private print as I should have supposed impossible at any time since the days of the Dunciad'. Furnivall became 'the most blackguardly of blockheads and most block-headed of blackguards'. In the summer of 1880 Furnivall resurrected the quarrel of 1876 about certain passages in the *Study of Shakespeare* which had been previously printed. Swinburne's book included a lengthy prose satire, 'Proceedings of the latest Shakespeare Society'.

In February 1881 Furnivall published an abusive pamphlet *The 'Co.' of Pigsbrook & Co.'* Swinburne replied to *The Athenaeum* on 16 February, and in letters of the time Furnivall becomes Flunkivall Brothelsbank. He wrote to Browning, who was nominally President of the New Shakspere Society, pointing out that Furnivall's pamphlet described Swinburne as 'a person of damaged character'. With his usual enjoyment of drawing lines in the sand Swinburne informed Browning that, if this imputation were true, 'it follows of course that I am unfit to hold any intercourse or keep up any acquaintance with you':

> ... if it is a lie, it follows equally of course that no person who remains in any way or in any degree associated with the writer of that pamphlet is fit to hold any intercourse or keep up any acquaintance with me.

Browning's reply is lost, but it must have been immediate because the next day, 21 February, Swinburne replied:

> You labour under an entire and I must be allowed to say a most unaccountable misapprehension if you imagine for one instant that I at all events – as you say – 'call upon you to take my part.' I have never in any case called upon any man to do anything of the kind. Having been publicly and personally insulted in a manner too infamous and blackguardly for description, I did call upon you – as any man with any sense of honour or self-respect would in my place be bound to call upon you, or upon any other acquaintance – to let me know whether or not, after this, your name is to remain in any way publicly associated with one which in my humble opinion it is degrading if necessary, and disgraceful if unnecessary, for a gentleman to pronounce, to transcribe, or to remember.

Browning remained associated with the Society.

The privacy of the regime at The Pines during the early 1880s has possibly been exaggerated by those who did not have the access to Swinburne they desired. Swinburne grew deafer and more reserved, prematurely aged since he was only 43. In March 1880 Swinburne met Isabel Burton and Mrs Lynn Linton in town, and they came to lunch a few days later. Isabel scribbled on the bottom of a letter from Swinburne to Lord Houghton that she found Swinburne 'looking so well and cheerful and we have been very merry'. On 28 April Swinburne gave a reading of *Studies in Song* to Watts, Austin Dobson, Arthur O'Shaughnessy, William Rossetti, Philip Marston, John Churton

12.2 Swinburne in middle age

Collins, and possibly Gosse. His mother visited in October and wrote
to Watts:

> It is the greatest possible comfort to me to have seen my very dear
> Son so well and happy. The contrast that it was to what I used to
> see him was something quite beyond words and I cannot say how

thankful I was – nor can I tell you how much I feel your care of him – and I am really quite happy about him. The return to the religious faith of his youth I feel is so much more hopeful when that fatal tendency from which he has suffered so much is got the better of.

The fatal tendency was of course alcohol, which Watts had proscribed, except for a bottle of Bass pale ale at midday lunch. As for religious belief, Lady Jane's pious wish was never to be satisfied. Watts was a free-thinker with a leaning toward nature mysticism. When Swinburne wrote of an 'edible and potable God' he offended Watts's sense of propriety rather than any real belief. Swinburne continued to argue about Christianity with correspondents such as John Morley, calling Christ the 'child-loving Socialist of Galilee' and maintaining 'that Christ was not a Christian, and certainly would not ... have been one if born within the Christian era'.

Swinburne's correspondence on religious as well as other matters continued to show the odd flash of his younger self: ribald remarks to Lord Houghton and satirical jibes as he explained to another correspondent that his family had quit Holmwood 'so that address is now ... a delusion and a snare, like the Christianity of Mrs. Bitcher Spewe or the Hellenism of Mr. R. W. Emerson'. Jowett came to lunch at The Pines and Swinburne read the Master his translation from Aristophanes' 'The Birds' (finished 19 October 1880). Watts and Swinburne returned the visit by seeing Jowett in Oxford. Swinburne wrote, 'I met one or two old friends and made one or two pleasant acquaintances.' Swinburne thought Balliol much improved since the 'dark days' when he had been an undergraduate.

By the autumn of 1880 Swinburne was writing *Mary Stuart*. Watts approved of the choice of subject. By the end of the year Swinburne was writing touchingly, 'there came a most lovely baby in arms here on a visit one day, and it beamed on me the minute our eyes met. But of all children out of arms Bertie is much the sweetest going at any price ... I don't know how to say what I feel about children – it is as if something of worship was mixed with love of them and delight in them ... ' Swinburne formed a lasting relationship with Bertie Mason, Watts's nephew.

The year 1881 began with a reading from his new poems, to which Ford Madox Brown and William Rossetti were invited, and Swinburne visited Rossetti on 7 January. Nichol stayed for a few days. Swinburne read James Thomson's *City of Dreadful Night* (1880), finding its author 'a man of genius' but some of the poetry having 'a vein of what can only be called vulgarity'. He also read Carlyle's *Reminscences* and was 'disgusted by the sour arrogance, egotism, and malevolence' of the book. Gosse's selection, *English Odes*, placed one of Swinburne's poems next to Patmore's 'To the Unknown Eros'. Swinburne declared he was amused at Patmore's 'ideas of lyric style and the structure of an ode', always committed to the requirement of form in poetry.

During the spring of 1881 Swinburne wrote an article on Keats for the *Encyclopaedia Britannica*. On 13 March Czar Alexander II was assassinated in St Petersburg. A delighted Swinburne told William Rossetti, 'I feel at peace with all or most men, and ready to make allowances for God.' To a republican the news of tyrannicide was as 'the news of a king's recovery from sickness to royalists'. Rossetti's feelings were 'considerably more mixed and tempered than yours'. Edward Trelawney had written to Rossetti, 'If you see Swinburne, remember me kindly to him, and say age prevented my calling on him, and I want him to write a tragedy on Charles I'. Swinburne commented that he had 'too much tragic work on hand with Mary Stuart to think of undertaking her grandson'.

Swinburne was disappointed by the reviews of *Studies in Song* and the sales of the *Heptalogia*. All the reviews except that of Watts either reviled or ignored the *Studies in Song*, and the latter had turned out a 'hopeless fiasco'. He had not forgotten his novels, for 'Watts thinks little but Nichol thinks much of them.' The *Encyclopaedia Britannica* commissioned an article on Marlowe, and he composed 'Athens: An Ode', 'an anti-Christian and anti-Russian' poem: 'Watts says the astute and practical Greeks will laugh at it and me – justly, he seems to think.'

On 22 April William and Lucy Rossetti had twins, Michael Ford and Mary Elizabeth. Swinburne responded with fifteen stanzas of 'Twins', 'April, on whose wings/Ride all gracious things' six days later. It was the type of sophisticated greetings-card verse Swinburne could reel off with ease. William Rossetti acknowledged the poem on the 29th, noting in his diary: 'received from Swinburne a long lyrical effusion on the birth of our twins: facile and taking (it seems on a first hasty perusal), but not very substantial'.

About a week before the end of April Bertie Mason left The Pines. Swinburne had grown very attached to the boy, reading him stories out of an illustrated Shakespeare, and writing the occasional poem based on things Bertie said. Bertie's absence plunged Swinburne into a state of abject deprivation in which his only solace was to write a poem for each day of the month Bertie was to be away. Swinburne had just turned 44, so this was hardly the dotage of an old man. The sequence was titled 'A Dark Month'. He expressed his feelings to Lady Jane, who was concerned at her son's reaction. Watts suggested she might have a word with Algernon. On 14 May she replied,

> I quite understand what you feel about Algernon but he has given
> me no opening, as you think it likely he may have done, to enable
> me to give him the little word of advice you suggest – he tells me
> that he has written '21 Poems of lamentation' on the subject of his
> dear little friend's absence which he calls a 'total eclipse of the
> Sun'. His love for that little friend amounts to devotion and I often
> hope that it may lead to the faith of his youth in some hidden way
> – for the love of, and the appreciation of innocent childhood is
> good and wholesome. You and no doubt his parents will guard the
> little child from any harmful views on that subject that Algernon
> might inadvertently lead him into.

It was an affection she had encouraged. On 28 February she had said, 'I
do so very much like all that you have written about him. The love of
children is a grand profession.' She goes on to say that she would like to
have Swinburne home for a while but is worried about him travelling
alone, which says more about her overprotection than it does about
Swinburne. A postscript adds, 'Your report of Algernon's health is most
satisfactory. What you say about his spoiling his writing by "not knowing when to stop" is so very true. I constantly deplore it!'

'A Dark Month' carried an epigraph from Hugo, 'La maison sans
enfants'. It open with Swinburne describing May as 'A month without
sight of the sun', himself 'hungering for the food of the sound/And
thirsting for joy of his voice'. His language grew ever more hyperbolic:
'Alas, what right has the dawn to glimmer,/What right has the wind to
do aught but moan?' However poor they are as poems there is no
doubting the pressure of feeling that provoked them. Swinburne's
hopes were disappointed. Bertie did not return until September, prompting Swinburne to pour forth his joy in 'Sunrise'. The episode had no
sequel; Swinburne was never again so mastered by an emotion for a
child.

On 11 June Swinburne attended the marriage of Houghton's daughter in London. By the end of June he had enough poems for a new book,
but sales of *Songs of the Springtides* had been disappointing, so no
immediate plans were made for publication. In August he worked on
Mary Stuart. Writing from Leigh House, Bradford-on-Avon, Lady Jane
lamented the fact that she had not seen her son for so long but builders
prevented her from entertaining anyone. On 19 August Swinburne had
John Churton Collins to lunch. After reading some of his work,
Swinburne and Collins walked over Putney Heath. They stood for some
time 'rapturously gazing at the scene from near the Church down on to
the valley beneath ... We talked incessantly: about the influence of
scenery on the emotions, he said it always calmed and made him perfectly happy.' Collins found it 'a most delightful walk – what a really
sweet character he is, a most lovable human soul, so generous, so

sympathetic, so noble'. Collins saw another side of the poet a few years later when he was embroiled in a controversy with Gosse.

On 24 September Swinburne dined with William Rossetti, 'chiefly because Swinburne, in his whimsical way, insisted on seeing the Twins. He has just now finished his Mary Stuart . . . and read us the final scene and 2 others: fine work, and perhaps hardly chargeable with over-lengthiness.' In October he finally made the trip to Bradford-on-Avon, staying with his mother and his aunt Charlotte Ashburnham. He told Watts he was 'well into the second canto of your Tristram' which has a love-making scene. 'It remains to be seen what verdict you will pro-nounce on my modest effort to paint a sylvan scene of unpretending enjoyment by moonlight.' By 21 October he had written a good part of the third canto and finished the final revision of *Mary Stuart*, published in November. During his stay he enjoyed being caught in gale-force winds:

> I went a good long way across country in the wind's teeth, but the return was the difficulty: I was twice blown off my legs from behind (once nearly caught up and whirled off the ground) . . . It was delicious . . . It was really rather nervous work passing under the trees, for quite considerable ones were split and dislimbed. But in the open it fully realized my idea of heaven.

In November he found time to parody Tennyson's 'Despair: A Dramatic Monologue', with 'Disgust: A Dramatic Monologue', and wrote the 'Note on the Character of Mary Queen of Scots', having told Stedman in April that he was contemplating writing her biography. In December he heard from Jowett, who said of *Mary Stuart*: 'I have read it through twice with great admiration. It has real dramatic power and contains some noble passages . . . I am sure that the poem will raise your reputa-tion.' He visited his mother at Lowndes Square and Lady Mary Gordon in Chelsea.

In January 1882 he told Henry Arthur Bright that *Mary Stuart* had been 'very coldly received' and corresponded with Oscar Wilde about Whitman. Of the former Swinburne once wrote, 'the only time I ever saw Mr. Wilde was in a crush at our acquaintance Lord Houghton's. I thought he seemed a harmless young nobody.' During February Swinburne produced more of *Tristram*, 'Eight Years Old' for Bertie Mason, and a sequence of 21 sonnets on the Elizabethan playwrights. Watts was writing a similar sequence on Shakespeare's plays. Swinburne reached his forty-fifth birthday feeling that 'for the last two years I have been stronger and harder at work . . . than ever I was in my life'.

On 7 April Watts went down to Birchington to be with Gabriel Rossetti during his final illness. He died on 9 April, apparently in Watts's arms. Swinburne was invited to the funeral which took place on

14 April but did not attend, instead elegizing his estranged friend in 'A Death on Easter Day'. Swinburne wrote to Scott,

> no one who ever loved the friend who died to me – by his own act and wish – exactly ten years ago can feel, I suppose, otherwise than sorrowfully content that the sufferer who survived the man we knew and loved should now be at rest. To this day I am utterly ignorant, and utterly unable to conjecture, why after our last parting in the early summer of 1872 he should have chosen suddenly to regard me as a stranger ... under the circumstances I felt that my attendance at his funeral could have been but a painful mockery.

Swinburne added, 'I do now – on the whole – strongly incline to believe in the survival of life – individual and conscious life – after the dissolution of the body. Otherwise I would not on any account have affected a hope or conviction I did not feel.' It was one of the few occasions in his letters that he made such a statement, hedged with qualifications. It was to be a dominant theme of his later poetry – the contemplation of death, the desire to penetrate its mystery, the awareness of unknowing, and the struggle to find a position which would satisfy both feeling and reason, a struggle which showed the poet in Swinburne had not been extinguished.

CHAPTER THIRTEEN

'The Measureless Music of Things'

In April 1882 Swinburne told Scott:

> I have just sent to the publishers the biggest book of verse – bar
> *Bothwell* – that ever I launched on the devoted heads of the public.
> Like your own volume, it contains poems on 'a little boy' – forty of
> them in all, besides others on babies ... so that I expect 'the
> Mothers of England' to rally round me on the publication of a
> volume in which, out of a total of one hundred poems, between
> forty and fifty are devoted to the praise of little children: though I
> cannot expect the approbation of the British Matron for certain
> passages – or indeed for one entire canto – of the leading poem,
> 'Tristram of Lyonesse,' in ten parts, ranging from about 800 to
> about 2000 lines.

Unfortunately, Watts's fears for the commercial appeal of a volume
comprising a single poem, especially after the poor reception of the
1880 poems, linked with anxiety about the sexually explicit second
canto, resulted in *Tristram of Lyonesse* being launched with a flotilla of
distracting and unseaworthy craft, among them 56 sonnets (21 on
English dramatists 1590–1650) in addition to the baby poems Swinburne
mentions. One of the 'Mothers of England' who rallied round the book
was Lady Jane, to whom Swinburne wrote on 19 July, 'I know you
cannot need to be assured how infinitely more to me than the applause
of all reviews on earth is a word of praise from you – above all, on the
subject of children.' Congratulations also came from Burne-Jones, who
said in June 1882, 'I cannot tell you how glorious I think it . . . I always
knew it was the very subject for you.'

Swinburne had started *Tristram* as long ago as December 1869. Its
'Prelude' had been separately published in 1871, and canto 1 in the
Gentleman's Magazine (1877) and the American *Poems and Ballads,
Second Series* (1878). Anthony Harrison has called it 'not only
Swinburne's finest poem with a medieval subject but also perhaps his
greatest single poem', and for John Rosenberg it is 'one of the great
erotic poems in English'. It has a unique centrality in Swinburne's
work, linking the fiery romanticism of his 1860s love poetry with his
later focus on landscape and sea. It can be read as a compendium of
his later themes which avoids much of the dead wood in the poetry he
wrote after 1879 (no babies, no politics, no Shakespeare). Despite its
imperfections, *Tristram* transcends the mere re-telling of a medieval

story. Swinburne pours his spirit into a legend which had fascinated
him from boyhood and, in so far as it is a celebration of consummated
love, it enables him, in poetry at least, to reverse the 'reverse experience' which had left his 'young manhood a barren stock'. He fulfilled
the promise of the 'Prelude', to 'give/Out of my life to make their dead
life live/Some days of mine' in more senses than one. Wherever
possible, Swinburne drew on personal experiences for the locations.
Descriptions of Tintagel and Kynance Cove were inspired by his visits
to Cornwall in 1864 and 1874. Northumberland featured too, and he
told Scott, 'you will admit the truthfulness – as far as it goes – of my
description of Bamborough Castle, and its surroundings', reminding
him of 'the lovely view of the three blue herons on the ledge of a sea-
rock' as they sailed to Grace Darling's lighthouse in September 1858;
herons that:

> Blue as the clear north heaven, clothed warm with light,
> Stood neck to bended neck and wing to wing
> With heads fast hidden under, close as cling
> Flowers on one flowering almond-branch in spring,
> Three herons deep asleep against the sun.

In canto 2, the lovers enjoy a brief idyll of solitude and love-making in
the woods:

> Only with stress of soft fierce hands she prest
> Between the throbbing blossoms of her breast
> His ardent face, and through his hair her breath
> Went quivering as when life is hard on death;
> And with strong trembling fingers she strained fast
> His head into her bosom; till at last,
> Satiate with sweetness of that burning bed,
> His eyes afire with tears, he raised his head
> And laughed into her lips; and all his heart
> Filled hers; then face from face fell, and apart
> Each hung on each with panting lips, and felt
> Sense into sense and spirit in spirit melt.

By canto 3, three years later, Tristram is alone in Brittany, struggling to
accept the loss of Iseult, until 'with the live earth and the living sea/He
was as one that communed mutually/With naked heart to heart of
friend to friend'. In canto 6 they escape to Northumberland for one last
period of happiness amid 'the mighty moorlands and the sea-walls
grey,/The brown bright waters of green fells that sing/One song to rocks
and flowers and birds on wing'. This canto includes a magical presentation of Merlin's imprisonment in the wood of Broceliande under the
spell of Nimue, where his soul is 'at one/With the ardent world's', his
'spirit of life reborn to mightier birth/ And mixed with things of elder
life than ours'. What in other versions (notably Tennyson's) is imprison-

ment becomes in Swinburne's minstrelsy an experience of transcendent union, where Merlin's heart:

> Hearing, is made for love's sake as a part
> Of that far singing, and the life thereof
> Part of that life that feeds the world with love:
> Yea, heart in heart is molten, hers and his,
> Into the world's heart and the soul that is
> Beyond or sense or vision . . .

This moment is analogous to others of fulfilment in later poems such as 'Loch Torridon', 'A Nympholept', 'A Swimmer's Dream' and 'The Lake of Gaube'. This ecstatic enjoyment of the natural world is apparent in canto 8 when Tristram swims at dawn:

> . . . toward the foam he bent and forward smote,
> Laughing, and launched his body like a boat
> Full to the sea-breach, and against the tide
> Struck strongly forth with amorous arms made wide
> To take the bright breast of the wave to his
> And on his lips the sharp sweet minute's kiss
> Given of the wave's lip for a breath's space curled
> And pure as at the daydawn of the world.

Typically of Swinburne, the chapel in which the remains of Tristram and Iseult are put after their deaths is not left to stand but crumbles into the sea.

Just as Handel's music helped to inspire *Atalanta in Calydon*, so Wagner inspired *Tristram*. On 15 November 1883 Swinburne informed Joseph Knight, 'nothing in music ever did produce upon me the effect produced by the first hearing – on the piano only, in private, of the overture or prelude to that opera' (that is *Tristan und Isolde*).

Tristram was dedicated to Watts, with a sonnet in which Swinburne wrote, 'There is a friend that as the wise man saith/ Cleaves closer than a brother.' Biographies of Swinburne have often dismissed Watts as too comic or reprehensible to be worth enquiry. But how did he achieve such a position in Swinburne's affections? We have seen how in 1872–73 Watts had pursued Swinburne's tangled publishing affairs with Hotten, presided over the transfer of rights to Chatto and helped Swinburne place single pieces with a variety of journals. In 1879 he had intervened decisively, taking up the late Admiral's role and removing Swinburne from his lodgings to a regime of domestic sobriety which restored his health.

Temperamentally Watts was fussy, untidy, caring to the point of being over-solicitous, ambitious but reluctant to publish, a prevaricator in his own affairs, romantic, sensitive, anxious to please, devoted, selfless, possessive and jealous. He was an early-rising workaholic who started many things and finished few. For years he hesitated over a biography of Rossetti. It never materialized. Nor did any substantial memoir of Swinburne, a man he knew for 47 years and lived with for 40. His novel *Aylwin* was in proofs fourteen years before it was published. He went on holidays with a large folder of unfinished manuscripts and books. A creature of habit, Watts enabled Swinburne at last to actualize his sense of order.

There was considerable common ground between them. They shared a large number of friends and acquaintances in literary and artistic London. Independent of Swinburne, Watts had a long, close relationship with Rossetti and he was often seen in the houses of Burne-Jones, Morris, Meredith, Westland Marston, the Burtons, Madox Brown, Whistler, Lord Houghton, even meeting Tennyson and George Eliot. In his day Watts was a respected critic and wrote poetry, and in later life became a best-selling novelist. As a literary figure he received as many letters as Swinburne. His first article appeared in 1873, his first in *The Athenaeum* in 1876, and in 1878 he edited a journal, *The Piccadilly*, with Whistler. Living with Watts, Swinburne believed he had on hand the opinion of someone he eventually (and ridiculously) called 'the first critic of our time, perhaps the largest-minded and surest-sighted of any age'. There were a number of occasions on which they would have been sitting at their respective desks at The Pines writing poems on the same theme or experience.

Both men had defining early experiences of the countryside and the sea: Swinburne with the Isle of Wight, the Channel and Northumbrian moors; Watts with East Anglia, the North Sea and the Fens. Child-like, both firmly believed in the importance of retaining an innocence of response. Watts wrote, 'the child's temper of wonder is the only true temper in which to look out upon the universe'. Both were hero-worshippers, Watts's heroes being George Borrow and Dante Gabriel Rossetti. Both had suffered the loss of a sibling, Swinburne in 1863 and Watts in the early 1870s when his brother died. Both were confirmed and disappointed bachelors, brooding on lost love, in Watts's case an emotional involvement as a young man with a gypsy girl. In his writings he alluded to 'a splendid East Anglian road-girl', and how 'between Englishmen of a certain type and gypsy women there is an extraordinary physical attraction', while *Aylwin* was written as a comment on 'Love's war with death' and on 'how terribly despair becomes intensified when a man has lost – or thinks he has lost – a woman whose love was the only light of his world'.

As an intellectual companion Watts had a less cosmopolitan and more conservative outlook. A vein of dogmatism lay behind the charming, accommodating manner. Though not to the same extent as

Swinburne, Watts revered Shakespeare and the Golden Age of Elizabeth I in poems such as 'Christmas at the Mermaid', and was proud of the fact that he came from the same part of England as Nelson. Watts's conviction that England had a special mission in the world influenced Swinburne's later poetry for the worse. Watts's education at school in Cambridge was probably broader and more practical than Swinburne's at Eton. Watts's father read papers to the British Association for the Advancement of Science and had a great interest in natural science.

Practical in legal affairs, Watts had an unorthodox religious outlook. He was a mystical free-thinker with a qualified belief in God and some experience with spiritualism and mesmerism. As a young man his beliefs may have been influenced by the Revd James Hunt's *An Essay on Pantheism* (1866), a wide-ranging look at comparative religion. Hunt was the curate of Watts's home town of St Ives in Huntingdonshire. The mysticism was stimulated by his uncle James Orlando Watts, who lived like a hermit among his books, with a passion for philology and the occult. He was personally known both to Swinburne and Thomas Purnell, who called him 'the scholar', and spent his last Christmas at The Pines. With his awareness of Sufism and Fitzgerald, Watts was equipped to converse with the Swinburne who had read about Islam and the *Mahabharata* in his early thirties.

Watts's mysticism was not of a contemplative, ascetic form, but romantic. His concept of a dark night of the soul was the absence of the Beloved, not the withdrawal of God. His optimistic Wordsworthian view of Nature was to some extent a positive influence on Swinburne's later poetry, for Swinburne's 'topographical' poems are often among his best. Watts did Swinburne's art a service in encouraging him to write poems such as 'By the North Sea', 'Loch Torridon' or 'A Nympholept', because in these Swinburne reconnects with a vital source of inspiration, his early passion for landscape and sea, and writes poems which are new achievements in his work rather than repetitions of poems already written. As Rosenberg suggested, in them he approximates to the intentionally blurred and diffuse painting of Turner. This does not mean they are mere description, a type of poetry Swinburne was well aware often led to justified charges of 'dullness'. Perhaps 'On the South Coast', 'March: An Ode' and 'A Channel Passage' are failures. But so equally would have been *Poems and Ballads, Third Series* (1889) if it had contained pale imitations of 'Dolores' or 'Hymn to Man'.

Early in July 1882 Swinburne dined with R. H. Horne and the Burtons, at George Bird's. His social life included visiting the Gosses, or seeing Purnell, the Lintons, Mrs Proctor, Jowett or Nichol. He still gave the occasional reading. In September Watts and Swinburne went to Guernsey, where Swinburne was bitterly disappointed to find Hugo absent from Peterport, but the beauty of the island and the pleasure of swimming almost atoned for this. On 6 September he enthused: 'we had the most delicious swim this morning in a bay walled in with precipices ... I would settle here if I could give up all company, and if the air were more bracing and less warm and relaxing.' The holiday inspired 'Les Casquets', and the roundels 'Insularum Ocelle', 'In Sark', and 'In Guernsey':

> Like children unworn of the passions and toils that wore us,
> We breast for a season the breadth of the seas that throng,
> Rejoicing as they, to be borne as of old they bore us
>   Across and along.

After their swim in Petit Bot Bay, Watts wrote 'A Morning Swim in Guernsey':

> Our glowing limbs, with sun and brine empearled,
> Seem born anew, and in your eyes, dear friend,
> Rare pictures shine, like fairy flags unfurled,
> Of child-land, where the roofs of rainbows bend
> Over the magic wonders of the world.

Between October and mid-November Swinburne stayed with his mother and sisters at Leigh House. He read the *New Testament* in Edward VI's version and judged that St Paul, not Christ, was the founder of Christianity. He 'wanted something big to do or at least attempt' such as 'the Life and Death of Cesare Borgia' but nothing came of this. News of George Powell's death reached him early in November. 'The poor fellow was one of the most obliging and kind-hearted of men, and wonderfully bright-spirited under severe trial and trouble. I shall always have a very tender and regretful remembrance of him.' After this visit Lady Jane told Watts, 'thanks to your care he seems a changed man. No words can say what a comfort it is to see him as he now is.' On 25 November *Le Figaro* published René Maizeroy's version of life at Swinburne and Powell's Étretât cottage in 1868–69, which Swinburne wrote to deny four days later.

In the last week of November Swinburne and Watts went to Paris for five days to see Hugo's *Le Roi s'amuse*, at the Théâtre Français. After a lifetime's devotion Swinburne finally met Hugo in person, presenting himself 'in a state of perturbation as well as delight before the greatest – I know – and I believe the best, man living ... After dinner, he drank my health with a little speech, of which – tho' I sat just opposite him – my accursed deafness prevented my hearing a single word.' Hugo likewise was partially deaf and Swinburne's hostess Tola Dorian had the unenviable task of facilitating communication. At dessert, Hugo drank Swinburne's health. Swinburne replied in kind and in the old aristocratic manner threw the glass over his shoulder.

Not understanding the gesture, Hugo was left muttering long after about the destruction of one of his best glasses. Swinburne saw other friends, among them Auguste Vacquerie, chief editor of the *Rappel*, and 'the Frenchman I most wanted to meet outside the Master's own peculiar circle – Leconte de Lisle, the poet, Hellenist, and free-thinker, a very noble and amiable old man'.

Swinburne spent much of February and March 1883 writing *A Century of Roundels* (published in June), dedicated to Christina Rossetti. Approximately a quarter of the poems were about children, there were elegies for Powell ('A Dead Friend', 'Past Days', and 'Autumn and Winter'), Wagner and Rossetti, and some nature pieces. It was an attempt at self-discipline, Swinburne having devised the eleven-line form by adapting it from the French *rondeaux*. Once started, he 'went on scribbling in it till in two months time I had a hundred of these samples ready for publication'.

In the spring of 1883 Swinburne visited Burne-Jones to see 'The Wheel of Fortune' before it went for exhibition at the Grosvenor Gallery. In June he wrote enthusiastically of Inchbold's paintings of the Lake of Geneva exhibited at the Royal Academy, and reviewed Hugo's *La Légende des Siècles*, part of *A Study of Victor Hugo* (1886). By 28 June he was at Leigh House. Lady Jane wrote, 'we have almost no neighbours we care about and when Algernon is with us, we keep as quiet as possible, his deafness makes him so shy and averse to making new acquaintances'. On 14 July Swinburne wrote to Watts, 'I find my Aunt Mary . . . has not had a copy sent her of the book. I am certain I told the dog Chatto always to send her an early copy of any book of mine. Pray take him by the ear and wring one from him.' It was duly sent and Lady Mary Gordon gave it to Mary Disney Leith for her forty-third birthday. Mary obviously enjoyed the poems because her *Original Verses and Translations* (1895) has several examples of Swinburne's roundel, including 'A Ride at St Andrews':

> And the firm hard ring of the hoof-beats heard on the sand:
>   No life but the wild sea life of the bird of the spray,
> And the strong fierce spirit that bears you, and bounds at
>   your hand,
> Across and away.

In September Swinburne and Watts went to Sidestrand on the Norfolk coast, lodging with a miller, Mr Jermy and his daughter Louie. An article in *The Daily Telegraph* called 'Poppyland' by Clement Shorter had extolled its beauty. Louie recalled that 'they were never in at the same time. When one came in the other went out. It was only by the merest chance that they ever sat down to dinner again. They never gave my puddings a chance.' Swinburne told his sister Alice, 'the whole place is fragrant with old-fashioned flowers, sweet-william and thyme and lavender and mignonette and splendid with sunflowers.'

During the winter of 1883 Swinburne wrote on Wordsworth and Byron, his opinion of Wordsworth now risen from what it was in the 1860s. Significantly for Swinburne's own political verse, Wordsworth is cited as 'royalist and conservative' but never ceasing to be 'in the deepest and most literal sense a republican; a citizen to whom the commonweal – the "common good of all" – was the one thing worthy of any man's and all men's entire devotion', a poet of singular 'high-minded loyalty to his native land'. This squaring of republicanism with unionism enabled Swinburne to write his later political poems believing he had not abandoned the politics of his youth. Morris invited him to join the Democratic Federation but Swinburne declined, writing on 21 November, 'what good I can do the cause we have in common will I think be done as well or better from an independent point of action and of view, where no other man can be held responsible for any particular opinion of mine, nor I for any particular opinion of his.'

He noted the extraordinary sunsets which followed the explosion of Krakatoa, which found their way into his 'A New-Year Ode to Victor Hugo'. In a letter to Georgiana Burne-Jones of March 1884 he wrote a brief paraphrase of a French skit on Victoria and John Brown, called 'Sir Brown: drame en 7 actes et 49 tableaux'. In March Swinburne went to see Burne-Jones with his mother, brother Edward and sisters, and in April dined at Mrs Ritchie's (Thackeray's daughter) and met the novelist Rhoda Broughton. In May he saw Aurelio Saffi, 'the surviving Triumvir of the Roman Republic', whose lectures he had attended in Oxford 26 years previously. When he offered a long poem on Hugo to the *Nineteenth Century*, its editor James Thomas Knowles wanted it cut down. For Swinburne, the request was unthinkable, and he promptly asked for his manuscript back. In June he wrote on Charles Reade, and 'Pelasgius', three sonnets 'against Jehovah and his two satellites, St. Paul and St. Augustine'. Contemplating a visit to Lucy Brown Rossetti, he confessed, 'I shall be only too happy to find you alone, as I dislike parties more than ever as I grow older and deafer'. After Watts visited Tennyson at Aldworth in Surrey in July and attended the funeral of his father in August, Swinburne and Watts made another visit to Sidestrand and Cromer in September 1884.

In November *A Midsummer Holiday and Other Poems* was published. Swinburne noted it took the number of poems he had published about Bertie to 50. It was undistinguished, except for the title-sequence, which has an unaccountable charm, like a set of faded picture-postcards from some unspoilt coast, stained with sand and smelling of the sea, or the nostalgia of a turn-of-the-century railway poster. Swinburne conjures 'cirques of hollow cliff', sea-down and headlands, gardens, 'the sandy strait of road where flowers run free', 'low pleached lanes', sunflowers in a mill-garden, the sun on the ocean, when to the cliff-walker 'golden spear-points glance against a silvershield'. He hymns the joy of the moment: 'As we give us again to the waters, the rapture of limbs that the waters enfold' with 'the rapture of spirit' that comes of being absorbed 'In the life everlasting of earth and of heaven, in the laws that atone and agree,/In the measureless music of things'. It is interesting to contrast Swinburne's line, 'a joy to the heart is a goal that it may not reach' with Mary Leith's 'Sweet to the soul is accomplished desire, saith the wise: he saith well' from 'A First Sight' (1894).

Swinburne carried on his literary correspondence with scholars such as A. H. Bullen and A. B. Grosart, staying with his mother at Leigh House in October. His mother and sisters were looking for somewhere to live in London for the winter on account of Charlotte's ill-health. At the end of November he saw the Burtons, and the Gosses before their departure to America.

On 13 December Swinburne started another of his plays, written impractically to be 'acted at the Globe, the Red Bull, or the Black Friars'. The fifth act of *Marino Faliero* 'could hardly have been found too untheatrical . . . by the audiences which endured and applauded the magnificent monotony of Chapman's eloquence'. In January 1885 he told William Rossetti it would be 'the most republican thing (bar certain *Songs before Sunrise*) I ever did'. He was sure that anyone could improve on Byron's handling of the subject. By 2 February he had written three acts – 'Watts thinks it, so far, the finest of my dramatic works' – and finished it on 17 March. It was published in May with a dedication to Aurelio Saffi. William Rossetti asked Watts on 25 May to tell Swinburne he had read it

> as being (in essence) an attack upon Tyranny, Oligarchy of the hereditary kind, and Priestcraft – and it is certainly treated with sustained splendour of diction and work of a kind of which Swinburne alone possesses the secret. As a dramatic presentment of the actual subject, I think Act 3, especially the earlier part of it, much the ablest thing in the drama – extremely fine indeed.

On his forty-eighth birthday Swinburne said happily, 'what stuff people talk about youth being the happiest time of life! Thank God . . . I am very much more than twice as happy now as I was when half my present age just twenty-four years ago.'

But on 22 May Victor Hugo died. For Swinburne it was like losing a second father. On 25 May he told Mrs Linton, 'I am trying to work off the first sense of stupid bewilderment by writing a short account of my dear Father and Master's work', speaking of how he had lost the gift which your dear 'father' and mine retained – and if ever there were manly men and heroes, were not they such! – the gift of tears, which women and children and Homeric heroes, and such men as Landor and Hugo do not lose. (If I could but 'cry like a child' – or a hero – I should be better again afterwards – like them.) Only I cannot quite understand yet how the sun manages to go on rising. Please don't show this to any one, but burn it.

'The Work of Victor Hugo' was published in magazine form in July and August 1885 and in *A Study of Victor Hugo*. Swinburne pondered the question of immortality:

When I think of his intense earnestness of faith in a future life and a better world than this, and remember how fervently Mazzini always urged upon all who loved him the necessity of that belief and the certainty of its actual truth, I feel very deeply that they must have been right – or at least that they should have been – however deep and difficult the mystery which was so clear and transparent to their inspired and exalted minds may seem to such as mine. They ought to have known, if any man ever did: and if they were right, I, whose love and devotion they requited with such kindness as I never could have really deserved, shall (somehow) see them again.

The year 1885 saw not only the death of Hugo but Lord Houghton (in August) and J. R. Woodford, Bishop of Ely, Swinburne's tutor of 1854–55. As he grew older, 'the dead become so alive and real to me. I have had dreams of my father and of Edith so vivid and delightful that they still seem as real, and almost as worth remembering, as many actual recollections.'

In June a foot injury prevented Swinburne from going out for several weeks but in July he was able to entertain the children's novelist Mary Louisa Molesworth, and Inchbold, who commiserated with him in his grief over Hugo. On 13 July he announced he and Watts were going north to the coast and thence to 'my cousin Sir J. Swinburne's in Northumberland'. If this trip had actually happened it would have been his first visit to Capheaton possibly since the early 1860s. In August the Burtons came to The Pines. In September and October, Swinburne, Watts, his sisters and Bertie went to Seaford, staying in Church Road. One day Swinburne and Theresa Watts were almost cut off by the tide. Hurrying back over the shingle and wet rocks, they reached safety 'drenched from head to foot by the blinding spray cast upon them by the incoming tide'. For holiday reading he had Thackeray and Mrs Linton's *Stabbed in the Dark*. As for the General Election, 'I have declined to give my vote for either party. The one cannot be trusted abroad, and the other cannot be trusted at home.'

The year closed with another set of epistolary ghosts coming back from the past to haunt Swinburne. Letters he had written to Howell

containing flagellation references came into the possession of the publisher George Redway. He notified Swinburne on 10 December, intimat-
ing that perhaps he would like them back. Redway planned an anthology,
Sea Song and River Rhyme, and wanted an original contribution from
Victoria's foremost laureate of the sea. Swinburne declined on 14 December, saying Watts would offer permission to reprint something in
return for the letters. In fact Redway did get a new poem, 'A Word for
the Navy', buying its copyright from Swinburne for one guinea on 1
July 1886. Redway printed the poem as a separate issue in August and
again in 1887 and 1896. It is not known whether there was an element
of blackmail involved. Watts contributed four sonnets to the book.
Ironically, the letters were preserved at The Pines and now reside in the
British Library. Feelings about Redway were not sufficiently bad to
prevent Watts giving Swinburne *Sea Song and River Rhyme*, inscribing
it 'To the Poet of the Sea on his fiftieth birthday' in 1887.

In 1886 Swinburne published *A Study of Victor Hugo* and a collection of essays, *Miscellanies*. He responded to the *Pall Mall Gazette*'s
request for a list of hundred great books by offering his own selection,
excluding any living writers. The list was headed by Shakespeare,
Aeschylus and selections from the Bible, Homer, Sophocles, Aristophanes,
Pindar, Lucretius, Catullus, Dante, Chaucer and Villon. By some slip,
he omitted Sappho. In March he met a man whose name was to be
forever dishonourably linked with his, the book-collector, bibliogra-
pher, and forger of rare pamphlets, Thomas J. Wise, who came to look
at Swinburne's Shelley editions. Wise was to be an occasional visitor
thereafter, eventually buying several thousand pounds' worth of manuscripts from Watts after Swinburne's death. In April Swinburne's brother
Edward and his wife Olga came to The Pines.

In July he went to Leigh House, and told Watts, 'I am neither surprised nor worried to hear of the unsuccess of my *Miscellanies*.' *Punch*
parodied his poem 'The Commonweal. A Song For Unionists' with
'The Common Squeal. A Song For Shriekers' on 10 July. On the 14th he
took a walk of over twelve miles 'through some of the most beautiful
woodlands by some of the most bewildering roads I ever saw'. He
wrote 'A Ballad of Bath', 'about the most difficult feat of sustained
rhythm and rhyme that I ever attempted'. In late September Watts and
Swinburne and Bertie went to Eastbourne, staying on 'its wild out-
skirts'. On Beachy Head, watching the birds wheeling in the sky, he
composed 'To a Seamew':

> When I had wings, my brother,
>   Such wings were mine as thine;
> Such life my heart remembers
> In all as wild Septembers

> As this when life seems other,
>   Though sweet, than once was mine;
> When I had wings, my brother,
>   Such wings were mine as thine.

With pride, Swinburne, nicknamed 'Seagull' as a boy, remembered his father, 'We, sons and sires of seamen,/Whose home is all the sea'. The domestic stability of his life at The Pines could not erase memories of the lost freedom of youth: 'We are fallen, even we, whose passion/On earth is nearest thine.'

On New Year's Day 1887 Swinburne told his mother he had started a drama

> in rhyme – founded on the legendary history of ancient Britain. The hero is the son of our first monarch, King Brute ... His son was Locrine – who came to grief through imprudently marrying two wives, and whose young daughter Sabrina became (and is now) the goddess of the river Severn (so called after her) in which she was drowned ... I mean to write it in all manner of rhymed metres, which I hope and expect will reduce all other critics to the verge of raving madness.

True to his word, Swinburne made his characters speak in couplets, Italian and Shakespearean sonnets, Chaucerian, Persian and elegiac metre, ottava rima, terza rima and an ABABBCC stanza. *Locrine* appeared in November, with a dedicatory poem to his sister Alice.

In February Philip Bourke Marston died and Swinburne memorialized him in 'Via Dolorosa' and a number of other poems, haunted by the pathos of a life blighted by blindness, the death of a sister and a fiancée. Watts wrote an obituary of Marston for *The Athenaeum* in which Swinburne's sonnet was included. He wrote to Havelock Ellis about Marlowe and criticized Arthur Symons's account of Massinger. In April he commented, 'I hardly ever go out.'

Swinburne's political opinions hardened noticeably in his fiftieth year. Gladstone became anathema to him for supporting Irish home rule, and Swinburne rebuffed those who argued he had rejected his republican principles. On 16 May he wrote to his mother,

> the first principle of a Republican is and must be Unity (without which liberty can only mean licence – or pure anarchy – or pretentious hypocrisy) and that Republicans ought in common consistency and honesty to be the first to protest against a party of anarchists and intriguers whose policy is to break up the state.

Karl Blind told Swinburne that Mazzini would have been 'utterly opposed to the dissolution of the Legislative union between Great Britain and Ireland', for 'how should Mazzini, of all men, have wished to see a kind of Roman "States of the Church" reared up in Ireland ... ?'

Swinburne's feelings about Ireland were inextricable from his detestation of Catholicism. On one occasion he even corrected his mother when she used the phrase 'religious error' of Catholic belief. He insisted, 'a creed which makes it a duty to murder innocent men, women, and children by tortures which I am sure you could not bear to read of is not an "error" – it is the worship of the principle of evil . . . Nero himself was a baby – a blessed innocent – compared to the Fathers of the Inquisition.'

The date 21 June 1887 was Victoria's Jubilee and, despite his earlier satirical jibes at the monarch, Swinburne now celebrated 'the blameless queen' in an ode. He was later surprised to hear the poem had been enjoyed by the Prince of Wales: 'I must say . . . that I think it nothing less than very generous of him – for, as Watts says, I never wrote anything more essentially republican in spirit and in tone.' On 28 June he reflected 'how more than satisfactorily the good Queen's Jubilee has gone off! Watts and I both think that the genuine and really beautiful success of it will have been – and will yet be, in its general and lasting influence – a heavy blow to the enemies of England.'

Just as telling was Watts's influence on *Selections from Swinburne* (1887), which, intended to revitalize Swinburne's flagging sales, was also a disowning of his poetic past. This was the first official selection of Swinburne's work, and its repression of his earlier poetry is of unrivalled audacity. All that survived from his poetry and drama of the 1860s were two extracts from *Atalanta*, 'Itylus' and an extract from *A Song of Italy*. From the 1870s came 'Hertha', 'In San Lorenzo', 'A Year's Burden' (*Songs before Sunrise*), one extract from *Bothwell*, two from *Erechtheus*, and 'A Ballad of Dreamland' and 'A Forsaken Garden' (*Poems and Ballads, Second Series*). The poetry Swinburne had published since 1880 comprised two-thirds of the book, often hacked into disparate sections with new and misleading titles. Presenting Swinburne as the laureate of the sea, nature and children, *Selections from Swinburne* was wholesome fare. As the only selection available in the United Kingdom in his lifetime, it multiplied through 20 editions until stopped in its tracks by Watts's death.

In his Preface to the 1913 edition, Watts stated that the book's peculiar interest is that 'the poems . . . were all chosen by Swinburne himself'. In fact, on 4 July 1887 Swinburne sent Mrs Molesworth a copy, saying the poems were 'chosen as much by Watts – or nearly so – as by myself'. The hasty parenthesis is revealing. He had admitted to giving away authority over his work and quickly corrects the impression. Whatever the responsibility of Watts, there is no doubt Swinburne became dismissive of the books on which his fame rested. In August, contemplating a second edition with additional poems, he insisted 'I will have no more *Atalanta* – there is quite enough already!'

Meanwhile, Watts was pre-empting the adverse comments of those readers who identified Swinburne with 'Laus Veneris', 'Dolores', and 'Hymn to Proserpine', by reviewing it anonymously in *The Athenaeum*. The *Selections* were 'admirable . . . as representative as possible in so voluminous a writer'. Anticipating objections to the removal of the 1866 poems, Watts wrote, 'it is a poet's balderdash that his more special admirers are sure to admire', and he attacked the fashion among young poets to feel that 'to extol other countries at the expense of their own is to be "aesthetic", "advanced" and "poetic"': 'the greatest poets, from Aeschylus to Dante, from Dante to Shakespeare . . . were inspired with the most intense love of country'. As for the extract from canto 6 of *Tristram*, he praised the description of the swim because it would have delighted Borrow! Watts had encouraged Swinburne into new poetic territory but the 1887 *Selections* was nothing less than closing the border behind him.

Swinburne's essay 'Whitmania' (published in August) is frequently cited as an example of Watts's baleful influence and Swinburne's violent rejection of his past views. According to Gosse, Watts hated Whitman 'most heartily'. Swinburne hoped that William Rossetti would see it, 'that it may be the privileged means (under Providence) of opening his eyes to the error of his ways'. He told Nichol it was Rossetti's fault for putting Walt 'only a little below Shakespeare'. 'Whitmania' was certainly intemperate but not a recantation. Swinburne's first use of the word 'Whitmania' was in 1872, and from the beginning he had had reservations about the formal qualities of Whitman's poetry and his tendency to be didactic: 'never before was high poetry so puddled and adulterated with mere doctrine in its crudest form'. In 1872 Swinburne had complained that Whitman's champions had a tendency to 'assume that if he be right all other poets must be wrong', and before 1867 Swinburne had compared Whitman with Blake in finding their work at times 'noisy and barren and loose, rootless and fruitless and informal'.

In May Swinburne received a presentation copy of Hardy's *The Woodlanders*. The two men felt a natural kinship and had an occasional but always cordial correspondence. In June he met Inchbold, having sent him the *Selections*, before going to Leigh House for the summer and marvelling at the vigour of his Aunt Julia on her ninety-second birthday. Having corrected the proofs of *Locrine*, he wrote an article on Marston and 'a poem which came upon me one day in the woodland beside the moor which I told you of – a sort of lyrical idyl in dialogue, called "Pan and Thalassius"'.

He returned to London on 23 August, following the death of one of his aunts. He was at Leigh House again by early October and parodied the moralizing he had once accused Wordsworth of being prone to, where 'all the divine life of things outside man is but as raw material for philosophic or theological cookery'. It was a walk along

> one of the most curious bits of scenery I know to the Christian thinker, a realized allegory. For, according to the route you take, in going or in returning, you pass from foul ugliness and worldly grime to divine glory of woodland and heavenly expanse of hillside open to the influences of heaven, or alas! alas! – vice versa. Let us pray, my friend, that our pilgrimage in this valley of trial may etc., etc.

It was November before Swinburne went to Lancing on the south coast, from where he penned long descriptive letters to his sister Alice. He was struck by Shoreham and its church, and returning at sunset noted how 'the whole glory of a most wonderful evening sky was reflected – and almost improved – in these tiny quiet pools or lakelets, twelve if not twenty times over'.

Swinburne published no books in 1888, but started a study of Ben Jonson, the first instalment of which was finished in March, and a number of poems. Among his friends he lost John William Inchbold in January and Mrs Proctor in March. Wise was now sending Swinburne forged pamphlets with the hope that he would accidentally authenticate them. 'Cleopatra' came in April, closely followed by 'Dead Love' and 'Siena'. 'I am quite certain, quite positive, that I never set eyes on the booklet before, nor heard of its existence,' said a bemused Swinburne, 'It is to me a fresh proof that the moral character of the worthy Mr. Hotten was . . . ambiguous.' In June he was saddened when his mother and sisters left Leigh House, a place he said he would remember with 'great affection and regret. I always liked it, but last summer I enjoyed the neighbourhood and my favourite walks so thoroughly that liking had passed into something like real love, such as I have hardly felt for any place since we left East Dene.' He declined an invitation from Nichol to visit him in Scotland, expressing his strong dislike of the train. At the end of July he finished 'The Armada', much to Watts's approval, who had written his own piece 'The Burden of the Armada' which Swinburne called 'a masterpiece of poetical narrative'.

More controversially, he penned a damning response to Whistler's 'Ten O'Clock Lecture' (reprinted in 1888) in the form of 'Mr Whistler's Lecture On Art' in June, apparently at the behest of Watts, who thought Whistler 'a bit of a charlatan'. Swinburne's objections to Whistler's championing of Japanese art may have sprung from a twisted patriotism but in writing this essay he betrayed both his friendship with Whistler and the younger self who wrote 'Before the Mirror'. Whistler replied, 'cannot the man who wrote Atalanta and the Ballads beautiful, – can he not be content to spend his life with *his* work . . . that he should stray about blindly in his brother's flower beds and bruise himself! . . . I have lost a confrère; but then I have gained an acquaintance – one Algernon Swinburne – "outsider" – Putney.' Swinburne read the letter 'livid with anger' and swore 'he would never speak to Whistler again'.

In the autumn he was still working on Jonson. He told Isabel of a visit to the Rossettis and how their children had played with him and wanted him to stay. 'They were all in that horrible earthquake at San Remo last year . . . But if people will go to the Riviera, what do they expect – or deserve?' Instead of the Riviera, Swinburne went to earthquake-free Lancing from 4 October to 3 November, for glorious swimming and sunsets. Among the poems inspired was 'Neap-tide', 'the exact picture of one particularly grim and dreary day last year'. The year 1888 ended with his composing a fine elegy 'In Memory of John William Inchbold', in which he celebrated his time with the painter in North Cornwall in the autumn of 1864.

In 1889 Swinburne saw two books through the press, *A Study of Ben Jonson* – about which he said, 'I never worked harder at anything, but I never was better satisfied with the result' – and *Poems and Ballads, Third Series* in May, dedicated to Scott. The title was probably chosen to increase sales, so the book would be associated with its forerunners in 1866 and 1878; it went through eight editions before Swinburne's death. Stronger than *A Midsummer Holiday*, it included the Inchbold elegy, 'Pan and Thalassius', 'A Word with the Wind', 'Neap-Tide' and 'The Interpreters'. It sounded the death-knell for the unfinished *Lesbia Brandon*, as seven border ballads originally part of that text were now wrenched from it and published.

It was an uneventful year. He went to Oxford in January to see Jowett. His mother was now living in London, but she stayed in Farnham, Surrey, for the summer, where Swinburne went in August. On 26 September Swinburne was seen on Wimbledon Common 'when the downpour was heaviest, about four o'clock . . . calmly marching along towards his resting place . . . he was wet through'. The reporter said Swinburne walked like a soldier, his gaze lowered, unless he saw any children, when 'his face is transfigured, and from his eyes there shines a light which is not of the earth'.

In October and November he had his third holiday at Lancing. He walked to Shoreham and came back by moonlight. There were babies and children on the esplanade as a substitute for those over which he cooed on Putney Hill. He told Alice on 30 October, 'to-day when I was in the sea it was like swimming into heaven – the glorious sunlight on and in the splendid broad rolling waves made one feel for the minute as if one was in another and better world'. On 11 November he described how he ran like a boy, tore off my clothes, and hurled myself into the water. And it was but for a few minutes – but I was in Heaven! The whole sea was literally golden as well as green – it was liquid and living sunlight in which one lived and moved and had one's being. And to feel that in deep water is to feel – as long as one is swimming out, if only a minute or two – as if one was in another world of life, and one far more glorious than even Dante ever dreamed of in his Paradise.

One of the strongest bonds between Swinburne and Watts was their feeling for the sea. In *Aylwin* Watts wrote,

> Those who in childhood have had solitary communings with the sea know the sea's prophecy. They know that there is a deeper sympathy between the sea and the soul of man than other people dream of. They know that the water seems nearer akin than the land to the spiritual world, inasmuch as it is one and indivisible, and has motion, and answers to the mysterious call of the winds, and is the writing tablet of the moon and stars.

Swinburne's time in Lancing inspired 'An Autumn Vision' (31 October) and 'A Swimmer's Dream' (4 November), 'begun in my head a little way off shore, out of pure delight in the sense of the sea':

> I lean my cheek to the cold grey pillow,
> The deep soft swell of the full broad billow,
> And close mine eyes for delight past measure,
>   And wish the wheel of the world would stand.

In 1890 Swinburne wrote articles on 'Notes of Travel – Alps and Pyrenees' by Hugo, Sir Walter Scott, Shirley and Davenport. Bertie Mason was now sixteen years old. On 20 June Swinburne wrote,

> what a privilege it is to have known a child as intimately as possible from the one age [that is, six] to the other, and not only to have won and obtained his regard (I don't want to brag, and say 'his affection', though perhaps I might), but to be told by his mother and his guardian that I have drawn him on . . . to enjoy and understand . . . Shakespeare and Molière as far as young boys can or ought to understand them – and that is most of the way – and Scott and Dickens altogether.

His relationship with his mother deepened. On 21 September he recalled how, in the summer of 1889, 'every morning my first thought was of delight that I was going to see you, and every night my last and strongest was one of thankfulness that I had had another day of you'. He was ever aware of time passing. In 1890 death claimed Richard Burton, for whom Swinburne wrote two elegies, William Bell Scott, and the long estranged Charles Augustus Howell.

The year 1891 was the 450th anniversary of Eton College. Swinburne was asked to write an ode and wrote one immediately, posting it on 10

March. Swinburne told William Rossetti, 'I jumped at the opportunity of throwing the name of their other typical naughty boy and disgrace to the orthodox traditions of the school full in the face of the authorities, who I trust will be in a due and proper rage (not for the first time, I should suppose) with both of us.' The 'naughty boy' was of course Shelley, but the ode is perfectly unobjectionable, unlike 'Eton: Another Ode', a flagellation poem he wrote about this time. He was invited to stay a night at Eton in late June but declined.

His mother became ill, and he stayed with her at Brockhampton Park in the Vale of Evesham in July and August. He went for 20-mile walks in heavy rain, and wrote the essay 'Social Verse'. On 31 July there was a family crisis. Edward had returned to England and was dying in London. Alice left for the city immediately but by the time she arrived he had died, aged 43. In April 1885 his mother had mentioned that Edward's health was poor and that a doctor had said, 'there is no positive illness but that his nervous system is very much lower than it should be, evidently from anxiety'. Swinburne wrote to Watts, 'it is strange to think at this time yesterday I had a brother by blood alive in the world, and now have none. I feel very thankful to you when I think I have one who is more to me and nearer than a brother.' As he contemplated the melancholy journey to Bonchurch for the funeral, Swinburne reflected that without Watts, 'how long since – how many years ago – I should have died as my poor dear brother has just died'. As for Edward's wife Olga Thumann, 'we do not even know where the woman is now: thank heaven, she will not be present to desecrate and irritate our sorrow'. On 2 August Swinburne wrote 'Life in Death' which begins, 'He should have followed who goes forth before us,/Last born of us in life, in death first-born'. After the funeral he returned to Brockhampton Park, later telling his mother, 'I was so glad to be at home – it is always home where you are – in those first days of sorrow, and to know you were glad to have me.' In the midst of this trouble, he found time to write 'A Birthday Ode. August 6, 1891' for Tennyson.

In the autumn of 1891 he and Watts went to stay at The Orchard, Niton, guests of Lady Mary Gordon. It was there he wrote a play, *The Sisters*. Something of the past was returning to him, like a pearl salvaged by a diver from a wreck.

'Deep Silence Answers'

At the end of January 1892 Swinburne had an unusual letter to answer. It was written from 27 Chesham Place, the Gordons' house in Chelsea:

> Cy merest dozen
>
> Anks thawfully for your kyind letter. Since you and Mr. Watts kyindly give us the choice of days (or doice of chays) may we name Wednesday all things being propitious? Tomorrow does not quite so well suit some of my mear Da's arrangements, & the foung yolks have wikelise some engagements. We were seadfully drorry not to go on Friday, & we could so horridly cry at cy mousin's kyind preparations having been vade in main!
>
> This little delay has allowed me more time to devote to your most interesting Eton book, even tho' it be only the tavings of a rug, or even the toping of a mug, it is exceptionally amusing to your mi, tho' I could dish that it wealt with a pater leriod. How many changes seem to have been made of late, tho' let us hope that it may never see a change in one respect & that it may be said of the birch as of the school 'Florebit'.
>
> With lany moves from Mimmy & all, & kind remembrances & thanks to cy m's 'Major' I remain
>
> E yr moving linor & coz
>
> Mary C. J. Leith

At some point in 1891 or earlier, Swinburne and Mary had renewed their correspondence for apparently the first time since the winter of 1864–65. It has been assumed that they had no contact until after the death of her husband. This letter suggests that Mary visited The Pines before her widowhood, not eighteen months after, as Fuller states. As we have seen, Swinburne had exchanged letters from time to time with Mary's mother, Lady Mary Gordon, sending her his books as they were published, and her letters had referred to 'Mun', as Mary was nicknamed. In 1883 she wrote, 'I am sure Mun will be amused to hear about your Eton friend though she had not the pleasure of sending either of her sons there.' Swinburne had stayed at The Orchard in the summer of 1874 and in 1891 with Watts, and the funerals of his father (1877) and Edward (1891) would have provided other opportunities for visits. For much of the year Lady Gordon lived in Chelsea.

This letter is one of three written in a cypher involving the transposition of the first letters of words, a game they probably devised when young. The correspondence is full of references to birching and Eton, with Mary casting herself as Swinburne's 'minor'. The next letter of

2 February 1893 recalls the time when Swinburne, aged eleven, was at Brooke Rectory, and her own novel *Trusty in Fight*, which she was revising. It reveals that Mary came to The Pines, made tea in Swinburne's room, and he gave her a book. In 1972 the Huntington Library acquired seventeen letters written by Swinburne to Mary between 1899 and 1902 in the same cypher, which confirm that flagellation was a subject of mutual interest. When Swinburne wrote the flagellatory 'Eton: Another Ode', it was dedicated 'To M.'. The letters invariably begin 'Cy merest dozen', which is elaborated with a phrase like 'that almost any fellow would have preferred to the postponement of an expected visit'. Swinburne's letters to Mary have a manic playfulness quite unlike letters to any other correspondent, as he revelled in comic family allusions and burlesque. Interpolated is a correspondence between fictional characters Frank Dilston and Reginald Clavering from *The Sisters*, and Freddy, Dick, Sig Thorburn and the Revd E. Thorburn from Mary's novel *Trusty in Fight*.

In the 25 years since her marriage had caused 'something of a gap in our correspondence', Mary Disney Leith had written ten novels and *A Martyr Bishop and other verses* (1878). Amongst many pious verses are poems of undefined regret for the past, such as 'Autumn' and 'Through the Years'. The most significant is 'Sketches from Recollection', a finely detailed poem written in the same stanza form as 'The Triumph of Time'. It describes 'A wide expanse of shifting ocean,/A wide expanse of breezy down/ . . . A nestling home in a sheltered bay' and then the shore, white cliffs, an old village church, the Solent, and 'our wanderings over the downs at even'. It concludes:

> And years roll onward, the years that sever
>   From times most sweet, as they wax and wane:
> Fairer days may be ours, but never
>   Shall those calm days return again
>   When in the cloudless summer weather
>   We wandered over those scenes together,
> Whose memory shall be a joy forever
>   To heighten gladness, to soothe in pain.

F. A. C. Wilson believed this was Mary's reply to Swinburne, reassuring him she had not forgotten their days together.

Wilson examined Mary's novels for what they might reveal about her character and relationship with Swinburne. He concluded that they were frequently disguised autobiography, that she often used a plot hinging on a young woman having to choose between marriage to a young, artistic but dangerous suitor and a less attractive older man, and through her fiction she strove to come to terms with the events of 1863–65, to justify her choice of Col. Disney Leith, to explore her ambivalent feelings toward Swinburne and to fantasize a different set of events.

Of *The Chorister Brothers* (1867) and *The Incumbent of Axhill* (1875) Wilson argued, 'it is surely unusual for a young bride to occupy herself with dreams of her rejected suitor's childhood and adolescence and to incorporate these in books in which her husband does not obtain a mention'. Mary took up personal themes once more in *Like His Own Daughter* (1883), *From Over The Water* (1884), *Rufus* (1886) and *Nora's Friends* (1889). Wilson saw *From Over The Water* as Mary's version of *Lesbia Brandon*. At one point the narrator explains, 'There never had been any attachment between Laura and her cousin. They had been friends and playmates from childhood, but nothing more, or were ever likely to be': 'She loved her cousin Lin – her old playfellow and lifelong friend – whether as lover or only as cousin with a kind of sisterly affection was perhaps not clear to herself.' In *Rufus* Mina hits Rufus in the face when he tries forcibly to embrace her. Wilson sees an ironic allusion to this in 'The Triumph of Time' when Swinburne writes, 'Would I have you change now, change at a blow,/Startled and stricken, awake and aware'. In *Under Cliff*, which has an Isle of Wight setting, the heroine marries the Swinburne figure at the end.

Wilson believed *Under Cliff* (1890) and *Trusty in Fight* (1893) as 'private communiqués' with Swinburne, along with his play *The Sisters*. These works were intended to enact some form of reconciliation between them after the disaster of 1864. But the reconciliation came first, perhaps some time toward the end of the 1880s, and these books evolved from it.

Trusty in Fight (1893) had Freddy Thorburn as a 'a highly romanticised version of Swinburne's adolescence', and 'Hatty, the sister-figure, receives the hero's flagellatory confidences during his vacations from school and also observes the punishments unwillingly inflicted by his benign and kindly father.' In one sequence Freddy is flagellated eighteen times in 43 pages. The novel captures the pious atmosphere of the Swinburne and Gordon families, and illustrates how 'from childhood onwards, for ethical and religious reasons, Mary felt moved by the idea of heroic suffering heroically borne'. Having first sketched it in 1863–64, 'it seems likely that she was inspired to rewrite it for publication by the fact of her renewal of relations with Swinburne'.

Mary was obsessed by these themes even after Swinburne's death. *A Black Martinmas* (1912) is the story of 'a Scottish girl who feels her father does not understand her, largely because he wishes to marry her off to a middle-aged family friend ... the heroine prefers another man but slowly comes to love and respect her father's candidate for her'. The heroine

> often regretted that she had not been born a boy. Hers was one of
> those girl-natures which have a good deal of the boy or man in
> their composition . . . neither a tomboy nor a hoyden, she cared for
> and sympathised with the aims and pursuits of men, while those of
> women, as such, did not actually appeal to her.

Wilson's general conclusion about Mary's fiction is that she 'remained
for many years desperately uncertain whether she had done rightly in
refusing Swinburne and that the decision of 1864 was insuperably
painful to her'.

In March 1892 Swinburne sent *The Sisters* to the press, 'a little tragedy
of modern life . . . which Mr. Watts tells me is too deficient in stage effect
and dramatic construction to be offered to you in the way of business', he
wrote to Herbert Beerbohm Tree, the actor and theatre manager. Swinburne
wrote the play in four weeks, and intended to make 'chance the tempter,
and a person who neither could or would have plotted to commit murder, a murderer by passive abstinence from warning or saving life'. Published in May, *The Sisters* was dedicated to Lady Mary Gordon with a
poem that describes The Orchard, where 'Between the sea-cliffs and the
sea there sleeps/A garden walled about with woodland'. *The Sisters* was
unusually autobiographical. On 20 July Swinburne remarked to Lucy
Rossetti, 'I will confess to you that I never cared so much about any of
my creatures – it went to my heart to despatch them – but what could I
do?' Swinburne's mother liked Redgie, 'which gave me more pleasure
than any review could, as I did think I had succeeded in making a nice
young fellow out of my own recollections and aspirations'.

The Sisters is set at Clavering Hall, Northumberland, in 1816. Reginald
Clavering has returned from Waterloo a scarred hero, an 'all but girl-
faced godling in the hall', in love with his cousin Mabel Dilston and she
secretly with him, which Anne discovers:

> And so you really mean to love the boy
> You played with, rode with, climbed with, laughed with, made
> Your tempter – and your scapegoat – when you chose
> To ride forbidden horses and break bounds
> On days forbidden.

Redgie feels he cannot tell her his love, being poor and without pros-
pects. Mabel calls Redgie 'The brightest, bravest, kindest, boy you
were/That ever let a girl misuse him'. He tells Frank that the previous
evening 'I asked her if she thought it possible/That two such baby
friends and playfellows, . . . /Could when grown up, be serious lovers'.
Mabel's reply was 'Hardly. No. Certainly not.' Frank is in love with
Mabel and jealous of Redgie, and Redgie is also loved by Anne. The
characters act out a tragedy written by Redgie at school, at the end of
which they are poisoned by Anne.

If there was a reconciliation with Mary around 1890, this seems to have set Swinburne thinking about his Capheaton days. Reginald Clavering appears in several flagellant pieces probably written at this time. 'Redgie's Return' is set on the first day of the school holidays and involves Redgie, Mabel, Frank and Sir Francis Dilston. 'The Swimmer's Tragedy' also has a Northumbrian setting and Redgie and Frank; Redgie is flogged for bathing in a forbidden pool. 'Redgie's Luck', subtitled 'A tragicomedy in 3 acts, 4 double acrostics, 16 scenes and 4 floggings', is set at Eton and to be acted 'April 1st 1893 at the Educational Theatre Birchington' – which suggests 1893 as a likely date of composition.

Swinburne's life at The Pines was governed by a routine which, if not as inflexible as it has been made out, was nevertheless fairly constant. At 10 a.m. he came down from his bedroom to his library on the first floor, breakfasted alone and read the paper. At 11 a.m. he walked up Putney Hill, pausing to admire the babies in their prams, among whose number was the future poet Robert Graves, before striking across Wimbledon Common. Swinburne walked in all weathers, without umbrella, coat or gloves, and had great pleasure from the Common, from the hawthorn blossom in spring and the frost and ice in winter. He walked every day except Sunday, when he found by experience there was too much risk of being recognized. In the Rose and Crown he had a beer, sitting apart from other customers. The landlord allowed him to dart into a private room if another customer disturbed his peace. At Wimbledon there was a newsagent he frequented, where he bought the occasional book. Lunch was at 1.30 p.m., and sometimes there would be friends or family present. If Swinburne liked the visitor he or she might be taken upstairs to his library, with the mosaic-topped table and the chair with golden rams' heads, and crammed with books, many piled on a long sofa. Otherwise, he took a siesta until 4 p.m. after which he worked for several hours. Around 6 p.m. he came down to the sitting room with a book and read aloud, usually from Dickens. Once he read Dickens aloud in the garden and a neighbour with a headache complained! Dinner was at 8 p.m., after which Swinburne went back to his room to work for several more hours. From time to time Watts and Swinburne would go out for lunch at the houses of friends.

Each year they took a holiday together and Swinburne would also stay with his mother. In July 1892 he saw her at Broxhead Warren, Alton, Hampshire, which she had leased until the end of September. There he started an essay, 'Victor Hugo: Notes of Travel' and wrote 'Astrophel. After Reading Sir Philip Sidney's Arcadia in the Garden of an Old English Manor House'. Watts and Swinburne probably went to the coast in late September.

Four days after Tennyson's death on 6 October, Swinburne sent his sympathies to Lady Tennyson, recalling 'the great kindness with which I was once received at Farringford when little more than a boy' in January 1858. He declined to attend the funeral at Westminster Abbey, for 'I hate all crowds and all functions, but especially the funereal kind beyond all decent expression.' He commemorated Tennyson in November with 'Threnody'.

Swinburne was generally thought to be the strongest candidate for the vacant Laureateship. Queen Victoria is alleged to have said to Gladstone, 'I am told that Mr. Swinburne is the best poet in my dominions', and Swinburne was the choice of the Prince of Wales. An article on the Laureateship in *The Times* on 17 October supported Swinburne, 'a master of verse who made the English tongue speak sonorously, and the melody of whose lines cannot lose their charm'. Four poets gave their vote anonymously in Swinburne's favour in the *Bookman* (one has since been identified as Yeats). Morris, whose name was also mentioned in the debate, told a friend, 'Bet you it is offered to Swinburne. Bet you he takes it.'

But the memory of *Poems and Ballads* still smouldered in some minds. *The Spectator*, for example, wrote that it would regret the choice of Swinburne for the Laureateship 'because we expect from him little further except melodious sound, and because we think his election would give new vogue to the sickly eroticism with which in his earlier career, he outraged canons that it is essential to maintain'. On 7 October Gladstone wrote to Lord Acton, 'The question of the succession comes before me with very ugly features. I have, as it happens, the old *Poems and Ballads* 1866. They are both bad and terrible. Have they been dropped? If they have is it a reparation?' Only if Swinburne were to withdraw these poems could he bring himself 'within the range of possibility'. Acton believed that Swinburne's appointment 'would stimulate the circulation of the offending volume (and condone it)'. Swinburne's extreme republicanism would be an offence to the Queen. In his opinion, 'Russia: An Ode' (1890) showed 'an unbroken consistency in evil in the mind and career of the man'. It would be 'an offence to Her Majesty's Imperial Brother and ally, to place in office involving appearance at Court, a man who clamours to have him murdered, and whose plea for Tyrannicide is not remote, or obscure, or unnoticed . . . '.

The publication of 'Russia: An Ode' in August 1890 had resulted in one M.P. tabling a question in the House of Commons on 5 August, 'whether Her Majesty's Government intend to prosecute Mr A. C. Swinburne, or the publisher or printer of the *Fortnightly Review* for his gross incitement to assassination of the Sovereign of a friendly nation'.

The Speaker had to call 'Order, order!' before responding, 'This House has no control over a poet's opinions.' By October Gladstone had made up his mind; he told Sir Henry Ponsonby, the Queen's secretary, that the appointment was 'absolutely impossible ... It is a sad pity; I have always been deeply impressed by his genius.'

Had he been offered the Laureateship, Swinburne would have turned it down. One of his favourite exclamations was, 'If ever I do degrade myself so far beneath the level of a very Bulgar, may I die – a Poet Laureate!' Watts later said that Swinburne's

> indignation knew no bounds at seeing his own name banded about by irresponsible correspondents and pressmen. It is true that the laureateship was never offered to him. Both sides in politics must have known that he would have rejected it with scorn ... I know he would have done so if an honorarium of £5000 a year had been offered to him for accepting it. So far from being annoyed by Lord Salisbury's appointment of Mr. Austin, Swinburne, strong as he was against the obsolete post of laureateship, approved, as I have often heard his say, of an appointment of a writer who was primarily an eminent publicist.

According to Gosse Swinburne's own choice was Canon Dixon or Lord De Tabley. But a number of Swinburne's occasional verses certainly could be laureate pieces, such as 'Music: An Ode', written for the opening of the new buildings of the Royal College of Music. The important thing was that he chose to write to them. The idea that he could be compelled to write to order was anathema to him. In January 1885 the editor of the *North American Review* asked Swinburne to write a poem for the Washington Monument to be delivered within the month. Swinburne received this proposal 'with equal amusement and astonishment. You must inform your American friends that I have not the honour to be a professional or official versifier ... '

In October 1892 Swinburne wrote 'Grace Darling', remembering how, 30 years before,

> I went with dear old Scott, who was hideously sick all the way out from Joyous Gard, to the lighthouse, where the heroine's old father who had rescued the shipwrecked crew from off the rocks while she kept the boat steady to take them in received us. Didn't you ever when a boy think how you would like of all things to keep or live in a lighthouse? I do to this day. Of course I mean if it's some miles out to sea and difficult to get at.

Sadly, Scott was soon 'dear' no longer. When his *Autobiographical Notes* were published Swinburne took great exception to some of Scott's comments about him, and wrote an angry letter to *The Academy* entitled 'The Poison of the Parasite'. Thereafter Scott was 'scorpion Scott', part of the menagerie of enemies that included 'polecat Howell', the 'bladder-broken vulture' Napoleon III, the 'butterfly' Whistler, the 'dog' Buchanan and the 'gap-toothed and hoary-headed ape' Emerson.

A more generous side of Swinburne's character is shown in his visit on 5 December to the bed-ridden sixteen-year-old son of Lady Brooke Bertram. 'I have called twice since, with books to amuse him – and have managed not to cry in his presence, though thinking of him and his gratitude and pleasure (at sight of me) has more than once made my eyes smart and moisten in private.' Swinburne's visits went on for months. Lady Bertram told Gosse she 'could tell you much of those many visits, his sense of humour, his reading of Dickens, the extraordinary humble way (and he so great!) in which he consulted Bertram about certain lines in his "Grace Darling", which he was then writing'.

In 1893 Jowett died, and Swinburne's 'Recollections of Professor Jowett' described his visits to Holmwood in the 1870s and the holiday together in Cornwall in 1874. John Nichol's death in 1894 passed without comment. Nichol had felt increasingly estranged from Swinburne, toward the end of his life selling some of his presentation copies of Swinburne's works. He had resented Swinburne's parody of his friend 'Owen Meredith' in the *Heptalogia* and wrote on 20 September 1890 of Swinburne, 'he has of late years become . . . an egotist'. In April 1894 Mary Leith's daughter-in-law Mildred, wife of her eldest son Alexander, died in childbirth. On 25 May Swinburne told Mary Molesworth, 'I have just written a little poem "to a baby kinswoman" who lost her mother a few days after her birth a few weeks ago – but I hear she is doing well, poor little pet, and she has most loving aunts to take thought for her'. In July Swinburne went to the Isle of Wight and by August was staying with his mother at Chestal, Dursley, Gloucestershire, checking the proofs of his third book of essays, *Studies in Prose and Poetry*. He read Chaucer and Heywood, visited Berkeley Castle, went for walks with Alice, and told Watts 'the day before your minor . . . played truant in very Etonian fashion'. The year ended with another loss, when Christina Rossetti died on 29 December. Swinburne composed an elegy for her, 'A New Year's Eve'. Just before he started to write, he looked out of the window and had 'never seen a more magnificent heavenful of stars'.

Apart from *Studies in Prose and Poetry*, 1894 saw the publication of *Astrophel and Other Poems*, dedicated to William Morris, whose Kelmscott Press had issued a beautiful edition of *Atalanta*. *Astrophel* contained a number of memorable poems such as 'Loch Torridon', 'A Nympholept', 'Elegy 1869–91' (for Richard Burton), along with 'Astrophel', 'An Autumn Vision', 'A Swimmer's Dream' and 'The Palace of Pan'. 'A Nympholept' is one of Swinburne's most atmospheric lyrics, evoking a hot summer woodland and the speaker's slow, inexorable possession by a sense of the God Pan, the 'terrene All'. Swinburne thought it 'one of the best and most representative things I ever did', a poem designed to 'render the effect of inland or woodland solitude – the splendid oppression of nature at noon which found utterance of old in words of such singular and everlasting significance as panic and nymph-olepsy'. It dramatizes the meeting of human consciousness with the mystery of existence beyond it and embodies Swinburne's core themes of power, powerlessness, fear, rapture and transcendence. The last stanza is one of the greatest moments in Swinburne's poetry:

> The terror that whispers in darkness and flames in light,
>   The doubt that speaks in the silence of earth and sea,
> The sense, more fearful at noon than in midmost night,
>   Of wrath scarce hushed and of imminent ill to be,
>   Where are they? Heaven is as earth, and as heaven to me
> Earth: for the shadows that sundered them here take flight;
>   And nought is all, as am I, but a dream of thee.

The ambiguity of the last line is brilliant: does the speaker dream Pan, the All? or does Pan dream the speaker? Numinous and hard-won (both by the speaker and the poet), here is a moment where the sense of self invading the Other or the Other invading the self is balanced in an ecstatic equilibrium. Its bliss is all the more poignant in a poet so often compelled to memorialize 'the flowing of all men's tears beneath the sky'.

On 4 June 1895 Swinburne described to his mother how he was

> making out a scheme for a narrative poem of King Arthur's time, founded on a beautiful tragic legend about two brothers – Knights of Northumberland. I have not finished my sketch of the story yet, but Walter likes the opening stanzas – inspired by the (late) hawthorns about here which are too lovely while they last ... I wish you could come and see and smell the haymaking in Wimble-don Park.

To William Rossetti he wrote, 'I have two poems on hand - one a little romance of chivalry, the other a lyric poem on the religions of the world, their glories and failures, and the one true faith that abides alone in all loyal men' ('The Altar of Righteousness').

A steady stream of visitors came to see the famous poet at The Pines. There are stories that Watts, resenting Swinburne's fame, tried to mo-nopolize their attention. When George Wyndham visited in 1891 Watts insisted on talking politics and read his own poems instead of allowing Swinburne to read his. Wyndham's impression was that Watts 'now considers Swinburne his own property'. In June 1895 Gosse brought the Dutch writer Maarten Maartens, who heard Swinburne read *The Tale of Balen*:

> It was too subjective an out-pour, and wearisomely impassioned, like a child's jump against a wall, but it was his appropriate utterance of his own creation. You felt the immediate concord between the travail and the bringing forth. At the first moment, however, when he ceased, I felt a poignant grief that it was over, a past experience in my life, an emotion of poetic sympathy I should never feel again. It had been very beautiful.
>
> Gloriously, and to me quite newly, direct; all the difference between seeing a beautiful woman and feeling her embrace.

Another visitor was William Rothenstein, who came on 10 August to draw a portrait:

> Swinburne gets up as I enter, rather like Lionel Johnson in figure, the same chétif boy, narrow shoulders and nervous twitch of the hands, which, however are strong and fine. A much fresher face than I would have imagined from accounts heard, a fine nose, a tiny glazed green eye, a curiously clear auburn moustache, and a beard of a splendid red. How young he looks, notwithstanding his years . . . When at last the sitting began, no sitter ever gave me so much trouble. For besides always changing his pose, he is so deaf, that he could not hear me; and after sitting a short time, a nervous restlessness seized on him, which held him the whole time . . . He speaks with the accent of an Oxford Don, and with a certain gaiety, with gracious and rather old-fashioned manners. He behaves charmingly to old Watts . . . He was like a schoolboy let out of school, when I said I would not bother him any longer.

During August Swinburne stayed with his family at The Rectory, Solihull, which they found 'a most sleepy place'. He carried on with *The Tale of Balen* and wrote letters to Watts, addressing Watts as 'major' and making jokes about getting swished for using a 'crib' for translation. By 25 August Lady Jane was back at 20 Ennismore Gardens in London. Morris continued to send Kelmscott books and William Rossetti dedicated an edition of his sister's poems to Swinburne. On 5 November Swinburne acknowledged a copy of *Jude the Obscure* sent by Hardy, which he found 'equally beautiful and terrible in its pathos'.

On 23 March he finished the dedicatory verses to *The Tale of Balen* for his mother. He referred to it as 'your poem', appropriately since, as he said to Mary Molesworth, 'she comes of a warlike house'. The feelings it stirred in him for his Northumbrian origins were sufficiently strong to enable him to send it on 9 June to Sir John Swinburne at Capheaton, since 'it is a Northumbrian story, as you may have seen, and so far deserving of a place in a Northumbrian library'. On 21 June Sir John invited Watts and Swinburne to visit Capheaton but it is unknown whether they ever did. The printers' copy for *The Tale of Balen* was made by Clara Reich, a young woman of 21 Watts had met in 1890 and between whom there had sprung up an unlikely romantic attachment. By the mid-1890s, Clara was a regular visitor to The Pines. When she was eventually introduced, she told Swinburne she had been born near Capheaton and Swinburne was delighted to meet a fellow Borderer. During the 1890s his Northumbrian roots became more significant to him than ever. This is apparent both from a discussion of the Brontës in November 1896 and the closing stanzas of *The Tale of Balen*, when Balen lies dying:

> He drank the draught of life's first wine
> Again: he saw the moorland shine,
> The rioting rapids of the Tyne,
>   The woods, the cliffs, the sea.
> The joy that lives at heart and home,
> The joy to rest, the joy to roam,
> The joy of crags and scaurs he clomb,
> The rapture of the encountering foam
>   Embraced and breasted of the boy . . .

In May Watts became Watts-Dunton by taking on his mother's maiden name. Swinburne received a Kelmscott *Chaucer* presented by Morris and Burne-Jones. In July he went to Barking Hall, Needham Market, in Suffolk, his mother's birthplace, to stay with his family. One letter of the time refers to Mary Leith, 'another dear friend, the nearest relative I have after my sisters, is off in a week or two for her annual sojourn in Iceland'. On 19 July Swinburne wrote 'The High Oaks, Barking Hall' for his mother's eighty-seventh birthday, and read Morris's *The Well at the World's End*. Though he did not especially like the air, he walked in the woods and noted how 'the biggest cedar on the lawn was like a ladder of light showing through a screen of shadow as it met the soft rainy gleam of sunset under heaps of cloud'. In September he worked on the 'Dedicatory Epistle' which would preface his *Collected Poems* in 1904.

On 3 October Morris died. 'My friendship with him began in '57 – think of that!' exclaimed Swinburne, 'and was never broken or ruffled for a moment . . . I felt stunned all the day after his death.' His mother sent her condolences to her son. On 26 November, after an illness of six weeks, Lady Jane Swinburne joined Edith, Charles Henry and Edward in death. Her youngest daughter Isabel reported, 'it had been a great and weary struggle ever since last Sunday but just the end was very rapid and painless, her vitality and strength were so great'. Swinburne went with Alice to Bonchurch for the funeral on 1 December, Charlotte kept from going by ill-health. Afterwards, outside the churchyard, Alice said to her brother they must be more and closer to each other than before, words which were still with Swinburne in 1897 when he wrote the haunting 'Barking Hall. A Year After'. In this poem he imagined how:

> Noon, dawn, and evening thrill
> With radiant change the immeasurable repose
> Wherewith the woodland wilds lie blest
> And feel how storms and centuries rock them still to rest.

The place was unchanged though his mother had gone. Comparing love to the sun, his feelings led him to write, 'Even earth and transient things of earth/Even here to him bear witness not of death but birth.' According to Gosse, Swinburne's grief was 'overwhelming, and it may be said that this formed the last crisis of his own life'.

Other losses followed. On 17 June 1898 Edward Burne-Jones died, severing Swinburne's last living contact with the Pre-Raphaelite days in the autumn of 1857 at the Oxford Union. On 30 June he told Isabel that he had a volume of poems ready which would be dedicated to Burne-Jones and Morris, though *A Channel Passage* was not published until 1904. He wrote an elegy for Mrs Lynn Linton who died in July. In January 1899 Charlotte died and was buried at Bonchurch. Alice wrote to a friend,

> it is a great consolation to us to feel that we have your prayers, we can see how merciful God has been to us in so many ways and it is a consolation to think that He has taken our dear sister from a life that was in many ways a continual mortification, (always borne with most cheerful patience), to the Rest, as we humbly hope and believe, of Paradise.

Isabel and Alice occasionally visited Mary Leith at Westhall, Aberdeen, as well as on the Isle of Wight. Mary's second son Robert was killed on active service in India on 21 April 1898 and on 22 April 1899 Mary's mother, Lady Mary Gordon, died. As their family circle diminished they wrote more frequently, exchanging jokes, and Swinburne offering Mary criticisms about her story 'The Cavemen'.

Lillah McCarthy described her visit to The Pines about this time:

> The house was smug and mid-Victorian ... When we came into the room – oh! the Victorian mustiness of it – Swinburne stood up and was very charming. He was dressed in shiny black from head to foot. His frock-coat fitted badly, his trousers were pulled up so high that they showed the tops of his elastic-sided boots. His arms hung so limp at his sides that they might have been boneless; but his head was astonishing, and his eyes seemed to betray the struggle which I came to see in his poetry – the struggle of the image to keep afloat in the mighty tide of his words ... Then he read, with a voice like a choric chant. The voice sounded strange and wonderful to me.

In June 1899 Swinburne wrote *Rosamund, Queen of the Lombards*. The play was dedicated to Mary, to whom Swinburne wrote on 11 September, 'you will recognize my Norse abhorrence of hot weather and southern climate here and there – how could our Northmen stand it!' The play was published on 26 October. A plan to reprint the *Heptalogia* came to nothing. This was the year of his last great poem, 'The Lake of Gaube'. His memories of that visit in the spring of 1862 were still vivid 30 years later. In a review of Hugo's *Notes of Travel* (1890) Swinburne described

> The fiery exuberance of flowers among which the salamanders glide like creeping flames, radiant and vivid, up to the very skirt of the tragic little pine-wood at whose heart the fathomless little lake lies silent, with a dark dull gleam on it as of half-tarnished steel, the deliciously keen and exquisite shock of a first plunge under its tempting and threatening surface, more icy cold than the sea in winter; the ineffable and breathless purity of the clasping water in which it seems to savour of intrusive and profane daring that a swimmer should take his pleasure till warned back by fear of cramp when but half way across the length of it ... the sport of catching and taming a salamander till it become the pleasantest as well as the quaintest of dumb four-footed friends; the beauty of its purple-black coat of scaled armour inlaid with patches of dead-leaf gold, its shining eyes and its flashing tongue ...

All these details find their way into the poem, which uses a three-part structure with varying metre and rhyme. The first part describes the flowers and the salamanders on the shores of the lake, the second part the swimmer who dives into the lake:

> As the bright salamander in fire of the noonshine exults and is glad
> of his day,
> The spirit that quickens my body rejoices to pass from the
> sunlight away,
> To pass from the glow of the mountainous flowerage,
> the high multitudinous bloom,
> Far down through the fathomless night of the water,
> the gladness of silence and gloom ...

The dive into the lake is a symbol of the confrontation with death. The diver survives the plunge and Swinburne closes the poem by saying that to all our questions about death, 'Deep silence answers: the glory/We dream of may be but a dream'. His imagery expresses a hope he could never express in prose except in the most qualified manner, as when he wrote that a child's devotion to the memory of her dead brother made him

> inclined to fancy that it may indicate – at least possibly – a revival and reunion after death. In spite of all the creeds and all the clergy on earth, I am not convinced of the contrary. Did you ever hear of the old parishioner who on being asked by her clergyman what she thought of his sermon against atheism replied – 'Ah, sir, it was a beautiful sermon – but still, begging your Reverence's pardon, I can't help thinking there is a God'?

14.1   Swinburne as an old man

It was in 1899 that Max Beerbohm visited The Pines. Swinburne was 'a strange small figure in grey, having an air at once noble and roguish, proud and skittish'. Despite grey hair that fringed his bald head he had 'something of a beautfully well-bred child, But he had the eyes of a god, and the smile of an elf'. E. V. Lucas called Swinburne's eyes 'fixed and mirthless'. When Richard Le Gallienne made a present of a scarce edition of Kyd which Swinburne only accepted after much persuasion,

> the boyish pleasure he showed in his new acquisition, I might say toy, was exhilarating to see. That eager boyishness, which, even as an old man, he never lost, was one of the most charming characteristics. His blues eyes seemed suddenly to flower in his face, and his whole countenance became so irradiated with interior light that one seemed to see the welling up of that deep lyric fount from which the most impassioned song in the English language had come.

A gift of lilies could spark the same response, taken from the hand of the giver 'as reverently as the communicant takes into his hands the consecrated bread of the sacrament . . . He bent his head over them in a rapture that was almost like a prayer . . . For many minutes he sat holding them, turning them this way and that, too rapt in his worship to speak or think of anything else.'

Swinburne was an idol to many of the writers of the 1890s, among them Arthur Symons, who visited The Pines several times. In 1900 Symons wrote of one encounter:

> Living, as he did, at a height higher than an eagle's flight, he showed it as often in his silences as in his words. And it was always there – in the strange green eyes that gazed in yours in a kind of abstract passion; in the face, that suggested the sense of flight, with its aquiline features . . . His voice, when he read his verse, was high-pitched; it was an ecstatic, a rapturous voice; it never went deep, but often up and up as he emphasised every word that had a special significance . . . His voice was not musical yet it was a beautiful voice; it did not ring many changes on the variations of the notes, but it was an inspired voice . . . I have heard many poets read their verse, but (save with the sole exception of Verlaine) never have I been so thrilled, so rooted in my chair, nor drawn in my breath.

In November Swinburne told Symons he no longer wished to write on imperial or patriotic subjects.

Leonard Woolf remembered how at Cambridge, with Thoby Stephen, Lytton Strachey and Clive Bell, he would walk in the evenings listening to the nightingales and chant poetry and 'more often than not it would be Swinburne' who was 'something of a legend and symbol to us in the early nineteen hundreds'. Woolf occasionally saw Swinburne in Putney. Once he was having his hair cut in a shop near Putney station:

> . . . the door opened and everyone, including the man cutting my hair, turned and looked at the tiny, fragile-looking figure in a cloak and large hat standing in the doorway. I remember very vividly the fluttering of the hands and fear and misery in the eyes. No one said anything, and after a moment the little figure went out and shut the door. 'That', said the barber, 'is Mr. Swinburne.'

In 1901 Swinburne wrote an essay on Dickens, who had been a 'household god' at East Dene. He had many social invitations but would turn them aside with 'I never go out from one year's end to another'. In July E. T. Cook came to lunch:

> Watts's room on the ground floor, where we had luncheon (all rather frowsy – anchovy sauce in streaks). Swinburne came in late – a short man and fat, now nearly bald. Both of them in carpet slippers. Swinburne very deaf – only addressable when T. Watts pulled chair round and shouted, 'Our friend here is speaking of Mat. Arnold.' This set him off talking in a curious falsetto, very emphatic voice (his hand shaking violently at meals and in a way like a child) . . . After lunch we went up to Swinburne's room on the first floor – stacked everywhere with books. He browsed around, showing me his treasures for about an hour – large paper Kelmscotts given him by W. Morris . . . Watts said Swinburne was a limpet – would never go anywhere except for seabathing.

On 6 October Swinburne wrote to William Sharp about a selection of his poetry Sharp was editing. He deprecated the 1866 poems, 'Ave Atque Vale' and *Atalanta*, preferring instead *Erechtheus*, adding, 'I would like to have seen one of what I call my topographical poems in full. The tiny scrap from Loch Torridon was hardly worth giving by itself.' By this time Swinburne felt the militant patriotism of 'The Armada' was better for boys than the classic pessimism of *Atalanta*.

Ever since his youth Swinburne had meditated writing something on the Borgias. At Oxford he filled several notebooks with part of a play about them. On 19 January 1902 he started writing a drama and spent some of that year researching the subject. All that came of it was the single act of *The Duke of Gandia* (1908). Otherwise he wrote a short essay on Shelley for *Chambers' Encyclopaedia*. Though distant from political issues, he signed a letter of protest on 19 June 1902 against the banning of any English performance of Maurice Maeterlinck's play 'Monna Vanna' and on 30 January another against the imprisonment of the Russian novelist Maxim Gorky.

On 4 April 1903 A. C. Benson came to The Pines. He described Swinburne as:

> a little pale, rather don-like man, quite bald, with a huge head and dome-like forehead, a ragged red beard in odd whisks, a small aquiline nose. He looked supremely shy but received me with a distinguished courtesy, drumming on the ground and uttering strange little whistling noises. He seemed very deaf. He was rather tremulous with his hands and clumsy. At first he said nothing, but gazed at intervals out of the window with a mild blue eye, and a happy sort of look . . . there was an odd bitter bookish scent about the room, which hung I noticed about him too . . . his little feet kicked spasmodically under the chair and he drummed on the table.

Benson thought Watts 'an egotistical, ill-bred little man', often leading the conversation back to himself, who considered Swinburne 'a mere boy still – and must be treated like one – a simple schoolboy, full of hasty impulses and generous thought'.

Swinburne's life went on: he wrote and corresponded on Elizabethan and Jacobean dramatists, walked over the Common, stood in drenching rain to watch birds on a lake; in the summers he paused where 'to see children playing in the hay carries me sixty years back'. A planned holiday at Lancing was cancelled when his sister Alice died on 30 September. In November Swinburne became dangerously ill with pneumonia but survived, albeit with weakened lungs. He spent the rest of 1903 and the early months of 1904 convalescing, thanking Hardy for sending *The Dynasts*, 'being still invalided and confined to one room for the purposes of sleeping and writing, though I go downstairs to dine and sup'. On 3 February he made his will, leaving everything to Watts. On 22 February he went out for the first time in months.

He was now 67 but age had not mellowed him in certain respects. When William Rossetti sent him a copy of Christina Rossetti's poems Swinburne replied that the book was beautiful 'but, good Satan! what a fearful warning against the criminal lunacy of theolatry! It is horrible to think of such a woman – and of so many otherwise noble and beautiful natures – spiritually infected and envenomed by the infernal and putrefying virus of the Galilean serpent'. Once when asked to be a godparent, Swinburne said, 'it would be impossible for me to take part, direct or indirect, in a religious ceremony which represents it as "a child of wrath" – words which seem to me the most horrible of all blasphemies – standing in need of human intervention to transmute it into "a child of grace".'

In the summer of 1904 Swinburne, Watts and Clara went to Cromer. At noon on the first day there Swinburne went out in a boat to swim in deep water. He came out of the water cold and tired. The sea did not have its usual invigorating effect. The same thing happened the next day. Swinburne said he was tired and looked unwell. He decided to give up trying to swim and reluctantly confined himself to walking along the beach or inland, sometimes alone or with Watts and Clara. The sea, which had inspired and thrilled him since the lost summers when his father threw him into the surf below East Dene, was now too much for him.

The year 1904 was a landmark for his publishing. His last collection of poems was *A Channel Passage*, a less interesting book than *Astrophel*, 'The Lake of Gaube' standing out, though it also had the haunting 'In a Rosary' and the 'Barking Hall' poems. Otherwise there were too many verses on England, politics, children and Elizabethan plays. Chatto issued Swinburne's *Collected Poems* in six volumes with a 'Dedicatory Epistle' in which Swinburne surveyed his life's work. His plays followed in five volumes a year later. In 1905 Watts encouraged Swinburne to publish *A Year's Letters* as *Love's Cross-Currents*. Swinburne wrote to William Rossetti on 21 August:

> if you glance at page 215 I think you may be reminded of a young fellow you once knew, and not see very much difference between Algie Harewood and Redgie Swinburne. Nothing in all my literary life has ever so much astonished me as the reception of this little old book. The first (small) impression was sold out on the day of publication . . . Reginald Harewood is otherwise rather a coloured photograph of . . . ACS.
> Yours,
> A. C. Swinburne

After a long courtship Watts-Dunton and Clara Reich married on 29 November. Swinburne thought it was all very jolly. If he was jealous of her relationship with Watts-Dunton he kept it to himself, drawing what solace he could from seeing Isabel, and Mary, 'my oldest and dearest relation and friend in the world'.

In 1907 Noyes celebrated Swinburne's seventieth birthday in verse in the *Fortnightly Review*. Noyes visited The Pines that year and marvelled at Swinburne's description of a walk by the North Sea over forty years before, for 'he remembered the most minute details of certain rock pools he had seen and described what he called "certain lozenges of colour" in them'. To William Rossetti on 14 April Swinburne wrote, 'I care no more than I ever did for flattery or notoriety or abuse: but I do not affect to be indifferent to the general evidence of the estimate which seems to be taken of my station and my work.' He saw the Nobel Prize go to Kipling, and in May he refused an honorary degree offered on behalf of Oxford University by Lord Curzon, just as in July 1908 he turned down a Civil List pension of £250 offered by Herbert Asquith. In March 1907 he told Symons, 'my magnum opus will be my book on the Elizabethan dramatists. I have put so much of my life, my thoughts, of my reading, of my research . . . into the production of this volume that I don't mind if it chances to be my last book of prose.' His prophecy for *The Age of Shakespeare* (1908) was correct.

On 6 October 1908 William Rossetti saw him for the last time; Swinburne looked 'in capital health, and is very erect, but has a look of age'. In 1909 Clara noticed Swinburne was coming in from his walk looking worn and tired, sometimes limping. On 1 April he went out for the last time, already showing signs of a cold caught when he was out in the rain. The next day he was confined to bed. Crossing his bedroom to get a book he collapsed and had to be lifted back to bed. A doctor arrived and announced that Swinburne was very ill. He was moved to his library on the first floor where he became delirious. When the nurse tried to give him oxygen, Swinburne beat it away with his hands until Watts-Dunton (who was himself ill) sent a message that it was like a sea-breeze. Semi-conscious, Swinburne would fling the blankets off and talk in Greek. Clara had 'a curious sense of hearing presaging chords of music which invaded me whenever I entered his room and found him either breathing heavily or moaning in broken accents in uneasy sleep'. Watts saw him for the last time on the evening of 9 April. Swinburne died of pneumonia at 10 a.m. the next day, having just turned 72.

Watts-Dunton wrote to Isabel, 'the end was certain this morning . . . but it came much more rapidly than anybody expected . . . he passed away, peacefully and with a happy smile upon his lips. The last I saw of him was last night, when I thought I never saw a man more happy and cheerful; and he might very well be so, for never was there a better man.' William Rossetti and his daughter Helen arrived that afternoon to pay their last respects. In death Swinburne seemed 'noble, calm, and lofty . . . more of intellectual dignity could not be found'. On 13 April he wrote in his diary, 'these few days I have been thinking of little other than Swinburne's death. That his essential work was done is a sufficiently obvious fact, but one grieves much the same.'

Swinburne's life had been a life not without controversy and his death was the same. Isabel wanted her brother to have a Church of England funeral. Though Watts-Dunton disliked the idea, he was reluctant to make an issue of it and mentioned this to Rossetti. After some thought Rossetti wrote on 11 April that Swinburne's wishes should be respected. Two days later Watts-Dunton answered that when Lady Jane died 'he decided to accept the affair as part and parcel of the huge grotesque mummery against which the single-handed struggle seemed to be useless. He was intensely fond of his mother and no doubt his reasoning got biased.' Rossetti thought the service would be 'absolutely wrong'. On 14 April Watts-Dunton wrote that Rossetti's queries

> fructified in my mind, and in the silent watches of the night there flashed upon my memory certain words of his in which he said, 'but with regard to myself, I should seem to be contradicting all my work if I consented to its being used over me'. I rose with a start from my bed and immediately remembered that I promised him it should not be done.

On 14 April he wrote to Isabel, 'the Church of England Burial Service cannot be read over Algernon's grave'. She refused to accept this. The next day Watts-Dunton wrote again,

> . . . up to his last moment he cherished the deepest animosity against the Creed which he felt had severed him from his most

beloved ties. Up to now I have kept from you this bitter fact, but
now I recall a promise I made to him if I survived him that the
Burial Service should never be read over his Grave ... If he had
made a slight matter of his antagonism against Christianity, as so
many free thinkers do, it would have been different but with him it
increased with his years and at the last (if I must say what I am
sorry to say) it was bitterer than ever.

Neither Watts-Dunton nor Isabel were well enough to attend the funeral in Bonchurch, though Mary Leith was there with her son Alexander, Clara Watts-Dunton, Sir John Swinburne, Morris's daughters, Bertie
Mason, Andrew Chatto, Hallam Tennyson, the Mayor of Newport and
Helen Rossetti, who left an account of Swinburne's last journey. She got
up at 6.30 a.m. and went to Waterloo 'to see the coffin placed in the
train':

> It was a glorious spring morning, the trees just beginning to burst
> into leaf and the almond blossom just out. The coffin arrived
> shortly after 8, and was placed in a 'luggage van' which showed no
> outward sign what kind of 'luggage' was within. Inside the van was
> draped in black. No crowd was at Waterloo Station to pay their
> last respects to the poet: the young poets and literati were in bed
> no doubt ... The small group of railway officials and journalists
> bared their heads as the coffin was placed in the train. Besides
> these there were (so far as I know) none but the party attending the
> funeral. I saw Mrs Watts-Dunton, attitudinising of course; I said a
> few words to her, but got into another carriage with Watts-Dunton's
> nephew (Mr Herbert Mason), the family lawyer Mr Arthur Moore,
> Mackenzie Bell, and a Miss Van de Spar. With Mrs Watts-Dunton
> were Sir John Swinburne, a fine-looking old gentleman with a
> strong family resemblance to the poet, Lord Gwyder (a cousin); Dr
> Lowry, another cousin, and Mr Chatto the publisher. May Morris
> and Mr Emery Walker were in another carriage. No public bodies
> – literary or political – were represented. The Mayor of Rome
> alone, in the name of his city, sent a wreath. There were several
> wreaths from private persons.
>
> The English are singularly lacking in any outward show of deco-
> rum on an occasion like this. The coffin was taken about from
> train to ship and ship to train on a common railway truck. No-one
> heeded it at Portsmouth. To me the most impressive sight was to
> see it on the ship, on a common truck it is true, but surrounded by
> flowers, with the splendid sea around and the blue serene sky
> above. It was lowered by the crane: then covered with a rough
> tarpaulin. At Ryde, again, none heeded the arrival of the silent
> traveller, whose tongue had once uttered such immortal words ...
>
> On arriving at Ventnor only two carriages had been provided ...
> There were considerable crowds at the station here and along the
> route, cameras etc. Here Swinburne was a local celebrity and his
> family had owned (and perhaps still did own) land!
>
> On reaching the cemetery young Mason gave me his arm, and
> we followed the coffin along with the other 'mourners' – To my

14.2 Swinburne's funeral

horror I suddenly became aware of a lugubrious chanting noise
and on looking round perceived that several carrion crows had
descended: a clergyman, in surplus get-up, was preceding the coffin
chanting psalms or whatever they are. On reaching the grave, and
the coffin being deposited, he (the Rector of Bonchurch) made a
little speech. He began by saying that he deeply regretted to an-
nounce that at a late hour yesterday he read a telegram from
Swinburne's executor saying that it was Swinburne's wish not to
have the burial service, that he however intended to show the
utmost respect to the memory of the dead poet, who whatever his
after opinions may have been, was nevertheless a baptised member
of our Church. He went on talking, but I felt perfectly ill with
disgust. Emery Walker, who was standing near me murmured 'scandalous'. I answered, 'It's disgraceful. I can't stand it.' When I heard
the wretch begin in his droning voice 'Man that is born of woman'
I quietly retired from the scene and going right away from the
vicinity of the grave plucked a branch of bay and some primroses
and violets which were growing about wild. When I saw that the
clergyman had finished I returned, and was one of the first to
throw flowers into the open grave. Again to my horror I saw the
coffin was covered with a purple pall on which was designed a
huge white cross, and I thought of his verses: 'Thou hast con-
quered, oh pale Galilean, and the world has grown grey from thy
breath'.

Helen Rossetti felt so disgusted by the affair that it was only after some
persuasion that she went to the gathering at a local hotel. She was not
alone in feeling that Swinburne had been betrayed. Even Sir John
Swinburne 'who did not feel so very strongly on the subject ... was
displeased'. A different view of the proceedings was given by Walter T.
Spencer, who said the Revd John Floyd Andrewes 'insisted on conduct-
ing the usual ceremony at the graveside. While he was reading there was
an arrival from London, who broke in on the scene with vehement
protests. The old clergyman had the good sense to proceed with the
service as though nothing untoward was happening, thereby averting
the unpleasant scene that everyone was beginning to fear.'

A short time afterward, Canon Mason, Vice-Dean of Canterbury
Cathedral, preached that 'much lustral water and the most precious of
all precious blood were needed to do away with the pollution which
Swinburne's poetry introduced into English literature'. The poets took a
different view, among them Thomas Hardy who, remembering 'The
passionate pages of his earlier years', visited Swinburne's grave in
Bonchurch in 1910 and penned his fine elegy 'A Singer Asleep'. In it
Hardy imagines Swinburne meeting Sappho, 'sighing to her spectral
form':

'O teacher, where lies hid thy burning line;
Where are those songs, O poetess divine

Whose very orts are love incarnadine?'
And her smile back: 'Disciple true and warm,
    Sufficient now are thine.'

Notes

In the following notes Lang refers to *The Swinburne Letters*, Peattie to *Selected Letters of William Michael Rossetti*, Gosse (1927) to the fourth edition of his *The Life of Algernon Charles Swinburne*, part of the Bonchurch Complete Works. Where an author has more than one reference in the bibliography sources are differentiated by year of publication. All letters by Swinburne or members of his family are from Lang unless otherwise indicated.

Introduction

1 'He was dead then': Bennett, 92.
2 'There are elusive hints': Apart from rumours that Watts-Dunton bullied Swinburne, a letter from Wise to Gosse of 9 January 1916 at the Harry Ransom Humanities Research Centre of the University of Austin at Texas reports that Clara Watts-Dunton's marriage was unconsummated, that she never slept at The Pines until after her husband's death, and that she had a drink problem. A letter from Wise to Gosse of 3 June 1915 (in the Brotherton Collection, Leeds) reveals that Isabel Swinburne found that Watts-Dunton often prevented her from seeing her brother, and that she thought Watts-Dunton had lived off Swinburne's money. The subject of bullying comes up in a letter of Gosse's dated 28 June 1909, also at Leeds.
3 'plague of mankind': White, 202.
4 'electric coma': Jay and Glasgow, 217.
   'he is our champion': Rossetti (1902), 255.
   'his sensitive face': Sharp, 440.
   'whenever I happen': Symons (1900), 20.
   'the eyes of a god': Hyder (1970), 237.
5 'the decadent, verbally sophisticated': Rosenberg, 145.

Chapter 1

7 'its salt . . . never of the sea': This is confirmed by a letter from E. Hope Lowry to Gosse of 24 December 1912 in the W. R. Perkins Library, Duke University. Swinburne told Julian Osgood Field a preposterous story that his father had taught him to swim by

taking him out on to the Solway Firth in a rowing boat, throwing him over the side and rowing away. See Field, 112.

'his delight in the water': Lafourcade (1928), I, 49.

9   'From earliest childhood': Gosse, 24–5.

'being Swinburne, he was of course': Wedmore, 64.

'His alarmed mother . . . might be harmful': See Peattie, 169n.

'such uncoordinated, involuntary': Ober, 51.

10 'It was a lovely place': James, 226–7.

12 'He was proud to be descended': For a genealogy of the Swinburnes see Hedley.

'was taken by his monk tutor': Geoffrey Scott, 184.

'remained staunchly Jacobite': Geoffrey Scott, 197.

'a foursquare design': Thomas, 8.

15 'the chaplain believed': Geoffrey Scott, 100.

'she married the diplomat': See Winning.

For Charles Henry Swinburne's naval career see Marshall's *Royal Naval Biography*, IV (2), 219–25.

17 'as his profession': Leith, 245.

'too sensible for any extravagances': James, 227.

18 'a pretty-featured, carroty haired spoilt boy': Lang III, 325n.

'Swinburne was a man . . . beneath contempt': Diary of Helen Angeli Rossetti, 25 April 1909. Quoted by permission of Signora Helen Guglielmini.

'the father of Swinburne's friend': See Wilson (1971), 241.

19 'exquisitely soft': Gosse, 290.

'boasted an exceptional library': See *The Times*, 2 May 1899, 12, for a report on a sale of part of the collection: 177 lots fetched £8595 5s.

20 'Alice was the most artistic': Williamson, 205.

'I don't like and never will read': Unpub. letter of Isabel Swinburne to B. E. Rosenthal, 24 September 1899, Eton College Library.

21 'in memory of Charles Swinburne': For this translation I am indebted to Mrs Rachel Chapman and to the Revd Alfred Tedman and his wife for drawing my attention to the inscription.

'our mothers': Leith, 3.

23 'a talented watercolourist': See Turley (1972). A number of her pictures are held in the Gordon archive at the Hartley Library, University of Southampton and in the County Record Office, Newport, Isle of Wight.

24 'suffered under Bonchurch Pilate': Holiday, 261.

'a large cousinhood gathered': Leith, 11.

'gradually became the poles': Lafourcade (1932), 18.

25 'In 1828, Swinburne's aunt': Louis, 9–10.

'had an impression': Sewell, 83.

'was for some time in a chronic state': Sewell, 88.

26 'there came an open split': Sewell, 94.

'Dickens stayed in Bonchurch': See Storey and Fielding, vol. 5, 572–613.

27 There are two letters by Ulrica Fenwick to Swinburne, dated 8 May and 18 May 1890 at the Harry Ransom Humanities Research Centre, University of Texas at Austin.

Chapter 2

28 'What a fragile little creature': Gosse, 11.

'venerable and imposing': Redesdale, 52–3.

'With the exception of the new College buildings': Redesdale, 59.

29 'so infinitely kind to me': Lang, IV, 321.

'modest, kind, and universally popular': A. C. Benson, 87–90.

'a good scholar': Gibson, 129n.

'I did my best for that ungodly boy': Winston, 35.

'very sympathetic attitude': Winston, 82.

'for I certainly was': By permission of the Edith S. and John S. Mayfield Collection, Special Collections Division, Georgetown University Library.

'a shock of red unbrushed hair': Fletcher, 14.

'Once, when Swinburne entered a class': Gosse, 13.

30 'sitting perched up': Gosse, 291.

'In a remarkable letter': Unpub. letter of Swinburne to Algernon Earle, husband to Mary Leith's third daughter Edith, 7 June 1906, Edith S. and John S. Mayfield Collection, Special Collections Division, Georgetown University Library.

'almost all Swinburne's': Gosse, 19.

'Sappho took possession': Gosse 22–3.

'delight and wonder . . . here at last': Unpub. letter of Swinburne to F. W. H. Myers of 18 August 1894. By permission of the Master and Fellows of Trinity College, Cambridge.

31 'As a lover and student': Lang, III, 229.

'My English tutor gave a prize': Meyers (1979).

'We used to take long walks': Gosse 292.

32 'I never wrote anything as autobiographical': Lang, VI, 38.

'greatly interested at the thought': Sewell, 106.

'Algernon adopted airs': Gosse, 20.

33 'particularly anxious to repel': Gosse, 17n.

'other boys would watch': Gosse, 292.

'He was of course bullied': James, 228–9.

'Kick him if you are near enough': Thomas, 22.

'once came to him': Salt, *TLS*, 25 Dec. 1919, 781.

34 'the poor lad was kept in bed': Coleridge, 40.

'Eton: Another Ode': British Library Ashley Ms. 5271.

For Swinburne's contributions to *The Pearl*, etc. see Forbes and Mendes. Mendes believes Swinburne may have been part of a group that produced the *Index Expurgatorius, Cythera's Hymnal* (1870) and *Harlequin, Prince Cherrytop* (1879).

35 'the impulse to play': McGann, 279.

36 'Come here, Master Bertram': Quoted by permission of the Provost and Fellows of Worcester College, Oxford.

37 'If I could have spoken': Quoted by permission of the Provost and Fellows of Worcester College, Oxford.

'Frank's Flogging': Quoted by permission of the Provost and Fellows of Worcester College, Oxford.

38 'I would give anything': Lang, I, 265.

'villain of the piece': Gibson, 127.

'another of what Cecil Y. Lang aptly calls': Thomas, 24.

'the taste for this punishment': Lang, VI, 244.

'It was, in my time': Lewis, 46–7.

39 'flogged him over the fallen trunk': Gibson, 125.

40 'Redgie's Luck': Quoted by permission of the Provost and Fellows of Worcester College, Oxford.

'My tutor caught me': Lang, VI, 254.

'I cannot help believing': Lang, VI, 247.

41 'had no more to do with': Lang, VI, 235.

'the masters at Eton': Ober, 64.

Blanche Warre Cornish: see *The Bookman* (June 1909), 126.

'a certain change took place': Gosse, 25.

'heard little of him': James, 229.

Edith Swinburne's letter: British Library Add. Ms. 70628 f.39–40.

42 'riding a little long-tailed pony': Minto, II, 14.

There is a mystery surrounding the date of Scott's meeting with Swinburne. In 1892 Swinburne said they met when he was 20 (that is, 1857) and in the Dedicatory poem of 1878 Swinburne writes that 21 years have elapsed. Scott's account puts the meeting in 1855.

'a gentle and delightful man': Gosse, 31.

'I kept him to stay with me': James, 229.

'greatly impressed with the simplicity of the boy': Gosse, 25.

Chapter 3

45   'in afternoon walked with Owen': Boyd, 114.
     'Not the tutor': Lang, I, 30n.
     'in some respects the most': Lafourcade (1932), 75.
     'Swinburne's first-term work': The comments by Robert Scott
     come from Examinations IVa 1852–68, Balliol College Archives.
48   'he is the most enthusiastic fellow': Lafourcade (1928), I, 126.
     'did not go in for games': Gosse, 33.
     'inoculate boys with his sinister tenets': James, 229.
50   'A slight girlish figure': Gosse, 34–5.
     'to-morrow I believe': Monsman, 363.
51   'nearly burst out laughing': Gosse, 40.
     'the rushing stream of Shelley's influence': Lafourcade (1927), 62.
     'Swinburne said Nichol gave him': Lafourcade (1928), I, 122.
     'the cause of foreign nationalities': Monsman, 372.
52   'a keen fine-witted man . . . religious matters': Peattie, 391.
     'A. C. Bradley told Gosse': Letter of 11 January 1916. British
     Library Ashley Ms. 5739, f.120.
     'we still managed to drink': Monsman, 382.
     'relishing those dramatists': Lang (1964), 198.
     'a terrific onslaught': Lang, V, 235–6.
53   'at present there seem only two people': Lang, I, 25.
54   'The Travelling of Thor': Quoted by permission of the Brotherton
     Collection, Leeds.
55   Extracts from Edwin Hatch's diary quoted by kind permission of
     the Master and Fellows of Pembroke College, Oxford.
     'young Swinburne called here': Lang, 15n.
57   'on account of persistently neglecting': Latin Register, Balliol Col-
     lege Archives. I am grateful to Ken Dowden for the translation of
     this and the two succeeding entries.
     'is clever and writes quaint ballads': Trevelyan, 141.
58   'he had been gated by the Dean': Gosse, 57.
     'I cannot leave England': Quoted by permission of the Berg Col-
     lection, New York Public Library.
     'Having received your farewell note': Quoted by permission of
     the Berg Collection, New York Public Library.
59   'mad and deafening': Surtees (1980), 26–7.
     'if . . . Swinburne "left"': Lafourcade (1932), 80.
     'Commoner Swinburne': Latin Register, Balliol College Archives.
62   'the most singular man': Lang, I, 30n.
63   'On August 25 the Chiswick Press': Nowell-Smith, 357–9.

'poor Papy': Charles Henry Swinburne's diary is in the Northumberland County Record Office.

Chapter 4

64   'he is much better suited': Oswald and Doughty, I, 385.
65   'overcame/My sight' from 'Three Faces', *A Century of Roundels* (1883).
     'The stories were to be called': See also Jones.
     'A Nine Days Wonder': British Library Add. Ms. 60398.
67   'sometimes twice or three times': Hyder (1970), 6.
     'an elderly lady': Thomas, 62.
     'guiding Swinburne through the Inferno': Praz, 226.
     'deliberately planned': Cassidy, 70.
68   'a curious fancy': Lang, I, 223n.
     'what the other possessed': Lafourcade (1932), 97.
     'Burton was a man': Brodie, 334.
     'both men had the same curious desire': Farwell, 268.
69   'the rest of the company': Gosse, 114.
     'In October he saw a production': Swinburne did in fact attend a staging of *The Merry Wives of Windsor* by Beerbohm Tree and in October 1892, *The Duchess of Malfi*.
70   'he collaborated with Swinburne': For 'The Laird of Waristoun' see Fisher.
     'the Coroner recorded a verdict': The notes to the inquest have probably not survived but see Violet Hunt for an account of it.
71   'the project entirely meets his own liking': Peattie, 121.
     'mountain lake shut in by solitary highlands': from Swinburne's essay 'John Ford'.
     'What go to India without *Sordello*!': This far travelled copy of Browning's poem now resides in the Armstrong Browning Library at Baylor University, Waco, Texas.
     'recited much from his own poems': Surtees (1980), 35.
72   'who seems to amaze small circles': Pope-Hennessy, 141n.
73   'after introducing into his reviews': Peattie 124.
74   'the subject seems to me': Lang (1964), 225.
     'a sort of parody': Mallock, 56. See also Sypher (1973) and Workman.
75   'a strange, quaint, grand old place': Cline (1970), I, 149.
     'Swinburne is strongly sensual': Lang, I, 48n–49n.
     'joined Rossetti at Swinburne's rooms': Lang, I, 54n.

77   'but de Sade confirmed Swinburne': Lafourcade (1932), 105.
      'Gosse's story of Swinburne proposing': For Gosse's source see
      my 'Swinburne's "Boo" Rides Again'. See also Mayfield (1953)
      who originally revealed Jane's age.
      'Once seeing Christine Spartali': Some versions say it was Maria.
      See Robertson, 13, and Anderson, 140.
78   'the duration of Swinburne's stay': Lang, I, 50n.
79   'found a good deal': Oswald and Doughty, II, 454–5.
      'Letters passed back and forth': These letters between Brown and
      Hunt are in the Angeli-Dennis Research Collection at British
      Columbia University Library.
80   'the American writer Henry Adams': Hyder (1970), 3–5.
      'why so early?' Trevelyan, 189–90.
82   'could sometimes talk Swinburne': Anderson, 130.
      'has ready a volume': Cline (1970), I, 199.
      'up the sloping lawn': Gosse, 90.
      'a sort of pseudo-Shelley': Hyder, 116.
      'in which, generally after a period': Gosse, 93.
83   'At 3 a.m. he had been awakened': Lang, VI, 240.
84   'our household consists . . . is seldom here': Oswald and Doughty,
      II, 482, 492.
      'I know next to nothing of Swinburne': Hyder (1970), 114.

Chapter 5

85   'he came up to see me': Sewell, 230.
      'Voice hoarse; neck slightly bent': Dubos, 71.
86   'the name given by the Greeks': Dubos, 71
87   'Throughout medical history': Dubos, 50.
      'it seems to me that with the decline': Dubos, 247–8, n.9.
90   'from the first conception': Lougy, xviii.
      'In our library, often alone': Leith, 19.
91   'Algernon is not much different': Lang, I, 100n.
      'he had quite a bad night': Lang, I, 96.
93   'It was not without surprise': See Swinburne, 'A Record of Friend-
      ship' (1920).
95   'partly shy and partly demonstrative': Peattie, 515.
      'I wish I were dating': Atkinson, 219–20.
96   'I hardly know how to give you': See Packer, 21–30.
97   'The autumn of that year': Leith, 25–6.
101   'the evidence, both internal and external': Lang (1959), 124. See
      Meyers (1993) for a list of key articles on Swinburne's lost love.

102   'a great sorrow': Gosse (1925), 11.
      'Speaking to me of this incident': Gosse, 78–9.
      'There were three poems': Mallock, 57.
103   'with extraordinary poignancy': Gosse (1912), 50.
106   'the extant manuscript': 'The Triumph of Time' is at Balliol Col-
      lege, Oxford.
107   'Mrs Hungerford Pollen told Gosse': Quoted by permission of the
      Special Collections Library, Duke University.
      'I know it is difficult': Leith, 4–5.
      For Mildred Leith's letter see *The Times*, 4 January 1969, 6.
109   'the marriage settlement': In the Gordon Archive, Hartley Li-
      brary, Southampton .
      'flags were displayed': See *Aberdeen Weekly Journal*, 20 July
      1849.
      'My marriage in 1865': Leith, 26–7.
      'She claimed one of her most valued wedding gifts': See Mayfield
      (1980), 34. Lafourcade (1930, xxii) writes of 'the book that he
      deposited, not perhaps without a secret sigh, among the wedding
      gifts of his cousin'.

Chapter 6

111   'as it was calculated': Oswald and Doughty, II, 529.
      'a keen sea breeze': Lafourcade (1930), vi–vii.
112   'such poetry as *Atalanta*': Rutland, 122.
114   'an overwhelming sense': Rutland, 124.
      'Swinburne was deeply instructed': Gosse, 109.
115   'life-long sorrow': Lang, VI, 83.
      'it is the greatest nuisance ... otherwise': Unpub. letters from
      Swinburne to Howell, Robert H. Taylor Collection, Manuscripts
      Division, Department of Rare Books and Special Collections,
      Princeton University Libraries.
116   'I cannot but congratulate ourselves': See *Memoirs of the Anthro-
      pological Society 1863–64* (1865), 308.
      'O, do not ask me if I can throw': See Brabrook, 57.
      'Swinburne ... elected a Fellow': Swinburne's membership only
      lapsed in 1905.
117   'though nothing of particular moment': Leith, 27.
      'an impenetrably close knot': Mills, 104–5.
      'kept by a disreputable old woman': Croft-Cooke, 75.
118   'a man whom I certainly did not esteem': Peattie, 544n.
119   'facile and spasmodically intense': Croft-Cooke, 41.

119   'The influence of Swinburne's unstable character': Reynolds, 13.
120   'our enjoyment was such': LeBourgeois, 91–5.
      'proved as unsatisfactory as might be expected': Reynolds, 11.
      'without exception the most extraordinary man': Du Maurier,
      235–6. This letter is dated April 1864 but, as Henderson points
      out, Swinburne did not return from Italy until 21 May. But
      George Du Maurier describes waking up the next day to find 'a
      healthy innocent little baby weighing over 20 pounds', presum-
      ably his second child, Guy Louis Du Maurier, born 13 May 1865.
      A date of 12 May 1865 for the meeting at Simeon Solomon's
      would bear out Armstrong's reference to already knowing *Atalanta
      in Calydon*.
      'A propos of Villon': Lamont, 163–4.
121   'Soon, something I had said': Mander, 58.
      'so long in the country': Unpub. letter of Swinburne to Joseph
      Knight, 19 November 1865, in the British Library.
123   'was extremely indignant': Notes by Gosse quoted by permission
      of the Special Collections Library, Duke University.
      'The remark you make on his behaviour': Trevelyan, 218–19.
124   'a deplorably vicious reputation': Trevelyan, 218.
125   'I went to see Swinburne yesterday': Lang, I, 141n.
126   'You know he has been warned': Lang, I, 142n.
127   'the wildest offers made me': Trevelyan, 223.
128   'in a very excited state': Lang, I, 155n.
129   'an incident involving members' top hats': See 'Algernon in Lon-
      don', an amusing parody of *Atalanta* in *The World*, May–June
      1876.
      'the only public speech': See Meyers (1988).
130   'we broke down together': Trevelyan, 237.
      'a very real and permanent misfortune': Gosse, 294.
      'On second thought I have made up my mind': Quoted by permis-
      sion of the Beinecke Rare Book and Manuscript Library, Yale
      University.

Chapter 7

135   'the bleak beauty of little words': Rosenberg, 132.
137   'that damned hound Payne': Letter of 7 August 1886 to Joseph
      Knight in the British Library.
      'on the title-page': Ellis (1930), 192.
138   'purgate his volume': Lang, I, 174–5n.
      'in high feather': Cline (1978), 23.

'if Mr. Swinburne would only modify': A copy of this letter is in the Chatto and Windus Archive, University of Reading.

140 'The Session of the Poets': Hyder (1970), 39–41.

'there is a terrible earnestness': Hyder (1970), 42–8.

141 'the despairing cry of the baffled voluptuary': Wise (1919), I, 162.

'rejoice in the advent': Thomson, 100–101.

'A very great poet has arisen': Peattie (1963), 363n.

'a better man of business than myself': Quoted by permission of the Edith S. and John S. Mayfield Collection, Special Collections Division, Georgetown University Library.

'I am, you will understand': Lang, I, 199.

142 'I fear the Philistines': Unpub. letter at Columbia University.

143 'vigorously written': Rossetti, 193–4.

'Swinburne's superiority': Peattie, 150.

144 'speaking of the qualities': Lang, I, 192.

145 'a rough time of it': Hyder (1933), 75.

'nothing more remarkable': Lafourcade (1932), 142.

146 'Swinburne is now in town again': Lang, I, 214n.

'as it acknowledges [Swinburne's] practical atheism': Peattie, 236n–7n.

147 'The old gentleman is kindly': Rossetti, 220–21.

148 'Mr Spartali the Greek consul': Unpub. letter of Ford Madox Brown in the British Library.

'the most nobly sustained lyric': Lang, I, 231.

149 'Don't lull us to sleep with songs': Lang, I, 236n.

'was quite thrown off his equilibrium': Surtees (1980), 46.

Chapter 8

151 'a clear headed and hearted woman': Lang, I, 233–4.

'his slender form': Beatty, 299.

152 'Mazzini urges him': Rossetti, 231.

'one of the finest and least understood': Sacks, 204.

153 'We were sitting after breakfast': Lang, I, 249–50n.

'an attack of insensibility': Peattie, 179n.

154 'How could you, as a Christian': Thwaite, 70–71.

156 'the attraction . . . lies': Mankovitz, 136.

'a true revolutionary' Mankovitz, 202.

157 'he will not last two years': Mankovitz, 215.

'had the keenest mind I ever': Mankovitz, 85.

'all about Menken calling': Falk, 201.

158 'To-day I have had such a letter': Lang, I, 276–7n.
'I am my own no longer': Lang, I, 277n.

159 'Woolner has been entertaining': Peattie, 193.
'Do write yourself': Lang, I, 278n.

161 'In his opinion there was a marked difference': See *Journal of the Anthropological Society* (1868), cxlv–cxlvi.

162 'I hear bye the bye': Cline (1978), 62.
'for five days past': Lang, I, 298.

163 'Hotten was still prepared': See Hotten's letter of 25 July 1868 in the Chatto and Windus Archive, Reading.
'I was walking along a corridor': Gosse, 164.
'so violently as to make a gash': Thwaite, 72.
'Mr Milnes made me go to lunch': See my 'The Admiral to the Rescue', 50.

164 'in capital spirits': Lang, I, 303n.
'a mysterious house': Lang, VI, 245. One of the books listed in Mendes is *The Mysteries of Verbena Lodge*.

165 'carried out to sea': Lang, I, 310n.

166 'The young Frenchman's impression': Henderson, 145–7.
'Powell later named the cottage': See an unpub. letter by Powell of 12 December 1868 in the Brotherton Collection, Leeds.

167 'excessively enthusiastic': Rossetti, 12 Jan. 1869.
'at which my governess looked shocked': Friswell, 78.

169 'The evenings were enlivened ... (Adelaide Kemble)': When Leighton took Kemble to Vichy and introduced her to Burton and Swinburne, he told her, 'One is a believer in Buddhism, the other in nothing; so you must not mind what they say.' See Augustus Hare, VI, 357.

Chapter 9

171 'I wept at the recital': Lang, II, 32.
'I never have professed myself': Peattie, 235.
'a poor old Italian man': Lang, II, 53–4.

172 'think none the worse of my feeling': Lang, II, 42–3.

173 'I sincerely deprecate the publication': Peattie, 237.

174 'one hears through it': Peattie, 244.

175 'most delightful as a lark': Peattie, 246.
'admired it exceedingly': Peattie, 237.

177 'It is most annoying to find': Oswald and Doughty, II, 810.
'Are you ever coming to London again?': Lang, II, 104.
'all the more now that I hear': Oswald and Doughty, II, 824.

'one of his maternal cousins': See Meyers (1979).

'your frequent use of Galilean machinery': Peattie, 254.

178 'For some while past': Peattie, 255.

'tell Ellis that the book': Peattie, 257.

179 'Gabriel had told me yesterday': Bornand, 7–8.

'after all, what is to be done': Oswald and Doughty, II, 872.

'an excuse was made': Bornand, 10.

180 'Swinburne was coming': Cline (1970), I, 418.

'raving with "delirium tremens"': Bornand, 16–17.

181 'there was a lot of unfinished burlesque': Unpub. letter from Swinburne to Thomson, 17 July 1870, Janet Camp Troxell Collection of Rossetti Manuscripts, Manuscripts Division, Department of Rare Books and Special Collections, Princeton University Libraries.

'is in Regent's Park': Gibson, 247.

183 'it is only last night': Peattie, 259.

'it is a great pity': Unpub. letter by Scott, 9 September 1870, British Library.

'Swinburne having breakfasted with Powell': Bornand, 33–4.

185 'negative use of eucharistic imagery': Louis, 12.

187 'He looks not well': Bornand, 54.

188 'I could not think why he seemed so cross': Ward, 116–17.

189 'I heard of the frightful scenes': Oswald and Doughty, III, 963.

Chapter 10

191 'to leave London feeling': See my 'The Admiral to the Rescue'.

192 'When you sent the M.S.': Lang, II, 158–9.

'there is a certain terrible inevitability': Murray, 213.

194 'I am rather afraid this vicinity': Bornand, 137.

'relapsed into his horrible drinking-habits': Bornand, 144.

195 'The Admiral says that the family': Bornand, 185.

'it was not ... a reply': Unpub. letter of Swinburne to Joseph Knight, 20 October 1872, British Library.

197 'little or no real idea of publishing it': Bornand, 194.

'highly desirable that he should': Bornand, 199.

198 'Swinburne enlivens the place': Abbott and Campbell, 34.

199 'I wanted you to help me': Abbott and Campbell, 36.

'His tappings at the door': E. F. Benson, 275.

201 'he is more amiable than I expected': Schweller and Petters, II, 246.

203 'for this proceeding': Unpub. letter, Brotherton Collection, Leeds.

'to listening to fiendish sonnets': Hake and Compton-Rickett (1918), 52–3.

204 The letter from Lady Mary Gordon of 19 May 1873 is in the Brotherton Collection, Leeds.

206 'the business relations with yourself': Lang, II, 256.
      'the country around is well-wooded': Hake and Compton-Rickett, 53.
      'I think he begins to be aware': Prest and Quinn, 243.
      The exchange between Watts and Chatto is in the Brotherton Collection, Leeds and the British Library.

207 'is coming to Cornwall': Unpub. letter of 1 January 1874 quoted by permission of the Jowett Copyright Trustees.

209 'behaved very well and showed no inclination to drink': Prest and Quinn, 252.

210 The letters from Percy Ashburnham and Lady Mary Gordon are quoted by permission of the Berg Collection, New York Public Library.

Chapter 11

213 'I cannot tell you what a pleasure': Unpub. letter of Anne Proctor, quoted by permission of Terry L. Meyers.

214 'there are to be met with': Hake and Compton-Rickett (1916), I, 136–7.

215 'The extreme dignity of Swinburne': Gosse, 206.

219 'Mun's *modest* little work': Quoted by permission of the Berg Collection, New York Public Library.

221 'the stinging saltiness': Douglas, 106.

222 'on the dull yellow foamless floor': Swinburne, 'Tennyson and Musset'.

223 Swinburne's letter of 26 December 1875 and the reply from E. A. Clowes quoted by permission of the Department of Special Collections, Stanford University Libraries.

224 'no non-Greek touch or allusion in it': Quoted by permission of the Jowett Copyright Trustees.
      'your greatest poem': Hake and Compton-Rickett (1916) I, 139.
      Collins's letter of 24 March 1876 is at the Harry Ransom Humanities Research Centre, University of Texas at Austin.
      'you have the sea always with you': Harrison's letter of 2 January 1876 quoted by permission of the Berg Collection, New York Public Library.

227 'an almost consummate piece of art': Lang, III, 277.

228 'I'm expecting Watts': Gosse, 216–17.
     'looking pasty-white': Spencer, 228. For Swinburne's visits to
     other bookdealers see Partington, 160.
229 'generally suffering from abuse': William Lestocq to Charles
     Haddon Chambers attached to a letter of 10 December 1916
     from Chambers to Gosse. Quoted by permission from the Sir W.
     E. Gosse papers, Special Collections Library, Duke University.
     'You always loved children': Unpub. letter of Howell, British
     Library.
     'marching about the Quadrangle': Gosse, 222.

Chapter 12

231 'To me Swinburne seemed': J. H. Ingram from a manuscript in
     the Brotherton Collection, Leeds.
232 'as a bed-ridden invalid': See letter to Thomas Allsop in Meyers
     (1979).
     'ill and worn': Bird and Rhys, 238–40.
233 'Can't we go now?': Hake and Compton-Rickett (1916), I, 102–3.
     'while fully aware': Lang, IV, 60n.
     'Watts gives me a melancholy account': Peattie, 376n.
237 'Wimbledon Common, at the eastern edge': Hutchinson, 193.
240 'looking so well and cheerful': Lang, IV, 135.
243 'If you see Swinburne': Peattie, 394.
     'received from Swinburne': Peattie, 398n.
244 'I do so very much': Unpub. letter by Lady Jane Swinburne,
     British Library.
     'rapturously gazing at the scene': Collins, 52.
245 'chiefly because Swinburne': Peattie, 400.
     'I have read it through twice': Unpub. letter by Jowett, 9 Decem-
     ber 1881, quoted by permission of the Berg Collection, New York
     Public Library and the Jowett Copyright Trustees.

Chapter 13

247 'I cannot tell you how glorious': Unpub. letter by Burne-Jones, 30
     June 1882, British Library.
     'not only Swinburne's finest': Harrison, 9.
     'one of the great erotic poems': Rosenberg, 135.
249 'nothing in music ever': Unpub. letter by Swinburne, 15 Novem-
     ber 1883, British Library.

250 'the child's temper of wonder': Hake and Compton-Rickett (1916), I, 268.

'a splendid East Anglian road-girl': Watts-Dunton, xv–xvi.

'how terribly despair becomes intensified': Douglas, 400–401.

251 'Watts's conviction': See Douglas, 273.

253 'In September Swinburne and Watts went to Sidestrand': In July 1883 Jowett was staying at Emerald Bank, Newlands, near Keswick. According to Abbott and Campbell (II, 256) and Gosse, Swinburne stayed there also, but Swinburne's letters do not yet corroborate this.

254 'they were never in at the same time': Lang, V, 37.

'what good I can do the cause': Kelvin, II, 246–7n.

255 'as being in (essence)': Peattie, 469.

262 'when the downpour was heaviest': *Pall Mall Budget* 26 September 1889, 1218, located by Terry L. Meyers.

263 'Those who in childhood': Douglas, 342.

264 'there is no positive illness': Unpub. letter by Lady Jane Swinburne, 18 April 1885, quoted by permission of the Brotherton Collection, Leeds.

Chapter 14

265 'Cy merest dozen': Fuller, 270.

'I am sure Mun will be amused': Unpub. letter of 14 March 1883, British Library.

266 For the Huntington Library letters see Birchfield (1980).

269 'Redgie's Return' is in Worcester College Library.

'the future poet Robert Graves': See Graves's 'Mad Mr. Swinburne' and A. P. Graves, *To Return To All That* (1932).

270 'Swinburne was generally thought': For a discussion of the Laureateship see Alan Bell and Frank C. Sharp.

271 'indignation knew no bounds': Unpub. letter of 9 June 1913, quoted by permission of the Brotherton Collection, Leeds.

'with equal amusement and astonishment': See Byars, 97.

272 'could tell you much of these many visits' Gosse, 279.

'he has of late years become': Greenberg, 261.

'to a baby kinswoman': See Turley (1982).

273 'now considers Swinburne his own property': Blunt, 68.

274 'Swinburne gets up as I enter': Lafourcade (1932), 276.

Sir John Swinburne's letter of 21 June 1896 is in the British Library. Swinburne's sisters did visit Capheaton towards the end of their lives.

275 'another dear friend': Lang, VI, 103.
'it had been a great and weary struggle': Unpub. letter of 27 November 1896. Quoted by permission of the Provost and Fellows of Eton College.

276 'it is a great consolation': Unpub. letter of 26 January 1899. Quoted by permission of the Provost and Fellows of Eton College.
'The house was smug and mid-Victorian': Lang, VI, 139n.

278 'a strange small figure in grey': Hyder (1970), 237.
'fixed and mirthless': E. V. Lucas, 140.

279 'the boyish pleasure': LeGallienne, 18.
'as reverently as the communicant': Kernahan, 26–7.
'Living, as he did': Beckson (1977), 208.
'more often than not it would be Swinburne': See Woolf, 167–70.

280 'Watts's room on the ground floor': Lang, VI, 152n.
The letter concerning Maeterlinck is at Yale; the letter about Gorky was printed in the *Morning Leader*, 31 January 1905.
'a little pale, rather don-like man': Benson, *Edwardian Excursions*, 107.

282 'he remembered the most minute details': Noyes, 507.

283 'up to his last moment': Peattie (1974).

284 'It was a glorious spring morning': From the diary of Helen Angeli Rossetti, quoted by permission of Signora Helen Guglielmini.

Select Bibliography

Anon. (1888, repr. 1995), *The Whippingham Papers*. Ware, Herts: Wordsworth Editions.

Atkinson, F. G. (1980), 'Some Unpublished Swinburne Letters', *Notes and Queries*, 27, 219–20.

Birchfield, James D. (1980), 'New Light on the Swinburne–Leith Correspondence', *Kentucky Review*, 1, (3), Spring, 52–63.

Byars, Julie A. (1973), 'Eight Unpublished Letters from A. C. Swinburne', *Notes and Queries*, 20, 95–7.

Fisher, Benjamin J. (1973), 'Rossetti and Swinburne in tandem: "The Laird of Waristoun"', *Victorian Poetry*, 11, 229–39.

Gosse, Edmund and Wise, Thomas J. (eds) (1925–27), *The Complete Works of Algernon Charles Swinburne*. 20 vols. London: Heinemann; New York: Gabriel Wells.

Hake, Thomas and Compton-Rickett, Arthur (eds) (1918), *The Letters of A. C. Swinburne*, London: John Murray.

Hughes, Randolph (ed.) (1942), *Lucretia Borgia*. London: Golden Cockerel Press.

―――― (ed.) (1950), *Pasiphae*. London: Golden Cockerel Press.

―――― (ed.) (1952), *Lesbia Brandon*. London: Falcon Press.

Hyder, Clyde K. (ed.) (1966), *Swinburne Replies*. New York: Syracuse University Press.

―――― (ed.) (1972), *Swinburne As Critic*. London and Boston: Routledge and Kegan Paul.

Lafourcade, Georges (1927), *Swinburne's Hyperion*. London: Faber and Gwyer.

―――― (ed.) (1930), *Swinburne's Atalanta in Calydon. A facsimile*. Oxford: Oxford University Press.

Lang, Cecil Y. (ed.) (1959–62), *The Swinburne Letters*. 6 vols. New Haven: Yale University Press; London: Oxford University Press.

―――― (ed.) (1964), *New Writings by Swinburne*. New York: Syracuse University Press.

Lougy, Robert E. (ed.) (1982), *The Children of the Chapel by Mary Gordon and Algernon Charles Swinburne*. Athens: Ohio University Press.

Mayfield, John S. (ed.) (1975), *Hide and Seek*. London: Stourton Press.

Meyers, Terry L. (1979), 'Further Swinburne Letters', *Notes and Queries*, 26, 313–20.

―――― (1988), 'Swinburne's Speech to the Royal Literary Fund', *Modern Philology*, 86 (2), 195–201.

Rooksby, Rikky (1991), 'Swinburne's Reginald', *Notes and Queries*, 236 (3), 322–3.

Schuldt, Edward P. (1976), 'Three Unpublished Balliol Essays of A. C. Swinburne', *Review of English Studies*, XXVII, 108, 422–30.

Swinburne, Algernon C. (1910), *A Record of Friendship*. London: privately printed.

Sypher, Francis J. (1973), 'Victoria's Lapse from Virtue: A Lost Leaf from Swinburne's "La Soeur de la Reine"', *Harvard Library Bulletin*, 21, 349–55.

———— (ed.) (1974), *Undergraduate Papers: An Oxford Journal*. New York: Delmar.

———— (ed.) (1976), *A Year's Letters by A. C. Swinburne*. London: Peter Owen.

Biography and Criticism

Beatty, Richmond C. (1934), 'Swinburne and Bayard Taylor', *Philological Quarterly*, 13, 297–9.

Beetz, K. H. (1982), *A. C. Swinburne. A Bibliography of Secondary Works, 1861–1980*. Metuchen, N.J. and London: Scarecrow Press.

Bird, Alice and Rhys, Ernest (1909), 'Two Evenings with Swinburne', *The Bibliophile*, 3 July, 238–41.

Cassidy, John A. (1964), *Algernon C. Swinburne*. New York: Twayne Publishers.

Croft-Cooke, Rupert (1967), *Feasting with Panthers*. London: W. H. Allen.

Forbes, Jill (1975), 'Two Flagellation Poems by Swinburne', *Notes and Queries*, 22, 443–5.

Fuller, Jean O. (1968), *Swinburne: A Critical Biography*. London: Chatto and Windus.

Gosse, Edmund (1912), 'Swinburne', *Portraits and Sketches*. London: Heinemann.

———— (1920), 'Swinburne and Kirkup', *The London Mercury*, III, December, 156–65.

———— (1925), *Swinburne. An Essay Written in 1875*. Edinburgh: Riverside Press.

———— (1927), *The Life of Algernon Charles Swinburne*. London: Heinemann. Volume XIX of the Bonchurch Complete Works.

Greenberg, Robert A. (1969), 'Swinburne's *Heptalogia* Improved', *Studies in Bibliography*, 22, 258–66.

Grosskurth, Phyllis M. (1963), 'Swinburne and Symonds: An Uneasy Literary Relationship', *Review of English Studies*, 14, 55, 257–68.

Hare, Humphry (1949), *Swinburne: A Biographical Approach*. London: Witherby.

Harrison, Anthony H. (1988), *Swinburne's Medievalism*. Baton Rouge and London: Louisiana State University Press.

———— (1990), 'Swinburne, Wordsworth, and the Politics of Morality', *Victorian Poets and Romantic Poems*. Charlottesville: Virginia University Press.

Henderson, Philip (1974), *Swinburne: The Portrait of a Poet*. London: Routledge and Kegan Paul.

Hutchings, Richard J. and Turley, Raymond V. (1978), *Young Algernon Swinburne*. Isle of Wight: Hunnyhill Press.

Hyder, Clyde K. (1933, rpr. 1984), *Swinburne's Literary Career and Fame*. New York: AMS.

———— (ed.) (1970), *Swinburne: the Critical Heritage*. London: Routledge and Kegan Paul.

Jones, Jason B. (1994), 'A Date and Source for Swinburne's "The Statue of John Brute"', *Notes and Queries*, 41 (3), 357.

Kernahan, Coulson (1917), 'A. C. Swinburne', *In Good Company*. London: John Lane, The Bodley Head.

Lafourcade, Georges (1928), *La Jeunesse de Swinburne*. Oxford: Oxford University Press.

———— (1932), *Swinburne: A Literary Biography*. London: Bells.

Lang, Cecil Y. (1959), 'Swinburne's Lost Love', *PMLA*, 74, March, 123–30.

———— (ed.) (1971), *Victorian Poetry*, 9, Spring–Summer. Swinburne issue.

LeBourgeois, John Y. (1973), 'Swinburne and Simeon Solomon', *Notes and Queries*, 20, 91–5.

Leith, Mary Disney (1917), *The Boyhood of Algernon Charles Swinburne*. London: Chatto and Windus.

Louis, Margot K. (1990), *Swinburne and his Gods*. London, Montreal and Buffalo: McGill-Queen's University Press.

Mayfield, John S. (1953), 'Swinburne's "Boo"' in *English Miscellany*, 4, Rome.

———— (1974), *Swinburneiana*. Maryland: Waring Press.

———— (1980), 'A Swinburne Collector in Calydon', *Quarterly Journal of the Library of Congress*, 37, 25–34.

McGann, Jerome J. (1972), *Swinburne: An Experiment in Criticism*. Chicago: University of Chicago Press.

McSweeney, Kerry (1981), *Tennyson and Swinburne as Romantic Naturalists*. Toronto and London: University of Toronto Press.

Meyers, Terry L. (1993), 'Swinburne Reshapes His Grand Passion: A Version by "Ashford Owen"', *Victorian Poetry*, 31 (1), 111–15.

Murray, Christopher D. (1983), *D. G. Rossetti, A. C. Swinburne and R. W. Buchanan. The Fleshly School Revisited*. Manchester: John Rylands University.

Nowell-Smith, Simon (1964), 'Swinburne's Queen-Mother and Rosamond', *Book Collector*, 357–9.

Noyes, Alfred (1957), 'Dinner at the Pines: Reminiscences of Swinburne', *Listener*, March, 57, 507–8.

Ober, William B. (1988), 'Swinburne's Masochism', *Boswell's Clap and other essays. Medical Analyses of Literary Men's Afflictions*. New York and London: Harper and Row.

Paglia, Camille (1991), 'Swinburne and Pater', *Sexual Personae*. Harmondsworth: Penguin.

Paley, Morton D. (1974), 'The Critical Reception of *A Critical Essay*', *Blake Newsletter*, 8, 32–7.

Panter-Downes, Mollie (1971), *At The Pines*. London: Hamish Hamilton.

Peattie, Roger W. (1963), 'William Michael Rossetti and the Defence of Swinburne's Poems and Ballads', *Harvard Library Bulletin*, 356–65.

———— (1973), 'Swinburne and his publishers', *Huntington Library Quarterly*, 36, 45–54.

———— (1974), 'Swinburne's Funeral', *Notes and Queries*, 21, 466–9.

Richardson, James (1988), *Vanishing Lives: Style and Self in Tennyson, D. G. Rossetti, Swinburne, and Yeats*. Charlottesville: University of Virginia Press.

Riede, David G. (1978), *Swinburne: A Study In Romantic Mythmaking*. Charlottesville: University of Virginia Press.

Rooksby, Rikky (1988), 'Swinburne Without Tears: A Guide to the Later Poetry', *Victorian Poetry*, 26 (4), 413–30. West Virginia University.

———— (1989), 'The Swinburne Collection at Balliol', *Victorians Institute Journal*, 17, 171–80. East Carolina.

———— (1990), 'The Swinburne Manuscripts at Worcester College Oxford', *Victorians Institute Journal*, 18, 175–83.

———— (1990), 'The Case of Commoner Swinburne', *Review of English Studies*, XLI (164), 510–20.

———— (1992), 'A Swinburne Tragedy', *Notes and Queries*, 237, 2, June, 185–7.

———— (1992), 'Upon the Borderlands of Being: Swinburne's Later Elegies', *Victorians Institute Journal*, 20, 137–58. East Carolina University.

———— (1993), 'Swinburne: The Admiral to the Rescue', *Notes and Queries*, 238 (1), 50–52.

———— (1993), 'Swinburne's "Boo" Rides Again', *Review of English Studies*, XLIV (173), 77–80.

———— (1993), 'Swinburne's *Lesbia Brandon* and the Death of Edith Swinburne', *Notes and Queries*, 238 (4), 487–90.

———— and Shrimpton, Nicholas (eds) (1993), *The Whole Music of Passion: New Essays on Swinburne*. Aldershot: Scolar Press.

———— (1997), 'A. C. Swinburne: A Nine Days Wonder', *Victorians Institute Journal*, 24. East Carolina.

Rosenberg, John D. (1967), 'Swinburne', *Victorian Poetry*, 11, 131–52.

Rutland, William (1931), *Swinburne as a Nineteenth Century Hellene*. Oxford: Blackwell.

Salt, Henry S. (1919), Letter to the *TLS*, 25 December, 781.

Scott, Geoffrey (1992), *Gothic Rage Undone*. Bath: Downside Abbey Press.

Sharp, William (1901), 'A Literary Friendship', *Pall Mall Magazine*, 25, 435–48.

Stedman, E. C. (1882), 'Some London Poets', *Harper's Monthly Magazine*, 64, May, 888–92.

Thomas, Donald (1979), *Swinburne: The Poet in his World*. London: Weidenfeld and Nicolson.

Thomson, James (1884), 'The Swinburne Controversy', *Satires and Profanities*, 99–104.

Turley, Raymond V. (1972), 'Swinburne and the Gordon Family', *Hampshire*, April, 49–50.

———— (1982), 'Swinburne's Baby Kinswoman', *Hampshire*, August, 52–6.

Various (1909), *The Bookman*, no. 213, vol. XXXVI (June). London: Hodder and Stoughton.

Watts-Dunton, Clara (1922), *The Home Life of Swinburne*. London: A. M. Philpotts.

Watts-Dunton, Theodore (1898, rpr. 1907), *The Coming of Love*. London: John Lane.

———— (1916), *Old Familiar Faces*. London: H. Jenkins.

Wedmore, Francis (1912), *Memories*. London: Methuen.

Wilson, F. A. C. (1968), 'Swinburne's Sicilian Blade', *North Dakota Quarterly*, 36 (4), 5–18.

———— (1969), 'The Character of Mary Gordon', *Literature and Psychology*, 19, 89–99.

———— (1970), 'Swinburne in love: Some Novels by Mary Gordon', *Texas Studies in Literature and Language*, 11, 1415–26.

———— (1971), 'Fabrication and Fact in Swinburne's *The Sisters*', *Victorian Poetry*, 9, 237–48.

———— (1971), 'Swinburne's Prose Heroines and Mary's Femmes Fatales', *Victorian Poetry*, 9, 249–56.

Wise, Thomas J. (1919, rpr. 1966), *A Bibliography of A. C. Swinburne*. 2 vols. London: Dawsons.

Workman, Gillian (1973), '"La Soeur de la Reine" and related Victorian Romances by Swinburne'. *Harvard Library Bulletin*, 21, 356–64.

General

Abbot, Evelyn and Campbell, Lewis (eds) (1897), *Life and Letters of Benjamin Jowett*. 2 vols. London: John Murray.

Allingham, H. and Radford, D. (eds) (1907), *William Allingham: A Diary*. London: Macmillan.

Anderson, Ronald and Koval, Anne (1994), *Whistler*. London: John Murray.

Angeli, Helen R. (1954), *Pre-Raphaelite Twilight*. London: Richards Press.

Beckson, Karl (ed.) (1977), *The Memoirs of Arthur Symons: Life and Art in the 1890s*. University Park, Pa. and London: Pennsylvania State University Press.

Beckson, Karl and Munro, John M. (eds) (1989) *Arthur Symons: Selected Letters 1880–1935*. London: Macmillan.

Bell, Alan (1972), 'Gladstone looks for a poet laureate', *TLS*, 21 July, 847.

Benson, A. C. (1924), *Memories and Friends*. London: John Murray.

Benson, E. F. (1985), *As We Were: A Victorian Peep-Show*. London: Hogarth Press.

Blunt, W. S. (1919), *My Diaries 1888–1900*. London: Martin Secker.

———— (1920), *My Diaries, Part Two, 1900–1914*. London: Martin Secker.

Bornand, Odette (ed.) (1977), *The Diary of W. M. Rossetti*. Oxford: Clarendon Press.

Boyd, A. K. (1948), *The History of Radley College 1847–1947*. Oxford: Basil Blackwell.

Brabrook, Sir E. (1932), *Some notes on his life*. London: privately printed.

Brodie, Fawn M. (1967, rpr. 1984), *The Devil Drives*. New York and London: W. W. Norton.

Clements, Patricia (1985), *Baudelaire and the English Tradition*. New Jersey: Princeton University Press.

Cline, C. L. (ed.) (1978), *The Owl and the Rossettis: Letters of Charles A. Howell and Dante Gabriel, Christina, and William Michael Rossetti*. University Park, Pa. and London: Pennsylvania State University Press.

————— (ed.) (1970), *The Letters of George Meredith*. 3 vols. Oxford: Clarendon Press.

Coleridge, Arthur D. (1896), *Eton In The Forties*. London: Richard Bentley and Son.

Collins, John (1992), *The Two Forgers: A Biography of Harry Buxton Forman and Thomas James Wise*. Aldershot: Scolar Press.

Collins, L. C. (ed.) (1912), *Life and Memoirs of John Churton Collins*. London: John Lane.

Daniels, Jeffery (ed.) (1985), *Solomon: A Family of Painters*. London: Inner London Educational Council.

Doughty, Oswald and Wahl, J. R. (eds) (1965), *The Letters of Dante Gabriel Rossetti*. 4 vols. Oxford: Oxford University Press.

Douglas, James (1904), *Theodore Watts-Dunton: Poet, Novelist, Critic*. London: Hodder and Stoughton.

Dubos, Jean and René (1953), *The White Plague*. London: Gollancz.

Du Maurier, Daphne (ed.) (1951), *The Young George Du Maurier*. London: Peter Davies.

Ellis, Stewart M. (ed.) (1923), *A Mid-Victorian Pepys: Letters and Memoirs of Sir William Hardman*. London: Palmer.

————— (ed.) (1930), *The Hardman Papers*. London: Palmer.

Falk, Bernard (1934), *The Naked Lady: A Biography of Adah Isaacs Menken*. London: Hutchinson.

Farwell, Byron (1963, rpr. 1990), *Burton: A biography of Sir Richard Francis Burton*. Harmondsworth: Penguin.

Field, Julian O. (1924), *Things I Shouldn't Tell*. London: Eveleigh Nash and Grayson.

Fletcher, C. R. L. (1922), *Edmund Warre*. London: John Murray.

Ford, Ford Madox (1979), *Memories and Impressions*. Harmondsworth: Penguin.

Friswell, Laura Hain (1906), *In The Sixties and Seventies*. Boston: Turner.

Gibson, Ian (1978), *The English Vice: Beating, Sex and Shame in Victorian England and After*. London: Duckworth.

Glasgow, Joanne and Jay, Karla (eds) (1992), *Lesbian Texts and Contexts: Radical Revisions*. London: Onlywomen Press.

Graves, A. P. (1932), *To Return To All That*. London: Jonathan Cape.

Graves, Robert (1959), *The Crowning Privilege*. Harmondsworth: Pelican.

Hake, Thomas and Compton-Rickett, Arthur (1916), *The Life and Letters of Theodore Watts-Dunton*. 2 vols. London: T. C. and E. C. Jack; New York: G. P. Putnam's Sons.

Hare, Augustus (1900), *The Story of My Life*. 6 vols. London: George Allen.

Hedley, W. Percy (1967), *Northumberland Families*. Newcastle: Society of Antiquaries of Newcastle-upon-Tyne.

Hellerstein, E. O., Hume, L. P. and Offen, K. M. (eds) (1981), *Victorian Women*. Brighton: Harvester.

Holiday, Henry (1914), *Reminiscences of My Life*. London: Heinemann.

Hudson, Derek (1974), *Munby: Man of Two Worlds*. London: Sphere.

Hunt, Violet (1932), *Wife to Mr Rossetti*. London: John Lane.

Hutchinson, Horace (1920), *Portraits of the Eighties*. London: Unwin.

James, Lionel (1945), *A Forgotten Genius: Sewell of St. Columba's and Radley*. London: Faber.

Kelvin, Norman (ed.) (1984–), *The Collected Letters of William Morris*. Princeton: Princeton University Press.

Lamont, L. M. (ed.) (1912), *Thomas Armstrong, C. B. A. Memoir*. London: Martin Secker.

LeGallienne, Richard (1951), *The Romantic 90s*. London: Putnam.

Lewis, John D. (1875), 'Eton Thirty Years Since', *Macmillan's Magazine*, May.

Lubbock, Percy (ed.) (1926), *The Diary of A. C. Benson*. London: Hutchinson.

Lucas, E. V. (1932), *Reading, Writing and Remembering*. New York: Harper.

Magnusson, Magnus (1980), 'On the Trail of an Obsession', *Magnus on the Move*. Edinburgh: MacDonald.

Mallock, W. H. (1920), *Memoirs of Life and Literature*. London: Chapman and Hall.

Mander, Rosalie (ed.) (1984), *Recollections of D. G. Rossetti and his circle by Henry Treffry Dunn*. Westerham: Dalrymple Press.

Mankowitz, Wolfgang (1982), *Mazeppa: The Lives, Loves and Legends of Adah Isaacs Menken*. London: Blond and Briggs.

Marsh, Jan (1989), *The Legend of Elizabeth Siddal*. London: Quartet Books.

——— (1991), *Elizabeth Siddal 1829–62*. Sheffield: Ruskin Gallery.

Marshall, John (1823–35), *Royal Naval Biography*. 4 vols. London: Longman, Hurst, Rees, Orme and Brown.

McLynn, F. (1990), *Burton: Snow Upon The Desert*. London: John Murray.

Mendes, Peter (1993), *Clandestine Erotic Fiction, A Bibliocritical Study*. Aldershot: Scolar Press.

Mills, Ernestine (ed.) (1912), *The Life and Letters of Frederic Shields*. New York: Longmans.

Minto, William (ed.) (1892), *William Bell Scott: Autobiographical Notes*. 2 vols. London: Osgood, McIlvaine.

Newall, Christopher (1993), *John William Inchbold*. Leeds: Leeds City Art Galleries.

Newman, T. and Wilkinson, R. (1991), *Ford Madox Brown and the Pre-Raphaelite Circle*. London: Chatto and Windus.

Quinn, Vincent and Prest, John (eds) (1987), *Dear Miss Nightingale: A Selection of Benjamin Jowett's Letters to Florence Nightingale*. Oxford: Clarendon Press.

Packer, Lorna Mona (1963), *The Rossetti–Macmillan Letters*. Berkeley: University of California Press; London: Cambridge University Press.

Partington, Winifred (1946), *Thomas J. Wise in the Original Cloth*. London: Hale, 1946.

Peattie, Roger W. (ed.) (1990), *Selected Letters of William Michael Rossetti*. University Park, Pa. and London: Pennsylvania University Press.

Pope-Hennessy, James (1951), *Monckton Milnes: The Flight of Youth*. London: Constable.

Praz, Mario (2nd edn 1951), *The Romantic Agony*. London and New York: Oxford University Press.

Redesdale, Lord (1915), *Memories*. London: Hutchinson.

Reynolds, Simon (1984), *The Vision of Simeon Solomon*. Stroud, Glos: Catalpa Press.

Robertson, W. Graham (1931), *Time Was*. London: Hamish Hamilton.

Rossetti, William M. (1903), *The Rossetti Papers 1862–70*. London: Sands and Co.

Sacks, Peter M. (1985), *The English Elegy*. Baltimore and London: Johns Hopkins University Press.

Schweller, H. M. and Peters, R. L. (eds) (1967–69), *The Letters of John Addington Symonds*. 3 vols. Detroit: Wayne State University Press.

Sewell, Eleanor L. (ed.) (1907), *The Autobiography of E. M. Sewell*. London: Longmans, Green.

Sharp, Frank C. (1996), 'William Morris and the Search for a Poet Laureate', *Journal of Pre-Raphaelite Studies*, 5 (Spring), 71–80, Toronto.

Smith, Denis Mack (1994), *Mazzini*. New Haven and London: Yale University Press.

Spencer, Walter T. (1923), *Forty Years in My Bookshop*. London: Constable.

Steer, Francis W. (ed.) (1958), *The Ashburnham Archives: A Catalogue*. Lewes: East Sussex County Council.

Storey, Graham and Kielding, K. J. (1965–7), *The Letters of Charles Dickens*. Oxford: Clarendon Press.

Surtees, Virginia (ed.) (1980), *The Diaries of George Price Boyce*. Norwich: Real World.

———— (ed.) (1981), *The Diary of Ford Madox Brown*. New Haven: Yale University Press.

Symons, Arthur (ed.) (1900), *Poetical Works of Mathilde Blind*. London: T. Fisher Unwin.

Thwaite, Ann (1985), *Edmund Gosse: A Literary Landscape*. Oxford: Oxford University Press.

Trevelyan, Raleigh (1978), *A Pre-Raphaelite Circle*. London: Chatto and Windus.

Waddington, Patrick (1994), *From Russian Fugitive to the 'Ballad of Bulgarie'*. Providence and Oxford: Berg.

Ward, Mrs Humphry [Mary A.] (1918), *A Writer's Recollections 1856– 1900*. London: Collins.

White, Norman (1992), *Hopkins. A Literary Biography*. Oxford: Clarendon Press.

Williamson, George C. (1921), *Behind My Library Door*. New York: Dutton.

Winning, Jean B. Von (1984), 'Swinburne's Aunt Emily', *Country Life* (76), 1217–18.

Winsten, Stephen (1951), *Salt and His Circle*. London: Hutchinson.

Winter, C. W. R. (1984), *The Manor Houses of the Isle of Wight*. Stanbridge: Dovecote Press.

Woolf, Leonard (1960), *Sowing: An Autobiography of the Years 1880– 1904*. London: Hogarth Press.

Woolford, John (ed.) (1972), *Poets and Men of Letters (Sale Catalogues of Libraries of Eminent Persons, vol. 6)*. London: Mansell.

Index